MULTIPLE SUBJECTS
ASSESSMENT FOR TEACHERS

Preparation Guide

by
Jerry Bobrow, Ph.D.
Stephen Fisher, M.A.

Contributing Authors
Allan Casson, Ph.D.
Harold D. Nathan, Ph.D.
Peter Z Orton, M.Ed.
Michele Spence, B.A.

ACKNOWLEDGMENTS

I would like to thank editor Michele Spence for editing, proofreading, and triple checking this very complex manuscript and for her overall invaluable assistance. I would also like to thank assistant editor Linnea Fredrickson for helping Michele wade through the many pages submitted. Finally, as always, I give special thanks to my wife, Susan, my daughter, Jennifer Lynn, and my sons, Adam Michael and Jonathan Matthew, for their patience and understanding as book deadlines approached.

Jerry Bobrow

Cover photograph by George Robinson/Tony Stone Images

ISBN 0-8220-2048-3
FIRST EDITION
© 1995 by Jerry Bobrow

preface

The MSAT examination is designed to evaluate subject-matter competence of applicants for Multiple Subject Teaching Credentials. The MSAT is a broad-range exam that includes these sections: Literature and Language Studies, Mathematics, History/Social Sciences, Visual and Performing Arts, Human Development, and Physical Education.

Because the MSAT requires you to use some skills and knowledge that you may not have used in many years, thorough preparation is the key to doing your best. This fact makes your study time more important than ever; it must be used effectively.

In keeping with the fine tradition of Cliffs Notes, this guide was developed by leading experts in the field of test preparation to give you the best preparation possible. The strategies, techniques, and materials presented in this guide have been researched, tested, and evaluated in MSAT preparation classes at many leading universities and colleges and are presently being used in the Bobrow Test Preparation Services MSAT classes offered at many California State Universities.

This guide is divided into five parts:

Part I: Introduction

A general description of the exam, format, questions commonly asked, and some basic overall strategies.

Part II: Analysis of Exam Areas

Focus on introducing and analyzing each subject area and question type with emphasis on suggested approaches and samples.

Part III: Review of Exam Areas

Intensive reviews in Literature and Language Studies, Mathematics, History/Social Sciences, Science, Visual and Performing Arts, Human Development, and Physical Education using a variety of methods including outlines, glossaries, and diagnostic tests in some areas.

Part IV: Two Full-Length Practice Tests

Two complete full-length practice tests with answers and in-depth explanations.

Part V: Supplemental Short Constructed-Response Practice

Additional practice with short constructed-response question types in all subjects.

This guide is not meant to substitute for comprehensive courses in each subject area, but if you follow the Study Guide Checklist on page v, review subject areas, and study regularly, you will get the best MSAT preparation possible.

study guide checklist

- ☐ 1. Read the MSAT information materials (registration bulletin, sample problem bulletin) available at the testing office of most undergraduate institutions.

- ☐ 2. Become familiar with the test Format, page 3.

- ☐ 3. Read General Description, MSAT Scoring, and Questions Commonly Asked about the MSAT, starting on page 4.

- ☐ 4. Learn the techniques of A Positive, Systematic Approach to multiple-choice and essay questions, starting on page 9.

- ☐ 5. Carefully read Part II: Analysis of Exam Areas, starting on page 21.

- ☐ 6. Review Literature and Language Studies, starting on page 141.

- ☐ 7. Review Mathematics, starting on page 151.

- ☐ 8. Review History/Social Sciences, starting on page 203.

- ☐ 9. Review Science, starting on page 277.

- ☐ 10. Review Visual and Performing Arts, starting on page 329.

- ☐ 11. Review Human Development, starting on page 357.

- ☐ 12. Review Physical Education, starting on page 373.

- ☐ 13. Strictly observing the time allotment take the Practice Test 1 Content Knowledge section, starting on page 399.

- ☐ 14. Check your answers, page 439, and carefully review explanations, starting on page 445.

- ☐ 15. Fill out the Analysis/Tally Sheet for Questions Missed, page 441.

- ☐ 16. Strictly observing time allotments, take both of the Practice Test 1 Content Area Exercises sections, starting on page 430.

- ☐ 17. Read the sample responses, starting on page 465, and use the evaluation sheet (page 442) to evaluate your responses.

☐ 18. Review weak areas as necessary.

☐ 19. Strictly observing time allotments, take Practice Test 2 in its entirety, beginning on page 481.

☐ 20. Check your answers, review the explanations, evaluate your essays, and fill in the analysis sheets as for Practice Test 1.

☐ 21. Review weak areas as necessary.

☐ 22. Review Part II: Analysis of Exam Areas, starting on page 21.

☐ 23. Complete and review the Supplemental Short Constructed-Response Questions in Part V, starting on page 559.

☐ 24. Carefully read The Final Touches, page 575.

contents

Part I: Introduction

Part II: Analysis of Exam Areas

Part III: Review of Exam Areas

Part IV: *Two Full-Length Practice Tests*

Part V: Supplemental Short Constructed-Response Practice

Part I:
Introduction

UPDATE: RECENT FORMAT CHANGE

FORMAT

Content Knowledge (Multiple-Choice Questions)	Number of Questions	Approximate % of Questions
I. Literature and Language Studies	24	20%
II. Mathematics	24	20%
III. Visual and Performing Arts	12	10%
IV. Physical Education	8	7%
V. Human Development	8	7%
VI. History/Social Studies	22	18%
VII. Science	22	18%
Time: 2 hours	*120 Questions*	

Content Area Exercises (Short Essay Questions)	Number of Questions
I. Literature and Language Studies	3
II. Mathematics	3
III. Visual and Performing Arts	2
IV. Physical Education	2
V. Human Development	2
VI. History/Social Studies	3
VII. Science	3
Time: 3 hours	*18 Questions*

Notice that the number of questions, timing, and order of sections has changed from those shown on pages 3 and 4.

General Description of the Exam: The Multiple Subjects Assessment for Teachers is composed of two sections.

- General Knowledge (120 multiple-choice questions), 2 hours
- Content Area Exercises (18 short essay questions), 3 hours

2

PREVIOUS FORMAT AND DESCRIPTION OF THE MSAT

PREVIOUS FORMAT

Content Knowledge (Multiple-Choice Questions)	Number of Questions	Approximate % of Questions
I. Literature and Language Studies	27	20%
II. Mathematics	27	20%
III. History/Social Sciences	24	18%
IV. Science	24	18%
V. Visual and Performing Arts	14	10%
VI. Human Development	9	7%
VII. Physical Education	9	7%
Time: 2 hours	*134 Questions*	

Content Area Exercises 1 (Short Essay Questions)	Number of Questions
I. Literature and Language Studies	4
II. Mathematics	4
III. Visual and Performing Arts	2
IV. Human Development	2
V. Physical Education	2
Time: 2 hours	*14 Questions*

Content Area Exercises 2 (Short Essay Questions)	Number of Questions
I. History/Social Sciences	4
II. Science	4
Time: 1 hour	*8 Questions*

PREVIOUS GENERAL DESCRIPTION

The Multiple Subjects Assessment for Teachers (MSAT) is designed to measure knowledge and higher-order thinking skills of prospective elementary school teachers. The MSAT focuses on the seven subject areas that are considered central to elementary educators and is composed of three parts.

- General Knowledge (134 multiple-choice questions)
- Content Area Exercises 1 (14 short essay questions)
- Content Area Exercises 2 (8 short essay questions)

There is no penalty for guessing, and the use of a nonprogrammable calculator is permitted on each section of the MSAT.

MSAT SCORING

MSAT Scoring on a Recent Exam

Section A: Content Knowledge (134 multiple-choice questions)	Scaled	Approximate % of Questions
Total possible score	200	
Passing score	156	67%
Minimum passing score	148	61%

Section B: Content Exercises 1 and 2 (22 short constructed-response essays) (66 points possible)	Scaled	Approximate % of Questions
Total possible score	200	
Passing score	155	55%
Minimum passing score	147	48%

Overall		
Total possible score	400	
Passing score	311	

Scoring can vary from test to test.

You pass if you achieve a passing score on both sections of the test—multiple-choice and short-answer essay. You can also pass if you score a minimum pass on one section *and* your total equals or exceeds the required passing total.

Scores for advancement to student teaching may vary depending on university requirements.

Short-Answer (Constructed-Response) Essays— 22 Questions

Each short-answer essay is scored 0–3. With 22 questions, there are 66 points possible. This raw score is then converted to a scaled score. Approximately 55% of the points possible is passing. Approximately 48% of the points possible is considered minimum pass. Minimum pass on the short-answer essay section is possible only if in the multiple-choice section you make a high enough score to get a total that equals or exceeds the required total.

Multiple-Choice—134 Questions

The number you get correct is converted to a scaled score. Correctly answering approximately two-thirds of the 134 questions is necessary to pass. Correctly answering approximately 61% of the 134 questions is a minimum pass. Minimum pass on the multiple-choice section is possible only if in the short-answer section you have a high enough score to get a total that equals or exceeds the required total.

General Information

- There is no penalty for guessing on multiple-choice or constructed-response questions. Answer all questions. Guess if necessary. Always attempt a response.
- You may use a calculator during the MSAT.
- You need not retake passed tests, but it may be to your benefit depending on your score.
- **The information above is subject to change.**

QUESTIONS COMMONLY ASKED ABOUT THE MSAT

What is the MSAT?

The Multiple Subjects Assessment for Teachers (MSAT) is the examination adopted by the Commission on Teacher Credentialing for evaluating subject-matter competence of applicants for the Multiple Subject Teaching Credential.

Who administers the MSAT?

The MSAT is a part of the Praxis Series, which is administered by Educational Testing Service (ETS) with guidelines drawn up by the California Commission on Teacher Credentialing.

When and where is the MSAT given?

The MSAT is administered statewide four times a year. You can get dates and test locations by contacting ETS Western Field Office at (510) 596-5500 for general information or 1(800) 772-9476 for services or specific information.

What materials should I take to the test?

Be sure to take with you your admission ticket, some form of photo and signature identification, several Number 2 soft lead pencils with good erasers, a calculator, and a watch to help pace yourself during the exam. No scratch paper, books, or other aids will be permitted in the test center.

What is included in the MSAT?

The sections of the MSAT include Literature and Language Studies, Mathematics, History and Social Sciences, Science, Visual and Performing Arts, Human Development, and Physical Education. Two hours are given for 134 multiple-choice questions and three hours for 22 short constructed-response essay questions.

What is a passing score?

On the September 1994 exam, a total passing score of 311 was necessary, with a minimum of 148 on the multiple-choice section and 147 on the short constructed-response essay sections. Passing scores may vary from test to test.

When will I get my score report?

Your test score will be mailed to you about four weeks after you take the test.

Can I take the MSAT more than once?

Yes. But remember, your plan is to pass on your first try.

Do I need to take both sections of the test?

You must pass both sections of the test. However, if you previously passed one section of the exam, you may take only the section you have not as yet passed. Thus, you do not have to pass both sections in one examination; you can achieve a total passing score in separate administrations. It may be advantageous to retake both sections, depending on your scores.

Should I guess on the test?

Yes! Since there is no penalty for guessing, guess if you have to. On the multiple-choice section, first try to eliminate some of the choices to increase your chances of choosing the right answer. But don't leave any of the answer spaces blank. On the short constructed-response essay section, be sure to give a response.

May I write on the test?

Yes! As scratch paper will not be provided, you must do all of your work in the test booklets. Your answer sheet for the multiple-choice section, however, must have no marks on it other than your personal information (name, registration number, etc.) and your answers.

How should I prepare?

Understanding and practicing test-taking strategies will help a great deal. A focused review of subject matter is invaluable. This guide gives you insights, review, and strategies for the question types. Some universities offer preparation programs to assist you in attaining a passing score. Check with them for further information.

How do I register or get more information?

The California Registration Bulletin is available at most college or university testing offices. Or you can get information by contacting ETS Western Field Office at (510) 596-5500 for general information or 1(800) 772-9476 for services or specific information.

TAKING THE MSAT: A POSITIVE, SYSTEMATIC APPROACH

STRATEGIES FOR THE GENERAL KNOWLEDGE (MULTIPLE-CHOICE) QUESTIONS

The General Knowledge section is composed of 134 multiple-choice questions with a time allotment of two hours. These questions are grouped by subject area.

Applying the "Plus-Minus" System

Many who take the MSAT don't get their best possible score because they spend too much time on difficult questions, leaving insufficient time to answer the easy questions. Don't let this happen to you. Since you have less than one minute per question, and each question is worth the same amount, use the following system to avoid getting stuck on any one question.

1. Answer easy questions immediately.

2. When you come to a question that seems "impossible" to answer, make a large minus sign (−) next to it on your test booklet.

3. Then mark a "guess" answer on your answer sheet and move on to the next question.

4. When you come to a question that seems solvable but appears too time consuming, mark a large plus sign (+) next to that question in your test booklet and register a guess answer on your answer sheet. Then move on to the next question.

Since your time allotment is just under one minute per question, a "time-consuming" question is a question that you estimate will take you more than one or two minutes to answer. But don't waste time deciding whether a question is a "+" or a "−." Act quickly, as the intent of the strategy is, in fact, to save you valuable time.

After you work all the easy questions, your **test booklet** should look something like this:

1.

+2.

3.

4.

−5.

+6.

etc.

5. After answering all the questions you can answer immediately (the easy ones), go back and answer your "+" questions. Change your "guess" on your answer sheet, if necessary, for those questions you are able to answer. You may instead wish to return briefly to the "+" questions in the same subject area before moving on to the next subject area. But do not spend too much time taking a second look at the "+" questions, or you will not complete the section.

6. If you finish the section and have rechecked your "+" questions, then you can either

    - Attempt those "−" questions, the ones that you considered "impossible."

    or

    - Don't bother with those "impossible" questions. Rather, spend your time reviewing your work to be sure you didn't make any careless mistakes.

7. Never spend more than about one minute on a question. If it looks like your question is going to take more than one minute, mark a plus or a minus, take your guess, and move on.

Remember, you do not have to erase the pluses and minuses you make in your question booklet. And be sure to fill in all your answer spaces—if necessary, with a guess. As there is no penalty for wrong answers, it makes no sense to leave an answer space blank.

Using the Elimination Strategy

Take advantage of being allowed to mark in your testing booklet. As you eliminate an answer choice from consideration, *make sure to mark it out in your question booklet* as follows:

(A̶)

?(B)

(C̶)

?(D)

Notice that some choices are marked with question marks, signifying that they may be possible answers. This technique will help you avoid reconsidering those choices you have already eliminated and will help you narrow down your possible answers. *These marks in your testing booklet do not need to be erased.*

Avoiding the "Misread"

Sometimes, a question may have different answers depending upon what is asked. For example,

If $6y + 3x = 14$, what is the value of y?

The question may instead have asked,

. . . what is the value of x?

Or a question could ask,

If $3x + x = 20$, what is the value of $x + 2$?

Notice that this question doesn't ask for the value of x, but rather the value of $x + 2$.

A question could be phrased as follows.

All of the following statements are true EXCEPT . . .

or

Which of the expressions used in the paragraph does NOT help develop the main idea?

Notice that the words EXCEPT and NOT change the above questions significantly.

To avoid "misreading" a question (and therefore answering it incorrectly), simply *circle* what you must answer in the question. For example, do you have to find x or $x + 2$? Are you looking for what is true or the *exception* to what is true? To help you avoid misreads, mark the questions in your test booklet in this way:

If $6y + 3x = 14$, what is the value of y?

If $3x + x = 20$, what is the value of $x + 2$?

All of the following statements are true EXCEPT . . .

Which of the expressions used in the paragraph does NOT help develop the main idea?

And, once again, *these circles in your question booklet do not have to be erased.*

Attacking the Multiple-Multiple-Choice Question

Some questions use a "multiple-multiple-choice" format. At first glance, these questions appear more confusing and more difficult than normal four-choice (A, B, C, D) multiple-choice questions. Actually, once you understand "multiple-multiple-choice" question types and technique, they are often easier than a comparable standard multiple-choice question. For example,

If x is a positive integer, then which of the following must be true?

    I. $x > 0$
    II. $x = 0$
    III. $x < 1$

(A) I only
(B) II only
(C) I and II only
(D) I and III only

Since x is a positive integer, it must be a counting number. Note that possible values of x could be 1, or 2, or 3, or 4, and so on. Therefore, statement I, $x > 0$, is always true. So next to I on your question booklet, place a T for *true*.

T I. $x > 0$
    II. $x = 0$
    III. $x < 1$

Now, realize that the correct final answer choice (A, B, C, or D) *must* contain *true statement I*. This eliminates (B) as a possible correct answer choice, as it does *not* contain true statement I. You should cross out (B) on your question booklet.

Statement II is *incorrect*. If x is positive, x cannot equal zero. Thus, next to II, you should place an F for *false*.

T I. $x > 0$
F II. $x = 0$
    III. $x < 1$

Knowing that II is false allows you to eliminate any answer choices that contain *false statement II*. Therefore, you should cross out (C), as it contains false statement II. Only (A) and (D) are left as possible correct answers. Finally, you realize that statement III is also false, as x must be 1 or greater. So you place an F next to III, thus eliminating choice (D) and leaving (A), I only. This technique often saves some precious time and allows you to take a better educated guess should you not be able to complete all parts (I, II, and III) of a multiple-multiple-choice question.

Understanding the Scoring—a Broad-Range Approximator

The following chart is designed to give you only an approximate score range for the multiple-choice section, not an exact score. When you take the actual MSAT, you will have questions that are similar to those in this book; however, some questions may be slightly easier or slightly more difficult. Needless to say, this variation may affect your scoring range.

Approximate Scaled Score	Raw Score
200–175	134–107
174–150	106–77
149–125	76–47
124–105	46–26
104–100	25–0

Keep in mind that this chart represents only an *approximate score range*. **The actual score conversion can change from test to test,** which would affect this broad-range approximation process.

Reviewing the Strategies

1. Remember that the test is composed of 134 questions covering seven subject areas. These 134 questions must be completed in two hours (approximately fifty seconds per question). Be sure to pace yourself accordingly.

2. You may wish to first complete the subject areas where you are best prepared. If you skip a question in a subject area, you may wish to return briefly to that question for a second look before you go to the next subject area. Never leave a question without at least filling in a guess response. Be careful when skipping subject areas to make sure that you are marking your answer in the correct space.

3. Try to answer all of the questions, but don't deliberate over any one question or group of questions at great length. Remember, each question is of equal value. If you are uncertain, use a process of elimination to choose your response. Since there are only four choices, if you can eliminate one or two, your guessing odds increase tremendously.

4. A common mistake is "misreading" the question. Be sure to focus on what the question is asking.

5. You are to select the "best" answer. This means the "best" of those given, which may not always be an "ideal" answer.

6. If the question gives a prompt, that is, a graph, cartoon, map, poem, or paragraph, you may wish to first read the question or questions that refer to that prompt (don't read the choices yet). Then go back and read the prompt, the question (again), and then the choices. Prereading the question can help you focus on what to look for in the prompt.

STRATEGIES FOR THE CONTENT AREA EXERCISES (SHORT CONSTRUCTED-RESPONSE ESSAY QUESTIONS)

The Content Area Exercises are composed of 22 short constructed-response essay questions in a total of three hours. This section is divided into a two-hour Content Area Exercises 1 test with 14 short essay questions and a one-hour Content Area Exercises 2 test with 8 short essay questions. There is a fifteen-minute break between the two exercises. The short essay questions are grouped by subject area.

Approaching the Questions

Briefly scan (read quickly) the group of questions allotted to the first subject area. Do **not** attempt to answer an individual question at this point. Simply scan for general content to decide which question you will work on first. Select the one that you feel the most comfortable with. If you take the questions out of order, be sure to attempt each question in the subject area before moving on to the next subject area. Be careful not to skip any questions. Next, scan the group of questions for the next subject area and decide which one you wish to attempt first. Continue with this process.

- Read and mark the question. That is, circle or underline what the question is asking. For example, does the question ask you to draw an inference or provide a conclusion? Does it ask you to compare or contrast two concepts, theories, time periods, or styles? How many examples are required (three contributing factors, two results, four types, etc.)?

- Restate the question to yourself before attempting to answer the item. It is essential that you clearly understand what the question is asking for.

- Quickly jot down, in the margin provided in the test booklet, pertinent facts and information needed to answer the question. You can use the cluster form, lists, phrases, or simply individual words. Do **not** attempt to make a complete outline of your answer. Time constraints (you have approximately eight minutes to read, analyze, and write) limit the effectiveness of detailed outlines.

Answering the Question

Follow these guidelines in writing your essay responses.

- Do **not** restate the question in your introductory sentence. This is considered unnecessary.

- Write in a clear, concise style. Be factual. Many questions call for an answer associated with causes, effects, and consequences.

- Answer all parts of an individual question. It's easy to skip part of the question under the time pressure. For example, listing two causes *but* forgetting to list the two results.

- Refer back to the question to make sure your answer is focused. Marking the question will help in maintaining focus.

- Essay answers will vary in length from about 50 to 150 words. Key words ("buzzwords") that are used in the field will often help display your knowledge of a subject.

- When you write your short answer, be very specific if you can and use one or two specific examples. Your answers will be more convincing and easier for you to write. For example, if you are asked to write about the short story, it may be much easier to base your answer on a story you know than to try to discuss the short story in general.

- Do **not** write an extended, definitive answer to any individual question that will take substantially longer than about eight minutes or that requires two full pages. The maximum score you can receive on any one question is three points. If you spend too much time on one question, you may not have time to adequately complete your other essays.

- Do **not** spend an inordinate amount of time on any individual factor in a question that asks for multiple factors. Your overall score will be based on your ability to answer all parts of the question, not simply *one* part.

- Answer each question. Before skipping a question, read it a few times to see if you gain insight concerning the question. The questions are generally designed so that you can receive partial credit if you have some knowledge of the subject. Partial answers will get partial credit. Even an answer that receives one point will be add to your total points.

- If you are completely unfamiliar with a question prompt, try a common-sense answer or *skip* the question. Do **not** get stuck. Recognize that by skipping a question you know nothing about, you will gain time for other questions.

- Unless specifically asked, do **not** write a conclusion or summary for any question. The question format does not normally require this type of response.

Checking Your Answer

Keep the following points in mind.

- Keep track of your time. Pace yourself. Make time to briefly scan your essays to make sure you've answered the question. Look for major errors in focus. Don't be overly concerned with minor spelling or grammar errors.

- Complete the entire essay booklet. Then, if time permits, review or reread your responses. **If possible, attempt an answer to every question.**

Understanding the Scoring and a Broad-Range Approximator

Papers are scored using the following scale. Readers understand fully the constraints on the writer taking this examination.

0— Blank papers, papers written on a totally different topic from the question on the exam, or papers that merely repeat or paraphrase the question.

1— Papers that misunderstand what the topic calls for.

Papers that fail to explain or support important points or parts of the topic.

Papers that reveal inadequate understanding of the subject matter related to the topic.

2— Papers that understand the topic adequately.

Papers that employ some supporting evidence when required.

Papers that deal with most of the requirements of the topics.

Papers that reveal adequate understanding of the subject matter.

3— Papers that thoroughly understand the topic.

Papers that deal with all parts of the assignment.

Papers that explain clearly and, when appropriate, support their conclusions.

Papers that reveal good understanding of the subject matter.

The following chart is designed to give you only an approximate range for the short constructed-response essay section, not an exact score. When you take the actual MSAT, you will have questions that are similar to those in this book; however, some questions may be slightly easier or slightly more difficult. Needless to say, this variation may affect your scoring range. To use this chart, each of your essays would have to be scored from 0 to 3. Since there are 22 essays, you could receive a possible 66 points. Then double this score. Thus, the top raw score would be 2×66, which is 132.

Approximate Scaled Score	Raw Score
200–182	132–104
181–156	103–72
155–130	71–42
129–105	41–15
104–100	14–0

Keep in mind that this chart represents only an *approximate score range.* **The actual score conversion can change from test to test,** which would affect this broad-range approximation process.

Analyzing a Question and Two Responses

Sample Question

Discuss several differences between Shakespearean drama and modern drama. Provide appropriate examples to support your answer.

Analysis of the Question

In analyzing this question, it is important to understand that you are being asked to discuss *only differences.* Often, in tests with time pressure, the test taker goes beyond the scope of the question (in this question, for example, by discussing *both* similarities and differences). Circling or underlining the key words and tasks given in the question will help you focus on what is required.

Before answering the question, try to recall pertinent information about dramas in general—setting, plot, theme, characterization, and so forth. More specifically, try to recall information about Shakespearean drama. Think of works that may be familiar to you, such as *Hamlet, Macbeth,* or *Romeo and Juliet.* Consider what general information from these works could assist you in answering the question, perhaps language, historical setting, or the use of metaphor. If you had to consider just one attribute of Shakespearean drama, what would it be? The lofty language? The use of poetry? Does this information help you in determining differences?

Think of distinctive qualities that characterize a modern drama. Consider the variety of plots, stage setting, the use of sound and lighting, and so forth.

Following are two very different responses to the sample question.

A "3" Response

The plays of Shakespeare are written in poetry and have a metrical pattern. The characters often speak in verse that sometimes rhymes. The language is more lofty and literary than that of modern drama and often relies heavily on metaphors and other figurative language to make a point. Shakespearean plays are often longer than modern plays and differ also in that they may have a historical base, have more complicated plots, and make considerable use of soliloquy. *Hamlet* and *Macbeth* are classic Shakespearean dramas.

Modern drama is not generally written in poetry. Instead its dialogue is colloquial. Modern plots may involve any aspect of life, and characters are drawn from everyday life.

A "1" Response

Shakespearean drama deals a lot with kings and queens and very involved plots. History is important. Examples are *Hamlet* and *Macbeth*. In modern drama, the plays can be serious or funny. But in most cases, the plays deal with regular life.

Reviewing the Strategies

1. You are to answer 14 questions in two hours in Content Area Exercises 1 and 8 questions in one hour in Content Area Exercises 2. This timing works out to about seven to eight minutes per question. Spend a little time orgainzing your response, making sure that you address the important points.

2. You may earn partial credit for an answer. Try to answer each question. Give a complete response when possible, but *at least* give a partial response.

3. Answer all parts of a question, but do not answer more than the question asks. You can earn a maximum score (three points) with a relatively brief response to most questions. Focus on the main point or points of the answer.

4. In answering a question, use the format that is requested in the question. For example, make a list if the questions elicits a list. Watch for key words like *list, compare,* and *describe* as you read the question. This will help you focus your response. Remember, it is not necessary to write a polished essay to answer every question, but do try to give a focused response.

5. Explain math questions conceptually; that is, describe how the answer is arrived at first, and then compute the answer. Or you may wish to compute the answer and then describe the steps you followed. Sometimes, computing the answer first will reinforce the process or give insight into the problem.

Part II:
Analysis of Exam Areas

LITERATURE AND LANGUAGE STUDIES

CONTENT

The Literature and Language Studies section concentrates on the components of written and oral expression and the elements of literature and language. Language studies include the operations of language development and its use in oral and written expression. Literature studies include both narrative and expository texts and the written materials of all disciplines. The scope of questions allows you to demonstrate your understanding and knowledge of literature and language. This section also tests your ability to use higher-order thinking skills in analyzing problems relevant to the topics and to apply the principles of the language arts in a variety of contexts.

Content Knowledge (Multiple-Choice)

The Content Knowledge (multiple-choice) test, which contains twenty-seven questions grouped together, covers the following major content areas and focuses on the topics listed under each. The approximate weight of each category is listed in parentheses.

1. **Literature (35 percent)**

   - concepts, conventions, and terminology of literature
   - basic assumptions and conventions of major literary genres, including children's literature
   - historical/social contexts of literature
   - various approaches associated with reading and interpreting literature

2. **Language and linguistics (35 percent)**

   - primary stages of language development, including significant factors that enhance or inhibit language development
   - historical and cultural factors that influenced the evolution of standard American English
   - applying the principles of linguistics in analyzing diverse textual contexts

3. **Oral and written communication (30 percent)**

   - applying various communication skills to the analysis and production of written text
   - applying communication skills to analyze oral discourse
   - demonstrating knowledge of the conventions of narration, exposition, reflection, and argumentation

- retrieving information from both print and nonprint sources
- interpreting written research reports

Content Area Exercises (Short Constructed-Response)

The four Literature and Language Studies short constructed-response questions generally conform to the following format.

- Three questions focus on content from the areas of literature, language and linguistics, and oral and written communication.
- One question tests content from one of these three areas.

These questions are designed to test your ability to

- discuss topics relevant to literature and language
- demonstrate critical thinking relevant to the topics
- apply an understanding of literature and language to pertinent issues, topics, and ideas
- analyze and evaluate passages from literature

SAMPLE QUESTIONS AND STRATEGIES FOR THE CONTENT KNOWLEDGE SECTION

Each of the following examples represents an area tested on the Literature and Language Studies multiple-choice segment. An analysis follows each question.

Literature

1. It is therefore to be steadily inculcated, that virtue is the highest proof of understanding, and the only solid basis of questions; and that vice is the natural consequence of narrow thoughts; that it begins in mistake and ends in ignominy.

   The style of this sentence is characterized by its use of
   (A) metaphysical images
   (B) overstatement
   (C) parallel phrases
   (D) subjunctive verbs

The correct answer is (C). The question calls for recognizing the *style* of the passage, that is, the techniques the author uses to convey meaning. In answering questions based on a written passage, it is often helpful to mark key points—here, for example, you might take note of and mark the connection between *virtue* and *understanding* and between *vice* and *narrow thoughts,* as well as the negative words concerning vice, *mistake* and *ignominy.* Even if you are not sure of the answer, you can use a process of elimination. Choice (A) is incorrect because there is no metaphysical imagery. There isn't sufficient information to choose overstatement (B). There is no use of the subjunctive in the passage (D). But parallel phrases are used: *that virtue is . . . that vice is* and *in mistake . . . in ignominy.*

2. All of the following correctly describe the ballad EXCEPT:
   (A) A ballad often rhymes abcb.
   (B) A ballad is a narrative poem.
   (C) A ballad often uses dialogue.
   (D) A ballad often uses learned language.

The correct answer is (D). Here, try to remember ballads you know and recall their names or techniques associated with them. For example, you might remember "Tom Dooley" and that a ballad is a poem that tells a story and originally was written to be sung. Choices (A), (B), and (C) *are* associated with a ballad, but learned language (D) is *not.* The language of a ballad is simple. It is a folk poem, not the product of sophisticated writers.

3. In a dramatic monologue, the speaker of the poem is usually
   (A) alone
   (B) speaking to a second person who does not reply
   (C) speaking to a second person who does reply
   (D) one of several speakers

The correct answer is (B). In a dramatic monologue, the speaker usually addresses one or more listeners, who do not speak. The person speaking reveals information about his or her character in this dramatic situation. A monologue is spoken by a single speaker (*mono*). A soliloquy is spoken by a single speaker who is alone (*solus*).

Questions 4–5 refer to the following poem.

> Gather ye rosebuds while ye may:
> Old time is still a-flying,
> And this same flower that smiles today
> Tomorrow will be dying.

4. The figure used in the third line of the poem is an example of
   (A) personification
   (B) simile
   (C) metaphysical conceit
   (D) irony

The correct answer is (A). Many literature questions test the ability to recognize the correct use of literary terminology. For example, knowing that a simile (B) is a comparison using *like* or *as* and that irony (D) is a technique in which a writer conveys a meaning opposite from the words actually used would allow you to eliminate both of these choices. Personification (A) gives human qualities to an inanimate object. Here, the flower is given the human quality of smiling.

5. The Latin phrase that best expresses the idea of this poem is
    (A) *Semper fidelis.*
    (B) *In vino veritas.*
    (C) *Carpe diem.*
    (D) *Cum grano sabis.*

The correct answer is (C). This is a difficult question. First, attempt to understand the direction of the poem. The promise of the day can quickly change (*flower that smiles . . . will be dying*). Therefore, the concept of time (*today . . . tomorrow*) is important. *Carpe diem* (C) means *seize the day,* that is, take advantage of present opportunity. The idea is commonplace in poetry.

6.   I am no poet here; my pen's the spout
                 Where the rain-water of my eyes run out.

    These lines, by a poet on the death of a friend, are an example of
    (A) metaphysical conceit
    (B) simile
    (C) feminine rhyme
    (D) understatement

The correct answer is (A). Note the negative reference (*I am no . . .*) and the figurative language (*rain-water of my eyes*). You can eliminate choice (B) because the lines contain no similes. You can eliminate (D) beacause the emotional quality of the words rules out understatement. The line is an example of metaphysical conceit. In this metaphor, the poet compares the poetry to a pen that pours out the poet's tears like a drain pipe. The poet is impressed with his ability.

7. Of the following lines of poetry, which is an iambic tetrameter?
    (A) And this alas is more than we would do
    (B) Mark but this flea and mark in this
    (C) Decaying more and more
    (D) And no birds sing

The correct answer is (B). In iambic tetrameter verse, there are four iambic (two syllables with the second stressed) feet. The first line is a pentameter (five feet), the third is a trimeter (three feet), and the fourth is a dimeter (two feet).

8. Arrange the following epic poems in the order in which they were written: *Paradise Lost,* the *Iliad,* the *Aeneid, Beowulf*
   (A) *Beowulf,* the *Iliad,* the *Aeneid, Paradise Lost*
   (B) the *Iliad,* the *Aeneid, Beowulf, Paradise Lost*
   (C) *Beowulf, Paradise Lost,* the *Iliad,* the *Aeneid*
   (D) the *Aeneid,* the *Iliad, Paradise Lost, Beowulf*

The correct answer is (B). In questions such as these, determining the first or last item in a series or which item came before or after another item can often allow you to eliminate most incorrect answer choices. Here, recognizing that the *Iliad* is a Greek epic written by the poet Homer places the *Iliad* before the *Aeneid,* an epic Roman work. *Beowulf* is an Old English poem and must come after the *Iliad* and the *Aeneid. Paradise Lost* was written by Milton in the seventeenth century. Simply recognizing that the *Iliad* was written first and *Paradise Lost* last would allow you to eliminate all incorrect answer choices.

Language and Linguistics

1. All of the following words or phrases could be used to define the word "persona" EXCEPT
   (A) protagonist
   (B) mask
   (C) second voice
   (D) alter ego

The correct answer is (A). The protagonist (hero or heroine) is one of the main characters of a literary work and is usually in conflict with the antagonist (villain). The other three choices are definitions of *persona.* The easiest way to answer this question, if you are not familiar with the word *persona,* is to realize that choices (B), (C), and (D) are synonyms and can therefore be eliminated.

2. Which of the following words or phrases could be used to introduce a clause that is to contradict or qualify what has gone before?
   (A) therefore
   (B) however
   (C) consequently
   (D) in addition

The correct answer is (B). Of the four words, only *however* suggests a contradiction of what has already been said. Words such as *but, despite,* and *although* would also meet the requirements of the question.

3. Of the following, which is an example of a periodic sentence?
   (A) I went to the store to buy milk and cash a check.
   (B) I wonder why the price of gasoline rises every summer and stays the same in winter.
   (C) According to state entomologists, the safest chemical to use to combat the fruit fly is Malathion.
   (D) Was the guard injured when the bank was robbed?

The correct answer is (C). A periodic sentence is one which is grammatically complete only at the end. The opposite is a loose sentence, one which is grammatically complete before the period or other end punctuation. In choices (A), (B), and (D), the sentences could end after *milk, rises,* and *injured,* respectively.

4. Which part of the word "prestidigitation" means "finger"?
   (A) presti
   (B) tid
   (C) digit
   (D) ation

The correct answer is (C). From general knowledge, you are probably aware that *digit* can refer to a *finger.* The word *prestidigitation* refers to the use of sleight of hand, quick movement intended for misdirection, as used by a magician.

5. The part of the word "synchronous" that means "time" is
   (A) chron
   (B) syn
   (C) sync
   (D) ronous

The correct answer is (A). *Chron* comes from the word *chronos,* which means *time.* The word *synchronous* is an adjective describing events that happen or states that exist at the same time.

6. The prefix "poly" is most likely to mean
   (A) again
   (B) partly
   (C) too little
   (D) many

The correct answer is (D). The prefix *poly* means *many, much, more than one,* as in the word *polygamy* (having two or more husbands or wives) or *polyglot* (speaking several languages).

Oral and Written Communication

1. The process by which a writer discovers ideas to write about is called both
   (A) content and message
   (B) deduction and induction
   (C) invention and prewriting
   (D) rhetoric and arrangement

The correct answer is (C). Here, you are being asked to determine a process that a writer uses to "discover" ideas. Therefore, you must look for an initial step. The older term for the idea-discovering process is *invention*. The term more often used today is prewriting.

2. The point in a plot where a rising action in which a conflict takes a decisive turn is called
   (A) hyperbole
   (B) enjambment
   (C) falling action
   (D) climax

The correct answer is (D). The turning point of a plot is its *climax*, which is followed by falling action. Other terms associated with the development of a narrative include setting, characterization, and denouement, which refers to the solution of a problem or the final outcome of the conflict in a literary work.

3. Read the following paragraph carefully and arrange the four sentences in the most coherent order.

   (1) But the effect will be unchanged. (2) Otherwise you might take the wrong pill or take a pill at the wrong time. (3) If you are taking several pills, be sure to pay close attention to the change in shape or color. (4) Changing from a brand-name medicine to a generic, you may find that the pill is a different shape or a different color.

   (A) 4–2–3–1
   (B) 2–3–1–4
   (C) 3–4–1–2
   (D) 4–1–3–2

The correct answer is (D). Sentence (1) logically follows sentence (4) because sentence (4) speaks of a change, and sentence (1) begins with *But* and comments on something that will remain unchanged. Sentence (2), which begins with *Otherwise*, logically follows sentence (3), which begins with *If*. And the sentence pair (3) and (2) logically follows the pair (4) and (1).

Questions 4–5 refer to the passage below.

Once I passed through a populous city imprinting my brain for future use with its shows, architecture, customs, traditions,
Yet now of all that city I remember only a woman I casually met there who detained me for love of me.
Day by day and night by night we were together—all else has long been forgotten by me.

4. The passage above is an example of
   (A) prose
   (B) free verse
   (C) blank verse
   (D) metered poetry

The correct answer is (B). This question deals with the techniques of poetry. This passage is an example of free verse, which is not rhymed and which does not have a regular metrical pattern. Blank verse (C) is, like this, unrhymed, but each line has only ten syllables. Although these lines lack regular meter, they are more rhythmic than most prose. If the passage were prose, there would be no capital letter in *Yet,* which does not begin a sentence, and there would be no break in the continuity of the printing.

5. The passage above was probably written by
   (A) Shakespeare
   (B) Milton
   (C) Wordsworth
   (D) Whitman

The correct answer is (D). By realizing that the passage is free verse, you can eliminate authors who wrote in a more formal meter. The passage is by Walt Whitman, perhaps the most celebrated writer of free verse. Shakespeare, Milton, and Wordsworth normally wrote in formal meters.

SAMPLE QUESTIONS AND STRATEGIES FOR THE CONTENT AREA EXERCISES

Following are representative Literature and Language Studies short constructed-response questions for each area covered. Strategies are included, as well as a sample response for each question.

Literature

> A slumber did my spirit seal
> I had no human fears:
> She seemed a thing that could not feel
> The touch of earthly years.
>
> (5) No motion has she now, no force,
> She neither hears nor sees;
> Rolled round in earth's diurnal course,
> With rocks, and stones, and trees.

1. As fully as possible, explain the circumstance of this poem, that is, who is speaking and what has happened. Discuss the use of contrast in the poem.

Strategy

Read and mark both of the tasks you are asked to perform, explain the circumstance of this poem (identify the speaker and what has happened) and discuss the contrast employed in the poem. As you read and mark the poem, ask questions about the meaning and use of words. If some words do not make sense to you, try to interpret them in a metaphorical sense. Consider the rhyme scheme and whether the poem tells a story.

Focus on the use of specific words and their function in the meaning of the poem. For example, consider the word *slumber* in line 1 and the separation from the human condition in lines 3 and 4 (*could not feel / The touch of earthly years*). In line 5, *no motion, no force,* and *neither hears nor sees* may be images associated with death. Note the negative words *no, neither,* and *nor,* which may suggest a contrast.

Sample Response

The gender of the speaker is not specified, but because the poem describes the loss of a woman, we may infer that the speaker is male. The first stanza describes the speaker's realization that "she" is dead and can no longer feel in a human way. The tense is the past. The second stanza, in the present tense, suggests a new reality for the woman. She has returned to the earth and has become a part of nature, just as much as the "rocks, stones, and trees."

The two stanzas contrast not only in the use of past and present tense, but also in that, in the first stanza, the speaker sees only the fact that the woman is dead, but by the end of the second stanza, he has realized that even though she, herself, has "no motion" and "no force," she shares in the movement of the "earth's diurnal course."

2. Discuss two techniques that an author can use to make a short story more interesting.

Strategy

Read the question twice, noting key points, before attempting to answer it. You might underline two techniques, short story, and interesting. Ask yourself what techniques might make *any* prose more interesting. For example, you might consider figurative language, multiple points of view, flashback, or foreshadowing and then decide on the two that seem most appropriate to the short story.

Sample Response

The use of flashback, a technique in which the narrative moves to a time prior to that of the main story, can make a short story more interesting. By using this technique, the author can reveal why characters are what they are and behave as they do by showing the reader details of their earlier lives.

Foreshadowing is a technique that uses clues to suggest events that have not yet occurred. It is often used to create suspense and thus make the story more interesting. Foreshadowing allows the author to link seemingly minor details to important events developed later in the story.

Questions 3–5 refer to the following poem. On the exam, you might find a question similar to any one of the three.

> When men shall find thy flower, thy glory pass,
> And thou, with careful brow sitting alone,
> Received hast this message from thy glass,
> That tells thee truth, and says that all is gone,
> (5) Fresh shalt thou see in me the wounds thou madest,
> Though spent thy flame, in me the heat remaining,
> I that have loved thee thus before thou fadest;
> My faith shall wax, when thou art in thy waning.
> The world shall find this miracle in me,
> (10) That fire can burn when all the matter's spent;
> Then what my faith hath been thyself shall see,
> And that thou wast unkind thou mayst repent.
> Thou mayst repent that thou hast scorned my tears,
> When winter snows upon thy golden hairs.

3. Describe the situation of this poem. Who is the speaker and the person addressed and what are their circumstances?

Sample Response

The speaker of this poem is a man addressing a beautiful young woman with whom he is in love. The young woman does not return the man's love, but he nevertheless vows to be faithful to her, even when she has grown old and is no longer beautiful. That the lady is still young is indicated by the verb tenses (the future tense of "shall find" and "shalt see") and by the phrase "before thou fadest." At the time of the poem, the lady's golden hair has not yet turned white.

4. Discuss the images the speaker uses to describe the woman and to describe his feelings.

Sample Response

The poem compares the lady's beauty to a flower (line 1), to a flame (line 6), and to the fuel that feeds the flame of the man's love (line 10) and describes her hair as golden (line 14). The man's love is compared to wounds (line 5), to heat (line 6), to faith (lines 8 and 11), and to a miracle (line 9). The most important source of images is religion, and the speaker's love is presented as a religious veneration of the lady. His love is miraculous because like a fire that burns without fuel, it will continue even after the beauty which inspired his love has faded away.

5. Discuss the rhetorical purpose of the poem. That is, what did the speaker hope to achieve by this poem and what are the methods he uses?

Sample Response

The purpose of the poem is to convince the lady to return the speaker's love while she is young and beautiful. The speaker makes his case by flattery (the lady is now as beautiful as a flower, is glorious) and more significantly, by asserting that his love is endless and by suggesting that the lady when she is old and no longer beautiful will regret that she did not accept such a love. He is saying, in effect, "You'll be sorry you refused a love like mine when you are old and gray."

Language and Linguistics

6. Standard American English is continually changing. Give three reasons for these changes.

Strategy

Note the task given. In this case, you are asked for three reasons. Next, note the prompt, the information given. Read this carefully. Focus on key words in the prompt. When writing your answer, use "buzzwords" when you can, that is, words that are used in the field and show a knowledge of the subject.

Sample Response

One reason that our language is changing is the necessity for new words to go with modern technology. As we invent or discover new items or processes, new names must be created to describe the items or processes accurately. For example, the word "taser" refers to a new electronic self-defense mechanism.

Another reason for the change is the infusion of words from foreign languages. As foreign words become used more frequently, they become part of our vocabulary. For example, the word "valet" comes from the French.

A third reason for the change is the inclusion of words that were once considered slang expressions. These slang expressions give new meanings to words. For example, the expression "chill out" doesn't mean to become cold but rather to become calm.

7. Explain and give four examples of how the same word can have different meanings.

Strategy

Note the tasks given. Underline or circle explain and four examples. Think of simple words that you have used in different ways. List your examples and give a few of their possible different meanings.

Sample Response

Words may have different meanings depending on the context in which they are used. For example, the word "hand" can mean a part of the human body or five playing cards in a game of poker. The word "tree" can mean a large plant or a diagram, as in a "family tree." The word "run" can mean to move quickly or a tear in a pair of stockings. The word "fan" can mean a device to help you keep cool or a person at a sports event.

Oral and Written Communication

8. List and discuss three factors that inhibit language acquisition.

Strategy

First, circle or underline the key words in the question. Notice that you need to list and discuss three factors. Next, focus on factors that inhibit language acquisition. If some factors don't immediately come to mind, think of factors that would *help* in language acquisition. Then write about how the absence of those factors would inhibit language acquisition.

Sample Response

Three factors that inhibit language acquisition are insufficient mental, emotional, and social growth.

Mental growth—As children grow mentally, they expand their ability to retain information. If this mental growth is slowed, words could be more difficult to learn and memorize.

Emotional growth—As children come in touch with expressing their feelings, their language base usually expands. If a child has inhibitions or emotional problems, this could slow his or her need or will to acquire language.

Social growth—As children learn to interact with other children, additional language becomes necessary. If this social growth is slowed and there is less interest or exchange, language growth may be inhibited.

9. As a child grows, in many respects communication becomes easier and more precise. Discuss a possible reason for this effect on communication.

Strategy

First, circle or underline the task to be completed. In this case, you are to discuss a possible reason. Next, focus on the prompt given. Notice the key words *communication becomes easier and more precise*. Try to think of examples where this is true. Sometimes, thinking of an example can help you find a reason.

Sample Response

As children get older, they experience many different people, items, and situations. They become more aware of similarities and differences. Since communication really depends on similar experiences or complementary experiences, children have, as they age, a larger and larger base from which to work. For example, if two children are discussing baseball hats, for good communication to occur, each must have had the experience of seeing a baseball hat or knowing what one is.

MATHEMATICS

CONTENT

The Mathematics section focuses on the fundamentals of mathematics and the ability to communicate the understanding of these fundamentals, to reason logically, and to solve problems using these fundamentals. Fundamentals of mathematics are defined as the mathematical background that an elementary school teacher must have. Because this section assesses reasoning and problem solving, only a minimal amount of computation is required. Nonprogrammable calculators are allowed to be used during the exam.

No knowledge of advanced-level mathematics is required for this exam, but real-life situations requiring a knowledge of several content areas will be used. Test takers should be familiar with commonly encountered terms in mathematics: prime numbers, factors, integers, ratio, area, perimeter, volume, parallel, perpendicular, polygon, etc.

All scratchwork is to be done in the test booklet. You should get used to this procedure because no scratch paper is allowed into the testing area.

Content Knowledge (Multiple-Choice)

The Content Knowledge (multiple-choice) test, which contains twenty-seven questions grouped together, covers the following major content areas and focuses on the topics listed under each. The approximate weight of each category is listed in parentheses.

1. **Numeration and number sense (20 percent)**

   - place value
   - cardinal and ordinal numbers
   - whole numbers
   - fractions
   - decimals
   - number concepts
   - problem solving

2. **Geometry, plane and solid (20 percent)**

   - angles
   - lines
   - parallelism
   - perpendicularity
   - congruence
   - similarity
   - polygons

3. Measurement (5 percent)

- estimation
- perimeter
- area
- volume
- mass
- weight
- time
- temperature
- angle measure
- English and metric systems of measurement

4. Algebraic concepts (10 percent)

- recognition and use of algebraic concepts
- identification and construction of formulas

5. Number theory (10 percent)

- set theory
- divisibility rules
- prime and composite numbers
- least common multiples
- greatest common divisors
- application to problem-solving situations

6. Real numbers and subsystems (20 percent)

- solving of word problems dealing with real-world situations
- working with different algorithms

7. Probability and statistics (15 percent)

- graphs, charts, and tables
- inferences
- basic problem solving
- predictions in probability and statistics

Content Area Exercises (Short Constructed-Response)

The four Mathematics short constructed-response questions ask test takers to summarize data, show strategies for solving problems, communicate mathematical concepts and ideas, and make generalizations. They generally conform to the following format.

- Three questions deal with probability and statistics, geometry, and the real number system and subsystems.
- One question is drawn from one of the following areas: measurement, algebra, number sense and numeration, number theory, and historical perspectives.

SAMPLE QUESTIONS AND STRATEGIES FOR THE CONTENT KNOWLEDGE SECTION

Each of the following examples represents an area tested on the Mathematics multiple-choice segment. Note that although the following questions are listed under their major content area, many questions may test more than one area. An analysis follows each question.

Numeration and Number Sense

1. In the following number, which digit is in the thousandths place?

6574.12398

(A) 2
(B) 3
(C) 5
(D) 9

The correct answer is (B). By underlining or circling what you are looking for, you will be sure that you are answering the right question. Here, it would be helpful to circle the key word *thousandths*. This is the kind of question which, under time pressure and testing pressure, may often be misread—in this case, perhaps, as *thousands*. Circling important words will minimize the possibility of misreading. To find the thousandths place, begin counting from the first number to the right of the decimal: tenths, hundredths, thousandths. The 3 is in the thousandths place. Your completed question might look like this after you mark the important words or terms.

1. In the following number, which ⬭digit⬭ is in the ⬭thousandths⬭ place?
6574.12③98

(A) 2
(B) ③
(C) 5
(D) 9

2. What is the correct order of the following from smallest to largest?

.6, .16, .66⅔, .58

(A) .6, .16, .66⅔, .58
(B) .58, .16, .6, .66⅔
(C) .16, .58, .6, .66⅔
(D) .66⅔, .6, .58, .16

The correct answer is (C). At times, questions may require you to compare the sizes of several decimals or of several fractions. If decimals are being compared, make sure that the numbers being compared have the same number of digits. (Remember, zeros to the far right of a decimal point can be inserted or eliminated without changing the value of the number.) Here, rewrite .6 as .60, giving all of the decimals the same number of digits: .60, .16, .66⅔, .58. Treating these as though the decimal point were not there (which can be done only when all the numbers have the same number of digits to the right of the decimal), the order is as follows: .16, .58, .60, .66⅔. Remember to circle important words in the question—here, *smallest to largest.*

3. What is the correct order of the following from smallest to largest?

$$⅝, ¾, ⅔$$

(A) ⅔, ¾, ⅝
(B) ⅔, ⅝, ¾
(C) ⅝, ⅔, ¾
(D) ¾, ⅝, ⅔

The correct answer is (C). Using common denominators,

$$⅝ = ¹⁵⁄₂₄$$

$$¾ = ¹⁸⁄₂₄$$

$$⅔ = ¹⁶⁄₂₄$$

Therefore, the order becomes ⅝, ⅔, ¾.

Using decimal equivalents,

$$⅝ = .625$$

$$¾ = .75 \text{ or } .750$$

$$⅔ = .66⅔ \text{ or } .666⅔$$

The order again becomes ⅝, ⅔, ¾

4. Which of the following is the best approximation of $(.889 \times 55)/9.97$ to the nearest tenth?
(A) 49.1
(B)   7.7
(C)   4.9
(D)   .5

The correct answer is (C). When you are asked to approximate, first check to see how far apart the answer choices are as a guide to how freely you can approximate. Notice here that the answers are not close. Now, making some quick approximations, $.889 \cong 1$ and $9.97 \cong 10$, which leaves the problem in this form:

$$\frac{1 \times 55}{10} = \frac{55}{10} = 5.5$$

The closest answer is (C), and it is therefore the correct answer. Notice that choices (A) and (E) are not reasonable. You could also use your calculator for this question to obtain an exact answer and then round to the nearest tenth.

5. What is the final cost of a watch that sells for $49.00 if the sales tax is 7%?
   (A) $49.07
   (B) $49.70
   (C) $52.00
   (D) $52.43

The correct answer is (D). Some questions, such as this one, need to be completely worked out. If you don't see a fast method but you do know that you could compute the answer, use your calculator. In this case, since the sales tax is 7% of $49.00,

$$7\% \text{ of } \$49.00 = (.07)(\$49.00) = \$3.43$$

The total cost of the watch is therefore

$$\$49.00 + \$3.43 = \$52.43$$

6. **Price List**

Top sirloin....................................... $2.99 per pound or 2 pounds for $5.00
Filet mignon................................... $4.00 per pound
London broil.................................. $1.79 per pound or 3 pounds for $5.00

Randy owns and manages Randy's Steakhouse. He needs to buy the following meats in order to have enough for the weekend business: 9 pounds of top sirloin, 8 pounds of filet mignon, and 7 pounds of London broil. What is the LEAST amount Randy can spend to buy the meat he needs for the weekend business?
   (A) $97.00
   (B) $71.44
   (C) $66.78
   (D) $54.99

The correct answer is (C). Here also you may wish to use your calculator.

top sirloin: 8 pounds + 1 pound
                = (4 × $5.00) + $2.99   (note: 2 pounds for $5.00)
                = $20.00 + $2.99
                = $22.99

filet mignon: 8 pounds
                = 8 × $4.00
                = $32.00

London broil: 6 pounds + 1 pound
                 = (2 × $5.00) + $1.79   (note: 3 pounds for $5.00)
                 = $10.00 + $1.79
                 = $11.79

Add to find the total.

$$\$22.99 + \$32.00 + \$11.79 = \$66.78$$

7. 51 × 6 could best be quickly mentally calculated by
   (A) 50 × 6 + 1
   (B) 51 + 51 + 51 + 51 + 51 + 51
   (C) (50 × 6) + (1 × 6)
   (D) (50 × 6) + 1/6

The correct answer is (C). Some problems, such as this one, may not ask you to solve for a numerical answer. Rather, you may be asked to set up the equation or expression without doing any solving, or you may be asked how to work a problem. A quick glance at the answer choices will help you know what is expected.

The quickest method of calculating 51 × 6 is to first multiply 50 × 6 (resulting in 300), then multiply 1 × 6 (resulting in 6), and then add them together (300 + 6 = 306). Answer choice (B) will also give the correct answer, but it is not the best way to *quickly* calculate the answer.

Geometry

1. If point P (1, 1) and point Q (1, 0) lie on the same coordinate graph, which of the following must be true?

   I. P and Q are equidistant from the origin.
   II. P is farther from the origin than P is from Q.
   III. Q is farther from the origin than Q is from P.

   (A) I only
   (B) II only
   (C) III only
   (D) I and II only

The correct answer is (B). In some problems, such as this, sketching diagrams or simple pictures can be very helpful because the diagram may tip off either a simple solution or a method for solving the problem. In this case, first draw the coordinate graph and then plot the points as follows.

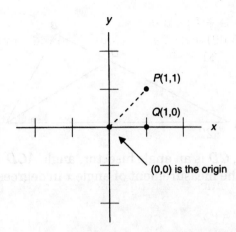

Only II is true. P is farther from the origin than P is from Q.

2. A hiking team begins at camp and hikes 5 miles north, then 8 miles west, then 6 miles south, then 9 miles east. In what direction must they now travel in order to return to camp?
   (A) North
   (B) Northeast
   (C) Northwest
   (D) West

The correct answer is (C). For this problem also, a diagram is very helpful.

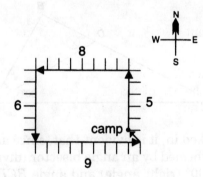

Thus, they must travel northwest (C) to return to camp. Note that in this case it is important to draw your diagram very accurately.

3.

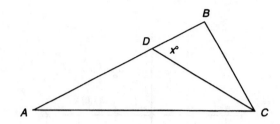

In the triangle above, *CD* is an angle bisector, angle *ACD* is 30°, and angle *ABC* is a right angle. What is the measurement of angle x in degrees?

(A) 30°
(B) 45°
(C) 60°
(D) 75°

The correct answer is (C). When you are given a diagram to work with, marking in that diagram as you read the question can save you valuable time. It can also give you insight into how to solve the problem because you will have the complete picture clearly in front of you.

Here, you should read the problem and mark as follows.

In the triangle above, *CD* is an angle bisector (*Stop and mark in the drawing*), angle *ACD* is 30° (*Stop and mark in the drawing*), and angle *ABC* is a right angle (*Stop and mark in the drawing*). What is the measurement of angle x in degrees? (*Stop and mark in or circle what you are looking for in the drawing.*)

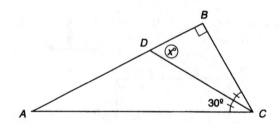

Now, with the drawing marked in, it is evident that, since angle *ACD* is 30°, angle *BCD* is also 30° because they are formed by an angle bisector (divides an angle into two equal parts). Since angle *ABC* is 90° (right angle) and angle *BCD* is 30°, then angle x is 60° because there are 180° in a triangle.

$$180 - (90 + 30) = 60$$

Always mark in diagrams as you read descriptions and information about them. This includes what you are looking for.

4.

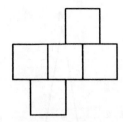

If each square in the figure above has a side of length 1, what is the perimeter of the figure?

(A) 8

(B) 12

(C) 14

(D) 16

The correct answer is (B). This is also a case in which marking in the diagram is helpful. Mark the known facts.

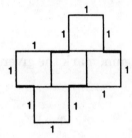

You now have a calculation for the perimeter: 10 *plus* the darkened parts. Now, look carefully at the top two darkened parts. They will add up to 1. (Notice how the top square may slide over to illustrate that fact.)

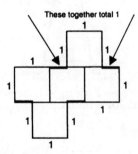

The same is true for the bottom darkened parts. They will add to 1. Thus, the total perimeter is 10 + 2, or 12.

5.

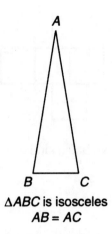

△ABC is isosceles
AB = AC

The perimeter of the isosceles triangle shown above is 42″. The two equal sides are each three times as long as the third side. What are the lengths of each side?
(A) 21, 21, 21
(B) 6, 6, 18
(C) 18, 21, 3
(D) 18, 18, 6

The correct answer is (D). Once again, mark the given information in the diagram.

Mark the equal sides.

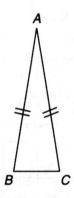

AB and *AC* are each three times as long as *BC*.

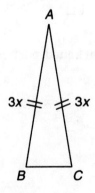

The equation for perimeter is

$$3x + 3x + x = 42$$

$$7x = 42$$

$$x = 6$$

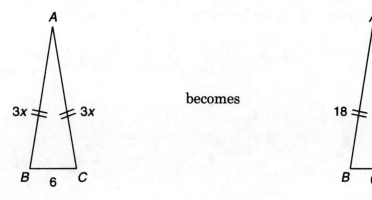

Note that this problem can also be solved by working from the answers. You know from the information given that two sides of the triangle are equal and that the two equal sides are both larger than the third side, which allows you to immediately eliminate answers (A), (B), and (C).

Measurement

1. Which of the following times gives approximately a 90° degree angle between the two hands of the clock?
   (A) 6:00
   (B) 7:00
   (C) 9:00
   (D) 11:00

The correct answer is (C). By simply sketching the times on a clock, it is evident that 9:00 gives an angle of approximately 90 degrees between the two hands.

2. If all sides of a square are doubled, the area of that square
   (A) is doubled
   (B) is tripled
   (C) is multiplied by 4
   (D) remains the same

The correct answer is (C) One way to solve this problem is to draw a square and then double all its sides. Then compare the two areas.

Your first diagram

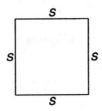

Doubling every side

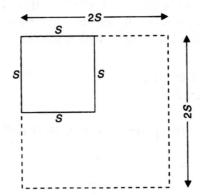

You can see that the total area of the new square will now be four times the original square.

3. What is the maximum number of milk cartons, each 2″ wide by 3″ long by 4″ tall, that can fit into a cardboard box with inside dimensions of 16″ wide by 9″ long by 8″ tall?
   (A) 18
   (B) 20
   (C) 24
   (D) 48

The correct answer is (D). Drawing a diagram, as shown below, may be helpful in envisioning the process of fitting the cartons into the box. Notice that 8 cartons will fit across the box, 3 cartons deep and 2 "stacks" high.

$$8 \times 3 \times 2 = 48 \text{ cartons}$$

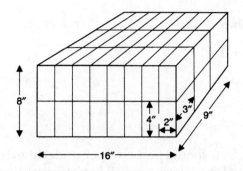

4.

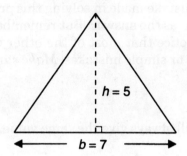

$h = 5$

$b = 7$

To find the area of the figure above, a student would use which of the following formulas?

   I. area = base times height
  II. area = ½ times base times height
 III. area = one side squared

(A) I only
(B) II only
(C) III only
(D) I and II only

The correct answer is (B). Notice that it is not necessary to use any of the numerical values given in the diagram. You are simply to answer how the problem is to be worked. In such cases, don't bother working the problem. It is a waste of your time.

5. Which equation can be used to find the perimeter, *P*, of a rectangle that has a length of 18 feet and a width of 15 feet?
(A) $P = (18)(15)$
(B) $P = 2(15)(18)$
(C) $P = (2)15 + 18$
(D) $P = 2(15 + 18)$

The correct answer is (D). In this question, as in the previous one, you should not work out a numerical answer. You need only identify the correct formula for doing so. The perimeter of the rectangle can be found by adding the length to the width and doubling this sum.

$$P = 2(15 + 18)$$

Algebraic Concepts

1. If $x + 6 = 9$, then $3x + 1 =$
   (A) 3
   (B) 9
   (C) 10
   (D) 34

The correct answer is (C). You should first circle or underline $3x + 1$ because this is what you are solving for. Solving for x leaves $x = 3$. Then substituting into $3x + 1$ gives $3(3) + 1$, or 10. The most common mistake made in solving this problem is to solve for x, which is 3, and *mistakenly choose* (A) as the answer. But remember, you are solving for $3x + 1$, not just x. You should also notice that most of the other choices would all be possible answers if you made common or simple mistakes. *Make sure that you are answering the right question.*

2. Which of the following will always give the same value as $a(b + c - d)$?
   (A) $ab - ac + ad$
   (B) $abcd$
   (C) $abc - d$
   (D) $ab + ac - ad$

The correct answer is (D).Substituting numbers for variables can often be an aid to understanding a problem. Remember to substitute simple numbers because *you* have to do the work. The above problem can be solved in this way. The problem shows the distributive property as a is distributed throughout the terms in the parentheses.

3. If $x > 1$, which of the following decreases as x decreases?

   I. $x + x^2$

   II. $2x^2 - x$

   III. $\dfrac{1}{x + 1}$

   (A) I only
   (B) II only
   (C) III only
   (D) I and II only

The correct answer is (D). This problem is most easily solved by taking each situation and substituting simple numbers. However, in the first situation (I. $x + x^2$), you should recognize that this expression will decrease as x decreases.

Trying $x = 2$ gives $2 + (2)^2 = 6$.

Now, trying $x = 3$ gives $3 + (3)^2 = 12$.

Notice that choices (B) and (C) are already eliminated because they do not contain I. You should also realize that now you need to try only the values in II. Because III is not paired with I as a possible choice, III cannot be one of the answers.

Trying $x = 2$ in the expression $2x^2 - x$ gives $2(2)^2 - 2$, or $2(4) - 2 = 6$.

Now, trying $x = 3$ gives $2(3)^2 - 3$, or $2(9) - 3 = 15$.

This expression also decreases as x decreases. Therefore, the correct answer is (D). Once again, notice that III should not be attempted because it is not one of the possible choices. Be sure to make logical substitutions. Use a positive number, a negative number, or zero when applicable to get the full picture.

4. Barney can mow the lawn in 5 hours, and Fred can mow the lawn in 4 hours. How long will it take them to mow the lawn together?
   (A) 5 hours
   (B) 4½ hours
   (C) 4 hours
   (D) 2⅔ hours

The correct answer is (D). Suppose that you are unfamiliar with the type of equation for this problem. Try the "reasonable" method. Since Fred can mow the lawn in 4 hours by himself, it will take less than 4 hours if Barney helps him. Therefore, choices (A), (B), and (C) are unreasonable and only choice (D) is possible.

Using the equation for this problem gives the following calculations.

$$\frac{1}{5} + \frac{1}{4} = \frac{1}{x}$$

In one hour, Barney could do ⅕ of the job, and in 1 hour, Fred could do ¼ of the job. Unknown $1/x$ is that part of the job they could do together in one hour. Now, solving, you calculate as follows.

$$\frac{4}{20} + \frac{5}{20} = \frac{1}{x}$$

$$\frac{9}{20} = \frac{1}{x}$$

Cross multiplying gives $\qquad 9x = 20$

Therefore, $\qquad x = {}^{20}\!/_9$ or $2\frac{2}{9}$

5. If $(x/4) + 2 = 22$, what is the value of x?
   (A) 40
   (B) 80
   (C) 100
   (D) 120

The correct answer is (B). If you cannot solve this algebraically, you could use the *work up from the choices* strategy. Start with (C), 100. What if $x = 100$?

$$(x/4) + 2 = 22$$
$$(100/4) + 2 \stackrel{?}{=} 22$$
$$25 + 2 \stackrel{?}{=} 22$$
$$27 \neq 22$$

Note that since 27 is too large, choice (D) will also be too large. Therefore, try (A). If (A) is too small, then you know the answer is (B). If (A) works, the answer is (A).

$$(x/4) + 2 = 22$$
$$(40/4) + 2 \stackrel{?}{=} 22$$
$$10 + 2 \stackrel{?}{=} 22$$
$$12 \neq 22$$

Since (A) is too small, the answer must be (B).

6. Harold's age is 3 years less than half Sue's age. If Harold is 9 years old, how old is Sue?

   Suppose S represents Sue's age. Which of the following equations can be used to find Sue's age?
   (A) $9 = (½)(S) - 3$
   (B) $9 - 3 = (½)(S)$
   (C) $9 = 3 - (½)(S)$
   (D) $3 - 9 = (½)(S)$

The correct answer is (A). This question, as other examples given, does not ask you to find a numerical answer. Rather you need only identify the formula that would be used to solve the problem. Changing the word sentence into a number sentence (equation),

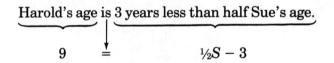

7. Rick is three times as old as Maria, and Maria is four years older than Leah. If Leah is z years old, what is Rick's age is terms of z?
   (A) $3z + 4$
   (B) $3z - 12$
   (C) $3z + 12$
   (D) $(z + 4)/3$

The correct answer is (C). Here, once again, you need not find the numerical answer.

$$z = \text{Leah's age}$$

$$z + 4 = \text{Maria's age}$$

$$3(z + 4) = \text{Rick's age}$$

$$3z + 12 = \text{Rick's age}$$

Number Theory

1. How many integers between 1 and 150 are divisible by both 4 and 5?
   - (A) 7
   - (B) 8
   - (C) 9
   - (D) 10

The correct answer is (A). If an integer is divisible by both 4 and 5, it must be divisible by 20. The integers between 1 and 150 that are divisible by 20 are 20, 40, 60, 80, 100, 120, and 140. So there are 7 integers between 1 and 150 that are divisible by both 4 and 5. Notice that here you should simply list the multiples of 20 between 1 and 150.

2. If x is a positive integer in the equation $12x = q$, then q must be a
   - (A) positive even integer
   - (B) negative even integer
   - (C) positive odd integer
   - (D) negative odd integer

The correct answer is (A). At first glance, this problem appears quite complex. But this question is one in which plugging in numbers greatly simplifies it. First, plug in 1 (the simplest positive integer) for x.

$$12x = q$$

$$12(1) = q$$

$$12 = q$$

Now, try 2.

$$12x = q$$

$$12(2) = q$$

$$24 = q$$

Try it again. No matter what positive integer is plugged in for x, q will always be positive and even.

3. What is the counting number that is less than 15 and when divided by 3 has a remainder of 1, but when divided by 4 has a remainder of 2?
    (A) 5
    (B) 8
    (C) 10
    (D) 12

The correct answer is (C). In this problem, it is most efficient to work from the answers and eliminate wrong answer choices. You can immediately eliminate (B) and (D) because they are divisible by 4, leaving no remainder. Choice (A) can also be eliminated because it leaves a remainder of 1 when divided by 4. Therefore, (C) is left as the correct answer. 10 leaves a remainder of 1 when divided by 3 and a remainder of 2 when divided by 4.

4. What is the greatest common factor of the numbers 18, 24, and 30?
    (A) 2
    (B) 3
    (C) 4
    (D) 6

The correct answer is (D). The largest number that divides evenly into 18, 24, and 30 is 6. As in the previous problem, you can work from the answers, but here, you should start with the largest answer choice beacause you're looking for the *greatest* common factor.

5.   1, 3, 6, 10, 15 . . .

    Which of the following is the next number in the series given above?
    (A) 20
    (B) 21
    (C) 25
    (D) 26

The correct answer is (B). Notice that the pattern here is based on the difference between the numbers.

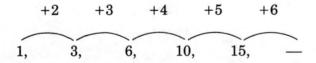

Therefore, the answer is 21.

Real Numbers and Subsystems

1. Together, a hat and coat cost $125. The coat costs $25 more than the hat. What is the cost of the coat?
   (A) $25
   (B) $50
   (C) $75
   (D) $100

The correct answer is (C). Circle the key words *cost of the coat*. To solve algebraically,

$$x = \text{hat}$$

$$x + 25 = \text{coat (cost \$25 more than the hat)}$$

Together they cost $125.

$$(x + 25) + x = 125$$

$$2x + 25 = 125$$

$$2x = 100$$

$$x = 50$$

But this is the cost of the *hat*. Notice that $50 is one of the answer choices, (B). Since $x = 50$, then $x + 25 = 75$. Therefore, the coat costs $75, which is choice (C). *Always answer the question that is being asked.* Circling the key word or words will help you do that.

2. A corporation triples its annual bonus to 50 of its employees. What percent of the employees' new bonus is the increase?
   (A) 50%
   (B) 66⅔%
   (C) 100%
   (D) 200%

The correct answer is (B). Let's use $100 for the normal bonus. If the annual bonus was normally $100, tripled it would now be $300. Therefore, the increase ($200) is ⅔ of the new bonus ($300). Two-thirds is 66⅔.

3. If a mixture is 3/7 alcohol by volume and 4/7 water by volume, what is the ratio of the volume of alcohol to the volume of water in this mixture?
   (A) 3/7
   (B) 4/7
   (C) ¾
   (D) 4/3

The correct answer is (C). "Pulling" information out of the word problem structure can often give you a better look at what you're working with, giving you additional insight into the problem. When pulling out information, actually write out the numbers and/or letters to the side of the problem, putting them into some helpful form and eliminating some of the wording. Here, the first bit of information that should be pulled out is what you're looking for—*ratio of the volume of alcohol to the volume of water*. Rewrite it as *A:W* and then into its working form, *A/W*. Next, you should pull out the volumes of each—$A = \frac{3}{7}$ and $W = \frac{4}{7}$

Now, the answer can be easily figured by inspection or substitution. Using $(\frac{3}{7})/(\frac{4}{7})$, invert the bottom fraction and multiply to get $\frac{3}{7} \times \frac{7}{4} = \frac{3}{4}$. The ratio of the volume of alcohol to the volume of water is 3 to 4.

4. Bill is ten years older than his sister. If Bill was twenty-five years of age in 1983, in what year could he have been born?
   (A) 1948
   (B) 1953
   (C) 1958
   (D) 1963

The correct answer is (C). The key words here are *in what year* and *could he have been born*. Thus, the solution is simple: $1983 - 25 = 1958$. Notice that the information used here is *twenty-five years of age* and *in 1983*. The fact about Bill's age in comparison to his sister's age is not needed.

5. John is 18 years old. He works for his father for $\frac{3}{4}$ of the year, and he works for his brother for the rest of the year. What is the ratio of the time John spends working for his brother to the time he spends working for his father per year?
   (A) $\frac{1}{4}$
   (B) $\frac{1}{3}$
   (C) $\frac{3}{4}$
   (D) $\frac{4}{3}$

The correct answer is (B). The key word *rest* points to the answer.

$$1 - \frac{3}{4} = \frac{4}{4} - \frac{3}{4} = \frac{1}{4} \text{ (the part of the year John works for his brother)}$$

Also, a key idea is the way in which the ratio is to be written. The problem becomes that of finding the ratio of $\frac{1}{4}$ to $\frac{3}{4}$.

$$\frac{\frac{1}{4}}{\frac{3}{4}} = \frac{1}{4} \div \frac{3}{4} = \frac{1}{\cancel{4}_1} \times \frac{\cancel{4}^1}{3} = \frac{1}{3}$$

Note that in this problem, as in the previous one, unnecessary information is provided—in this case, John's age.

Probability and Statistics

1. What is the probability of throwing two dice in one toss so that they total 11?
   - (A) ⅙
   - (B) ¹⁄₁₁
   - (C) ¹⁄₁₈
   - (D) ¹⁄₃₆

The correct answer is (C). If you don't know a formal method to solve probability problems, you can try some possibilities. Set up what could happen, but set up only as much as you need to. Here, you should simply list all the possible combinations resulting in 11 (5 + 6 and 6 + 5) and realize that the total possibilities are 36 (6 × 6). Thus, the probability equals

$$\frac{\text{possibilities totaling 11}}{\text{total possibilities}} = \frac{2}{36} = \frac{1}{18}$$

2. What is the probability of tossing a penny twice so that both times it lands heads up?
   - (A) ⅛
   - (B) ¼
   - (C) ⅓
   - (D) ½

The correct answer is (B). The probability of throwing a head in one throw is

$$\frac{\text{chances of a head}}{\text{total chances (1 head + 1 tail)}} = \frac{1}{2}$$

Since you are trying to throw a head *twice*, multiply the probability for the first toss ½ times the probability for the second toss (again ½). Thus, ½ × ½ = ¼, and ¼ is the probability of throwing heads twice in two tosses. Another way of approaching this problem is to look at the total number of possible outcomes:

	First Toss	*Second Toss*
1.	H	H
2.	H	T
3.	T	H
4.	T	T

Thus, there are four different possible outcomes. There is only one way to throw two heads in two tosses. Thus, the probability of tossing two heads in two tosses is 1 out of 4 total outcomes, or ¼.

3. How many combinations are possible if a person has 4 sports jackets, 5 shirts, and 3 pairs of slacks?
   (A) 4
   (B) 5
   (C) 12
   (D) 60

The correct answer is (D). Since each of the 4 sports jackets may be worn with 5 different shirts, there are 20 possible combinations. these may be worn with each of the 3 pairs of slacks for a total of 60 possible combinations. Stated simply, $5 \times 4 \times 3 = 60$ possible combinations.

SAMPLE QUESTIONS AND STRATEGIES FOR THE CONTENT AREA EXERCISES

Following are representative Mathematics short constructed-response questions from areas covered. Strategies and a sample response are included with each question.

Probability and Statistics

1.   **Total: 20 Days of Vacation**

   10 days of sightseeing
   5 days of shopping
   4 days of relaxing and swimming
   1 day of travel

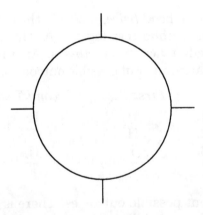

Use the circle above to construct a pie chart showing the percentages to reflect the breakdown of vacation days. Explain the reason for the size of each of the sections.

Strategy

First, circle or underline what you are being asked to do. In this problem, you are being asked to <u>construct a pie chart</u> and to <u>explain the reason for the size of each of the sections</u>. Next, carefully review the information given, keeping in mind that the total in a pie chart is 100%. When constructing a pie chart, always start by keeping in mind that 50% is half of the circle and 25% is a quarter of the circle. Then place or draw the largest amount or section first.

Sample Response

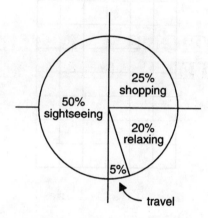

10 days of sightseeing out of 20 total is 10/20 = 1/2 = 50%.
5 days of shopping out of 20 total is 5/20 = 1/4 = 25%.
4 days of relaxing and swimming out of 20 total is 4/20 = 1/5 = 20%.
1 day of travel out of 20 total is 1/20 = 5%.

2. If Sara flips a two-sided coin three times, what are the odds of getting three heads in a row? Explain how you arrived at your answer.

Strategy

First, circle or underline what you are being asked to do. In this problem, you are being asked to find the <u>odds</u> and <u>explain</u> how you got them. Next, solve the problem showing your work. Note the steps that you used to get the answer. Explaining your procedure—the steps—will complete the task.

Sample Response

When Sara flips the coin the first time, the odds of getting heads is 1 out of 2, or ½. Since each flip is independent of the next flip, you multiply the odds for each independent event. There are 3 independent events, so the odds are ½ × ½ × ½ = ⅛. So the odds of Sara getting three heads in a row are 1 out of 8.

3.
Car Sales: 1950–1990

1950—100 cars sold
1960—200 cars sold
1970—300 cars sold
1980—400 cars sold
1990—300 cars sold

Use the grid below to graph the information given above. Explain your procedure in graphing.

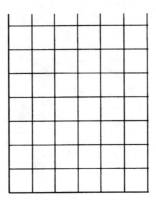

Strategy

First, underline or circle what you are being asked to do. In this case, you are being asked to graph and explain. Next, carefully review the information given to graph. Note the major categories or groups. Decide what major relationship the graph is supposed to show so that you will properly label each side. Check the numbers given and notice the range.

Sample Response

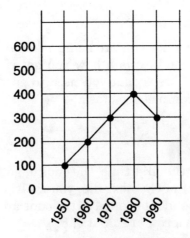

The vertical numbers on the left side of the graph represent the number of cars, starting with 0 and increasing by steps of 100. The horizontal numbers along the bottom of the graph indicate the years of sales starting with 1950.

Since there were 100 cars sold in 1950, the graph would be appropriately marked at the 100 line directly above the 1950 line. 1960 would be marked at the 200 line. 1970 would be marked at the 300 line. 1980 would be marked at the 400 line. And 1990 would be marked at the 300 line.

Geometry

4.

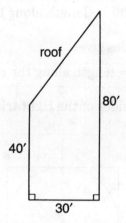

The cross-sectional diagram of a downtown office building shown above has the dimensions given. What is the length along the roof? Explain your method of arriving at the answer.

Strategy

First circle or underline what you are being asked to find and what else you must do. In this problem, you are being asked to find the <u>length along the roof</u> and to <u>explain your method</u>. Next, you should carefully read the information given. In geometry problems, you should mark the diagrams and fill in as many dimensions as possible. Since you are being asked to solve and explain, show your steps and describe your method in finding the answer. Finally, make sure that you have answered the question and completed the task given.

Sample Response

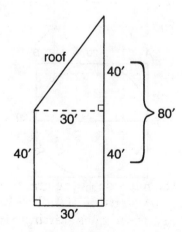

By drawing a line which divides the diagaram into two parts—a rectangle and a right triangle—the length of the roof can be determined. The upper triangular section has a base of 30 feet and a height of 40 feet. Using the Pythagorean theorem for right triangles,

$$30^2 + 40^2 = (\text{length along the roof})^2$$

$$900 + 1600 = (\text{length along the roof})^2$$

$$2500 = (\text{length along the roof})^2$$

Taking the square roots of both sides gives

$$50 = \text{length along the roof}$$

You could also recognize that the sides of the right triangle are in a 3-4-5 ratio, which is commonly found in right triangles.

5.

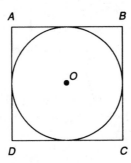

If the radius of circle O inscribed in square $ABCD$ as shown above is 10 inches, what is the perimeter of square $ABCD$? Explain how you arrived at your answer.

Strategy

First, circle or underline the task. You are being asked to find the underline{perimeter} and underline{explain} your procedure. Next, mark the diagram and fill in the given information. Since the outside figure is a square, you should mark each of the sides as equal. Solve the problem, paying special attention to the steps you use. Explaining these steps will complete your task.

Sample Response

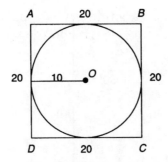

By looking at the diagram, it is obvious that the radius, which is 10 inches, is equal to one-half the length of one of the sides. Therefore, one side is 20 inches. Since the circle is inscribed in a square, and all sides of a square are equal, each side is 20 inches. The perimeter is the sum of all sides, or 20 + 20 + 20 + 20 = 80 inches.

Real Numbers and Subsystems

6. One way to multiply 103 × 17 is to multiply 100 × 17 and then 3 × 17 and add the results. Without calculating, how do you know that this method will work? Explain the method and then check by calculating the results.

Strategy

Circle or underline the tasks given. In this problem, you are given more than one task—explain the method and check by calculating. Notice that the problem says "without calculating," so some insight into the method is necessary. If you do not spot the method without calculating, calculate the answer and work backward. Often, you will understand the insight involved after calculating an answer.

Sample Response

The method used here is really the distributive property. Since 103 × 17 is really (100 + 3)(17), you could simply distribute as follows.

$$(100 \times 17) + (3 \times 17)$$

To check the answer, multiply 103 × 17, giving 1751. Since 100 × 17 is 1700 and 3 × 17 is 51, the total is 1751. Since both answers are the same, the method has been checked.

7.

×	3		9	
2				
			45	55
7		42		
	27		81	

The table above gives the operation involved, some of the numbers involved in the operation, and some of the outcomes. Fill in the table completely and explain your method.

Strategy

First, circle or underline what you are being asked to do. In this case, you are being asked to fill in the table and explain your method. Carefully check the operation involved and then the numbers in the columns. Next, check the numbers given in the table and look for the relationships between them or patterns.

Sample Response

×	3	6	9	11
2	6	12	18	22
5	15	30	**45**	**55**
7	21	**42**	63	77
9	**27**	54	**81**	99

Since the operation in the table is multiplication, some of the numbers can be filled in by simply multiplying. But some of the column headings must be discovered by dividing. For example, if 7 times something is 42, then the top number in that column is 6 because 42 divided by 7 is 6. These are the steps used.

Algebraic Concepts

8. If $x + y = 12$, and x is an integer greater than 12, what are the possible values of y? Explain your answer.

Strategy

First, circle or underline what you must find. In this problem, you are looking for possible values of y and an explanation of your answer. Next, review the information or equation given. If possible, solve the equation; if not, plug in values for one or both of the variables. When plugging in, watch for patterns in the outcomes. Make sure that you fulfill all of the tasks given.

Sample Response

If x is greater than 12, then y must always be a negative integer. Substituting 13 for x, you can see that for $13 + y$ to equal 12, y would have to be -1. Substituting 14 for x, you can see that for $14 + y$ to equal 12, y would have to be -2. If you try more numbers that are greater than 12, you will see that the pattern continues and that the value of y will always be negative.

9. Simplify the expression $4x + 3y + 4x + 2y$. Explain your method.

Strategy

Always circle or underline what you are being asked to do. In this case, you are being asked to <u>simplify the expression</u> and <u>explain your method</u>. Note the variables given and focus on the procedure. List the steps as you go through the process.

Sample Response

The expression $4x + 3y + 4x + 2y$ can be simplified to $8x + 5y$. Since you can combine only like terms, that is, x's with x's and y's with y's, you should rearrange and regroup the terms as follows: $(4x + 4x) + (3y + 2y)$. Now, combining like terms gives $4x + 4x$ is $8x$ and $3y + 2y$ is $5y$. So the simplified version is $8x + 5y$.

USING YOUR CALCULATOR

The MSAT allows the use of calculators, and you should take a calculator to the test. Even though no question will require the use of a calculator—that is, each question can be answered without a calculator—in some instances, using a calculator will save you valuable time.

You should

- Bring your own calculator, since you can't borrow one during the exam.

- Bring a calculator even if you don't think you'll use it.

- Make sure that you are familiar with the use of your calculator.

- Make sure that your calculator has new, fresh batteries and is in good working order.

- Practice using your calculator on some of the problems to see when and where it will be helpful.

- Check for a shortcut to any problem that seems to involve much computation. But use your calculator if it will be time effective. If there appears to be too much computation or the problem seems impossible without the calculator, you're probably doing something wrong.

- Before doing an operation, check the number that you keyed in on the display to make sure that you keyed in the right number. You may wish to check each number as you key it in.

- Before using your calculator, set up the problem and/or steps on your paper. Write the numbers on paper as you perform each step on your calculator. (It is generally safer not to use the memory function on your calculator.)

- Be sure to carefully clear the calculator before beginning new calculations.

Be careful that you

- Don't rush out and buy a sophisticated calculator for the test.

- Don't bring a calculator that you're unfamiliar with.

- Don't bring a pocket organizer, hand-held mini-computer, laptop computer, or calculator with a typewriter-type keypad or paper tape.

- Don't bring a calculataor that requires an outlet or any other external power source.

- Don't bring a calculator that makes noise.

- Don't try to share a calculator.

- Don't try to use a calculator on every problem.

- Don't become dependent on your calculator.

Take advantage of being allowed to use a calculator on the test. Learn to use a calculator efficiently by practicing. As you approach a problem, first focus on how to solve that problem, and then decide if the calculator will be helpful. Remember, a calculator can save you time on some problems, but also remember that each problem can be solved without a calculator. Also remember that a calculator will not solve a problem for you by itself. You must understand the problem first.

HISTORY/SOCIAL SCIENCES

CONTENT

The History/Social Sciences section concentrates on significant historical events and issues and basic social science concepts. Because of the multidisciplinary approach of this section, almost all multiple-choice and constructed-response questions require knowledge of both history and the social sciences. Also, using higher-level/critical-thinking skills is essential in answering the majority of questions in this area. A number of questions will require exercising critical-thinking skills in demonstrating an understanding of charts, graphs, tables, maps, political cartoons, original documents, and short quotations.

Content Knowledge (Multiple-Choice)

The Content Knowledge (multiple-choice) test, which contains twenty-four questions grouped together, covers the following major content areas and focuses on the topics listed under each. The approximate weight of each category is listed in parentheses. Because answering almost every question in the Content Knowledge test requires an understanding of both history and the social sciences, the weights for both areas total 100 percent.

Historical Fields

1. **California history (10 percent)**

   - overview of the geographic regions
   - Native-American customs, ceremonies, and demographics
   - European exploration and colonization
   - Spanish and Mexican rule
   - the gold rush
   - westward expansion and statehood
   - growth through World War I and World War II
   - development to the present

2. **United States history (45 percent)**

   - Native-American peoples
   - exploration and colonization
   - issues leading to the American Revolution
   - the "new-nation" period
   - growth of the republic
   - the Civil War and Reconstruction
   - post-Reconstruction

- immigration in the early twentieth century
- the industrialization of America (causes and consequences)
- World War I and World War II (causes and consequences)
- the nuclear age and the Cold War (causes and consequences)
- America in the last quarter of the twentieth century

3. World history (40 percent)

- the prehistoric period
- the development of early civilizations
- the classical civilizations of Greece and Rome
- the development of the great religions of the world
- feudal society in Europe and Japan
- the development of the Chinese and Indian empires
- kingdoms and cultures of sub-Saharan Africa
- the rise of Islam
- Central American and South American civilizations
- the development and expansion of European nations
- colonialism, nationalism, imperialism, and independence in the nineteenth and twentieth centuries
- political ideology in the twentieth century and its impact on world events

4. Nonhistorical perspective (5 percent)

- social science questions not directly posed in historical context

Social Science Fields

1. Government and politics (20 percent)

- political ideology and theories (such as absolutism, communism, socialism, and democracy)
- United States government and the American political system

2. Geography (35 percent)

- emphasis on physical, cultural, political, economic, and regional geography
- map and globe reading
- the geographical setting of an area (understanding how geography and history are interconnected)

3. Economics (25 percent)

- basic economic concepts (such as supply and demand, inflation, and recession)
- the government's role in the economy

4. **Anthropology and sociology (20 percent)**
   - terminology
   - research methodology and techniques
   - general concepts related to humans and society (human culture and social organization)
   - cultural change

Content Area Exercises (Short Constructed-Response)

The four History/Social Sciences short constructed-response questions generally conform to the following format.

- One question focuses on United States history and geography.
- One question centers on United States history and political science.
- One question is devoted to world history and geography.
- One question is based on any historical period and economics.

SAMPLE QUESTIONS AND STRATEGIES FOR THE CONTENT KNOWLEDGE SECTION

Each of the following examples represents an area tested on the History/Social Sciences multiple-choice segment. An analysis follows each question.

Historical Fields

California History

1. Cesar Chavez is most closely associated with political reforms in which of the following areas?
   (A) Unionization of migrant farm workers
   (B) Bilingual education for Hispanic students
   (C) Medical treatment for the indigent and homeless
   (D) Voter registration for undocumented aliens

The correct answer is (A). In answering the question, first attempt to place Cesar Chavez in a historical time period, which is often sufficient to give you a historical perspective. Cesar Chavez attempted to unionize migrant (seasonal) farm workers in the early 1960s. He was able to accomplish many of his political objectives through a nationwide boycott of the California lettuce and grape industries to force growers to compromise at the bargaining table. You could quickly eliminate choice (D) because only citizens of the United States can register to vote. Undocumented aliens or documented aliens (workers possessing a green card legally permitting them to work in the United States) are not American citizens. Choices (B) and (C) concerned Chavez, but the focus of his work was always the migrant farm worker. The question asks for the area *most* associated with Chavez. By establishing the United Farm Workers union (UFW), Chavez provided a political forum and powerful collective-bargaining agency for migrant workers. Those who joined the UFW were not only Hispanics; many Filipino and Anglo workers also readily joined. Prior to Chavez's efforts, migrant workers were intimidated by the power of agribusiness. Chavez's belief in nonviolence, coupled with his brilliant political acumen and popular support, resulted in better pay and working conditions for migrant workers.

2. The legal basis on which the United States obtained California from Mexico in 1848 was
   (A) annexation
   (B) purchase
   (C) treaty
   (D) revolt

The correct answer is (C). This is a fact-recall type question. A number of test questions are at this level; however, the majority test higher-level thinking skills. The Treaty of Guadalupe Hidalgo (1848), which ended the Mexican-American War, handed over all lands between Texas and the Pacific to the United States, including California. Acquisition of California fulfilled the vision of an American empire stretching from the Atlantic to the Pacific, the "Manifest Destiny" of the United States. Texas was acquired through annexation (A) in 1845. Purchase (B) enabled the United States to obtain Louisiana from France in 1803, a small strip of land south of the Gila River from Mexico (the Gadsden Purchase) in 1853, and Alaska from Russia in 1867.

3. Which of the following was the most important food of the Indians occupying the foothill regions of California prior to historic contact?
   (A) Yucca plants
   (B) Fish and large game
   (C) Seeds and berries
   (D) Acorn nuts

The correct answer is (D). In analyzing this question, you must recognize the limiting factors in the question (food, foothill regions, historic contact), which allows you to eliminate obviously wrong answers. The most important and only reliable food for the majority of California Indians, including Indians of the foothills, was acorn nuts. You can eliminate (B) because coastal and river Indians, not foothill Indians, would have eaten fish, and few Indians included large game animals as a regular part of their diet. While seeds and berries (C) were a part of the Indians' diet because grasses and wild oats covered many hills and valleys and while yucca plants were used as both a food and a basket source, prior to European contact (1500s), it was the acorn (the nut of the oak tree) that was the Indians' staple food source. Almost all California Indians depended on acorn meal because oaks grew in most parts of California. After pounding the acorn kernel into a powder, Indians used water to leach the acorn's bitter tannic acid. The resulting meal could be boiled into a mush, baked into cakes, or stored.

United States History

1. Which of the following had the most revolutionary impact on the economic development of the West during the nineteenth century?
   (A) The long drive
   (B) The invention of barbed wire
   (C) The refrigerated railroad car
   (D) The steamboat

The correct answer is (B). To analyze this difficult question, you must recognize that the term *revolutionary* implies a substantial and far-reaching impact. Also, you must take into consideration the concept of the economic development of the West (a geographic area) and the time frame (all of the 1800s). You can eliminate (A), moving cattle from one area to another (for example from Texas to Wyoming), and (C), the refrigerated railroad car (invented in the late nineteenth century), because neither was revolutionary in the economic development of the West. The steamboat (D) affected the economic development of the Mississippi basin but is too limited an answer to be correct. But barbed wire was revolutionary in its economic impact on the West because it doomed the open cattle range, making it possible for thousands of homesteaders to fence off land to prevent roaming cattle from destroying crops. The commercial practicality of barbed wire, made possible by the machine invented by J. F. Glidden in 1874, by 1890 resulted in much open-range land being privately owned, encouraging the development of stock farming, centralization, and town building. Some historians compare the importance of barbed wire in the West to that of the cotton gin in the South.

2. "Remember the *Maine*" best exemplifies which of the following philosophies?
   (A) Jingoism
   (B) Nationalism
   (C) Imperialism
   (D) Isolationism

The correct answer is (A). Some questions may call for recognizing the historical context of a term or quotation. By recognizing that *remembering* a historic event (for example, "Remember the Alamo") is usually associated with a rallying cry for action, you can eliminate (D). Isolationism implies a lack of action. Jingoism is characterized by a bellicose foreign policy and preparation for military action. When the battleship *Maine* was mysteriously blown up in Havana harbor (1898), the American press, led by William Randolph Hearst's *New York Journal,* demanded war against Spain. The Hearst press at the time was often referred to as the "jingo" press because their sensationalized reporting of events ("yellow journalism") often heightened war fervor. Imperialism (C), the policy of extending power into foreign regions, does not consistently suggest the same aggressive and warlike spirit of jingoism.

3. The American Colonization Society encouraged emancipation and subsequent Negro emigration to
   (A) the West Indies
   (B) Liberia
   (C) Ghana
   (D) Canada

The correct answer is (B). Here you need to realize that the American Colonization Society was part of the early abolitionist movement. The Society believed that Southerners would be encouraged to free their slaves if "white supremacy" weren't threatened by the presence of free Negroes in the South. Abolitionists formed the Society in 1816 with the express purpose of transporting freed Negroes to what would become Liberia (along the Gold Coast of Africa) and raised money to emancipate slaves and support them there. After 1840, the Society was unable to obtain the necessary funds because of antipathy to their efforts both in the North and in the South. Ultimately, several thousand Negroes were transported to Liberia. While abolitionists encouraged runaway blacks to escape to Canada (D), this was never an objective of the Society. A question related to this one might ask for the first independent black African country (Liberia) or why the efforts of the Society failed (the paternalistic attitude that limited emigration would "solve" the injustices of slavery).

4. With the ratification of the Eighteenth Amendment, Prohibition became the "law of the land." However, in the 1920s, many Americans who were normally law-abiding citizens openly disregarded this law. Which of the following most accurately explains this reaction?
   (A) The law was not in agreement with the mores of society.
   (B) Jail terms were a deterrent to this criminal behavior.
   (C) Indoctrination as a social norm was ineffective.
   (D) The cultural relativity of the law was questioned.

The correct answer is (A). This question demonstrates the multidisciplinary aspect of the History/Social Sciences test (in this case, history and sociology). To answer the question, you must look for an answer that explains why normally law-abiding citizens disregarded and disobeyed a law. Eliminate (B) because it contradicts information suggested; it would seem, in this case, that jail terms probably were *not* deterrents. An understanding of the time period (the "Roaring Twenties") would eliminate (C); the failure to indoctrinate (manipulate thinking) would not adequately explain the reaction to Prohibition. When laws are not in agreement with the mores of society (the social norms that provide the moral standards of behavior), the law will be widely disobeyed. In the case of Prohibition, there was a disparity between the ideal norm (behavior that is desired) and the real norm (behavior that consistently occurs). The general disregard for Prohibition and lack of enforcement eventually led to its repeal in 1933 (the Twenty-first Amendment). Cultural relativity (D) concerns the variation in customs from one culture to the next.

World History

1. Thomas Malthus, in his provocative essay "The Principle of Population," theorized that the disparity between the food supply and the number of people in need of sustenance would be even greater if not for
   (A) contraceptive devices used for population control
   (B) the advancement of medical knowledge
   (C) the efforts of "enlightened nations" in providing aid to third-world countries
   (D) positive checks such as war, plague, and famine

The correct answer is (D). To answer this question, you must place Malthus at the end of the eighteenth century. His pessimistic essay (1798) argues that population increases according to a geometric progression (2, 4, 8, 16, . . .), but food increases arithmetically (1, 2, 3, 4, . . .). Malthus believed that this scenario would result in population growth far outstripping the available food supply. He stated that this tendency could be checked by two types of circumstances: positive checks such as war, disease, and poverty and preventive checks such as moral restraint and religious practice. Malthus specifically ruled out birth control (A) on moral grounds. Neo-Malthusians cite parts of Africa (such as Somalia, Ethiopia, and Sudan) and parts of Asia (such as India, Pakistan, and Bangladesh) to exemplify the consequences of Malthusian theory.

2. The principal objective of Russia's desire to expand in the direction of the Ottoman Empire was to
   (A) gain permanent access to the Mediterranean Sea
   (B) gain control over the Caspian Sea
   (C) prevent the formation of an Austro-Prussian military alliance
   (D) limit the influence of Islam and reestablish Christian rule

The correct answer is (A). This question requires understanding of the role of geography in political decision making. Russia was landlocked and did not have a geographical outlet to the Mediterranean. You must also recognize that the Ottoman Empire was centered in Turkey, whose borders include the Black Sea (north) and the Mediterranean Sea (south). Historically, a characteristic of Russian foreign policy from the seventeenth century onward was to obtain permanent access to the Mediterranean. A port on the Black Sea would allow Russia to better control its own destiny. Britain and other European countries, however, prevented the territorial expansion of Russia in the direction of Turkey. The European objective was to maintain the current balance of power. The most notable attempt by Russia to upset the balance resulted in Russian defeat during the Crimean War (1853–56). Historically, the Ottomans played a significant role in European politics. By the middle of the sixteenth century, the Ottomans controlled not only Turkey but most of southeastern Europe, the Crimea, Iran, and a majority of the Middle East. However, by the nineteenth century, the Ottoman Empire was contemptuously referred to as the "Sick Man of Europe" and depended on English intervention (especially directed against Russia) for its political survival. You could eliminate choice (B) by recognizing that the Caspian Sea was part of Russia's traditional borders.

3. As early as the thirteenth century, manorialism, as an economic and social way of life, declined primarily due to the
   (A) geographic isolation of the large manors from port cities
   (B) expansion of home industries
   (C) decrease in agricultural output
   (D) revival of international trade following the Crusades

The correct answer is (D). You are expected to be familiar with significant world events—in this case the late Middle Ages, feudalism, and the decline of manorialism. During the Middle Ages, the manor was the basic unit of economic life, and feudalism was the basic political unit. Manorialism was geared to an agriculture-based economy (almost all goods and services were produced at the manor). As a result of the Crusades, there was marked revival in international trade, necessitating a change in the land-based feudal economic system, the decline of manorialism, a movement toward a money economy, and the development of merchant-based trade centers, craft guilds, and towns.

4. Ancient Egypt and Mesopotamia are essentially different in all of the following EXCEPT
   (A) the predictability of their river system
   (B) natural protection against foreign invaders
   (C) a bureaucratically administered state
   (D) length of dynastic rule

The correct answer is (C). This question calls for understanding the similarities and differences between two ancient civilizations and knowledge of the geography of each. You can arrive at the correct answer through a *process of elimination*. Choice (A) is incorrect because in Egypt the Nile's *annual* floods were predictable, while in Mesopotamia (modern-day Iraq), floods were often unpredictable and destructive. Choice (B) is incorrect because Egypt's natural barriers (desert and sea), as well as its isolation from other civilizations, greatly hindered foreign invaders, while the flat plains of Mesopotamia invited invasion. Consider the succession of political power in the region (Sumeria, Babylonia, Assyria, Persia, . . .) as opposed to Egypt, which remained a distinct political entity. The *only* common characteristic listed is bureaucratic government. The pharaoh of Egypt and the kings of Mesopotamia ruled through the privileged class of nobles and priests.

5. Historically, the division of Africa into colonies and protectorates by Europe in the nineteenth century is similar to the American government's Indian removal policy during the same period because
   (A) the ruling government followed a policy of isolation and extermination
   (B) rival groups were often enclosed in the same geographic area
   (C) economic development was not accomplished until exploitation ended
   (D) the main political objective was assimilation with the white race

The correct answer is (B). Here, you should attempt to eliminate obvious misstatements. When an answer has two parts and you *know* that one of them is false, eliminate the answer. For example, choice (A) is a gross exaggeration. Although isolation was a component of the U.S. Indian removal policy, extermination was not (although it might have been favored by individuals in government). Choice (D) is incorrect. Assimilation with the white race may have been an objective of U.S. policy in the late nineteenth century, but it was not in the European colonization of Africa. Although choice (C) is possible, only choice (B) specifically addresses the question. Rival Indian tribes were often forcibly settled in the same geographic area. The removal of the Cherokee and Seminoles to lands that bordered the more warlike Plains Indians, for example, resulted in both cultural and geographic displacement. In Africa, tribal boundaries were often arbitrarily drawn, primarily to further economic exploitation of the colonial area.

Nonhistorical Perspective

1. A proponent of the theory that human nature is an expression of innate aggression would most likely favor which of the following statements?
   (A) Territories are established through mutual cooperation and negotiation.
   (B) Much of the evidence used to substantiate innate aggression is not relevant to human behavior.
   (C) Innate aggression is a biological characteristic of humans.
   (D) Territoriality can be explained ritualistically.

The correct answer is (C). This question could be answered through a process of elimination. The theory of innate aggression holds that in the human species territoriality and aggressiveness are biologically linked (as you might deduce from the term *innate*). Eliminate choices (A) and (B) because they are inconsistent with the view of a proponent of this theory. Eliminate choice (D) by recognizing that rituals are learned and therefore are not innate traits. Such books as *On Aggression* by Konrad Lorenz, *The Naked Ape* by Desmond Morris, and *African Genesis* by Leo Frobeenius support the view that humans are genetically belligerent and violent.

Social Science Fields

Government and Politics

1. A power <u>not</u> written into the Constitution but exercised by the Supreme Court as early as 1803 is
   (A) implied power
   (B) judicial review
   (C) the power to determine the number of justices on the Supreme Court
   (D) the power to decide cases involving disputes between states

The correct answer is (B). Here, you need to understand the evolution of political power among the three branches of government. Judicial review was not provided for in the Constitution but was exercised by the Supreme Court in the famous *Marbury* v. *Madison* case (1803). Judicial review refers to the power of the federal courts to interpret the Constitution and to declare acts of Congress unconstitutional. Judicial review allows the courts to exercise "checks and balances" over the legislative and executive branches. In *McCulloch* v. *Maryland* (1819), the Supreme Court affirmed the right of Congress to use implied powers (A) and exercise the "necessary and proper" clause of Article I. The power to determine the number of Supreme Court justices (C) is given to Congress.

2. During the period 1948–60, the term "puppet government" was most closely associated with which of the following pairs?
   (A) USSR : Afghanistan
   (B) USSR : Yugoslavia
   (C) USSR : East Germany
   (D) USSR : Cuba

The correct answer is (C). The term *puppet government* implies that a nation is not sovereign, or autonomous, in its actions. Following World War II, most of Eastern Europe was dominated by the Soviet Union. Churchill used the term *iron curtain* in 1946 to characterize Soviet control over this region. The question calls for recognizing the area most dominated by the Soviet Union. You can eliminate choice (A) because Russian intervention in Afghanistan was primarily in the 1980s. Choices (B) and (D) are incorrect because Yugoslavia under Tito and Cuba under Castro generally pursued an independent political course, although Cuba relied on Russian economic support to maintain its political system. East Germany, however, was dominated by the Soviet Union. Russian motivation to control Eastern Europe during this time derived from both the fear of a reunited Germany and the historical desire to create "buffer zones" between Russia and the West.

3. Which of the following was the most effective political weapon used in the United States to defeat pending civil-rights legislation throughout the twentieth century?
   (A) Organizing political-action committees composed of conservative Democrats and reactionary Republicans
   (B) The use of the filibuster
   (C) Grass-roots campaigns to intimidate supporters of civil-rights legislation
   (D) Controlling important congressional committees to prevent favorable civil-rights legislation from being debated

The correct answer is (B). For this question, you need an understanding of political history. The term *pending* tells you that the legislation in question was before Congress. Throughout the twentieth century, the filibuster (unlimited debate on a bill) has been the most effective political weapon used to defeat pending civil-rights legislation, effectively strangling the democratic process by delaying or preventing a vote. While a filibuster is taking place, no other bills can be considered, and the only way to limit it is with a successful cloture vote, which requires a sixty-percent majority to pass. In 1957, Senator Strom Thurmond of South Carolina spoke for a record twenty-four hours in a successful effort to defeat a civil-rights bill. The historic 1964 Civil Rights Act was filibustered, but a cloture vote was passed, allowing a favorable vote. Many civil-rights bills that passed the House died in the Senate due to the effectiveness of the filibuster.

Geography

1.

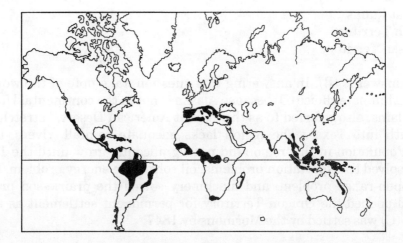

The shaded areas on the map best represent which of the following vegetative zones?
(A) Tropical rain forest
(B) savanna and grasslands
(C) marshes and wetlands
(D) deciduous forest

The correct answer is (A). To answer this question, you must recognize the demarcation of the equator and the climate associated with land in that area. Most of tropical rain forests, which constitute nearly half of the forested area of the earth, lie on or near the equator. Deciduous forests (D) are found throughout the world. A related question might ask about the political and economic implications of continued exploitation of the rain forests.

2. Considering the physical geography of California, a farmer would most likely use local rainfall to water crops in which of the following valleys?
(A) The Sacramento Valley
(B) The Imperial Valley
(C) The Coachella Valley
(D) The San Joaquin Valley

The correct answer is (A) This question calls for an understanding of the precipitation patterns and river systems of California. By associating the Sacramento Valley with the Sacramento delta (the largest runoff area in the state), it would be logical to conclude that a farmer in the Sacramento Valley would be the most likely to use rainfall for irrigation (in the form of runoff). While the Sacramento Valley receives between ten and twenty inches of precipitation a year, the mountain areas that surround it receive between thirty and ninety inches, providing adequate runoff. The other choices are dry farming areas, which receive less than twenty inches of rainfall annually (the San Joaquin Valley receives less than ten) and which are dependent on irrigation from other sources for crop production.

3. The last area settled in the continental United States was the
   (A) Oregon Territory
   (B) Great Plains
   (C) Utah Territory
   (D) Alaska Territory

The correct answer is (B). In answering this question, take note of the words *last* and *continental*. Eliminate choice (D) because Alaska is not in the continental United States. The Great Plains, also referred to as the "Great American Desert," stretches from the Dakotas south into Texas. The region lacks adequate rainfall, rivers, timber, and vegetation. Population in this region did not significantly grow until the 1880s, when the railroad solved transportation problems, oil solved the energy problem, barbed wire solved the open-range problem, and machinery solved the prairie-sod problem. The Oregon Trail opened the Oregon Territory for permanent settlement as early as the 1830s. Utah (C) was settled by the Mormons by 1847.

Economics

1. Shortly after the Constitution went into effect, Alexander Hamilton proposed a protective tariff in order to
   (A) raise revenue from foreign sources
   (B) protect American shipping
   (C) protect the wages of American labor
   (D) encourage American manufacturing

The correct answer is (D). To answer this question, you must understand the term *protective tariff,* which, like a regular tariff, is a tax on goods entering a country. But the purpose of a protective tariff is to safeguard a domestic industry from foreign competition, not simply to raise revenue. Therefore, in the historical context of the question, you should eliminate choice (A). While choices (B) and (C) are possible answers because a protective tariff might have some effect on them, neither addresses *Hamilton's purpose* in proposing the tariff in the 1790s—to protect American manufacturing to further the economic independence of the new nation.

2. The purchasing power of the dollar during a period of deflation tends to
   (A) fall
   (B) rise
   (C) remain constant
   (D) not be affected by supply and demand

The correct answer is (B). You should be aware that during *in*flationary times, the purchasing power of the dollar declines. So you can correctly assume that during *de*flationary times, the purchasing power of the dollar would *not* fall, eliminating choice (A). Deflation is a period of falling prices caused by a decline in both demand and purchasing power. However, as prices fall, the purchasing power of the dollar rises, without a decline in the quality of goods or services. Choice (D) can be eliminated because supply and demand *always* affect the marketplace.

3. In the United States, a sales tax on a necessity is an example of a
   (A) direct tax
   (B) proportional tax
   (C) progressive tax
   (D) regressive tax

The correct answer is (D). A sales tax on a necessity (food, clothing, gasoline, etc.) is an example of a regressive tax. The tax has a greater impact on the poor than on others because a sales tax on a necessity takes a greater percentage of a poor person's income than of a wealthier person's income. The personal income tax is an example of a direct tax (A) because it is paid directly to a state or to the federal government. The personal federal income tax is also an example of a progressive tax (C) because the tax rate increases as the tax base increases.

Anthropology and Sociology

1. In the Zuni culture, the bride and groom reside with the kin group of the bride. Such families are
   (A) matriarchal
   (B) matrilineal
   (C) matrilocal
   (D) endogamous

The correct answer is (C). This question requires understanding the meaning of a word. But even if you are unfamiliar with the term *matrilocal,* note the connection between the word *reside* in the question and the implication of locality in *matrilocal.* Matrilocal residence results when the husband and wife reside in the home or geographic area of the bride's family. *Matriarchal* (A) refers to authority residing with the female head of the family. *Matrilineal* (B) refers to inheritance or determination of descent through the female line. *Endogamous* (D) refers to marriage that is restricted to a specific group.

2. The *nouveau riche* may display luxury items in a highly visible manner. For example, during the course of a party, they may light expensive cigars with twenty-dollar bills. These actions are most clearly examples of
   (A) marginal adaptation
   (B) conspicuous consumption
   (C) benevolent despotism
   (D) infantile sensationalism

The correct answer is (B). By recognizing that the terms in (C) and (D) are not relevant to the question, you can quickly eliminate them. *Conspicuous consumption,* a term used by Thorstein Veblen in *The Theory of the Leisure Class,* describes the consumption of wealth, goods, and services primarily for the purpose of display and implies that an individual can obtain status when luxury goods are consumed in a highly visible manner. The Indians of the Pacific Northwest practiced a similar custom called the potlatch.

3. A study revealed that lynchings in the South in the early 1900s increased when the price of cotton decreased. A sociologist seeking an explanation for this behavior would most likely explain the actions as the result of
   (A) negative stereotyping
   (B) aggression
   (C) scapegoating
   (D) self-fulfilling prophecies

The correct answer is (C). Here, you must recognize a cause-and-effect relationship. The term that *best* describes this action is *scapegoating*. By definition, a scapegoat is one who is made to shoulder the blame for the problems of others. Historically, during times of economic or political stress, scapegoating against religious, ethnic, and racial groups (viewed as different from the mainstream) often takes place. Choice (B) is incorrect because *aggression* is too vague to best answer the question. However, the term *displaced aggression* would be an acceptable answer were it offered because it is, in effect, the outcome of scapegoating. Viewing an individual with a negative stereotype (A) would encourage scapegoating but would not necessarily result in it.

SAMPLE QUESTIONS AND STRATEGIES FOR THE CONTENT AREA EXERCISES

Following are representative History/Social Sciences short constructed-response questions from each area covered. Strategies and a sample response are included with each question.

U.S. History and Geography

1. Discuss why the United States failed to ratify the Treaty of Versailles. Include in your answer the political climate in the United States, the international scene, specific terms of the treaty, and geographic factors that influenced the decision.

Strategy

The question asks why the United States didn't ratify the Treaty of Versailles. Note the items that should be included in your answer (political opposition in the United States, world politics, terms of the treaty, geographic link).

Before attempting to answer the question, consider what you know about treaties in general—they are made between countries and link those countries politically and possibly militarily; in the United States, the Senate must ratify all treaties; examples of modern treaties would include the North Atlantic Treaty Organization (NATO) and the Strategic Arms Limitation Treaty (SALT). Consider in general why there might be opposition to a treaty—fear of involvement in foreign problems, costs, mistrust of the treaty partner, and so forth. Consider the location of Versailles—France.

By establishing a historical perspective, even if you are not completely familiar with this treaty, you may be able to include enough pertinent information in your answer to receive partial credit. Remember, most short constructed-response questions are designed so that a person with a reasonably broad social-sciences background will receive at least partial credit for an answer.

Now you must decide how many of the general factors concerning treaties that you recalled might apply to the Treaty of Versailles.

Sample Response

The Treaty of Versailles, signed in 1919, ended World War I. Wilson's Fourteen Points were very idealistic and called for a just peace, not retribution. His proposal included a League of Nations and an end to secret negotiations. The European leaders (the "Big Four") rejected many of Wilson's proposals. Most terms of the treaty dealt harshly with Germany—for example, large reparations, a "war-guilt clause," demilitarization of the Rhineland, and loss of territory.

Wilson left the Republican-controlled Senate out of the European peace process. Since the Senate would have to ratify the treaty, this mistake proved fatal. Also, the country was strongly isolationist following World War I. For people in the United States, isolated geographically from Europe, the possibility of being forced into a foreign war was the antithesis of acceptable American foreign policy.

U.S. History and Political Science

2. With reference to the U.S. Constitution, explain the difference between enumerated and implied powers. Explain the significance of *McCulloch* v. *Maryland* in determining the constitutionality of implied powers.

Strategy

The question asks (1) the difference between enumerated and implied powers and (2) how a court case applies to implied powers.

Before attempting to answer the question, consider definitions for the terms *enumerated* (stated) and *implied* (not specifically stated). Since the question refers to the Constitution, simply listing powers that are *stated* in the original Constitution (coining money, regulating commerce, and so forth) and listing *implied* powers (those that must be interpreted in order to be carried out—for example, passing environmental-safety laws and providing controls over nuclear energy) would provide partial credit. *McCulloch* v. *Maryland* is a court decision that you would be expected to be familiar with (as are *Marbury* v. *Madison* and *Brown* v. *Board of Education*.)

Sample Response

Enumerated powers are those powers of Congress specifically stated in Article I, Section 8, of the Constitution, ranging from collecting taxes to declaring war. The legal basis for implied powers is found in the "necessary and proper" clause, which gives Congress the authority to make all laws that are necessary and proper to carry out all stated powers.

The McCulloch case (1819) addressed the extent to which the national government could use implied powers in carrying out governmental decisions. In this case, it was determined that Maryland could not tax a federal bank, even though the bank was located on state property. In effect, this decision prohibited a state from taxing a federal institution. The significance of the decision is that it strengthened the national government and affirmed the concept of national supremacy.

World History and Geography

3. Discuss two significant factors that contributed to the fall of the Roman Empire. Include in your answer approximate dates, key events, and geographic references.

Strategy

The question asks for two factors that led to the fall of Rome. Note the items that need to be included in your answer (dates, key events, geography).

Before attempting to answer the question, consider factors that might lead to the fall of any empire (war, failing economy, climatic changes, civil unrest, and so forth). Ask yourself why Rome would fall. (At this point, you're trying to place the question in historical perspective.) Decide how many of the general factors you've listed might apply to the fall of Rome.

You might recall the century Rome fell (fifth century A.D.), or that *barbarians* were responsible for sacking Rome, or that the *army* had undergone far-reaching changes, or that *Christianity* was a factor.

Sample Response

The decline leading to the fall of Rome began in the third century A.D. but gained momentum during the fourth and fifth centuries. The weakness of the Roman emperors during this period was a primary factor, especially after Constantine moved the capital to Byzantium (on the Bosporus) in A.D. 330. The emperors who remained in Rome were generally weak and politically ineffective and often depended on bribing the army to stay in power.

The deterioration of the army was also a major factor. It was no longer an honor for sons of Roman aristocrats to serve as officers. The presence of mercenaries, who did not have a true stake in the success of Rome and often demanded land as compensation, weakened the economic and political system, which encouraged barbaric Germanic tribes such as the Visigoths, Saxons, Lombards, and Vandals to threaten first the Roman frontier and then Rome itself.

Here is an additional world history and geography short constructed-response question. (Note, however, that there will be only one such question on the exam.)

4. Discuss the truth of this statement: Homer's epic poem the *Odyssey* is an important source of information about Greek history. Include in your answer geographic references, religious practices, and approximate dates.

Strategy

Note that the question asks you to determine the *truth* of the statement. Ask yourself how any piece of literature can provide a glimpse of the history of a period. Before answering the question, attempt to recall information about Homer (when he lived, what he wrote about) and what you know about ancient Greece (belief in gods as determiners of humans' fate, influence of the Mediterranean, mythology, . . .). What images do you recall from the *Odyssey*? (Odysseus, the Trojan War, Zeus, Poseidon, . . .)

Sample Response

In one sense, the *Odyssey* is not a good factual source of historical information. It has been questioned whether Homer existed at all and, if he did, whether he wrote the *Odyssey*. And the writer, whoever he may be, did not deal, in this poem, with the Trojan War (or any historical event) in anything but the sketchiest of terms, instead detailing the travels of the mythical hero Odysseus after that time on his return to Ithaca. (There is also some historical question as to whether there was a Trojan War, but many now believe that it did occur.)

The *Odyssey* is, however, a storehouse of information concerning Greek customs and religion. The poem is rich in detail about the importance of the gods in the lives of the Greeks and the concept of fate. Two examples of such detail include the control of Odysseus by Zeus and the attack on Odysseus's ship by Poseidon. Examples of detail concerning social life include the importance of gifts, loyalty, and hospitality and the inappropriateness of greed and excessive love of luxury (as evidenced by the suitors of Odysseus's wife, Penelope).

History and Economics

5. Explain how the laws of supply and demand operate in the American marketplace.

Strategy

Restate the question. How do economic principles operate in a capitalist market-place? Before you attempt to answer this question, consider what you know about the American market system. It is a market economy; that is, the marketplace essentially determines what people buy and how much they pay for their goods. How does government affect the economic system? Who controls the economy? (the marketplace) Who determines product availability? Can you define *profit* and *price*?

Remember, adequately answering part of a question will give you partial credit (even if you simply define the terms).

Sample Response

The American economy is essentially a money economy. The more people want a product, the more they are willing to pay for it, encouraging suppliers to produce more of the goods because increased demand at higher prices will be advantageous to the supplier.

The law of demand states that, other things being equal, the quantity of any good which people are ready to buy varies inversely with its price. As the price of a good gets lower, the quantity demanded of that good increases, and as the price of a good rises, the quantity demanded falls.

The law of supply states that, other things being equal, the quantity of any good offered for sale varies directly with its price. At higher prices, suppliers offer more goods for sale; at lower prices, suppliers offer fewer goods for sale.

SCIENCE

CONTENT

The Science section focuses on primary scientific concepts, principles, and interrelationships in the context of real-life problems and significant science phenomena and issues. The Science questions in both the multiple-choice and the short-constructed response sections test the following three skills.

- the explanation and application of concepts

- process skills, such as interpreting a stimulus, ordering and categorizing material, and relating, inferring, or applying information found in various stimuli

- designing an experiment or investigating information necessary to explain an experiment

Content Knowledge (Multiple-Choice)

The Content Knowledge (multiple-choice) test, which contains twenty-four questions grouped together, covers the following three major content areas and focuses on the topics listed under each. The approximate weight of each category is listed in parentheses.

1. **Life sciences (33–34 percent)**

   - *cellular biology,* including the structure and function of cells and their organelles, genes and gene functions, energy sources and processes, and biologically significant molecules

   - *biology of organisms,* including life forms, the structure and function of organs and organ systems, and the basic principles of heredity

   - *ecology,* including interrelationships in the biosphere and the characteristics of ecosystems, energy flow in biological communities, and the characteristics of biological communities

   - *evolution,* including evolutionary mechanisms, evolutionary patterns and determining evidence for evolutionary change, and the history of life as related to the geological timeline

2. **Geosciences (33–34 percent)**

   - *astronomy,* including planetary systems, the solar system, stars, galaxies, and cosmology

   - *geology,* including internal and external earth processes, earth materials and land forms, and earth history and its life forms

- *meteorology,* including the composition and structure of the atmosphere, weather and climate, and atmospheric movement

- *oceanography,* including chemical, biological, geological, and physical characteristics and processes

3. Physical sciences (33–34 percent)

- *matter,* including its characteristics, structure, and physical and chemical properties

- *reactions and interactions,* including changes in matter, kinetic theory, chemical reactions, oxidation and reduction, acids and bases, chemical bonding, and the role of catalysts

- *macromechanics,* including periodic, straight line, projectile, and circular motion; Newtonian physics, including motion, gravity, weight, mass, and conservation of energy

- *energy,* including fossil and nonfossil sources, transformations, and heat

- *electricity and magnetism,* including circuits, static and current electricity, and magnetic principles and applications

- *wave phenomena,* including motion and the applications of and principles underlying the electromagnetic spectrum, mirrors, lenses, and sound production

- *modern physics and nuclear chemistry,* including principles of relativity, radioactivity, fission, and fusion

Content Area Exercises (Short Constructed-Response)

The four Science short constructed-response questions cover each of the following four major content areas and focus on the topics listed under each.

1. Life sciences

- *biology of organisms,* including the structure and function of organ systems, life forms, and the basic principles of heredity

- *ecology,* including interrelationships in the biosphere, the characteristics of ecosystems, and energy flow and characteristics in biological communities

- *evolution,* including mechanisms and patterns, evidence for evolutionary change, and the history of life as related in the geological timeline

2. Geosciences

- *geology,* including internal and external earth processes, earth materials and land forms, and earth history and its life forms

3. Physical sciences

- *matter,* including its characteristics, structure, and chemical and physical properties

- *energy,* including energy sources, transformations, and heat

- *electricity and magnetism,* including circuits, static and current electricity, and magnetic principles and applications

4. Science, technology, and society
- The questions in this area are developed from content from the life sciences, geosciences, or physical sciences as outlined above.

SAMPLE QUESTIONS AND STRATEGIES FOR THE CONTENT KNOWLEDGE SECTION

Each of the following examples represents an area tested on the Science multiple-choice segment. An analysis follows each question.

Life Sciences

1. Which of the following organisms are most truly independent in obtaining nourishment?
   (A) Bighorn sheep
   (B) Palm trees
   (C) Humans
   (D) Salamanders

The correct answer is (B). In answering this question, you should particularly note (or underline, circle, or bracket) the words *most truly independent* and *nourishment.* True independence suggests not being subject to control by others or not requiring or relying on something else. Nourishment is food. Obtaining food independently is most associated with green plants because they are the only organisms that can manufacture food (obtaining energy from sunlight and storing that energy as sugar). Since palm trees are the only green plants listed, that is the correct answer. All organisms depend on a food chain to obtain nourishment, but all food chains must begin with green plants (the producers). Animals are either primary or secondary consumers and must get their energy from eating plants or other animals.

2. When a mutation in a gene occurs in an individual, it will not have an effect on the group unless the
   (A) environment changes
   (B) threat of predators is reduced
   (C) individual lives long enough to breed
   (D) mutation increases the variability of the group

The correct answer is (C). In analyzing the question, mark the terms *mutation, gene,* and *effect*. If the wording of a question is confusing, restate it—in this case, perhaps as "What factors would cause a mutation *not* to have an effect on a group?" For a mutation to be passed on, the genetic material must be passed on through breeding. A mutation is the result of a change in the makeup of the chromosomes, which contain the genes that determine the characteristics of an organism. When changes occur in sex cells, the result can be significant. Mutations can be both successful and unsuccessful, with beneficial changes being preserved through natural selection.

3. Enzymes are proteins that are essential during metabolism. Which of the following best summarizes the importance of enzymes in the metabolic process?
   (A) They are secreted by the endocrine glands and regulate many bodily functions.
   (B) They permit certain chemical reactions to proceed at significant speeds.
   (C) They transfer energy from one complex molecule to another complex molecule.
   (D) They release stored energy to all parts of the body.

The correct answer is (B). In this question, you might mark the terms *enzymes* and *metabolic process* and attempt to recall relevant information about them. Metabolism is the sum of the chemical and physical processes in living organisms and provides the basis for energy transfer, cell maintenance, and growth. Enzymes act as catalysts during the metabolic process, and without them, many of the body's chemical reactions would not occur fast enough (B). The body uses enzymes to control its many thousands of chemical reactions, including the burning of food; lipase, for example, is an enzyme that helps in the digestion of fats.

4. Ozone depletion is a serious environmental danger. Which of the following is not a true statement regarding ozone depletion?
   (A) It was detected over the Antarctic region.
   (B) It has the potential to change the genetic structure of phytoplankton.
   (C) It is directly linked to a rise in the average temperature of the earth.
   (D) It could lead to an increase in skin cancer.

The correct answer is (C). Here, you are looking for *incorrect* information regarding ozone depletion; the answer choices include three true statements and one false statement. In this format, when you recognize an answer choice as a true statement, eliminate it. The breakdown of the ozone layer is primarily the result of an increase in chlorofluorocarbons (CFCs, such as are found in refrigeration and insulation products) in the atmosphere. Eliminate choice (A) because ozone depletion *was* detected over Antarctica. Eliminate choice (B) because an increase in ultraviolet (UV) radiation, which the ozone layer blocks, *could* alter the genetic makeup of the tiny organisms at the beginning of the food chain. Eliminate choice (D) because that same increase in UV *could* lead to an increase in skin cancer. But choice (C) is *not* true and is thus the correct answer. Ozone depletion is not generally associated with the greenhouse effect (a warming trend caused by an increase in atmospheric carbon dioxide).

Geosciences

1. Igneous rocks are found throughout the world. Which of the following processes yields an igneous rock?
   (A) Accumulations on a coral reef
   (B) Tremendous pressure over an extended period of time
   (C) The laying down of deposits one on top of the other
   (D) The eruption of a volcano

The correct answer is (D). Answering this question correctly requires your recognizing the geologic process that results in the formation of igneous rocks. Attempt to eliminate incorrect answers based on your general understanding of rock types. For example, the information in choice (B) relates to metamorphic rocks and that in choice (C) to sedimentary rocks. A coral reef (A) is the result of the buildup of once-living things. Lava from an erupting volcano (D) is molten rock which can reach a temperature of approximately 1200 degrees Celsius. An igneous rock is produced by the solidification of molten rock, which cools and becomes solid either deep within the earth or at the earth's surface.

2. Taking all things into consideration and on a global scale, which of the following is the primary factor determining climate?
   (A) The atmospheric conditions in the area
   (B) The latitude of the area
   (C) The meeting of warm and cold air masses
   (D) Mountain barriers

The correct answer is (B). The question calls for identifying a climate determiner having global significance. The term *climate* refers to the long-term weather patterns of a large geographical area and takes into account temperature, humidity, and precipitation. Of the choices given, latitude is the best determiner of climate as it is consistently and directly correlated with temperature. The equator, at zero degrees latitude, generally has a tropical climate (warm and wet); at the extreme northern and southern latitudes (polar regions), the climate is very cold and dry. Choice (A) is a possible answer, but atmospheric conditions are generally influenced by latitude. Mountain barriers (D), as well as water currents, elevation, and so forth, obviously affect climate, but for this question, latitude is the *best,* most comprehensive answer.

3. A spacecraft uses its engines to escape the earth's gravitational pull. Once in space, the spacecraft does not need its engines to stay in orbit. Which of the following best explains why an astronaut in orbit is weightless?
   (A) The spacesuit creates an air-free environment.
   (B) The gravitational attraction of the moon balances that of the earth.
   (C) The earth's gravity pulls the spacecraft and the astronauts equally, but no force pulls the astronauts to the spacecraft.
   (D) Mass is decreased due to the weaker gravitational pull.

The correct answer is (C). This question can be answered through a process of elimination. For example, eliminate choice (A) because an individual in an air-free environment would suffocate and choice (D) because mass remains constant even though location changes. (Note, however, that weight can change, for example between the earth and the moon, because weight is a function of gravity.) Although the question is introduced with information on gravity, its real focus is on weightlessness. In a spacecraft, an astronaut becomes weightless when centrifugal force (created by orbiting the earth) precisely counterbalances the gravitational pull of the earth.

Physical Sciences

1. Which of the following best demonstrates the theory that molecules are always in motion?
   (A) A spoonful of sugar is added to a cup of cocoa, and the cocoa becomes sweet in all parts of the cup.
   (B) A small stone is dropped into a glass of water and falls straight to the bottom.
   (C) An ice cube is placed in a cold container and melts very slowly.
   (D) A drop of oil is added to a pan of water, and the oil floats to the top.

The correct answer is (A). Recognizing that choice (B) represents the effect of gravity and that choice (C) represents a change in the state of matter would help you eliminate both because neither would best be explained by molecular motion. Understanding the properties of mixtures would eliminate choice (D). The correct answer addresses the movement of molecules in distributing the sugar to all parts of the cup. Similar distribution would result if a gas were released in a corner of a room. The gas would soon diffuse throughout the room as its molecules are evenly distributed.

2. Which of the following solutions would make litmus paper turn red?
   (A) Liquid drain opener
   (B) Salt water
   (C) Vinegar
   (D) Lye

The correct answer is (C). Litmus paper changes color to red when dipped in an acid and to blue when dipped in a base. The acid or alkaline strength of a solution is measured by the pH scale (in which H represents hydrogen, as acids and alkalis have different hydrogen concentrations). The pH scale measures from 1 to 14, with 1 being the most acidic, 7 neutral, and 14 most alkaline. Recognizing this would allow you to eliminate any nonacids as possible answers. Drain opener (A) usually contains lye (D), which is strongly alkaline; salt water (B) also is alkaline. Of the choices given, only vinegar is acid.

3. Which statement best explains the following example? As a car is driven at high speeds for a long duration, the size of the tires temporarily increases.
   (A) Gases can be compressed to small volumes by pressure.
   (B) As the temperature of a gas increases, the volume increases.
   (C) When the pressure exerted on a gas is greatest, the volume is greatest.
   (D) A compressed gas pushes out equally in all directions.

The correct answer is (B). The size, or volume, of the tires increases because the friction between the tires and the road causes heat. The increase in temperature increases the volume of the air in the tires, expanding them. Charles's law states that as temperature increases (at a fixed pressure) so does volume. Choice (A) is a correct statement, but it does not answer the question. Gases can be compressed, but the opposite happens in the tire example. Choice (C) is a misstatement.

4. A nuclear reactor that powers an electric generating plant relies on
   (A) cold fusion
   (B) fission
   (C) fusion
   (D) fission and fusion

The correct answer is (B). All nuclear reactors in use today obtain their energy through nuclear fission, which releases energy when a heavy nucleus splits into smaller fragments. You should eliminate cold fusion (A) because this process is in only the experimental stages as an alternative source of energy. (Cold fusion does not rely on thermonuclear heat energy input to generate nuclear energy; the hydrogen isotopes necessary for cold fusion are obtainable from ocean water.) In nuclear fusion (C), tremendous energy is released when very light nuclei unite to form a heavier nucleus. Stars, including the sun, derive their energy from nuclear fusion, as do hydrogen bombs.

Other Skills Tested

Investigating Information Necessary to Explain an Experiment

1. A student conducts an experiment to demonstrate changes that would possibly take place in the air in a sealed greenhouse containing many plants. Which of the following is the most likely result of this experiment?

   I. The air becomes poorer in carbon dioxide.
   II. The air becomes poorer in oxygen.
   III. The air becomes richer in carbon dioxide.
   IV. The air becomes richer in carbon monoxide.

   (A) I only
   (B) II only
   (C) II and III only
   (D) III and IV only

The correct answer is (A). Before answering this question, visualize the situation given. Ask youself questions such as these. What constitutes a sealed greenhouse? What is its environment? How does a greenhouse influence plant growth? Note that in a "multiple-multiple-choice" question, if you know that any one of the four statements (I–IV) is false (or that any one of the four is true in a question using <u>not</u>), you can quickly eliminate any answer choice containing that statement. For example, here it should be apparent that carbon monoxide, a poison, would not be characteristic of a greenhouse environment (statement IV). Eliminate (D) because it contains IV. You should also recognize that in a greenhouse (sealed or unsealed), photosynthesis takes place. Green plants combine carbon dioxide and water from the atmosphere (in the presence of sunlight) and release glucose (sugar), oxygen, and water as by-products. Because plants use carbon dioxide and water, the air would be poorer in these compounds but richer in oxygen. So statement II is untrue, and you can eliminate both (B) and (C) because they contain II, leaving only (A) as a possible answer. The quickest way to answer this particular question, however, is to realize that statement I is true and thus must be in the correct answer choice. Since I appears *only* in choice (A), that must then be the correct answer.

Processing Skills

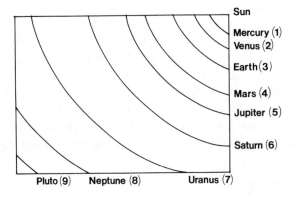

	Average Density (grams/cubic centimeter)	Surface Temperature (degrees C)	Diameter at Equator (kilometers)
(1)	5.3	345 to −175	5,000
(2)	5.2	500	12,100
(3)	5.6	10	12,800
(4)	4.0	−30 to −90	6,787
(5)	1.34	−150	142,800
(6)	0.70	−180	120,000
(7)	1.3	−190	51,800
(8)	1.7	−215	49,000
(9)	?	−230	6,000

Question 1 is based on the diagram and table above and the following information.

Objects float in water if they are lighter than an equal volume of water. An object with a density of 1.0 g/cm³ has a volume equal to that of the water it displaces.

1. Which planet or planets would be able to float if there were a water source large enough to hold it or them?
   (A) Mercury
   (B) Venus
   (C) Saturn
   (D) Jupiter and Uranus

The correct answer is (C). You need only the data presented in the diagram, table, and given information to correctly answer this question. You need no outside knowledge. The information given indicates that an object with a density of less than 1.0 g/cm³ will float in water. Therefore, the surface temperature and diameter sections of the table are irrelevant in answering this question. Saturn is the only planet listed with a density of less than 1.0 (0.70 g/cm³) and could theoretically float.

SAMPLE QUESTIONS AND STRATEGIES FOR THE CONTENT AREA EXERCISES

Following are representative Science short constructed-response questions from each area covered. Strategies and a sample response are included with each question.

Life Sciences

1. Discuss three general examples to support the statement that most of our energy comes from the sun. Include specific information to support your answer.

Strategy

Restate the question. What examples can you give to demonstrate how the sun's energy is used? For example, how is the sun related to various energy sources (fossil and nonfossil, solar power)? What about photosynthesis? Is the statement valid? Does most of our energy really come from the sun?

Simply listing three accurate examples, even without a discussion, will give you partial credit. Be sure not to expand on one example in great detail and fail to leave time for the remaining examples.

Start your answer with a concise, factual statement. For clarity, give each of the three examples its own paragraph.

Sample Response

All food chains are dependent on the sun. Photosynthesis enables green plants to manufacture their own food. A green plant uses chlorophyll in the presence of sunlight to convert carbon dioxide and water (from the air) into sugars (glucose) and oxygen.

Energy from the sun initiates the hydrologic (water) cycle. The heat from the sun causes evaporation. Warm, moist air rises and condenses into clouds. When the clouds are saturated, precipitation falls as rain or snow.

Energy from the sun is also linked to alternative sources of energy. Solar heating cells change sunlight into electricity. Winds are caused by temperature differentials due to the solar heating of the air. Hydroelectricity is produced from moving water and is linked to the sun.

Geosciences

2. Briefly discuss three reasons that the earth's atmosphere limits the usefulness of optical telescopes. Include refracting and reflecting telescopes in your answer, as well as relevant supporting information.

Strategy

You can receive a reasonable score on this question even if you can't differentiate between refracting and reflecting telescopes. Consider what optical telescopes (or any telescopes) are generally used for—to look at celestial objects. Consider what might limit the telescope's effectiveness in looking at stars—light, clouds, etc. Remember that some questions, to be adequately answered, may require more space than that needed for others.

Sample Response

Optical telescopes use lenses and mirrors to study light rays from distant objects. All optical telescopes have light-gathering power. Refracting telescopes produce an image using two or more convex lenses which focus at a single point. Reflecting telescopes produce an image using lenses and concave mirrors. Both produce enlarged images of distant objects. The largest astronomical telescopes contain parabolic mirrors.

The earth's atmosphere contains water molecules, dust, clouds, and a variety of pollutants. The earth's atmosphere filters out visible light from outer space. Also, the industrial light of urban areas makes atmospheric viewing difficult because it interferes with the light-gathering potential of optical telescopes.

The earth's atmosphere creates optical unsteadiness and aberrations, and therefore, clear magnifications greater than 2000 are difficult to achieve. Also, layers of air move because of temperature variations, which causes further aberrations.

Physical Sciences

3. Using scientific terminology, explain why a vacuum bottle can keep hot things hot or cold things cold.

Strategy

Before answering the question, consider the shape and structure of a Thermos (vacuum) bottle. (It has a double wall that encloses a vacuum—a nearly air-free environment.) Recall terms that are associated with keeping things hot or cold (insulation, conduction of heat, etc.).

Sample Response

A Thermos, also called a vacuum bottle, blocks the three processes through which heat is transferred—that is, conduction, convection, and radiation.

The Thermos works efficiently because it is double walled, with a vacuum between the walls. Heat cannot be conducted or convected easily because there are few air molecules to move around in a vacuum.

The inside of the bottle has a shiny surface that acts like a mirror and reflects the heat (either inside or outside the container) back to its source. This limits heat loss or gain by radiation.

Thermos bottles also minimize heat loss or gain by having a small mouth, which limits heat transfer. The stopper is made of a good insulating material like cork or plastic.

Science, Technology, and Society

4. Design an experiment based on distillation that would take a gallon of ocean water and purify it. What materials would be needed? What will be the result?

Strategy

Consider these questions. How could you purify ocean water? What is its composition? How could you get salt and other impurities out of the water? What does heat have to do with it? When you distill something, what actually is taking place?

Sample Response

A distillation experiment is designed to separate substances in a liquid through vaporization. Ocean water is composed of a substantial amount of salt. Distillation is usually carried out in an apparatus called a still, which requires a boiler, a condenser, and a receiver.

Heat the ocean water until it reaches its boiling point. As the ocean water boils, it begins to evaporate and change from a liquid into a gas, in the form of water vapor. The gas goes through tubing to a collector container. The container sits in ice, which accelerates the condensation from water vapor back to liquid (or from a gas to a liquid).

The condensed water is pure water. Salt and other impurities remain as a residue in the original pan. Salt has a higher boiling point than water and therefore doesn't evaporate with the water.

VISUAL AND PERFORMING ARTS

CONTENT

The Visual and Performing Arts section focuses on music, the visual arts, dance, and drama/theater. Each content area is given equal treatment.

Content Knowledge (Multiple-Choice)

The multiple-choice questions in the Content Knowledge test emphasize the following instructional components.

- *aesthetic perception* (recognizing, in an artistic element, the nuances of light, color, sound, movement, and composition; responding to an art element directly and metaphorically)

- *aesthetic valuing* (understanding the intellectual, emotional, and philosophic foundation for making judgments about the arts)

- *creative expression* (recognizing and interpreting artworks holistically; recognizing in an artwork the interrelationship among ideas, feelings, values, and personal experiences)

- *cultural heritage* (interpreting artworks in a cultural and historical setting; recognizing the cultural diversity of the art world)

The questions in this section include visual stimuli (such as pictures and diagrams) when appropriate and relevant. Some items test understanding of the multicultural and multiethnic nature of the arts. You must also be familiar with basic terminology, concepts, and issues of the art world.

The Content Knowledge (multiple-choice) test, which contains fourteen questions grouped together, covers the following three major categories and focuses on the abilities listed under each. The approximate weight of each category is listed in parentheses.

1. Aesthetic perception/creative expression (40 percent)

- know the basic vocabulary of art
- understand elements, design principles, and fundamentals of art

2. Cultural heritage (40 percent)

- make judgments based on recognizing the geographical origin of artworks
- differentiate among a variety of art styles
- draw comparisons between and among artworks based on their historical, social, emotional, and artistic contexts

95

3. Aesthetic valuing (20 percent)
- understand the meaning of artworks
- evaluate aesthetic criteria inherent in a work of art
- apply appropriate criteria in evaluating works of art

Content Area Exercises (Short Constructed-Response)

The two Visual and Performing Arts short constructed-response questions may come from any of the four art areas covered in the multiple-choice section: music, visual arts, dance, and drama/theater. These questions assess your ability to analyze, assess, interpret, and synthesize art from any of the four areas.

SAMPLE QUESTIONS AND STRATEGIES FOR THE CONTENT KNOWLEDGE SECTION

Each of the following examples represents an area tested on the Visual and Performing Arts multiple-choice segment. An analysis follows each question.

Music

1. Rhythm is the flow of music in
   (A) time
   (B) space
   (C) form
   (D) harmony

The correct answer is (A). *All* music moves in time, not space. Music must be internalized "as it goes by." After a composition has been completed, one must evaluate it in *retrospect,* necessitating the development of a musical memory. In other art forms, the viewer has the luxury of analyzing the piece in detail, since it exists in space. Each musical composition has a rhythm, a beat, a pulse, which exists in time. Form (C) is the overall structure of a piece. Harmony (D) is the combination of tones which accompany the main theme (melody).

2. Which of the following sections include the largest number of instruments in a traditional orchestra?
   (A) Brass
   (B) String
   (C) Percussion
   (D) Woodwind

The correct answer is (B). Try to visualize orchestras you have seen. Without the string section, you would have a band, not an orchestra. The string section is usually composed of a minimum of ten first violins, eight second violins, six violas, four cellos, and two basses. In the brass section (A) are usually four French horns, two trumpets, three trombones, and one tuba. In the percussion section (C) are usually timpani (kettle-drums) and two or three other percussion instruments (such as xylophone, chimes, and glockenspiel). In the woodwind section (D) are usually two flutes, two oboes, two clarinets, and two bassoons.

3. Which of the following would <u>not</u> be considered an American "functional" folk instrument?
   (A) The spoons
   (B) The harmonica
   (C) The jug
   (D) The washboard

The correct answer is (B). A functional folk instrument is a familiar household item that is used to make music. Although the harmonica is a well-traveled instrument often used in folk music, it would not be classified as functional because its primary purpose is to make music. Folk music often relies on informal, homemade instruments, which have roots in the music traditions of the British Isles and Africa. The spoons are often used to accompany American fiddle and folk tunes. The washboard and jug are popular in African-American jazz, blues, and "jug" bands.

Visual Arts

1. Which of the following is <u>not</u> a characteristic of the cubist movement of the early twentieth century?
   (A) Employment of linear perspective rather than reassembled space
   (B) Incorporation of sharp edges and straight lines, depicting nature in geometric terms
   (C) Use of themes from the art of primitive peoples
   (D) Depiction of subjects by the use of solid shapes and detailed textures

The correct answer is (A). The cubists, greatly influenced by Paul Cézanne, *rejected* linear perspective in favor of a mobile perspective that used geometric planes and allowed objects to be depicted from several vantage points at the same time. The cubists also rejected the hyperemotional art of early expressionists such as Paul Gauguin, who often depicted nature unrealistically, with skies of nearly any color, trees of blue, and the ground of various shades of orange. Choices (B), (C), and (D) are characteristics of the cubists.

2. The axis line in a painting is
   (A) an imaginary line connecting only the strongest and weakest figures
   (B) the median line within a figure
   (C) used only when dealing with circular objects
   (D) an imaginary line that controls the path of eye movement through a composition

The correct answer is (D). The axis line is the imaginary line resulting from the subtle unity achieved in a painting by placing objects in such a way that the eye follows a path through the composition. The starting point is also the focal point. The eye, in viewing a logically sequenced painting, will begin at the focal point, follow the path, and then, once again, focus on the starting point.

3.

In the drawing above, which area of shading best represents a halftone?
(A) A
(B) B
(C) C
(D) D

The correct answer is (B). The position of the light source determines the direction of the shadow. The shadows are always on the side opposite the light. A halftone is a middle value. The highlight (A) is the lightest value. The core shadow (C) is the darkest value. Choice (D) represents the *cast* shadow, which takes the shape of the surface on which it falls.

Dance

1. Historically, the traditional shape of a folk dance was based on the
   (A) triangle
   (B) square
   (C) circle
   (D) figure eight

The correct answer is (C). The traditional circle shape of almost all folk dances evolved from early Stone Age ritual dance, in which the circle epitomized the tapping of magic power. The encircling motion of the dancers allowed the group to surround an object or person. Folk dances, associated with the history of a people, employed this design, since it fostered a community spirit and allowed increased dancer interaction.

2. Ballet can take many forms. In comparison to a dramatic ballet, a nondramatic ballet emphasizes
   (A) dancing that is based on classical Greek models
   (B) dancing without telling a story
   (C) poetic and lyrical styles that speak to graceful flights of fancy
   (D) fewer technical conventions than traditional ballet

The correct answer is (B). Nondramatic ballet emphasizes dance that does not tell a story. Instead, the dance movement, including its expressive qualities, is the centeral focus. Dramatic ballet often follows classical models based on common themes. Both dramatic and nondramatic ballet allow for differing styles that could emphasize lyrical qualities.

3. Dance history includes, in part, the contributions made by individual choreographers. George Balanchine, often referred to as the most influential American choreographer of the twentieth century, has become synonymous with a particular style of ballet. Which of the following would be <u>inconsistent</u> with the radical innovations associated with Balanchine?
   (A) Ballets that lack a definable plot, have few characterizations, and incorporate stark decor
   (B) Female body types that accentuate the limbs and dances that employ "leggy," thin dancers
   (C) Dance techniques that emphasize heel-floor contact instead of toe-floor contact to increase a dancer's speed
   (D) Limiting the number of on-stage dancers in order to emphasize dancer-to-audience interaction and unobstructed movement

The correct answer is (C). Balanchine (1904–83) emphasized increased floor contact with the toes rather than the heels. Heel-floor contact restricts speed and therefore limits rapid change in direction. Balanchine redefined and modified traditional ballet techniques in order to focus on attributes which would increase speed. For example, in executing allegro (fast-moving) steps, he relied on increased toe-floor contact, enhancing the dancer's ability to make the quick movements necessary to fast-tempo dancing. Balanchine ballets were often plotless (A), allowing the viewer to concentrate on the speed of the dance rather than an evolving story line. The choreography was best suited to lean body types (B), accentuating the limbs.

Drama/Theater

1. Which of the following theater conventions would have been considered unusual during Elizabethan times?
   (A) The lowering of a curtain to indicate the end of an act
   (B) Boys and men playing all female roles
   (C) The use of box-office revenues, rather than money from rich patrons, as primary financial support of the theatrical troupe
   (D) Audiences generally composed of all classes of society

The correct answer is (A). A convention is a generally recognized practice that an audience in a particular culture accepts as authentic or legitimate. Such conventions govern theatrical details, convincing audiences of the "truth" of a performance, and may be markedly different from one era or culture to another. An Elizabethan audience (sixteenth-century England) would have considered it unusual for a lowered curtain to signal the end of an act. At this time, plays were not divided into acts but were marked by continuous action as one scene flowed into the next. The Elizabethan audience *would* expect to see boys or young men in the female roles (B). During this time, box-office revenues were the troupe's primary financial support (C), and the audience was socially and economically diverse, with people from all walks of life attending the performances (D).

2. The "flowering" of Western culture is often associated with the Golden Age of Greece (fifth century B.C.) and the city of Athens. Which of the following was <u>not</u> associated with Athenian classical Greek theater during this time?
   (A) The protagonist in a tragedy, as the events unfold, experiences a sudden reversal in personal fortune and a catastrophic end.
   (B) The most prominent playwrights were Aeschylus, Sophocles, and Socrates.
   (C) The thematic material could be presented as drama, tragedy, comedy, or satyr play.
   (D) Festivals of original dance, song, and plays were presented to honor the Greek god Dionysus.

The correct answer is (B). The most famous Greek playwrights during the classical period were Aeschylus, Sophocles, Euripides, and Aristophanes. Socrates was one of the great philosophers of the period. The other choices were associated with Athenian theater at this time. The protagonist is, as a tragedy develops, in conflict with the antagonist, or villain, and undergoes a reversal in fortune and a catastrophic end. In a satyr play (C), a burlesque, the chorus was often dressed as the half-man, half-goat mythical satyr. In fact, during the festival of Dionysus, a playwright was expected to submit three tragedies and a satyr play. The City Dionysia, a celebration to honor Dionysus (the god of fertility, wine, and rebirth), was one of the most important theatrical events of the Golden Age of Greece.

3. Which of the following would be the LEAST appropriate play for which to use a thrust stage?
   (A) A production that calls for elaborate setting and scene changes
   (B) A modern drama that deals with an internal problem/solution
   (C) A script that requires audience-actor interaction
   (D) A play that includes a dramatic soliloquy

The correct answer is (A). A thrust stage extends into the audience's seating area, allowing the audience to "surround" it. Such an arrangement does not lend itself to elaborate setting or scene changes. In fact, it was the need for more elaborate staging that prompted the development of the proscenium stage. Audience-actor interaction (C) is a primary advantage of a thrust stage. A dramatic soliloquy (D) is a monologue performed by an actor alone on the stage, which would work well on the thrust stage.

SAMPLE QUESTIONS AND STRATEGIES FOR THE CONTENT AREA EXERCISES

Following are representative Visual and Performing Arts short constructed-response questions from each area covered. Strategies and a sample response are included with each question.

Music

1. Other than in musical style, briefly compare and contrast an opera and a musical.

Strategy

Before answering the question, try to recall both general and specific information about these performances. What operas are you familiar with? (perhaps *Madame Butterfly, The Magic Flute, William Tell,* or the folk opera *Porgy and Bess*) What is the subject matter of most operas? (dramatic themes, drama set to music) What about staging? What can you recall about musicals? (use of both songs and spoken dialogue) Notice that the question asks you *not* to talk about musical style.

Sample Response

Both operas and musicals are staged stories. Both employ costumes, scenery, soloists, dancers, and chorus. Certainly in both, <u>music</u> is the medium which connects all elements. However, there are major differences between the two theatrical forms.

In an opera, there may be spoken dialogue, but usually, the music is continuous. The emphasis in an operatic stage performance is less upon dialogue; instead, the vocal skills of the singers are displayed.

In comparison, a musical is a form in which there is much <u>spoken dialogue</u>, highlighted with songs. The focus in a musical is upon the <u>acting</u> and story line, rather than the singer. Since its beginnings, musical theater has integrated drama, music, chorus dancing, and soloists.

Visual Arts

2.

In the painting above, identify the probable historical period from the subject matter and style. Briefly discuss the design techniques (such as texture, background, brush strokes, and balance).

Strategy

Although you should always analyze a picture carefully, it is easy to overanswer a visual prompt question, so as always, be mindful of time. Here, consider whether the subject matter gives clues to the time period or artist. Look at the composition (the arrangement of physical elements in the painting). Is it symmetrical or asymmetrical? Look at the background. Decide if techniques are evident and what they are. Does the picture have a theme? Why might the figure be gazing in a particular direction?

Sample Response

The subject matter and style are representative of the Renaissance period.

The main figure is placed flatly against the background. The picture is balanced on each side by an equal amount of space. The illusion of depth is weak in spite of the distant trees. The figure is placed strongly in the foreground, and there is no indication of a middle ground. The background serves merely as a decorative drop to create balance and to fill space.

The eye of the viewer follows the figure in a continuous cycle, starting and ending on the figure's face. The repetitive linear texture of the velvety dress complements and aligns with the flowing structure of the robe. The figure is modeled in light and dark values so that it appears solid, round, and lifelike.

Dance

3. All cultures incorporate dance as a form of expression. Briefly describe the development of ritual dance as practiced by Stone Age cultures. Include in your answer the function of ritual dance and the characteristics of fertility and hunting ritual dance.

Strategy

Mark key terms in the question—in this case, *ritual dance, Stone Age, fertility,* and *hunting.*. Before beginning your response, think about why cultures use rituals of all kinds. Recall modern rituals and consider possible similarities with ancient rituals (such as purpose or setting). Simply defining the terms *ritual dance, fertility,* and *hunting* in a primitive context would give you partial credit.

Sample Response

The function of ritual dance is to influence the deities and control the direction of natural events. Ritual dance was also used as a physical manifestation in casting magic spells.

Fertility dances were performed by all Stone Age cultures. These dances represented the most basic of human concerns and recognized human dependence on nature. Ritual dance represented the natural rhythm of the seasons (dances were most common before the planting and harvest seasons) and was an attempt to assure prosperity for present and future generations.

Some dances were intended to create hunting magic. Male dancers, dressed in animal skins and adorned with body paint, would dance and chant to create the proper magic. The animal dance was the link between the natural and the supernatural worlds. The gods were called on to protect the hunters and provide animals for a successful hunt.

Drama/Theater

4. Playwrights often adapt familiar plays and themes to contemporary settings. Briefly compare the historical settings and one theme common to *West Side Story* and Shakespeare's *Romeo and Juliet.*

Strategy

Before writing the short answer, try to recall information pertinent to both stories—plots, endings, details. You might remember movie versions of both. Note that the question asks you to discuss only two items—the historical settings and *one* common theme.

Sample Response

Romeo and Juliet is set in fifteenth-century Verona, Italy. West Side Story is set in New York City during the 1950s. West Side Story is essentially a contemporary retelling of the Shakespearean tragedy.

One parallel theme of the plays concerns the feuding of families. In Romeo and Juliet, the Montagues and the Capulets are the families who vie for political control. In West Side Story, the feuding "families" are divided by both race and a desire for control. The Puerto Ricans are the Sharks, and the Anglos are the Jets, both groups fighting to protect their established "turf." In both plays, the children are the recipients and victims of their parents' intolerance and hatred.

HUMAN DEVELOPMENT

CONTENT

The Human Development section measures the basic skills and knowledge that elementary school teachers must have in order to recognize and effectively respond to a variety of teaching situations. The test stresses the developmental needs of students rather than the academic information taught to them. The teacher is expected to be knowledgeable in this field in order to interpret and make assessments regarding student behavior and to plan appropriate teaching strategies in both affective and cognitive domains to facilitate a child-centered and nurturing environment. This section also measures the ability to recognize and understand issues concerning individual differences and human diversity.

Content Knowledge (Multiple-Choice)

The Content Knowledge (multiple-choice) test, which contains nine questions grouped together, covers the following five major content areas and focuses on the topics listed under each. The approximate weight of each category is listed in parentheses.

1. **Theory, including implications and applications (20 percent)**

   - behavioral development
   - cognitive development
   - social learning
   - psychosocial development

2. **Research, including implications and applications (30 percent)**

   - family attachments and influences
   - temperament and personality
   - influences affecting achievement
   - antisocial (aggressive) and prosocial behavior
   - intelligence testing and intellectual behavior
   - play activities
   - moral and character development
   - substance abuse and its effects on the unborn child

3. **Major developmental perspectives (15 percent)**

   - continuity and discontinuity
   - nature and nurture
   - child-centered and adult-directed learning

4. **Gathering and applying information (10 percent)**
    - assessment of children (formal and informal)
    - ethical issues confronting educators

5. **Human diversity (25 percent)**
    - questions composed of the above content areas as they pertain to diverse populations

Content Area Exercises (Short Constructed-Response)

The two Human Development short constructed-response questions generally conform to the following format.

- One question tests understanding of significant developmental theories and research.
- One question tests understanding of the influences of various sources of human diversity on growth and development.

SAMPLE QUESTIONS AND STRATEGIES FOR THE CONTENT KNOWLEDGE SECTION

Each of the following examples represents an area tested on the Human Development multiple-choice segment. An analysis follows each question.

Theory

1. A ten-year-old child of average development is learning to play chess. According to Piaget's operational period of stage development, the child would <u>not</u> be able to
    - (A) choose a response in reaction to an opponent's move
    - (B) think four moves ahead and imagine potential combinations
    - (C) complete an end game by checkmating an opponent
    - (D) understand the basic instructions and follow the rules of the game

The correct answer is (B). Piaget's stages of cognitive development are ordered into four periods: sensorimotor (0–2 years), preoperational (2–7 years), period of concrete operations (7–11 years), and period of formal operations (11+ years). During the period of concrete operations, logical operations can be applied to concrete problems. The rules of a variety of games can be learned and applied; however, complex deductions are not possible until a child enters the period of formal operations. Choice (C) is not the *best* answer because there is insufficient information regarding the end game (number of pieces, position on the board, number of moves to checkmate the opponent) to determine the level of complex reasoning needed to complete the game. Even if you don't know Piaget's theory, you could answer this question correctly. Since there can be only one right answer, that answer must, logically, be the most difficult task listed, thinking far ahead and identifying complex possibilities.

2. According to Piaget's cognitive development theory, egocentrism would most likely
   (A) characterize children who are selfish
   (B) limit the intuitive growth of children
   (C) encourage a global view of familiar surroundings
   (D) explain why children are able to use logical rules to deal with problems

The correct answer is (B). Egocentrism, according to Piaget, indicates that children generally view the world from the reference point of their own perspective. Egocentrism, then, would limit intuitive cognitive development, since it inhibits a child from using knowledge objectively. Piaget's "three-mountain problem" demonstrates the limiting aspects of egocentric behavior. In the experiment, a four year old (given various options) will invariably choose examples that correspond to the child's view of the world. Egocentrism is characteristic of children in the preoperational stage (ages two to seven).

Research

1. Which of the following is in the correct chronological order of language acquisition?
   (A) Cooing, phonetic expansion, initial inflection, single words
   (B) Cooing, initial inflection, single words, phonetic expansion
   (C) Initial inflection, cooing, phonetic expansion, single words
   (D) Phonetic expansion, cooing, single words, initial inflection

The correct answer is (A). It should be apparent that in a progression from the simple to the more complex, cooing would be the beginning of language acquisition and single words (of the choices given) would be the most complex. Therefore, through a process of elimination, you could arrive at the correct answer. Cooing sounds are prelinguistic and appear in children at about three months. Phonetic expansion is associated with the babbling stage. The one-word stage of language development is characteristic of the linguistic period.

2. Research indicates that the right and left hemispheres of the brain are characterized by dominant functions and abilities. Which of the following would not be a dominant function of the left hemisphere of the brain?
   (A) Language and speech
   (B) Spatial organization
   (C) Logic
   (D) Sequential organization

The correct answer is (B). Spatial organization is a right-brain function. Right-brain individuals see the whole of things. The left hemisphere of the brain is generally associated with verbal concepts, rules, and judgments. The part, rather than the whole, is emphasized. Other dominant left-hemisphere functions include logic and organizational skills. The right hemisphere of the brain is strongly connected to emotions. Patterns are also emphasized, as are creativity, fantasy, and aesthetics. You could answer this question correctly even if you don't know about the functions of the right and left hemispheres of the brain. If you realize that choices (C) and (D) are logically similar functions, you are left with only two possible answers.

Major Developmental Perspectives

1. The most important principle that a teacher should follow when initiating a program of positive reinforcement is to
   (A) punish negative behavior and reward positive behavior
   (B) provide regular opportunity for socially acceptable behavior
   (C) make sure that the reward comes immediately after the appropriate behavior
   (D) provide peer approval and recognition

The correct answer is (C). Positive reinforcement is most effective in strengthening behavior when the reward comes immediately after the desired response. Choice (B) does not address the concept of immediate rewards; however, providing positive opportunities is an important factor in any reinforcement program. Choice (A) is incorrect because rewards tend to be more effective than punishment in changing behavior. Negative reinforcement (punishment) is often associated with perpetuating self-image problems. Punishment can also reinforce deviant behavior.

Gathering and Applying Information

1. An educational researcher is attempting to correlate an individual's intelligence-test scores in childhood with achievement in adult life. The research strategy that would best investigate any correlation between the variables is
   (A) cross-sectional
   (B) experimental
   (C) longitudinal
   (D) a case study

The correct answer is (C). A longitudinal research design investigates an individual through time. Historically, longitudinal studies have been used to challenge the belief that intelligence is a static and unchanging characteristic. In an experimental design (B), the researcher manipulates one factor or variable while holding constant all other factors that might influence an outcome. The cross-sectional approach (A) investigates subjects of different ages simultaneously for the purpose of understanding the relationship among variables such as age, experience, and behavior. A case study (D) is an extensive study of a single case using all available data about an individual.

Human Diversity

1. Three teacher groups were asked to participate in an educational study. Group 1 was asked to describe a normal sixth-grade student. Group 2 was asked to describe a mentally retarded sixth-grade student. Group 3 was asked to describe a hyperkinetic sixth-grade student.

   The three groups then viewed a videotape of a sixth-grade student. At the end of the study, the three groups were asked to describe the characteristics of the child viewed on the videotape. All groups described the child on the videotape as similar in characteristics to the child they had described at the start of the study. However, all three groups had actually observed the same videotape.

What is the best explanation for the behavior described above?
(A) The experiment was flawed because the research conditions were arranged deliberately.
(B) The observer did not know whether the child being observed was from the experimental or the control group.
(C) Teachers are not trained to make clinical judgments on emotional behaviors.
(D) The expectations of the observer caused an error in observation.

The correct answer is (D). Even in well-trained educators, preconceived biases can influence objectivity. By first having to describe a child without considering other external factors, the observer subconsciously developed a "vested" interest in the outcome of the experiment. Stereotypical attitudes on the part of teachers can profoundly influence judgments that affect student learning.

SAMPLE QUESTIONS AND STRATEGIES FOR THE CONTENT AREA EXERCISES

Following are representative questions from the two areas tested by the Human Development short constructed-response questions. Strategies and a sample response are included with each question.

Developmental Theories and Research

1. What does Maslow's self-actualization theory suggest about factors that influence student achievement? Give appropriate examples to support your answer.

Strategy

This is a difficult question because it requires specific information in order to answer it. However, even if you lack some of that specific information, you might consider general factors that influence student achievement (or anyone's achievement)—both external and internal factors such as environment and attitude. Also, you might attempt to define self-actualization. For example, the term *self* refers to the individual, and the term *actual* means existing in fact, not merely potential. Therefore, you could arrive at the term *self-motivating* as a possible entry to the essay. The point is that before leaving the answer blank, think about the question. Remember, accurate information, no matter how limited, will result in partial credit.

Sample Response

Abraham Maslow developed a hierarchy of human needs that progress from physiological needs (basic needs such as food, water, and clothing) and safety needs (the need for an orderly, nonthreatening environment) to the meta-needs of self-actualization (self-esteem needs). Maslow referred to the basic needs as deficiency needs.

He theorized that an individual could not attain higher needs until basic lower-level needs were satisfied. He referred to the meta-needs as growth needs. When an individual reaches self-actualization, the person is capable of being self-motivating, independent, and creative.

By recognizing the hierarchical link between motivation and achievement, a teacher can influence the direction of learning. A child who feels loved will perform at higher expectation levels. Also, a child will attempt to meet a teacher's expectations of him or her, whether positive or negative.

Influences of Various Sources of Human Diversity on Growth and Development

2. Assume that there is a need to increase student interaction in your fifth-grade classroom. Briefly discuss why a teacher needs to look at student interaction in the classroom. Include in your answer five methods to accomplish this increase in interaction.

Strategy

Before answering the question, visualize a typical classroom configuration (parallel rows). Ask yourself what teaching strategies would limit student interaction (lecture, individual reports, etc.) and what strategies would alter this pattern (cooperative learning groups, reconfiguring the room arrangement, etc.) Be sure to note the number of methods required.

Sample Response

Introspective teachers always look at their teaching patterns and adjust them as needed. For example, a teacher must guard against talking/lecturing too much. In such a setting, students are passive rather than active learners. Also, if a teacher recognizes students who are lonely or overly aggressive, teaching strategies can be designed to integrate those students into the classroom activities. Improving relationships in the classroom is a fundamental goal of effective teachers. To increase student interaction, the following methods could be implemented.

1. Institute cooperative learning groups.

2. Develop cooperative class projects such as debates and plays.

3. Shift from a lecture format.

4. Alter the traditional parallel-row seating arrangement; instead, incorporate a concentric-circles approach or a four-desk, contiguous-square configuration.

5. Develop teaching strategies that avoid direct teacher-child interaction and, instead, emphasize student-student strategies.

PHYSICAL EDUCATION

CONTENT

The Physical Education section focuses on knowledge and understanding of the three major categories included in a comprehensive physical education program. This section of the test measures your ability to evaluate movement education and to recognize the physical, biological, and social sciences in the context of

- understanding the nature and purpose of physical education activities and their place in the physical education curriculum

- evaluating and interpreting the performance level and physical characteristics of physical education students

- making decisions regarding the conduct and needs of students in physical education classes

Content Knowledge (Multiple-Choice)

The Content Knowledge (multiple-choice) test, which contains nine questions grouped together, covers the following three major content areas and focuses on the topics listed under each. The approximate weight of each category is listed in parentheses.

1. **Movement concepts and forms (40–50 percent)**

   - *fundamental movements and movement concepts,* including nonlocomotor and manipulative movements and concepts of space, time, effort, and quality in the context of movement education

   - *fitness,* including skill- and health-related fitness and conditioning

   - *movement forms,* including traditional and nontraditional games in the context of individual, dual, and team games/sports as well as tumbling and gymnastics

2. **Physical and biological science foundations (30–40 percent)**

   - growth and development, motor learning, kinesiology, and exercise physiology

3. **Social science foundations (10–20 percent)**
   - social and psychological aspects of physical education

Content Area Exercises (Short Constructed-Response)

The Physical Education short constructed-response questions generally require you to demonstrate mastery of one or more of the following abilities.

- describing the characteristics of movement forms
- assessing/diagnosing student growth based on given data
- designing/prescribing movement routines based on specific goals

The two questions in this section generally conform to the following format.

- One question deals with movement concepts and forms.
- One question deals with a fitness-related topic.

Note that categories 2 and 3 of the multiple-choice questions (physical and biological science foundations and social science foundations) are *not* included in the short constructed-response topics.

SAMPLE QUESTIONS AND STRATEGIES FOR THE CONTENT KNOWLEDGE SECTION

Each of the following examples represents an area tested on the Physical Education multiple-choice segment. An analysis follows each question.

Movement Concepts and Forms

1. Which locomotor transport skill is described in the following example?

   The balance is on one foot; the body is then thrust forward into space, with the individual landing on the same foot as the takeoff foot.

   (A) Hop
   (B) Skip
   (C) Gallop
   (D) Jump

The correct answer is (A). Visualize the locomotor movement described. The hop is the only choice listed that uses only one foot. Hopping is a basic structured locomotor movement. In hopping, both the body lean and the position of the hands help balance the movement of landing on one foot. Skipping (B) is a series of step-hops done with alternate feet.

2. Which of the following is not a measurable element of heath-related fitness?
   (A) Cardiorespiratory endurance
   (B) Body composition
   (C) Coordination
   (D) Musculoskeletal fitness

The correct answer is (C). Health-related fitness is associated with disease and illness prevention by the maintenance of a healthy lifestyle. As a physical education term, health-related fitness is not directly related to sports skills such as dribbling a basketball or catching a football but rather to such things as body composition, muscular endurance, and flexibility. Coordination (C), the ability to perform motor tasks on demand quickly and efficiently, is fundamentally a motor-performance fitness attribute. Motor-performance fitness is associated with agility, balance, power, speed, and strength.

3. Which of the following is the correct order from simplest to most complex in an elementary tumbling program?
   (A) Balance stunts, individual stunts, animal movements, inverted balance
   (B) Animal Movements, balance stunts, inverted balance, individual stunts
   (C) Animal movements, inverted balance, balance stunts, individual stunts
   (D) Inverted balance, animal movements, individual stunts, balance stunts

The correct answer is (B). Note that in ordering items from simplest to most complex, knowing the first or last item in the series allows you to quickly eliminate incorrect answers. In this case, knowing that individual stunts (of the choices given) are the most difficult activity, leaves only (B) and (C) as possible answers.

4. Which of the following is the correct formula to calculate your target heart rate for aerobic activity?
   (A) The number 220 minus your age multiplied by 0.70 equals the target heart rate.
   (B) The number 200 plus your age multiplied by 0.50 equals the target heart rate.
   (C) Your weight minus your age multiplied by 1.0 equals the target heart rate.
   (D) Your pulse rate added to your weight divided by 2 equals the target heart rate.

The correct answer is (A). When considering health-related fitness, the target heart rate is generally set at seventy percent of an individual's maximum heart capacity. The purpose of reaching and maintaining a target heart rate is to reach a level in which the aerobic training will most benefit the cardiovascular system. The formula is arrived at by taking the number 220 (which represents the maximum heart rate for an excellently trained, young individual), subtracting your age, and taking seventy percent of that figure as your target heart rate for aerobic activities. Maintaining the target heart rate (in health-related fitness) is achieved through long-duration and low-intensity activities.

Physical and Biological Science Foundations

1. A second grade physical education activity involves throwing a bean-bag through a target placed fifteen feet from the student. The performance objective of this activity most likely emphasizes
   (A) gross-motor coordination
   (B) object-handling skills
   (C) cross-lateral throwing movement
   (D) static balance

The correct answer is (C). Visualize a student performing this skill. You should eliminate static balance (D) because the term implies a stationary activity. While object-handling skills (B) are necessary for this activity, they would not be emphasized. (Juggling is a good example of object-handling skills.) The emphasis in this activity is on throwing. One of the performance objectives involved in practicing with a bean-bag is to develop cross-lateral coordination and throwing for accuracy. In cross-lateral throwing, the student steps forward with the foot opposite the throwing hand, transferring weight and increasing strength and distance. Gross-motor activities (A) involve the whole body (running, jumping, etc.).

2. Which of the following is not a true statement regarding isometric exercise?
   (A) Isometric exercises are useful for building strength.
   (B) Isometric exercises involve a held contraction against an immovable base.
   (C) Isometric exercises can be performed in virtually any location and with little, if any, danger of injury.
   (D) Isometric exercises are considered a comprehensive fitness program because specific muscle groups can be worked independently.

The correct answer is (D). The value of isometric exercises is in producing strength in a relatively short time. Isometric exercises are *not* considered comprehensive because they are designed to "work" only one muscle group at a time. In isometrics, a muscle group contracts against an immovable object. *Isotonic* exercises usually involve the use of weights or heavy calisthenics.

3. A male in his early forties has a physical exam before attempting a regular exercise program. The results of the physical include the following data: a serum cholesterol level of 200, a diastolic blood pressure of 82, a resting pulse rate of 70, a family history of heart attack in one grandparent at the age of 70, height of 5 feet 9 inches, and weight of 170 pounds.

   What is the most logical fitness program for this individual to participate in?

   (A) No program. The individual is at cardiovascular risk.
   (B) A limited program. The individual has at least two cardiovascular risk factors.
   (C) A moderate program. The individual's family history indicates a potential problem.
   (D) A full program. The individual is in apparent good health.

The correct answer is (D). The individual described is in good health and would be able to begin a progressively strenuous exercise program. Although one might argue that 170 pounds might be slightly heavy (the body structure is not mentioned), this would be reason to start a regular exercise program. The other data from the physical are quite satisfactory. A cholesterol level above 200 is considered a moderate health risk; one above 240 is a high risk factor. A diastolic blood pressure of 90 would be considered high risk. The family history does not represent a limiting factor in pursuing an exercise program; heart disease in only one grandparent at age 70 would not be considered unusual.

Social Science Foundations

1. A female junior high school student frequently refuses to dress for her physical education class. The teacher is not making much headway in convincing the student that her behavior is inappropriate. The teacher recognizes that this student is overweight and withdrawn. Of the following examples, which is the most accurate statement in explanation of the student's behavior?
   (A) The student is being influenced by a peer group that considers dressing for physical education "uncool."
   (B) The student is exhibiting self-esteem problems.
   (C) The student has experienced negative reinforcement in previous P.E. classes.
   (D) The teacher should use the class to improve student interaction.

The correct answer is (B). A significant factor in interpreting this question is the fact that the student is overweight and withdrawn. It should be apparent that one of the goals of an elementary physical education program is to improve self-esteem. Not dressing for P.E. is a recurring problem. Strategies to encourage overweight individuals to dress for the class would include such things as conferencing with the student to determine the cause of the problem, involving the student directly in the activities, suggesting weight-loss programs, and showing the student how physical education can promote healthy lifestyle choices. Although choice (D) does not explain the student's behavior, this would be an appropriate direction for the teacher to take.

2. Which of the following best describes an appropriate guideline for planning a physical education program?
   (A) The activities should be nonvigorous to encourage active participation by all students.
   (B) Proportional emphasis should be placed on basic movement, rhythmics, stunts and tumbling, and selected sports.
   (C) Program goals should emphasize the affective and cognitive domain but de-emphasize the psychomotor domain.
   (D) The program should be geared to exposure to rather than mastery of a skill.

The correct answer is (B). In planning a successful physical education program, balanced and varied progression is essential. Such a program would incorporate proportional emphasis on basic movement and encourage a broad range of activities. Choice (A) is incorrect because an effective program has to consider vigorous physical activity in order to promote growth and physical fitness. Choice (D) is incorrect because mastery of a skill is the expected outcome in any sound educational program (including physical education).

SAMPLE QUESTIONS AND STRATEGIES FOR THE CONTENT AREA EXERCISES

Following are representative Physical Education short constructed-response questions. Strategies and a sample response are included with each question.

Movement Concepts and Forms

1. A bean-bag can be used as a physical education manipulative tool. How can bean-bag activities reinforce perceptual-motor abilities at the lower primary grades? Include specific perceptual-motor, performance-based objectives used in movement education to support your answer.

Strategy

Visualize a bean-bag activity (such as throwing and catching) Consider the advantages of using a bean-bag and the perceptual-motor abilities involved (such as balance and hand-eye coordination). Consider why manipulatives are used in a physical education program and what the performance-based objectives are likely to be (student demonstration of a skill).

Sample Response

Bean-bag activities advance perceptual-motor skills in facilitating improved hand-eye coordination, balance, laterality, sensory perceptions, and proper body imaging. They also promote kinesthetic awareness and sensory functioning in vision, hearing, and touch. The manipulative aspects of the bean-bag are conducive to early primary exploration. Bean-bags are flexible and soft and greatly reduce the fear factor in catching objects.

An example of a bean-bag activity improving hand-eye coordination and laterality is throwing the bean-bag over one's head and clapping one's hands before catching the bag. In locomotor and nonlocomotor activities, the bean-bag could be used for balance—for example, balancing the bean bag on various body parts while transversing an area.

Fitness-Related Topic

2. How is aerobic fitness related to overall health fitness? Include appropriate examples to support your answer.

Strategy

Recall what you already may know about this topic. For example, aerobic activities involve continuous motion and are related to cardiovascular fitness. Consider what the term *aerobic* means (related to the presence of oxygen). Recall some aerobic activities.

Sample Response

Health fitness is directly related to preventing and remediating the degenerative aspects of disease. Instituting an aerobic-fitness program of the proper duration, intensity, and frequency can improve overall health fitness. Oxygen-based aerobic activities, such as jogging, cycling, swimming, and low-impact aerobic dancing, are designed to be continuous so as to reach and maintain a target heart rate. Aerobic activities should be performed at least three times a week for thirty minutes or more at a time. The key result of aerobics is improved cardiovascular fitness and increased oxygen intake; other results include a stronger heart muscle, lower heart rate, and reduced blood pressure. Such exercise also improves strength and endurance and decreases body fat.

CHARTS, GRAPHS, MAPS, CARTOONS, AND DIAGRAMS

Some questions on the MSAT require you to understand and use information given in charts, graphs, maps, cartoons, and/or diagrams. The following section will give you some insight into how to approach these question types.

CHARTS, TABLES, AND GRAPHS

Strategies

A chart, table, or graph is given so that you can refer to it. Look for trends or changing patterns that might appear. Also, look for additional information and key words or headings that are included. In dealing with this type of question, you should do the following.

- Focus on understanding the important information in the chart, table, or graph.

- Don't memorize the information; refer to it when you need to.

- Sometimes, skimming the questions first can be helpful. This will tell you what to look for.

- Quickly, but carefully, examine the whole graph and all additional information before you start to answer questions. Make sure that you understand the information given.

- Read the question or questions and possible choices and notice the key words. Decide on your answer from the information given.

- Sometimes, the answer to a question is available in extra information given with a graph (headings, scale factors, legends, etc.). Be sure to read and understand this information.

- Look for the obvious large changes, high points, low points, trends, etc. Obvious information often leads to an answer. Unless you are told otherwise, use only the information given in the chart or graph.

Charts and Tables

Charts and tables are often used to give an organized picture of information, or data. Be sure that you understand *what is given*. Column headings and line items give the important information. These titles give the numbers meaning.

Mathematics

Questions 1–4 refer to the following chart.

BURGER SALES FOR THE WEEK OF AUGUST 8–14

Day	Hamburgers	Cheeseburgers
Sunday	120	92
Monday	85	80
Tuesday	77	70
Wednesday	74	71
Thursday	75	72
Friday	91	88
Saturday	111	112

1. On which day were the most hamburgers sold?
   (A) Sunday
   (B) Monday
   (C) Thursday
   (D) Saturday

The correct answer is (A). First, pay special attention to what information is given in the chart. This chart shows the number of "Burger Sales for the Week of August 8–14." The days of the week are given along the left side of the chart. The number of *hamburgers* for each day is given in one column and the number of *cheeseburgers* in the other column. To answer this question, you must simply be able to read the chart. The most hamburgers were sold on Sunday (120).

2. On which day were the most burgers sold (hamburgers and cheeseburgers)?
   (A) Sunday
   (B) Monday
   (C) Friday
   (D) Saturday

The correct answer is (D). To answer this question, you must understand the chart and do some simple computation. Working from the answers is probably the easiest method.

   (A) Sunday $120 + 92 = 212$
   (B) Monday $85 + 80 = 165$
   (C) Friday $91 + 88 = 179$
   (D) Saturday $111 + 112 = \underline{223}$

Another method is to *approximate* the answers.

3. On how many days were more hamburgers sold than cheeseburgers?
   (A) 7
   (B) 6
   (C) 5
   (D) 4

The correct answer is (B). To answer this question, you must compare the sales for each day. Hamburgers outsold cheeseburgers every day except Saturday.

4. If the pattern of sales continues,
   (A) the weekend days will have the fewest number of burger sales next week
   (B) the cheeseburgers will outsell hamburgers next week
   (C) generally, when hamburger sales go up, cheeseburger sales will go up
   (D) hamburgers will be less expensive than cheeseburgers

The correct answer is (C). To answer this question, you must notice one of the trends. Most days that hamburger sales go up, cheeseburger sales go up (with the exception of Saturday to Sunday).

Science

Questions 5–6 refer to the following chart.

THE PLANTS

Plant Group	Chlorophyll	Leaves	Seeds	Flowers
Fungi	no	no	no	no
Algae	yes	no	no	no
Ferns	yes	yes	no	no
Gymnosperms	yes	yes	yes	no
Angiosperms	yes	yes	yes	yes

5. Which of the following plant groups has chlorophyll and leaves but no seeds or flowers?
   (A) Algae
   (B) Ferns
   (C) Gymnosperms
   (D) Angiosperms

The correct answer is (B). This table shows what each basic plant group does and doesn't have. Notice that the plant groups are listed along the left and the items (characteristics) are given at the top of each column. To answer this question you must be able to read the chart. Ferns have a *yes* in the chlorophyll and leaves columns and a *no* in the seeds and flowers columns. So ferns have chlorophyll and leaves but no seeds or flowers.

6. Which of the following is the most complex plant group?
   (A) Fungi
   (B) Algae
   (C) Gymnosperms
   (D) Angiospserms

The correct answer is (D). To answer this question, you must understand that, on this table, the plant group with the *most characteristics* will be the *most complex.*. Angiosperms (D) have chlorophyll, leaves, seeds, and flowers and would be considered the most complex.

7.

TEMPERATURE OF OBJECTS IN °C

Absolute zero	−273
Oxygen freezes	−218
Oxygen liquifies	−183
Water freezes	0
Human body	37
Water boils	100
Wood fire	830
Iron melts	1535
Iron boils	3000

As shown in the table above, the difference in temperature between the point at which oxygen freezes and the point at which iron melts is
(A) 1317
(B) 1535
(C) 1718
(D) 1753

The correct answer is (D). To answer this question, you must be able to read the chart and do some simple calculations. The freezing temperature of oxygen is −218 degrees centigrade. Iron melts at 1535 degrees centigrade. To find the difference between the two you must subtract.

$$1535 - (-218) = 1535 + 218 = 1753$$

Graphs

Information may be displayed in many ways. The three basic types of graphs you should know are bar graphs, line graphs, and pie graphs (or pie charts).

Bar Graphs

Bar graphs convert the information in a chart into separate bars or columns. Some graphs list numbers along one edge and places, dates, people, or things (individual categories) along another edge. Always try to determine the *relationship* between the columns in a graph or chart.

History/Social Sciences

1.

Number of Delegates Committed to Each Candidate

Candidate 1 has approximately how many more delegates committed than does Candidate 2?
(A) 150
(B) 200
(C) 250
(D) 400

The correct answer is (C). To understand this question, you must be able to read the bar graph and make comparisons. Notice that the graph shows the "Number of Delegates Committed to Each Candidate," with the numbers given along the bottom of the graph in increases of 200. The names are listed along the left side. Candidate 1 has approximately 800 delegates (possibly a few more). The bar graph for Candidate 2 stops about three quarters of the way between 400 and 600. Now, consider that halfway between 400 and 600 would be 500. So Candidate 2 is at about 550.

$$800 - 550 = 250$$

Science

2.

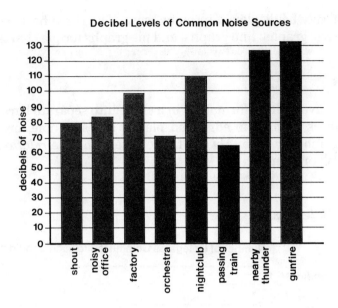

The graph above shows the average decibel levels associated with various common sources of noise. Listening to high levels of noise for a long time can damage the eardrum and cause loss of hearing.

According to the graph above, which of the following sources of noise would be most likely to damage the eardrum?
(A) An orchestra
(B) A passing train
(C) Nearby thunder
(D) Gunfire

The correct answer is (D). To answer this question, you must be able to read the graph and understand the information included. Notice that the decibels of noise are listed along the left-hand side in increases of 10. The common sources of noise are listed along the bottom of the graph. Since gunfire has the highest decibel rating, it is usually the loudest of the choices. This would cause it to be the most likely to damage the eardrum.

Line Graphs

Line graphs convert data into points on a grid. These points are then connected to show a relationship between the items, dates, times, etc. Notice the slopes of lines connecting the points. These lines will show increases and decreases. The sharper the slope *upward,* the greater the *increase.* The sharper the slope *downward,* the greater the *decrease.* Line graphs can show trends, or changes, in data over a period of time.

History/Social Sciences

Questions 3–4 refer to the following graph.

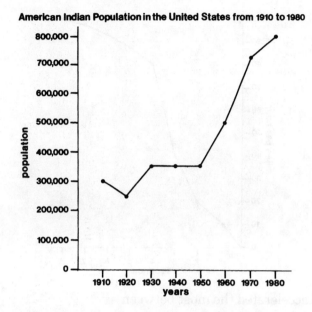

American Indian Population in the United States from 1910 to 1980

3. In which of the following years were there about 500,000 American Indians?
   (A) 1940
   (B) 1950
   (C) 1960
   (D) 1970

The correct answer is (C). To answer this question, you must be able to read the graph. The information along the left side of the graph shows the number of Indians in increases of 100,000. The bottom of the graph shows the years from 1910 to 1980. You will notice that in 1960 there were about 500,000 American Indians in the United States. Using the edge of your answer sheet like a ruler will help you see that the dot in the 1960 column lines up with 500,000 on the left.

4. During which of the following time periods was there a decrease in the American Indian population?
   (A) 1910 to 1920
   (B) 1920 to 1930
   (C) 1930 to 1940
   (D) 1960 to 1970

The correct answer is (A). Since the slope of the line goes *down* from 1910 to 1920, there must have been a decrease. If you read the actual numbers, you will notice a decrease from 300,000 to 250,000.

Mathematics

5.

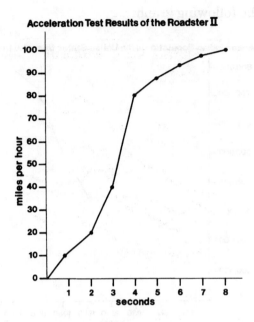

Acceleration Test Results of the Roadster II

The Roadster II accelerated the most between
(A) 1 and 2 seconds
(B) 2 and 3 seconds
(C) 3 and 4 seconds
(D) 4 and 5 seconds

The correct answer is (C). To answer this question, you must understand how the information is presented. The numbers on the left side of the graph show the speed in miles per hour (mph). The information at the bottom of the graph shows the number of seconds. The movement of the line can give important information and show trends. The *more the line slopes upward,* the *greater the acceleration.* The greatest slope upward is between 3 and 4 seconds. The Roadster II accelerates from about 40 to about 80 mph in that time.

Mathematics and History/Social Sciences

Questions 6–7 refer to the following line graph.

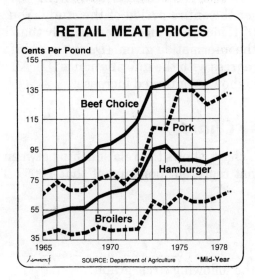

RETAIL MEAT PRICES

SOURCE: Department of Agriculture   *Mid-Year

6. A pound of hamburger in 1975 cost approximately how much more than it did in 1970?
   (A) 20 cents
   (B) 25 cents
   (C) 30 cents
   (D) 35 cents

The correct answer is (A). A line graph shows the relationship between two or more items. This question calls for comparing the price of hamburger in 1975 with the price of hamburger in 1970. You are asked to determine the *approximate price increase during the given period.* To answer the question, you must be able to see the differences among the four items listed on the chart. Notice that the lower horizontal line indicates the time reference as given in years 1965 to 1978. Each line extending from it represents a one-year increment. The vertical line on the far left gives the price, or cents per pound (35¢ to $1.55 per pound). Each line extending from it represents a 20¢ increment (35¢ to 55¢; 55¢ to 75¢, etc.). In 1975, hamburger sold for slightly more that 85¢ per pound. The price increase from 1970 to 1975 was approximately 20¢ per pound.

7. Which of the following is an accurate statement based on the information provided in the chart?
   (A) The figures for mid-year 1978 indicate a downward trend in retail meat prices.
   (B) Pork prices increased more gradually than broiler prices.
   (C) More hamburger was sold than beef choice.
   (D) The figures for mid-year 1978 indicate a continued increase in retail meat prices.

The correct answer is (D). To answer this question, you must be able to determine the *one* statement that is consistent with the information provided in the graph. Mid-year

1978 is shown by the continuation of the lines representing meat prices beyond the 1978 line. Notice that all lines represent an *upward* trend. Choice (A) does not agree with the data in the chart. Choice (B) asks you to compare two items to see which one showed the most consistent price over the entire period of the study. You should notice that pork prices, especially since 1971, increased more dramatically than broiler prices. Choice (C) cannot be supported by the information given. (*Do not* read information into the chart.) The only statement that agrees with the information is (D). All meat prices, as shown by the mid-year 1978 prices, show a continued increase.

Circle Graphs (Pie Charts)

A circle graph, or pie chart, shows the relationship between the whole circle (100%) and the various slices that represent portions of that 100%. The larger the slice, the higher the percentage.

Mathematics

Questions 8–10 refer to the following circle graph.

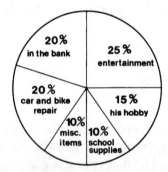

How John Spends His Monthly Paycheck

8. John spends one quarter of his monthly paycheck on
   (A) his hobby
   (B) car and bike repair
   (C) entertainment
   (D) school supplies

The correct answer is (C). To answer this question, you must be able to read the graph and apply some simple math. Notice how the information is given in the graph. Each item is given along with the percent of money spent on that item. Since one quarter is the same as 25%, entertainment is the one you are looking for.

9. If John receives $100 on this month's paycheck, how much will he put in the bank?
   (A) $2
   (B) $20
   (C) $35
   (D) $60

The correct answer is (B). To answer this question, you must again read the graph carefully and apply some simple math. John puts 20% of his income in the bank. 20% of $100 is $20. So he will put $20 in the bank.

10. The ratio of the amount of money John spends on his hobby to the amount he puts in the bank is
    (A) 1/2
    (B) 5/8
    (C) 2/3
    (D) 3/4

The correct answer is (D). To answer this question, you must use the information in the graph to make a ratio.

$$\frac{\text{his hobby}}{\text{in the bank}} = \frac{15\%}{20\%} = \frac{15}{20} = \frac{3}{4}$$

Notice that the ratio of 15%/20% reduces to 3/4.

Mathematics and History/Social Sciences

Questions 11–12 refer to the following pie charts.

**Distribution of Earned Degrees
By Field of Study**

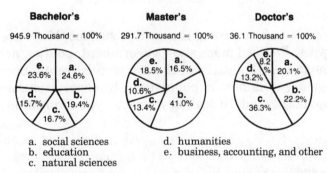

Bachelor's

945.9 Thousand = 100%

e. 23.6% a. 24.6%
d. 15.7% b. 19.4%
c. 16.7%

Master's

291.7 Thousand = 100%

e. 18.5% a. 16.5%
d. 10.6% b. 41.0%
c. 13.4%

Doctor's

36.1 Thousand = 100%

e. 8.2% a. 20.1%
d. 13.2% b. 22.2%
c. 36.3%

a. social sciences
b. education
c. natural sciences
d. humanities
e. business, accounting, and other

11. Which field of study received the smallest number of earned master's degrees?
    (A) Social sciences
    (B) Education
    (C) Natural sciences
    (D) Humanities

The correct answer is (D). Remember that a circle graph, or pie chart, shows the relationship between the whole circle (100%) and the slices or parts of that 100%. The larger the slice, the higher the percentage. A circle graph makes it easy to see the relationship among the parts that make up the total graph. Two or more circle graphs can be used in the same example to show many relationships. In this question, you must find the field of study that received the *smallest* number of *master's* degrees. You can see that the humanities, with 10.6% of the total amount, is the correct answer. Notice that with the data given, you could have calculated the *number* of master's degrees earned in the humanities, although to answer this question, you do not need to. 291.7 thousand equals 100% (see the information above the circle graph); therefore, 10.6% of 291,700 would be approximately 30,920 earned degrees. This information could be calculated for each segment of the pie chart.

12. In comparing bachelor's degrees to doctor's degrees, which field of study shows the greatest percentage change?
    (A) Education
    (B) Natural sciences
    (C) Humanities
    (D) Business, accounting, and other

The correct answer is (B). To answer this question, you must compare total *percentage changes*. If the question asked you to find the *negative percentage change* (percentage loss), the correct answer would have been (D). (Business showed a 15% reduction in earned degrees.) From the chart, you can see that choices (B) and (D) show the greatest percentage change. Choice (B) shows approximately a 20% change, while choice (D) shows approximately a 15% change.

MAPS

Strategies

A map can represent all or part of the earth's surface. Maps are usually classified into four general types. Political maps show government, politics, and political parties. Physical maps show the earth's surface, climate, and currents. Special-purpose maps show products, vegetation, minerals, population, transportation, and the like. Relief maps show the shape of the land. In dealing with this type of question, you should do the following.

Consider the geographic factors.

- Location of the event
- Size of the area involved
- Geographic relationship of the area to other concerned places (How far apart are the places? In what direction?)
- Important water areas
- Means of access to the area (How can we get to the area?)
- Physical factors such as mountains and plains
- Natural resources which play a part
- Soil, climate, and rainfall

Consider the human factors.

- Industries of the area
- Trade and other relations with the outside world
- Available means of transportation
- Size and location of population
- Large cities concerned in the event
- Racial, religious, and other factors involved
- Developments from history

To understand a map, you must first become familiar with the information presented on the map. For instance, the title, legend, scale, direction, longitude, and latitude are all important to interpret a map. The legend is particularly important because it usually explains the symbols used on a map. You should notice the main points of the map first and then look at the finer detail.

Mathematics and History/Social Sciences

Questions 1–2 refer to the following map.

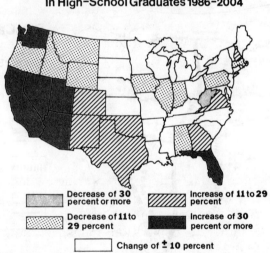

**Percent Change by State
In High–School Graduates 1986–2004**

The map above uses different shadings to show how the percentage of high school graduates will increase or decrease in each state in an eighteen-year period.

1. According to the map, which of the following will occur in the most states?
   (A) A decrease of 30% or more
   (B) A decrease of 11% to 29%
   (C) A change of about 10%
   (D) An increase of 11% to 29%

The correct answer is (C). To answer this question, you must understand the map and the legend given. The legend, or key, at the bottom of the map shows what each different type of shading stands for. Read this information carefully. Now, simply count the number of states that have the same type of shading. You may have noticed that most of the states have no shading, so most states have a change of about 10%.

2. According to the map, generally the greatest increase is expected in the
   (A) Southeast
   (B) Midwest
   (C) Northwest
   (D) Southwest

The correct answer is (D). The dark shading reflects the greatest increase. Most of the dark shading occurs in the lower left-hand corner of the map—the Southwest. If you look for trends, you might immediately notice that most states with large increases are in the Southwest.

History/Social Sciences

Questions 3–4 refer to the following map.

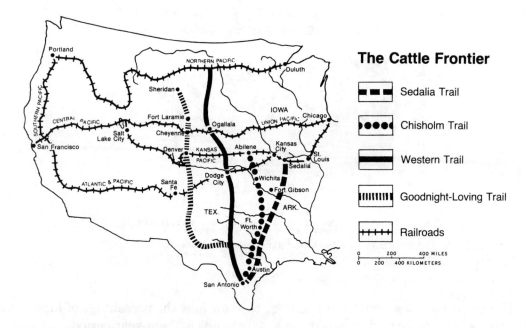

3. Which trail connected the Northern Pacific Railroad with San Antonio?
   (A) The Sedalia Trail
   (B) The Chisholm Trail
   (C) The Goodnight-Loving Trail
   (D) The Western Trail

The correct answer is (D). The Western Trail is the only trail that connects with the Northern Pacific. Notice that the legend and the title "The Cattle Frontier" are clues to the historical importance of this special-purpose map. You can see that many questions can be made from data included in this map. For instance, what would be the importrance of having a western trail cross a major railroad line? Possible answers could include the fact that towns would develop around the connecting point or that the railroad could be used to bring western cattle to various markets.

4. If you were to leave St. Louis with a final destination of Portland, the most logical route would be to
   (A) go by rail to Santa Fe; connect by rail with the Atlantic & Pacific and Southern Pacific; proceed by rail to Portland
   (B) go by rail to Chicago; go by rail to the Central Pacific and Southern Pacific connection; proceed by rail to Portland
   (C) go by rail to Denver; go by trail to connect with the Central Pacific; proceed by rail to Portland
   (D) go by rail to Sedalia; go by trail to the Atlantic & Pacific connection at Santa Fe; proceed by rail to Portland

The correct answer is (B). You can quickly eliminate choices (C) and (D) because they use trails to connect with various railroads. Using a trail with unpredictable road conditions and traveling by wagon would be far slower than traveling by a longer rail route. Choice (B) is the most *direct* rail route to Portland. Look for the shortest route before you eliminate each possible answer.

CARTOONS

A political cartoon represents an amusing or satiric picture of people, places, or things and is used to make a special point about or to deride some subject of popular interest.

Strategies

In considering a political cartoon, identify the event used and look for the point of view of the cartoonist, that is, what the cartoonist is trying to say. Remember that most good political cartoonists are critics who comment on the social issues that face the United States and the world. To deal with questions based on a political cartoon, you should do the following.

- Become familiar with the symbols used in political cartoons. For example, the "donkey" represents the Democratic Party; the "elephant" is a symbol of the Republican Party; the "dove" is a symbol of peace; the "hawk" is a symbol of war; and "Washington D.C." and "Uncle Sam" are symbols of the United States government.

- Try to understand the meaning of the statement, if any, that goes with the political cartoon. This statement is often a clue to the cartoonist's attitude.

History/Social Sciences

1.

"NOTICE HOW MUCH MORE REFINED?"

How does the cartoonist feel about neutron nuclear weapons?
(A) Nuclear weapons are necessary if the United States is to maintain the current balance of power with Russia.
(B) Neutron nuclear weapons are not as deadly as conventional nuclear weapons.
(C) The military is responsible for developing nuclear weapons.
(D) Advanced nuclear designs cannot change the deadly nature of nuclear weapons.

The correct answer is (D). In this political cartoon, a comparison is drawn between neutron nuclear weapons and nonneutron nuclear weapons. The symbols are clues to the cartoonist's point of view. Notice that the "refined," or technically advanced, neutron bomb still represents death and destruction. The neutron bomb is dressed in the "cloak of death"; the refined cigarette holder still produces a "mushroom cloud" (a mushroom cloud is a symbol of the destructive nature of the bomb). The question asked by the military—"Notice how much more refined?"—is an indication that the cartoonist considers refinements in nuclear weapons as nothing but more "sophisticated" killing devices. In other words, in the cartoonist's point of view, a "refined" nuclear weapon is still a nuclear weapon.

DIAGRAMS

Sometimes information will be given in a simple diagram or picture.

Strategies

When a diagram or picture is given, you should look for its main emphasis. Also look for key words, markings, directions of arrows, distances, and so forth. Look for both the obvious and the unusual. In dealing with questions based on diagrams or pictures, you should keep the following in mind.

- You may wish to skim the question or questions before looking at the diagram.

- Examine the diagram carefully. Make sure that you understand the information given.

- Read any additional information given carefully.

- Don't try to memorize the diagram.

Science

1.

CROSS SECTION OF THE ATLANTIC OCEAN

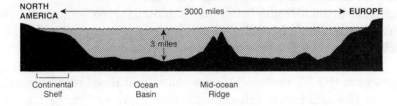

According to the diagram, all of the following are true EXCEPT:
(A) Europe does not have a continental shelf.
(B) The mid-ocean ridge is about halfway between the two continents.
(C) The ocean basin is of fairly consistent depth.
(D) The mid-ocean ridge is less than three miles high.

The correct answer is (A). To answer this question, you must understand the information given in the diagram. You must also notice that you are looking for what is *not* true. Choice (A) is *not* true. Europe *does* have a continental shelf, although it appears smaller than that of North America. Notice also that only the continental shelf of North America is marked in the diagram. You must analyze this diagram to see that this marking is showing *one example*. Notice that the ocean basin is also marked on only one side of the mid-ocean ridge, but there is an ocean basin on the other side. By careful inspection, you will see that all of the other choices are *true*, so you can eliminate them.

2.

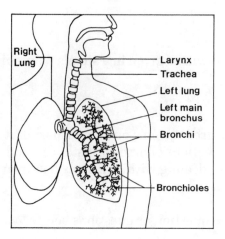

Air enters the body through the nose and mouth and passes into the throat. Next, it goes into the larynx and then to the trachea (windpipe). The trachea branches into two main bronchi. Each main bronchus leads to a lung, which also contains many smaller bronchi and bronchioles. Inside these lungs, oxygen enters the bloodstream while, at the same time, carbon dioxide leaves the blood and enters the lungs to be breathed out.

From the information given above, which of the following is the path of carbon dioxide as it is exhaled?
(A) Larynx/trachea/main bronchus/bronchi/bronchioles
(B) Bronchioles/bronchi/main bronchus/trachea/larynx
(C) Trachea/larynx/main bronchus/bronchioles
(D) Bronchi/larynx/trachea/main bronchus/bronchioles

The correct answer is (B). To answer this question, you must understand not only the diagram, but also the additional information given. By *reversing* the process of air coming into the lungs, you will get the path *out of* the lungs. Carbon dioxide is exhaled starting from the bronchioles to the bronchi to the main bronchus to the trachea to the larynx.

Mathematics

3.

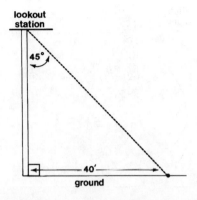

As pictured in the diagram above, Felipe has built a lookout station but does not know the height of the station from the ground. Felipe climbs to the top of the station and spots a coin 40 feet from the base of the station. He accurately marks the angle of his sight as 45 degrees (as shown above). From this information, he correctly determines the height of the lookout station as

(A) 20 feet
(B) 30 feet
(C) 40 feet
(D) 80 feet

The correct answer is (C). To answer this question, you must understand the diagram and apply some basic geometry. Since the lookout station is shown to be vertical, or 90 degrees, to the ground, and the angle of sight is 45 degrees, then the third angle must be 45 degrees. This is because there are 180 degrees in a triangle. Now, since two of the angles in a triangle are equal, it is an isosceles triangle and the sides opposite those angles are also equal. So the sides opposiste the 45 degrees are each 40 feet.

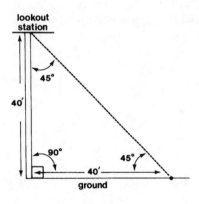

Part III:
Review of Exam Areas

LITERATURE AND LANGUAGE STUDIES REVIEW

ANALYZING POEMS AND PROSE

ANALYZING POEMS

Some students have trouble with sight-reading poetry because they don't know where to start. They see the word "death" in the first line and "tomb" in the third and jump to the conclusion that this poem (which, in fact, is a sentimental lover's pitch to a woman who has turned him down) must be about mortality and spend the next ten minutes trying to make the poem fit these gloomy expectations.

To avoid premature conclusions, and to prepare yourself for the kind of question that both the Content Knowledge section and Content Area Exercises may ask, try going through each poem asking the following questions in something like this order.

What is the dramatic situation?

Who is the speaker? Or who are the speakers? Is the speaker a male or a female? Where is he or she? When does this poem take place? What are the circumstances?

Sometimes you'll be able to answer all of these questions: The speaker is a male psychopath living in a remote cottage, probably in Renaissance Italy, who has strangled his mistress and is sitting with her head propped upon his shoulder (Browning's "Porphyria's Lover"). Sometimes you'll be able to answer only a few and sometimes only vaguely: The speaker is unnamed and unplaced and is speaking to an indeterminate audience. No matter. Already you've begun to understand the poem.

What is the structure of the poem?

What are the parts of the poem and how are they related to each other? What gives the poem its coherence? What are the structural divisions of the poem?

In analyzing structure, your best aid is the punctuation. Look first for the complete sentences indicated by periods, semicolons, question marks, or exclamation points. Then ask how the poem gets from the first sentence to the second and from the second to the third. Are there repetitions such as parallel syntax or the use of one simile in each sentence? Answer these questions in accordance with the sense of the poem, not by where a line ends or a rhyme falls.

Think about the logic of the poem. Does it, say, ask questions, then answer them? Or develop an argument? Or use a series of analogies to prove a point? Understanding the structure isn't just a matter of mechanics. It will help you to understand the meaning of the poem as a whole and to perceive some of the art, the formal skills that the poet has used.

What is the theme of the poem?

You should now be able to see the point of the poem. Sometimes a poem simply says "I love you"; sometimes the theme or the meaning is much more complex. If possible, define what the poem says and why. A love poem usually praises the loved one in the hope that the speaker's love will be returned. But many poems have meanings too complex to be reduced to single sentences.

Are the grammar and meaning clear?

Make sure you understand the meaning of all the words in the poem, especially words you thought you knew but which don't seem to fit in the context of the poem. Also make sure you understand the grammar of the poem. The word order of poetry is often skewed, and in a poem, a direct object may come before the subject and the verb. ("His sounding lyre the poet struck" can mean a poet was hit by a musical instrument, but as a line of poetry, it probably means the poet played his harp.)

What are the important images and figures of speech?

What are the important literal sensory objects, the images, such as a field of poppies or a stench of corruption? What are the similes and metaphors of the poem? In each, exactly what is compared to what? Is there a pattern in the images, such as a series of comparisons all using men compared to wild animals? The most difficult challenge of reading poetry is discriminating between the figurative ("I love a rose"—that is, my love is like a rose, beautiful, sweet, fragile) and the literal ("I love a rose"—that is, roses are my favorite flower).

What is the tone of the poem?

Tone is a slippery word, and almost everyone has trouble with it. It's sometimes used to mean the mood or atmosphere of a work, although purists are offended by this definition. Or it can mean a manner of speaking, a tone of voice, as in "The disappointed coach's tone was sardonic." But its most common use as a term of literary analysis is to denote the inferred attitude of an author. When the author's attitude is different from that of the speaker, as is usually the case in ironic works, the tone of voice of the speaker, which may be calm, businesslike, even gracious, may be very different from the satiric tone of the work, which reflects the author's disapproval of the speaker. Because it is often very hard to define tone in one or two words, questions on tone do not appear frequently on multiple-choice exams, but an essay topic may well ask for a discussion of the tone of a poem or a passage of prose.

What literary devices does the poem employ?

The list of rhetorical devices that a writer might use is enormous. The terms you should know are metaphor, simile, and personification.

What is the prosody of the poem?

You need to know the basics about about the rhyme, meter, and sound effects of poetry.

ANALYZING PROSE

In the event that you're asked to analyze prose, you might deal with the issues of genre (the kind of work, such as short story or essay), content, structure, and style.

Genre

From what kind of work is the selection taken? Is it fiction or nonfiction?

If you're dealing with a work of fiction, chances are you'll have to think about the character or characters in the passage, while a work of nonfiction probably focuses on an issue, on an idea, or on the narrator, him or herself.

Narrator

Whether the passage is from a work of fiction or of nonfiction, you must be aware of who is speaking and what his or her attitudes are toward the characters or the subject of the passage. If you can, identify who is speaking, where and when, why, and to whom.

Subject

Then ascertain what the purpose of the passage is. Is it to present an argument or to introduce a character? To cajole, or entertain, or stir to action? If you can define an author's purpose clearly, most of the questions on the interpretation of meaning will fall neatly into place.

Structure

The normal units of prose are the sentence and the paragraph. As with a poem, try to see how each part advances the progress of the whole. How are the sentences and paragraphs related to each other and to the passage as a whole.

Style

The style of prose is determined by diction, imagery, figurative language, and syntax—all matters you deal with in the analysis of poetry. In addition, the analysis of prose is certain to raise questions about the rhetoric of a passage, that is, its use of words to persuade or influence a reader.

GLOSSARY

Following are important literature and language terms.

Allegory—A story in which people, things, and events have another meaning. An example of allegory is Orwell's *Animal Farm*.

Allusion—A reference in a work of literature to something outside the work, especially to a well-known historical or literary event, person, or work. Lorraine Hansberry's title *A Raisin in the Sun* is an allusion to a phrase in a poem by Langston Hughes. In *Hamlet*, when Horatio says, "ere the mightiest Julius fell," the allusion is to the death of Julius Caesar.

Ambiguity—Multiple meanings a literary work may communicate, especially two meanings that are incompatible.

Apostrophe—Direct address, usually to someone or something that is not present. Keats's "Bright star! would I were steadfast" is an apostrophe to a star.

Attitude—A speaker's, author's, or character's disposition toward or opinion of a subject. For example, Hamlet's attitude toward Gertrude is a mixture of affection and revulsion, changing from one to the other within a single scene.

Autobiography—An author's account of his or her own life.

Biography—An accurate history of a single person.

Climax—Normally the point of highest interest in a novel, short story, or play. As a technical term of dramatic composition, the climax is the place where the action reaches a turning, where the rising action, the complication of the plot, ends and the following action, the resolution of the plot, begins.

Comedy—A dramatic form intended to amuse the audience. Usually, a comedy moves from an unhappy situation to a happy resolution. The word *comedy* is now also applied to genres other than drama, such as the novel, film, or television show.

Connotation—The implications of a word or phrase, as opposed to its exact meaning (denotation). Both *China* and *Cathay* denote a region in Asia, but to a modern reader, the association of the two words are different.

Convention—A device of style or subject matter so often used that it becomes a recognized means of expression. For example, a lover observing the literary love conventions cannot eat or sleep and grows pale and lean.

Denotation—The dictionary meaning of a word, as opposed to connotation.

Diction—Word choice. Essay questions on a passage of prose or a poem could ask you to talk about diction or about "techniques" that include diction. Any word that is important to the meaning and the effect of a passage can be used in your essay. These words are also *details*.

Didactic—Explicitly instructive.

Digression—The use of material unrelated to the subject of a work.

Epigram—A pithy saying, often using contrast. The epigram is also a verse form, usually brief and pointed.

Euphemism—A figure of speech using indirection to avoid offensive bluntness, such as *deceased* for *dead* or *remains* for *corpse*.

Figurative language—Writing that uses figures of speech (as opposed to literal language or that which is actual or specifically denoted) such as metaphor, simile, and irony. Figurative language uses words to mean something other than their literal meaning. "The black bat night has flown'" is figurative, with the metaphor comparing night and a bat. "Night is over" says the same thing without figurative language. No real bat is or has been on the scene, but night is like a bat because it is dark.

Genre—A literary form, such as essay, novel, or poem. Within genres like the poem, there are also more specific genres based upon content (love poem, nature poem) or form (sonnet, ode).

Grotesque—Characterized by distortions or incongruities. The fiction of Poe is often described as grotesque.

Hyperbole—Deliberate exaggeration, overstatement. As a rule, hyperbole is self-conscious, without the intention of being accepted literally. "The strongest man in the world" or "a diamond as big as the Ritz" are hyperbolic.

Imagery—The images of a literary work; the sensory details of a work; the figurative language of a work. Imagery has several definitions, but the two that are paramount are the visual, auditory, or tactile images evoked by the words of a literary work or the images that figurative language evokes.

Irony—A figure of speech in which intent and actual meaning differ, characteristically praise for blame or blame for praise; a pattern of words that turns away from direct statement of its own obvious meaning. The term *irony* implies a discrepancy. In *verbal irony* (saying the opposite of what one means), the discrepancy is between statement and meaning. Sometimes, irony may simply understate, as in "Men have died from time to time . . ."

Jargon—The special language of a profession or group. The term *jargon* usually has pejorative associations, with the implication that jargon is evasive, tedious, and unintelligible to outsiders.

Literal—Not figurative; accurate to the letter; matter of fact or concrete.

Lyrical—Songlike; characterized by emotion, subjectivity, and imagination.

Metaphor—A figurative use of language in which a comparison is expressed without the use of a comparative term like *as, like,* or *than*. A simile would say, "night is like a black bat"; a metaphor would say, "the black bat night." When Romeo says, "It is the east, and Juliet is the sun," his metaphors compare her window to the east and Juliet to the sun.

Narrative techniques—The methods involved in telling a story; the procedures used by a writer of stories or accounts. *Narrative techniques* is a general term which asks you to discuss the procedures used in the telling of a story. Examples of the techniques you might use are point of view, manipulation of time, dialogue, or interior monologue.

Novel—A fictional narrative in prose of considerable length. Shorter works are called novellas, and even shorter ones are called short stories.

Omniscient point of view—The vantage point of a story in which the narrator can know, see, and report whatever he or she chooses. The narrator is free to describe the thoughts of any of the characters, to skip about in time or place, or to speak directly to the reader.

Oxymoron—A combination of opposites; the union of contradictory terms. Romeo's line "feather of lead, bright smoke, cold fire, sick health" has four examples of the device.

Parable—A story designed to suggest a principle, illustrate a moral, or answer a question. Parables are allegorical stories.

Paradox—A statement that seems to be self-contradicting but, in fact, is true. The figure in a Donne sonnet that concludes "I never shall be chaste except you ravish me" is a good example of the device.

Parody—A composition that imitates the style of another composition normally for comic effect. A contest for parodies of Hemingway draws hundreds of entries each year.

Personification—A figurative use of language which endows the nonhuman (ideas, inanimate objects, animals, abstractions) with human characteristics.

Plot—The interrelated actions of a play or a novel which move to a climax and a final resolution.

Point of view—Any of several possible vantage points from which a story is told. The point of view may be omniscient, limited to that of a single character, or limited to that of several characters. And there are other possibilities. The teller may use the first person and/or the third person

Rhetorical question—A question asked for effect, not in expectation of a reply. No reply is expected because the question presupposes only one possible answer.

Rhetorical techniques—The devices used in effective or persuasive language. The most common examples include devices like contrast, repetitions, paradox, understatement, sarcasm, and rhetorical question.

Satire—Writing that seeks to arouse a reader's disapproval of an object by ridicule. Satire is usually comedy that exposes errors with an eye to correcting vice and folly. Examples of satire can be found in the novels of Charles Dickens, Mark Twain, or Joseph Heller.

Setting—The background to a story; the physical location of a play, story, or novel. The setting of a narrative will normally involve both time and place.

Simile—A directly expressed comparison; a figure of speech comparing two objects, usually with *like, as* or *than*. It is easier to recognize a simile than a metaphor because the comparison is explicit: my love is like a fever; my love is deeper than a well; my love is as dead as a doornail.

Soliloquy—A speech in which a character who is alone speaks his or her thoughts aloud. A monologue also has a single speaker, but the monologuist speaks to others who do not interrupt. Hamlet's "To be, or not to be" and "O! what a rogue and peasant slave am I" are soliloquies.

Stereotype—A conventional pattern, expression, character, or idea. In literature, a stereotype could apply to the unvarying plot and characters of some works of fiction (those of Barbara Cartland, for example) or to the stock characters and plots of many of the greatest stage comedies.

Strategy (or **rhetorical strategy**)—The management of language for a specific effect. The strategy or rhetorical strategy of a poem is the planned placing of elements to achieve an effect. The rhetorical strategy of most love poems, for example, is deployed to convince the loved-one to return the speaker's love. By appealing the the loved-one's sympathy ("If you don't return my love, my heart will break."), or by flattery ("How could I not love someone as beautiful as you?"), or by threat ("When you're old, you'll be sorry you refused me."), the lover attempts to persuade the loved-one to love in return.

Structure—The arrangement of materials within a work; the relationship of the parts of a work to the whole; the logical divisions of a work. The most common principles of structure are series (A, B, C, D, E), contrast (A vs. B, C vs. D, E vs. A), and repetition (AA, BB, AB). The most common units of structure are—play: scene, act; novel: chapter; poem: line, stanza.

Style—The mode of expression in language; the characteristic manner of expression of an author. Many elements contribute to style, and if a question calls for a discussion of style or of "stylistic techniques," you can discuss diction, syntax, figurative language, imagery, selection of detail, sound effects, and tone, using the ones that are appropriate.

Syllogism—A form of reasoning in which two statements are made and a conclusion is drawn from them. A syllogism begins with a major premise ("All tragedies end unhappily.") followed by a minor premise ("*Hamlet* is a tragedy.") and a conclusion ("Therefore, *Hamlet* ends unhappily.").

Symbol—Something that is simultaneously itself and a sign of something else. For example, winter, darkness, and cold are real things, but in literature they are also likely to be used as symbols of death. Yorick's skull is a symbol of human mortality, and Melville's white whale is certainly a symbol, but exactly what it symbolizes has yet to be agreed upon.

Theme—The main thought expressed by a work.

Thesis—The theme, meaning, or position that a writer undertakes to prove or support.

Tone—The manner in which an author expresses his or her attitude; the intonation of the voice that expresses meaning. Tone is described by adjectives, and the possibilities are nearly endless. Often a single adjective will not be enough, and tone may change from chapter to chapter or even line to line. Tone may be the result of allusion, diction, figurative language, imagery, irony, symbol, syntax, and style.

Tragedy—Now defined as a play with a serious content and an unhappy ending. Shakespeare's *Hamlet* or Miller's *Death of a Salesman* are examples.

MATHEMATICS REVIEW

INTRODUCTION TO THE MATHEMATICS REVIEW

The following pages are designed to give you an intensive review of the basic skills used on the MSAT Mathematics section, Arithmetic, algebra, geometry, axioms, properties of numbers, terms, and simple statistics are covered. Before you begin the diagnostic review tests, it would be wise to become familiar with basic mathematics terminology, formulas, and general mathematical information, a review of which begins below. Then proceed to the arithmetic diagnostic test, which you should take to spot your weak areas. Then use the arithmetic review that follows to strengthen those areas.

After reviewing the arithmetic, take the algebra diagnostic test and once again use the review that follows to strengthen your weak areas. Next, take the geometry diagnostic test and carefully read the complete geometry review.

Even if you are strong in arithmetic, algebra, and geometry, you may wish to skim the topic headings in each area to refresh your memory of important concepts. If you are weak in math, you should read through the complete review.

SYMBOLS, TERMINOLOGY, FORMULAS, AND GENERAL MATHEMATICAL INFORMATION

Common Math Symbols and Terms

Symbol References:

= is equal to	≥ (≧) is greater than or equal to
≠ is not equal to	≤ (≦) is less than or equal to
> is greater than	∥ is parallel to
< is less than	⊥ is perpendicular to

Natural numbers—the counting numbers: 1, 2, 3, . . .

Whole numbers—the counting numbers beginning with zero: 0, 1, 2, 3, . . .

Integers—positive and negative whole numbers and zero: . . . −3, −2, −1, 0, 1, 2, . . .

Odd numbers—numbers not divisible by 2: 1, 3, 5, 7, . . .

Even numbers—numbers divisible by 2: 0, 2, 4, 6, . . .

Prime number—number divisible by only 1 and itself: 2, 3, 5, 7, 11, 13, . . .

Composite number—number divisible by more than just 1 and itself: 4, 6, 8, 9, 10, 12, 14, 15, . . . (0 and 1 are neither prime nor composite)

Squares—the results when numbers are multiplied by themselves, $(2 \cdot 2 = 4)$ $(3 \cdot 3 = 9)$: 1, 4, 9, 16, 25, 36, . . .

Cubes—the result when numbers are multiplied by themselves twice, $(2 \cdot 2 \cdot 2 = 8)$ $(3 \cdot 3 \cdot 3 = 27)$: 1, 8, 27, . . .

Math Formulas

Triangle
Perimeter $= s_1 + s_2 + s_3$
Area $= \frac{1}{2}bh$

Square
Perimeter $= 4s$
Area $= s \cdot s$, or s^2

Rectangle
Perimeter $= 2(b + h)$, or $2b + 2h$
Area $= bh$, or lw

Parallelogram
Perimeter $= 2(l + w)$, or $2l + 2w$
Area $= bh$

Trapezoid
Perimeter $= b_1 + b_2 + s_1 + s_2$
Area $= \frac{1}{2}h(b_1 + b_2)$, or $h\left(\dfrac{b_1 + b_2}{2}\right)$

Circle
Circumference $= 2\pi r$, or πd
Area $= \pi r^2$

Pythagorean theorem (for right triangles) $a^2 + b^2 = c^2$

The sum of the squares of the legs of a right triangle equals the square of the hypotenuse.

Cube
Volume $= s \cdot s \cdot s = s^3$
Surface area $= s \cdot s \cdot 6$

Rectangular Prism
Volume $= l \cdot w \cdot h$
Surface area $= 2(lw) + 2(lh) + 2(wh)$

Important Equivalents

$\frac{1}{100} = .01 = 1\%$	$\frac{1}{3} = .33\frac{1}{3} = 33\frac{1}{3}\%$
$\frac{1}{10} = .1 = .10 = 10\%$	$\frac{2}{3} = .66\frac{2}{3} = 66\frac{2}{3}\%$
$\frac{1}{5} = \frac{2}{10} = .2 = .20 = 20\%$	$\frac{1}{8} = .125 = .12\frac{1}{2} = 12\frac{1}{2}\%$
$\frac{3}{10} = .3 = .30 = 30\%$	$\frac{3}{8} = .375 = .37\frac{1}{2} = 37\frac{1}{2}\%$
$\frac{2}{5} = \frac{4}{10} = .4 = .40 = 40\%$	$\frac{5}{8} = .625 = .62\frac{1}{2} = 62\frac{1}{2}\%$
$\frac{1}{2} = \frac{5}{10} = .5 = .50 = 50\%$	$\frac{7}{8} = .875 = .87\frac{1}{2} = 87\frac{1}{2}\%$
$\frac{3}{5} = \frac{6}{10} = .6 = .60 = 60\%$	$\frac{1}{6} = .16\frac{2}{3} = 16\frac{2}{3}\%$
$\frac{7}{10} = .7 = .70 = 70\%$	$\frac{5}{6} = .83\frac{1}{3} = 83\frac{1}{3}\%$
$\frac{4}{5} = \frac{8}{10} = .8 = .80 = 80\%$	$1 = 1.00 = 100\%$
$\frac{9}{10} = .9 = .90 = 90\%$	$2 = 2.00 = 200\%$
$\frac{1}{4} = \frac{25}{100} = .25 = 25\%$	$3\frac{1}{2} = 3.5 = 3.50 = 350\%$
$\frac{3}{4} = \frac{75}{100} = .75 = 75\%$	

Measures

Customary System, or English System

Length

12 inches (in) = 1 foot (ft)
3 feet = 1 yard (yd)
36 inches = 1 yard
1760 yards = 1 mile (mi)
5280 feet = 1 mile

Area

144 square inches (sq in) = 1 square foot (sq ft)
9 square feet = 1 square yard (sq yd)

Weight

16 ounces (oz) = 1 pound (lb)
2000 pounds = 1 ton (T)

Capacity

2 cups = 1 pint (pt)
2 pints = 1 quart (qt)
4 quarts = 1 gallon (gal)
4 pecks = 1 bushel

Time

365 days = 1 year
52 weeks = 1 year
10 years = 1 decade
100 years = 1 century

Metric System, or The International System of Units

Length—meter

Kilometer (km) = 1000 meters (m)
Hectometer (hm) = 100 meters
Dekameter (dam) = 10 meters

  Meter
10 decimeters (dm) = 1 meter
100 centimeters (cm) = 1 meter
1000 millimeters (mm) = 1 meter

Volume—liter

Common measures
1000 milliliters (ml, or mL) = 1 liter (l, or L)
1000 liters = 1 kiloliter (kl, or kL)

Mass—gram

Common measures
1000 milligrams (mg) = 1 gram (g)
1000 grams = 1 kilogram (kg)
1000 kilograms = 1 metric ton (t)

Some Approximations

Meter is a little more than a yard
Kilometer is about .6 mile
Kilogram is about 2.2 pounds
Liter is slightly more than a quart

Math Words and Phrases

Words that signal an operation:

Addition

- Sum
- Total
- Plus
- Increase
- More than
- Greater than

Multiplication

- Or
- Product
- Times
- At (sometimes)
- Total (sometimes)

Subtraction

- Difference
- Less
- Decreased
- Reduced
- Fewer
- Have left

Division

- Quotient
- Divisor
- Dividend
- Ratio
- Parts

Mathematical Properties and Basic Statistics

Some Properties (Axioms) of Addition

- *Commutative* means that the *order* does not make any difference.

$$2 + 3 = 3 + 2$$
$$a + b = b + a$$

NOTE: Commutative does *not* hold for subtraction.

$$3 - 1 \neq 1 - 3$$
$$a - b \neq b - a$$

- *Associative* means that the *grouping* does not make any difference.

$$(2 + 3) + 4 = 2 + (3 + 4)$$
$$(a + b) + c = a + (b + c)$$

The grouping has changed (parentheses moved), but the sides are still equal.

NOTE: Associative does *not* hold for subtraction.

$$4 - (3 - 1) \neq (4 - 3) - 1$$
$$a - (b - c) \neq (a - b) - c$$

- The *identity element* for addition is 0. Any number added to 0 gives the original number.

$$3 + 0 = 3$$
$$a + 0 = a$$

- The *additive inverse* is the opposite (negative) of the number. Any number plus its additive inverse equals 0 (the identity).

$$3 + (-3) = 0; \text{ therefore, } 3 \text{ and } -3 \text{ are inverses}$$
$$-2 + 2 = 0; \text{ therefore, } -2 \text{ and } 2 \text{ are inverses}$$
$$a + (-a) = 0; \text{ therefore, } a \text{ and } -a \text{ are inverses}$$

Some Properties (Axioms) of Multiplication

- *Commutative* means that the *order* does not make any difference.

$$2 \times 3 = 3 \times 2$$
$$a \times b = b \times a$$

NOTE: Commutative does *not* hold for division.

$$2 \div 4 \neq 4 \div 2$$

- *Associative* means that the *grouping* does not make any difference.

$$(2 \times 3) \times 4 = 2 \times (3 \times 4)$$
$$(a \times b) \times c = a \times (b \times c)$$

The grouping has changed (parentheses moved), but the sides are still equal.

NOTE: Associative does *not* hold for division.

$$(8 \div 4) \div 2 \neq 8 \div (4 \div 2)$$

- The *identity element* for multiplication is 1. Any number multiplied by 1 gives the original number.

$$3 \times 1 = 3$$
$$a \times 1 = a$$

- The *multiplicative inverse* is the reciprocal of the number. Any number multiplied by its reciprocal equals 1.

$$2 \times \tfrac{1}{2} = 1; \text{ therefore, 2 and } \tfrac{1}{2} \text{ are inverses}$$
$$a \times 1/a = 1; \text{ therefore, } a \text{ and } 1/a \text{ are inverses}$$

A Property of Two Operations

- The *distributive property* is the process of distributing the number on the outside of the parentheses to each number on the inside.

$$2(3 + 4) = 2(3) + 2(4)$$
$$a(b + c) = a(b) + a(c)$$

NOTE: You cannot use the distributive property with only one operation.

$$3(4 \times 5 \times 6) \neq 3(4) \times 3(5) \times 3(6)$$
$$a(bcd) \neq a(b) \times a(c) \times a(d) \text{ or } (ab)(ac)(ad)$$

Some Basic Terms in Statistics

- To find the arithmetic *mean,* or average, simply total the numbers and divide by the number of numbers.

Find the arithmetic mean of 3, 5, 6, 7, and 9. The total is $3 + 5 + 6 + 7 + 9 = 30$. Then divide 30 by 5, giving a mean, or average, of 6.

- To find the *mode,* look for the most frequently occurring score or measure.

Find the mode of these scores: 3, 5, 5, 5, 6, 7. The mode is 5, since it appears most. If there are two modes, distribution of scores is called *bimodal*.

- To find the *median,* arrange the scores or numbers in order by size. Then find the middle score or number.

Find the median of these scores: 2, 5, 7, 3, 6. First arrange them in order by size: 7, 6, 5, 3, 2. The middle score is 5; therefore, the median is 5. If the number of scores is even, take the average of the two middle scores. Find the median of these scores: 2, 5, 7, 4, 3, 6. First arrange them in order by size: 7, 6, 5, 4, 3, 2. The two middle numbers are 4 and 5; therefore, the median is $4\tfrac{1}{2}$.

- The *range* of a group of scores or numbers is calculated by subtracting the smallest from the largest.

Find the range of the scores, 3, 2, 7, 9, 12. The range is $12 - 2 = 10$.

ARITHMETIC

ARITHMETIC DIAGNOSTIC TEST

Questions

1. $6 = ?/4$

2. Change $5\frac{3}{4}$ to an improper fraction.

3. Change $\frac{32}{6}$ to a whole number or mixed number in lowest terms.

4. $\frac{2}{5} + \frac{3}{5} =$

5. $\frac{1}{3} + \frac{1}{4} + \frac{1}{2} =$

6. $1\frac{3}{8} + 2\frac{5}{6} =$

7. $\frac{7}{9} - \frac{5}{9} =$

8. $11 - \frac{2}{3} =$

9. $6\frac{1}{4} - 3\frac{3}{4} =$

10. $\frac{1}{6} \times \frac{1}{6} =$

11. $2\frac{3}{8} \times 1\frac{5}{6} =$

12. $\frac{1}{4} \div \frac{3}{2} =$

13. $2\frac{3}{7} \div 1\frac{1}{4} =$

14. $.07 + 1.2 + .471 =$

15. $.45 - .003 =$

16. $\$78.24 - \$31.68 =$

17. $.5 \times .5 =$

18. $8.001 \times 2.3 =$

19. $.7\,\overline{)\,.147}$

20. $.002\,\overline{)\,12}$

21. ⅓ of $7.20 =

22. Circle the larger number: 7.9 or 4.35.

23. 39 out of 100 means:

24. Change 4% to a decimal.

25. 46% of 58 =

26. Change .009 to a percent.

27. Change 12.5% to a fraction.

28. Change ⅜ to a percent.

29. Is 93 prime?

30. What is the percent increase of a rise in temperature from 80° to 100°?

31. Average 0, 8, and 10.

32. $8^2 =$

33. Approximate $\sqrt{30}$.

Answers

1. 24
2. $^{23}/_4$
3. $5^2/_6$ or $5^1/_3$
4. $^5/_5$ or 1
5. $^{13}/_{12}$ or $1^1/_{12}$
6. $4^5/_{24}$
7. $^2/_9$
8. $10^1/_3$
9. $2^2/_4$ or $2^1/_2$
10. $^1/_{36}$
11. $^{209}/_{48}$ or $4^{17}/_{48}$
12. $^1/_6$
13. $^{68}/_{35}$ or $1^{33}/_{35}$
14. 1.741
15. .447
16. $46.56
17. .25
18. 18.4023
19. .21
20. 6000
21. $2.40
22. 7.9
23. 39% or $^{39}/_{100}$
24. .04
25. 26.68
26. .9% or $^9/_{10}$%
27. $^{125}/_{1000}$ or $^1/_8$
28. 37.5% or $37^1/_2$%
29. No
30. 25%
31. 6
32. 64
33. 5.5 or $5^1/_2$

ARITHMETIC REVIEW

Rounding Off

To round off any number:

1. Underline the place value to which you're rounding off.
2. Look to the immediate right (one place) of your underlined place value.
3. Identify the number (the one to the right). If it is 5 or higher, round your underlined place value up 1. If the number (the one to the right) is 4 or less, leave your underlined place value as it is and change all the other numbers to its right to zeros. *For example:*

Round to the nearest thousands:

345,678   becomes 346,000

928,499   becomes 928,000

This works with decimals as well. Round to the nearest hundredth:

$$3.4\underline{6}78 \quad \text{becomes } 3.47$$

$$298,435.0\underline{8}3 \quad \text{becomes } 298,435.08$$

Place Value

Each position in any number has *place value*. For instance, in the number 485, 4 is in the hundreds place, 8 is in the tens place, and 5 is in the ones place. Thus, place value is as follows:

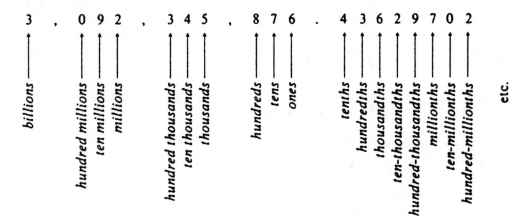

Fractions

Fractions consist of two numbers: a *numerator* (which is above the line) and a *denominator* (which is below the line).

$$\frac{1 \text{ numerator}}{2 \text{ denominator}} \quad \text{or} \quad \text{numerator } \tfrac{1}{2} \text{ denominator}$$

The denominator lets us know the number of equal parts into which something is divided. The numerator tells us how many of these equal parts are contained in the fraction. Thus, if the fraction is ⅗ of a pie, then the denominator 5 tells us that the pie has been divided into 5 equal parts, of which 3 (numerator) are in the fraction.

Sometimes it helps to think of the dividing line (in the middle of a fraction) as meaning "out of." In other words, ⅗ would also mean 3 "out of" 5 equal pieces from the whole pie.

Common Fractions and Improper Fractions

A fraction like ⅗, where the numerator is smaller than the denominator, is less than one. This kind of fraction is called a *common fraction*.

But sometimes a fraction may be more than one. This is when the numerator is larger than the denominator. Thus, ¹²⁄₇ is more than one. This is called an *improper fraction*.

Mixed Numbers

When a term contains both a whole number (such as 3, 8, or 25) and a fraction (such as ½, ¼, or ¾), it is called a *mixed number*. For instance, 5¼ and 290¾ are both mixed numbers.

To change an improper fraction to a mixed number, you divide the denominator into the numerator. *For example:*

$$\frac{18}{5} = 3\tfrac{3}{5} \qquad 5\overline{)18} \\ \frac{15}{3}$$

To change a mixed number to an improper fraction, you multiply the denominator times the whole number, add in the numerator, and put the total over the original denominator. *For example:*

$$4\tfrac{1}{2} = \tfrac{9}{2} \qquad 2 \times 4 + 1 = 9$$

Reducing Fractions

A fraction must be reduced to *lowest terms*. This is done by dividing both the numerator and denominator by the largest number that will divide evenly into both. For example, ¹⁴⁄₁₆ is reduced by dividing both terms by 2, thus giving us ⅞. Likewise, ²⁰⁄₂₅ is reduced to ⅘ by dividing both numerator and denominator by 5.

Adding Fractions

To add fractions, you must first change all denominators to their *lowest common denominator* (LCD)—the lowest number that can be divided evenly by all the denominators in the problem. When you have all the denominators the same, you may add fractions by simply adding the numerators (the denominator remains the same). *For example:*

$$\frac{3}{8} = \frac{3}{8} \qquad\qquad \frac{1}{4} = \frac{3}{12}$$
$$+\frac{1}{2} = \frac{4}{8} \leftarrow \left\{\begin{array}{l}\text{one-half is}\\\text{changed to}\\\text{four-eighths}\end{array}\right. \qquad +\frac{1}{3} = \frac{4}{12} \quad\left\{\begin{array}{l}\text{change both}\\\text{fractions to}\\\text{LCD of 12}\end{array}\right.$$
$$\frac{7}{8} \qquad\qquad\qquad \frac{7}{12}$$

In the first example, we changed the ½ to ⁴⁄₈ because 8 is the lowest common denominator, and then we added the numerators 3 and 4 to get ⅞.

In the second example, we had to change both fractions to get the lowest common denominator of 12, and then we added the numerators to get ⁷⁄₁₂. Of course, if the denominators are already the same, just add the numerators. *For example:*

$$\tfrac{6}{11} + \tfrac{3}{11} = \tfrac{9}{11}$$

Adding Mixed Numbers

To add mixed numbers, the same rule (find the LCD) applies, but make sure that you always add the whole number to get your final answer. *For example:*

$$2\frac{1}{2} = 2\frac{2}{4} \leftarrow \begin{cases} \text{one-half is changed} \\ \text{to two-fourths} \end{cases}$$
$$+ \; 3\frac{1}{4} = 3\frac{1}{4}$$
$$5\frac{3}{4}$$
$$\begin{cases} \text{remember to add the} \\ \text{whole numbers} \end{cases}$$

Subtracting Fractions

To subtract fractions, the same rule (find the LCD) applies, except that you subtract the numerators. *For example:*

$$\frac{7}{8} = \frac{7}{8} \qquad \frac{3}{4} = \frac{9}{12}$$
$$- \; \frac{1}{4} = \frac{2}{8} \qquad - \; \frac{1}{3} = \frac{4}{12}$$
$$\frac{5}{8} \qquad\qquad \frac{5}{12}$$

Subtracting Mixed Numbers

When you subtract mixed numbers, sometimes you may have to "borrow" from the whole number, just like you sometimes borrow from the next column when subtracting ordinary numbers. *For example:*

$$6\overset{4\;\;11}{\cancel{5}1}$$
$$- \; 129$$
$$522$$

$$4\overset{3\frac{7}{6}}{\cancel{1}\frac{1}{6}}$$
$$- \; 2\frac{5}{6}$$
$$1\frac{2}{6} = 1\frac{1}{3}$$

you borrowed 1
from the 10's
column

you borrowed one in
the form of $\frac{6}{6}$ from
the 1's column

To subtract a mixed number from a whole number, you have to "borrow" from the whole number. *For example:*

$$6\_\_ = 5\frac{5}{5} \leftarrow \begin{cases} \text{borrow one in the form of} \\ \frac{5}{5} \text{ from the 6} \end{cases}$$
$$- \; 3\frac{1}{5} = 3\frac{1}{5}$$
$$2\frac{4}{5}$$
$$\begin{cases} \text{remember to subtract the} \\ \text{remaining whole numbers} \end{cases}$$

Multiplying Fractions

Simply multiply the numerators; then multiply the denominators. Reduce to lowest terms if necessary. *For example:*

$$\frac{2}{3} \times \frac{5}{12} = \frac{10}{36} \qquad \text{reduce } \frac{10}{36} \text{ to } \frac{5}{18}$$

This answer has to be reduced as it wasn't in lowest terms.

Canceling when multiplying fractions: You could first have "canceled." That would have eliminated the need to reduce your answer. To cancel, find a number that divides evenly into one numerator and one denominator. In this case, 2 will divide evenly into 2 in the numerator (it goes in one time) and 12 in the denominator (it goes in 6 times). *Thus:*

$$\frac{\overset{1}{\cancel{2}}}{3} \times \frac{5}{\underset{6}{\cancel{12}}} =$$

Now that you've canceled, you can multiply out as you did before.

$$\frac{\overset{1}{\cancel{2}}}{3} \times \frac{5}{\underset{6}{\cancel{12}}} = \frac{5}{18}$$

Remember, you may cancel only when *multiplying* fractions.

Multiplying Mixed Numbers

To multiply mixed numbers, first change any mixed number to an improper fraction. Then multiply as previously shown. To change mixed numbers to improper fractions:

1. multiply the whole number by the denominator of the fraction
2. add this to the numerator of the fraction
3. this is now your numerator
4. the denominator remains the same

$$3\frac{1}{3} \times 2\frac{1}{4} = \frac{10}{3} \times \frac{9}{4} = \frac{90}{12} = 7\frac{6}{12} = 7\frac{1}{2}$$

Then change the answer, if in improper fraction form, backed to a mixed number and reduce if necessary.

Dividing Fractions

To divide fractions, invert (turn upside down) the second fraction and multiply. Then reduce if necessary. *For example:*

$$\frac{1}{6} \div \frac{1}{5} = \frac{1}{6} \times \frac{5}{1} = \frac{5}{6} \qquad \frac{1}{6} \div \frac{1}{3} = \frac{1}{6} \times \frac{3}{1} = \frac{3}{6} = \frac{1}{2}$$

Simplifying Fractions

If either numerator or denominator consists of several numbers, these numbers must be combined into one number. Then reduce if necessary. *For example:*

$$\frac{28 + 14}{26 + 17} = \frac{42}{43} \quad \text{or}$$

$$\frac{\frac{1}{4} + \frac{1}{2}}{\frac{1}{3} + \frac{1}{4}} = \frac{\frac{1}{4} + \frac{2}{4}}{\frac{4}{12} + \frac{3}{12}} = \frac{\frac{3}{4}}{\frac{7}{12}} = \frac{3}{4} \times \frac{12}{7} = \frac{36}{28} = \frac{9}{7} = 1\frac{2}{7}$$

Decimals

Fractions may also be written in decimal form by using a symbol called a *decimal point*. All numbers to the left of the decimal point are whole numbers. All numbers to the right of the decimal point are fractions with denominators of only 10, 100, 1000, 10,000, etc., as follows:

$$.6 = \frac{6}{10} = \frac{3}{5} \qquad .0007 = \frac{7}{10,000}$$

$$.7 = \frac{7}{10} \qquad .00007 = \frac{7}{100,000}$$

$$.07 = \frac{7}{100} \qquad .25 = \frac{25}{100} = \frac{1}{4}$$

$$.007 = \frac{7}{1000}$$

Adding and Subtracting Decimals

To add or subtract decimals, just line up the decimal points and then add or subtract in the same manner you would add or subtract regular numbers. *For example:*

$$23.6 + 1.75 + 300.002 = \quad \begin{array}{r} 23.6 \\ 1.75 \\ 300.002 \\ \hline 325.352 \end{array}$$

Adding in zeros can make the problem easier to work:

$$\begin{array}{r} 23.600 \\ 1.750 \\ 300.002 \\ \hline 325.352 \end{array}$$

and

$$54.26 - 1.1 = \quad \begin{array}{r} 54.26 \\ -\ 1.10 \\ \hline 53.16 \end{array}$$

and

$$78.9 - 37.43 = \begin{array}{r} \overset{8}{7}8.\overset{}{\cancel{9}}\overset{1}{}0 \\ -37.4\ 3 \\ \hline 41.4\ 7 \end{array}$$

Whole numbers can have decimal points to their right. *For example:*

$$17 - 8.43 = \begin{array}{r} \overset{6}{1}\overset{9}{7}.\overset{}{\cancel{0}}\overset{1}{}0 \\ -\ 8.4\ 3 \\ \hline 8.5\ 7 \end{array}$$

Multiplying Decimals

To multiply decimals, just multiply as usual. Then count the total number of digits above the line which are to the right of all decimal points. Place your decimal point in your answer so there is the same number of digits to the right of it as there was above the line. *For example:*

$$\begin{array}{r} 40.012 \leftarrow 3\ \text{digits} \\ \times\quad 3.1 \leftarrow 1\ \text{digit} \\ \hline 40012 \\ 120036 \\ \hline 124.0372 \leftarrow 4\ \text{digits} \end{array}$$

{total of 4 digits above the line that are to the right of the decimal point

{decimal point placed so there is same number of digits to the right of the decimal point

Dividing Decimals

Dividing decimals is the same as dividing other numbers, except that if the divisor (the number you're dividing by) has a decimal, move it to the right as many places as necessary until it is a whole number. Then move the decimal point in the dividend (the number being divided into) the same number of places. Sometimes you may have to add zeros to the dividend (the number inside the division sign).

$$1.25\overline{)5.} = 125\overline{)500.}\ \ \overset{4.}{}$$

or

$$0.002\overline{)26.} = 2\overline{)26000.}\ \ \overset{13000.}{}$$

Changing Decimals to Percents

To change decimals to percents:

1. move the decimal point two places to the right and
2. insert a percent sign

$$.75 = 75\% \qquad .05 = 5\%$$

Changing Percents to Decimals

To change percents to decimals:

1. eliminate the percent sign and
2. move the decimal point two places to the left (sometimes adding zeros will be necessary)

$$75\% = .75 \qquad 5\% = .05$$
$$23\% = .23 \qquad .2\% = .002$$

Changing Fractions to Percents

To change a fraction to a percent:

1. multiply by 100 and
2. insert a percent sign

$$1/2 = (1/2) \times 100 = 100/2 = 50\%$$
$$2/5 = (2/5) \times 100 = 200/5 = 40\%$$

Changing Percents to Fractions

To change percents to fractions:

1. divide the percent by 100,
2. eliminate the percent sign, and
3. reduce if necessary

$$60\% = 60/100 = 3/5 \qquad 13\% = 13/100$$

Changing Fractions to Decimals

To change a fraction to a decimal simply do what the operation says. In other words, 13/20 means 13 divided by 20. So do just that (insert decimal points and zeros accordingly):

$$20\overline{)13.00}^{.65} = .65 \qquad 5/8 = 8\overline{)5.000}^{.625} = .625$$

Changing Decimals to Fractions

To change a decimal to a fraction:

1. move the decimal point two places to the right,
2. put that number over 100, and
3. reduce if necessary

$$.65 = 65/100 = 13/20$$

$$.05 = 5/100 = 1/20$$

$$.75 = 75/100 = 3/4$$

Read it: .8
Write it: 8/10
Reduce it: 4/5

Finding Percent of a Number

To determine percent of a number, change the percent to a fraction or decimal (whichever is easier for you) and multiply. Remember, the word "of" means multiply.

What is 20% of 80?

$$(20/100) \times 80 = 1600/100 = 16 \text{ or } .20 \times 80 = 16.00 = 16$$

What is 12% of 50?

$$(12/100) \times 50 = 600/100 = 6 \text{ or } .12 \times 50 = 6.00 = 6$$

What is 1/2% of 18?

$$\frac{1/2}{100} \times 18 = (1/200) \times 18 = 18/200 = 9/100 \text{ or } .005 \times 18 = .09$$

Other Applications of Percent

Turn the question word-for-word into an equation. For "what" substitute the letter x; for "is" substitute an *equal sign;* for "of" substitute a *multiplication sign.* Change percents to decimals or fractions, whichever you find easier. Then solve the equation.

18 is what percent of 90?

$$18 = x(90)$$
$$18/90 = x$$
$$1/5 = x$$
$$20\% = x$$

10 is 50% of what number?

$$10 = .50(x)$$
$$10/.50 = x$$
$$20 = x$$

What is 15% of 60?

$$x = (15/100) \times 60 = 90/10 = 9$$
$$\text{or} \quad .15(60) = 9$$

Finding Percentage Increase or Percentage Decrease

To find the *percentage change* (increase or decrease), use this formula:

$$\frac{\text{change}}{\text{starting point}} \times 100 = \text{percentage change}$$

For example:

What is the percentage decrease of a $500 item on sale for $400?

Change: $500 - 400 = 100$

$$\frac{\text{change}}{\text{starting point}} \times 100 = \frac{100}{500} \times 100 = \frac{1}{5} \times 100 = 20\% \text{ decrease}$$

What is the percentage increase of Jon's salary if it went from $150 a month to $200 a month?

Change: $200 - 150 = 50$

$$\frac{\text{change}}{\text{starting point}} \times 100 = \frac{50}{150} \times 100 = \frac{1}{3} \times 100 = 33\tfrac{1}{3}\% \text{ increase}$$

Prime Numbers

A *prime number* is a number that can be evenly divided by only itself and 1. For example, 19 is a prime number because it can be evenly divided only by 19 and 1, but 21 is not a prime number because 21 can be evenly divided by other numbers (3 and 7).

The only even prime number is 2; thereafter any even number may be divided evenly by 2. Zero and 1 are *not* prime numbers. The first ten prime numbers are 2, 3, 5, 7, 11, 13, 17, 19, 23, and 29.

Arithmetic Mean, or Average

To find the *average* of a group of numbers:

1. add them up and
2. divide by the number of items you added

For example:

What is the average of 10, 20, 35, 40, and 45?

$$10 + 20 + 35 + 40 + 45 = 150$$
$$150 \div 5 = 30$$

The average is 30.

What is the average of 0, 12, 18, 20, 31, and 45?

$$0 + 12 + 18 + 20 + 31 + 45 = 126$$

$$126 \div 6 = 21$$

The average is 21.

What is the average of 25, 27, 27, and 27?

$$25 + 27 + 27 + 27 = 106$$

$$106 \div 4 = 26\frac{1}{2}$$

The average is $26\frac{1}{2}$.

Median

A *median* is simply the middle number of a list of numbers after it has been written in order. (If the list contains an even number of items, average the two middle numbers to get the median.) For example, in the following list—3, 4, 6, *9*, 21, 24, 56—the number 9 is the median.

Mode

The *mode* is simply the number most frequently listed in a group of numbers. For example, in the following group—5, 9, 7, 3, 9, 4, 6, 9, 7, 9, 2—the mode is 9 because it appears more often than any other number.

Squares and Square Roots

To *square* a number, just multiply it by itself. For example, 6 squared (written 6^2) is 6×6 or 36. 36 is called a perfect square (the square of a whole number). Any exponent means multiply by itself that many times. *For example:*

$$5^3 = 5 \times 5 \times 5 = 125$$

$$8^2 = 8 \times 8 = 64$$

Remember, $x^1 = x$ and $x^0 = 1$ when x is any number (other than 0).

Following is a list of perfect squares:

$0^2 = 0$	$5^2 = 25$	$9^2 = 81$
$1^2 = 1$	$6^2 = 36$	$10^2 = 100$
$2^2 = 4$	$7^2 = 49$	$11^2 = 121$
$3^2 = 9$	$8^2 = 64$	$12^2 = 144$ etc.
$4^2 = 16$		

Square roots of nonperfect squares can be approximated. Two approximations you may wish to remember are:

$$\sqrt{2} \cong 1.4$$

$$\sqrt{3} \cong 1.7$$

To find the *square root* of a number, you want to find some number that when multiplied by itself gives you the original number. In other words, to find the square root of 25, you want to find the number that when multiplied by itself gives you 25. The square root of 25, then, is 5. The symbol for square root is $\sqrt{}$. Following is a list of perfect (whole number) square roots:

$$\sqrt{0} = 0 \qquad \sqrt{16} = 4 \qquad \sqrt{64} = 8$$
$$\sqrt{1} = 1 \qquad \sqrt{25} = 5 \qquad \sqrt{81} = 9$$
$$\sqrt{4} = 2 \qquad \sqrt{36} = 6 \qquad \sqrt{100} = 10 \quad \text{etc.}$$
$$\sqrt{9} = 3 \qquad \sqrt{49} = 7$$

Square Root Rules

Two numbers multiplied under a radical (square root) sign equal the product of the two square roots. *For example:*

$$\sqrt{(4)(25)} = \sqrt{4} \times \sqrt{25} = 2 \times 5 = 10 \text{ or } \sqrt{100} = 10$$

and likewise with division:

$$\sqrt{\frac{64}{4}} = \frac{\sqrt{64}}{\sqrt{4}} = \frac{8}{2} = 4 \text{ or } \sqrt{16} = 4$$

Addition and subtraction, however, are different. The numbers must be combined under the radical before any computation of square roots may be done. *For example:*

$$\sqrt{10 + 6} = \sqrt{16} = 4 \qquad (\sqrt{10 + 6} \text{ does } not \text{ equal } [\neq] \sqrt{10} + \sqrt{6})$$

or $\quad \sqrt{93 - 12} = \sqrt{81} = 9$

Approximating Square Roots

To find a square root which will not be a whole number, you should approximate. *For example:*

Approximate $\sqrt{57}$

Because $\sqrt{57}$ is between $\sqrt{49}$ and $\sqrt{64}$, it will fall somewhere between 7 and 8. And because 57 is just about halfway between 49 and 64, $\sqrt{57}$ is therefore approximately 7½.

Approximate $\sqrt{83}$

$$\overset{9}{\sqrt{81}} < \sqrt{83} < \overset{10}{\sqrt{100}}$$

Since $\sqrt{83}$ is slightly more than $\sqrt{81}$ (whose square root is 9), then $\sqrt{83}$ is a little more than 9. Since 83 is only two steps up from the nearest perfect square (81) and 17 steps to the next perfect square (100), then 83 is ²⁄₁₉ of the way to 100.

$$\tfrac{2}{19} \cong \tfrac{2}{20} = \tfrac{1}{10} = .1$$

Therefore, $\qquad\qquad\qquad\qquad \sqrt{83} \cong 9.1$

Simplifying Square Roots

To simplify numbers under a radical (square root sign):

1. factor the number to two numbers, one (or more) of which is a perfect square,
2. then take the square root of the perfect square(s), and
3. leave the others under the $\sqrt{}$

Simplify $\sqrt{75}$

$$\sqrt{75} = \sqrt{25 \times 3} = \sqrt{25} \times \sqrt{3} = 5\sqrt{3}$$

Simplify $\sqrt{200}$

$$\sqrt{200} = \sqrt{100 \times 2} = \sqrt{100} \times \sqrt{2} = 10\sqrt{2}$$

Simplify $\sqrt{900}$

$$\sqrt{900} = \sqrt{100 \times 9} = \sqrt{100} \times \sqrt{9} = 10 \times 3 = 30$$

Signed Numbers (Positive Numbers and Negative Numbers)

On a number line, numbers to the right of 0 are positive. Numbers to the left of 0 are negative, as follows:

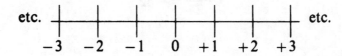

Given any two numbers on a number line, the one on the right is always larger, regardless of its sign (positive or negative).

Addition of Signed Numbers

When adding two numbers with the same sign (either both positive or both negative), add the numbers and keep the same sign. *For example:*

$$\begin{array}{r} +5 \\ + +7 \\ \hline +12 \end{array} \qquad \begin{array}{r} -8 \\ + -3 \\ \hline -11 \end{array}$$

When adding two numbers with different signs (one positive and one negative), subtract the numbers and keep the sign from the larger one. *For example:*

$$\begin{array}{r} +5 \\ + -7 \\ \hline -2 \end{array} \qquad \begin{array}{r} -59 \\ + +72 \\ \hline +13 \end{array}$$

Subtraction of Signed Numbers

To subtract positive and/or negative numbers, just change the sign of the number being subtracted and then add. *For example:*

$$\begin{array}{r} +12 \\ -\ +4 \\ \hline \end{array} \qquad \begin{array}{r} +12 \\ +\ -4 \\ \hline +8 \end{array} \qquad \begin{array}{r} -19 \\ -\ +6 \\ \hline \end{array} \qquad \begin{array}{r} -19 \\ +\ -6 \\ \hline -25 \end{array}$$

$$\begin{array}{r} -14 \\ -\ -4 \\ \hline \end{array} \qquad \begin{array}{r} -14 \\ +\ +4 \\ \hline -10 \end{array} \qquad \begin{array}{r} +20 \\ -\ -3 \\ \hline \end{array} \qquad \begin{array}{r} +20 \\ +\ +3 \\ \hline +23 \end{array}$$

Multiplying and Dividing Signed Numbers

To multiply or divide signed numbers, treat them just like regular numbers but remember this rule. An odd number of negative signs will produce a negative answer. An even number of negative signs will produce a positive answer. *For example:*

$$(-3)(+8)(-5)(-1)(-2) = +240$$
$$(-3)(+8)(-1)(-2) = -48$$

$$\frac{-64}{-2} = +32$$

$$\frac{-64}{2} = -32$$

Parentheses

Parentheses are used to group numbers. Everything inside parentheses must be done before any other operations. *For example:*

$$50(2 + 6) = 50(8) = 400$$

When a parenthesis is preceded by a minus sign, change the minus to a plus by changing all the signs in front of each term inside the parentheses. Then remove the parentheses. *For example:*

$$6 - (-3 + a - 2b + c) =$$
$$6 + (+3 - a + 2b - c) =$$
$$6 + 3 - a + 2b - c = 9 - a + 2b - c$$

Order of Operations

If multiplication, division, powers, addition, parentheses, etc., are all contained in one problem, the order of operations is as follows:

1. parentheses
2. powers and square roots
3. multiplication
4. division } whichever comes first, left to right

5. addition
6. subtraction } whichever comes first, left to right

For example:

$10 - 3 \times 6 + 10^2 + (6 + 1) \times 4 =$

$10 - 3 \times 6 + 10^2 + (7) \times 4 =$ (parentheses first)

$10 - 3 \times 6 + 100 + (7) \times 4 =$ (powers next)

$10 - 18 + 100 + 28 =$ (multiplication)

$-8 + 100 + 28 =$ (addition/subtraction, left to right)

$92 + 28 = 120$

An easy way to remember the order of operations *after parentheses* is: *Please My Dear Aunt Sarah* (*P*owers, *M*ultiplication, *D*ivision, *A*ddition, *S*ubtraction).

ALGEBRA DIAGNOSTIC TEST

Questions

1. Solve for x: $x + 5 = 17$

2. Solve for x: $4x + 9 = 21$

3. Solve for x: $5x + 7 = 3x - 9$

4. Solve for x: $mx - n = y$

5. Solve for x: $\dfrac{r}{x} = \dfrac{s}{t}$

6. Solve for y: $\dfrac{3}{7} = \dfrac{y}{8}$

7. Evaluate: $3x^2 + 5y + 7$ if $x = -2$ and $y = 3$

8. Simplify: $8xy^2 + 3xy + 4xy^2 - 2xy =$

9. Simplify: $6x^2(4x^3y) =$

10. Simplify: $(5x + 2z) + (3x - 4z) =$

11. Simplify: $(4x - 7z) - (3x - 4z) =$

12. Factor: $ab + ac$

13. Solve for x: $2x + 3 \leq 11$

14. Solve for x: $3x + 4 \geq 5x - 8$

Answers

1. $x = 12$
2. $x = 3$
3. $x = -8$
4. $x = (y + n)/m$
5. $x = \dfrac{rt}{s}$
6. $y = {}^{24}\!/_7$ or $3\frac{3}{7}$
7. 34

8. $12xy^2 + xy$
9. $24x^5y$
10. $8x - 2z$
11. $x - 3z$
12. $a(b + c)$
13. $x \leq 4$
14. $x \leq 6$

ALGEBRA REVIEW

Equations

An *equation* is a relationship between numbers and/or symbols. It helps to remember that an equation is like a balance scale, with the equal sign (=) being the fulcrum, or center. Thus, if you do the *same thing to both sides* of the equal sign (say, add 5 to each side), the equation will still be balanced. To solve the equation $x - 5 = 23$, you must get x by itself on one side; therefore, add 5 to both sides:

$$\begin{array}{r} x - 5 = 23 \\ +5 \quad +5 \\ \hline x \quad\; = 28 \end{array}$$

In the same manner, you may subtract, multiply, or divide *both* sides of an equation by the same (nonzero) number, and the equation will not change. Sometimes you may have to use more than one step to solve for an unknown. *For example:*

$$3x + 4 = 19$$

Subtract 4 from both sides to get the $3x$ by itself on one side:

$$\begin{array}{r} 3x + 4 = 19 \\ -4 \quad -4 \\ \hline 3x \quad\;\; = 15 \end{array}$$

Then divide both sides by 3 to get x:

$$\frac{3x}{3} = \frac{15}{3}$$

$$x = 5$$

Remember: Solving an equation is using opposite operations, until the letter is on a side by itself (for addition, subtract; for multiplication, divide, etc.).

Understood Multiplying

When two or more letters, or a number and letters, are written next to each other, they are understood to be *multiplied*. Thus, $8x$ means 8 times x. Or ab means a times b. Or $18ab$ means 18 times a times b.

Parentheses also represent multiplication. Thus, $(a)b$ means a times b. A raised dot also means multiplication. Thus, $6 \cdot 5$ means 6 times 5.

Literal Equations

Literal equations have no numbers, only symbols (letters). *For example:*

$$\text{Solve for } Q\text{: } QP - X = Y$$

First add X to both sides:

$$\begin{array}{r} QP - X = Y \\ +\,X \qquad +\,X \\ \hline QP \quad\;\; = Y + X \end{array}$$

Then divide both sides by P:

$$\frac{QP}{P} = \frac{Y + X}{P}$$

$$Q = \frac{Y + X}{P}$$

Again opposite operations were used to isolate Q.

Cross Multiplying

$$\text{Solve for } x\text{: } \frac{b}{x} = \frac{p}{q}$$

To solve this equation quickly, you cross multiply. To cross multiply:

1. bring the denominators up next to the opposite side numerators and
2. multiply

$$\frac{b}{x} = \frac{p}{q}$$

$$bq = px$$

Then divide both sides by p to get x alone:

$$\frac{bq}{p} = \frac{px}{p}$$

$$\frac{bq}{p} = x \quad \text{or} \quad x = \frac{bq}{p}$$

Cross multiplying can be used only when the format is two fractions separated by an equal sign.

Proportions

Proportions are written as two fractions equal to each other.

Solve this proportion for x: $\dfrac{p}{q} = \dfrac{x}{y}$

This is read "p is to q as x is to y." Cross multiply and solve:

$$py = xq$$

$$\frac{py}{q} = \frac{xq}{q}$$

$$\frac{py}{q} = x \text{ or } x = \frac{py}{q}$$

Evaluating Expressions

To *evaluate* an expression, just insert the value for the unknowns and do the arithmetic. *For example:*

Evaluate: $2x^2 + 3y + 6$ if $x = 2$ and $y = 9$

$$2(2^2) + 3(9) + 6 =$$
$$2(4) + 27 + 6 =$$
$$8 + 27 + 6 = 41$$

Monomials and Polynomials

A *monomial* is an algebraic expression that consists of only one term. For instance, $9x$, $4a^2$, and $3mpxz^2$ are all monomials.

A *polynomial* consists of two or more terms; $x + y$, $y^2 - x^2$, and $x^2 + 3x + 5y^2$ are all polynomials.

Adding and Subtracting Monomials

To *add* or *subtract monomials,* follow the same rules as with regular signed numbers, provided that the *terms are alike:*

$$
\begin{array}{r}
15x^2yz \\
-18x^2yz \\
\hline
-3x^2yz
\end{array}
\qquad 3x + 2x = 5x
$$

Multiplying and Dividing Monomials

To *multiply monomials*, add the exponents of the same terms:

$$(x^3)(x^4) = x^7$$

$$(x^2y)(x^3y^2) = x^5y^3$$

$$-4(m^2n)(-3m^4n^3) = 12m^6n^4 \text{ (multiply numbers)}$$

To *divide monomials*, subtract the exponents of the like terms:

$$\frac{y^{15}}{y^4} = y^{11} \qquad \frac{x^5y^2}{x^3y} = x^2y \qquad \frac{36a^4b^6}{-9ab} = -4a^3b^5$$

Remember: x is the same as x^1.

Adding and Subtracting Polynomials

To *add or subtract polynomials*, just arrange like terms in columns and then add or subtract:

$$
\begin{array}{ll}
\text{Add:} & \begin{array}{r} a^2 + \ ab + \ b^2 \\ 3a^2 + 4ab - 2b^2 \\ \hline 4a^2 + 5ab - \ b^2 \end{array}
\end{array}
$$

$$
\begin{array}{ll}
\text{Subtract:} & \begin{array}{r} a^2 + b^2 \\ (-) \ 2a^2 - b^2 \\ \hline \end{array} \quad \rightarrow \quad \begin{array}{r} a^2 + \ b^2 \\ + \ -2a^2 + \ b^2 \\ \hline -a^2 + 2b^2 \end{array}
\end{array}
$$

Multiplying Polynomials

To *multiply polynomials*, multiply each term in one polynomial by each term in the other polynomial. Then simplify if necessary:

$$(3x + a)(2x - 2a) =$$

$$
\begin{array}{r}
2x - 2a \\
\times \ \ 3x + \ a \\
\hline
+2ax - 2a^2 \\
6x^2 - 6ax \\
\hline
6x^2 - 4ax - 2a^2
\end{array}
\qquad
\begin{array}{l}
\text{similar to}
\end{array}
\qquad
\begin{array}{r}
23 \\
\times 19 \\
\hline
207 \\
23 \\
\hline
437
\end{array}
$$

Factoring

To *factor* means to find two or more quantities whose product equals the original quantity. Two types of factoring you should know are

A. *Factoring out a common factor*

$$\text{Factor: } 2y^3 - 6y$$

1. find the largest common monomial factor of each term and
2. divide the original polynomial by this factor to obtain the second factor (the second factor will be a polynomial)

For example:

$$2y^3 - 6y = 2y(y^2 - 3)$$
$$x^5 - 4x^3 + x^2 = x^2(x^3 - 4x + 1)$$

B. *Factoring the difference between two squares*

$$\text{Factor: } x^2 - 144$$

1. find the square root of the first term and the square root of the second term and
2. express your answer as the product of: the sum of the quantities from step 1, times the difference of those quantities

For example:

$$x^2 - 144 = (x + 12)(x - 12)$$
$$a^2 - b^2 = (a + b)(a - b)$$

Inequalities

An *inequality* is a statement in which the relationships are not equal. Instead of using an equal sign (=) as in an equation, we use > (greater than) and < (less than), or ≥ (greater than or equal to) and ≤ (less than or equal to).

When working with inequalities, treat them exactly like equations, EXCEPT: if you multiply or divide both sides by a negative number, you must *reverse* the direction of the sign. *For example:*

$$\text{Solve for } x: \quad 2x + 4 > 6$$

$$\begin{array}{r} 2x + 4 > 6 \\ -4 \quad -4 \\ \hline 2x \quad\; > 2 \end{array}$$

$$\frac{2x}{2} > \frac{2}{2}$$

$$x > 1$$

Solve for x: $-7x > 14$ (divide by -7 and reverse the sign)

$$\frac{-7x}{-7} < \frac{14}{-7}$$

$$x < -2$$

$3x + 2 \geq 5x - 10$ becomes $-2x \geq -12$ by opposite operations. Divide both sides by -2 and reverse the sign.

$$\frac{-2x}{-2} \leq \frac{-12}{-2}$$

$$x \leq 6$$

GEOMETRY

GEOMETRY DIAGNOSTIC TEST

Questions

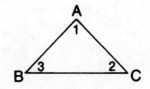

1. Name any angle of this triangle three different ways.

2. A(n) _____ angle measures less than 90 degrees.

3. A(n) _____ angle measures 90 degrees.

4. A(n) _____ angle measures more than 90 degrees.

5. A(n) _____ angle measures 180 degrees.

6. Two angles are complementary when their sum is _____.

7. Two angles are supplementary when their sum is _____.

8. In the diagram, find the measures of ∠a, ∠b, and ∠c.

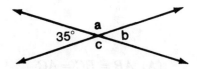

9. Lines that stay the same distance apart and never meet are called _____ lines.

10. Lines that meet to form 90 degree angles are called _____ lines.

11. A(n) _____ triangle has three equal sides. Therefore, each interior angle measures _____.

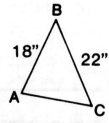

12. In the triangle, AC must be smaller than _____ inches.

13. In the triangle, which angle is smaller, $\angle A$ or $\angle C$?

14. What is the measure of $\angle ACD$?

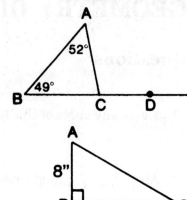

15. What is the length of AC?

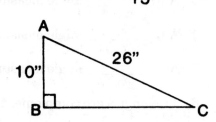

16. What is the length of BC?

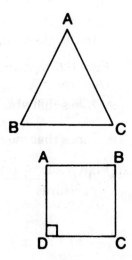

17. Name each of the following polygons:

(A) $AB = BC = AC$
    $\angle A = \angle B = \angle C = 60°$

(B) $AB = BC = CD = AD$
    $\angle A = \angle B = \angle C = \angle D = 90°$

(C) $\overline{AB} \parallel \overline{DC}$
$AB = DC$
$\overline{AD} \parallel \overline{BC}$
$AD = BC$
$\angle A = \angle C$

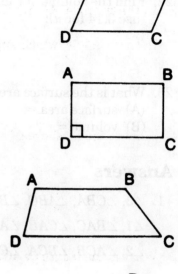

(D) $AB = DC$
$AD = BC$
$\angle A = \angle B = \angle C = \angle D = 90°$

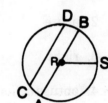

(E) $\overline{AB} \parallel \overline{DC}$

18. Fill in the blanks for circle R:
   (A) $\overline{RS}$ is called the _____.
   (B) $\overline{AB}$ is called the _____.
   (C) $\overline{CD}$ is called a _____.

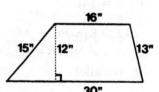

19. Find the area and circumference for the circle ($\pi \cong 22/7$):
   (A) area =
   (B) circumference =

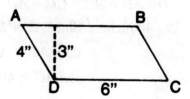

20. Find the area and perimeter of the figure:
   (A) area =
   (B) perimeter =

21. Find the area and perimeter of the figure ($ABCD$ is a parallelogram):
   (A) area =
   (B) perimeter =

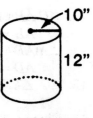

22. Find the volume of the figure if $V = (\pi r^2)h$
(use 3.14 for π):

23. What is the surface area and volume of the cube?
    (A) surface area =
    (B) volume =

Answers

1. $\angle 3, \angle CBA, \angle ABC, \angle B$

   $\angle 1, \angle BAC, \angle CAB, \angle A$

   $\angle 2, \angle ACB, \angle BCA, \angle C$

2. acute

3. right

4. obtuse

5. straight

6. $90°$

7. $180°$

8. $a = 145°$
   $b = 35°$
   $c = 145°$

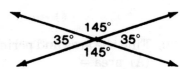

9. parallel

10. perpendicular

11. equilateral, $60°$

12. 40 inches. Since $AB + BC = 40$ inches

    then $AC < AB + BC$

    and $AC < 40$ inches

13. ∠C must be the smaller angle, since it is opposite the shorter side *AB*.

14. ∠*ACD* = 101°

15. *AC* = 17 inches

16. Since △*ABC* is a right triangle, use the Pythagorean theorem:

$$a^2 + b^2 = c^2$$

$$10^2 + b^2 = 26^2$$

$$100 + b^2 = 676$$

$$b^2 = 576$$

$$b = 24''$$

17. (A) equilateral triangle
    (B) square
    (C) parallelogram
    (D) rectangle
    (E) trapezoid

18. (A) radius
    (B) diameter
    (C) chord

19. (A) area = πr^2

    $= \pi(7^2)$

    $= {}^{22}\!/_7(7)(7)$

    = 154 square inches

    (B) circumference = πd

    $= \pi(14)$ $d = 14''$, since $r = 7''$

    $= {}^{22}\!/_7(14)$

    $= 22(2)$

    = 44 inches

20. (A) area = ½(a + b)h

    = ½(16 + 30)12

    = ½(46)12

    = 23(12)

    = 276 square inches

    (B) perimeter = 16 + 13 + 30 + 15 = 74 inches

21. (A) area = bh

    = 6(3)

    = 18 square inches

    (B) perimeter = 6 + 4 + 6 + 4 = 20 inches

22. volume = $(\pi r^2)h$

    = $(\pi \cdot 10^2)(12)$

    = 3.14(100)(12)

    = 314(12)

    = 3768 cubic inches

23. (A) All six surfaces have an area of 4 × 4, or 16 square inches, since each surface is a square. Therefore, 16(6) = 96 square inches in the surface area.

    (B) volume = side × side × side, or 4^3 = 64 cubic inches.

GEOMETRY REVIEW

Plane geometry is the study of shapes and figures in two dimensions (the plane).

Solid geometry is the study of shapes and figures in three dimensions.

A point is the most fundamental idea in geometry. It is represented by a dot and named by a capital letter.

Lines

- A straight *line* is the shortest distance between two points. It continues forever in both directions. A line consists of an infinite number of points. It is named by any two points on the line. The symbol ↔ written on top of the two letters is used to denote that line.

This is line *AB*:

It is written: $\overleftrightarrow{AB}$

A line may also be named by one small letter. The symbol would not be used.

This is line *l*:

- A *line segment* is a piece of a line. A line segment has two endpoints. It is named by its two endpoints. The symbol — written on top of the two letters is used to denote that line segment.

This is line segment *CD*:

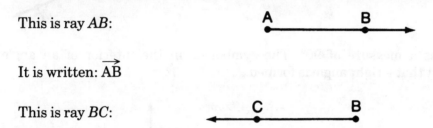

It is written: $\overline{CD}$

Note that it is a piece of $\overleftrightarrow{AB}$

- A *ray* has only one endpoint and continues forever in one direction. A ray could be thought of as a half-line. It is named by the letter of its endpoint and any other point on the ray. The symbol → written on top of the two letters is used to denote that ray.

This is ray *AB*:

It is written: $\overrightarrow{AB}$

This is ray *BC*:

It is written: $\overleftarrow{BC}$ or $\overleftarrow{CB}$

Note that the direction of the symbol is the direction of the ray.

Angles

- An *angle* is formed by two rays that start from the same point. That point is called the *vertex;* the rays are called the *sides* of the angle. An angle is measured in degrees. The degrees indicate the size of the angle, from one side to the other.

In the diagram, the angle is formed by rays *AB* and *AC*. *A* is the vertex.

$\overrightarrow{AB}$ and $\overrightarrow{AC}$ are the sides of the angle.

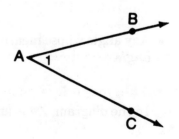

The symbol ∠ is used to denote an angle.

- An angle can be named in various ways:
  1. By the letter of the vertex—therefore, the angle above could be named ∠A.
  2. By the number (or small letter) in its interior—therefore, the angle above could be named ∠1.
  3. By the letters of the three points that formed it—therefore, the angle above could be named ∠BAC, or ∠CAB. The center letter is always the letter of the vertex.

Types of Angles

- *Adjacent angles* are any angles that share a common side and a common vertex.

In the diagram, ∠1 and ∠2 are adjacent angles.

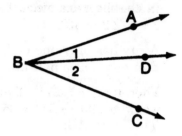

- A *right angle* has a measure of 90°. The symbol ∟ in the interior of an angle designates the fact that a right angle is formed.

In the diagram, ∠ABC is a right angle.

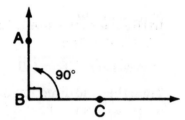

- Any angle whose measure is less than 90° is called an *acute angle*.

In the diagram, ∠b is acute.

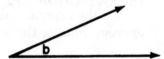

- Any angle whose measure is larger than 90°, but smaller than 180°, is called an *obtuse angle*.

In the diagram, ∠4 is an obtuse angle.

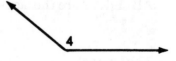

- A *straight angle* has a measure of 180°.

In the diagram, ∠*BAC* is a straight angle (also called a line).

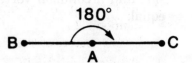

- Two angles whose sum is 90° are called *complementary angles*.

In the diagram, since ∠*ABC* is a right angle, ∠1 + ∠2 = 90°.

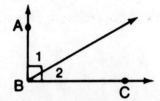

Therefore, ∠1 and ∠2 are complementary angles. If ∠1 = 55°, its complement, ∠2, would be: 90° − 55° = 35°.

- Two angles whose sum is 180° are called *supplementary angles*. Two adjacent angles that form a straight line are supplementary.

In the diagram, since ∠*ABC* is a straight angle, ∠3 + ∠4 = 180°.

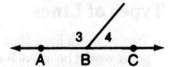

Therefore, ∠3 and ∠4 are supplementary angles. If ∠3 = 122°, its supplement, ∠4, would be: 180° −122° = 58°.

- A ray from the vertex of an angle that divides the angle into two equal pieces is called an *angle bisector*.

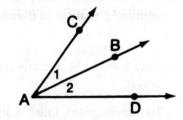

In the diagram, $\overrightarrow{AB}$ is the angle bisector of ∠*CAD*. Therefore, ∠1 = ∠2.

• If two straight lines intersect, they do so at a point. Four angles are formed. Those angles opposite each other are called *vertical angles*. Those angles sharing a common side and a common vertex are, again, *adjacent angles*. Vertical angles are always equal.

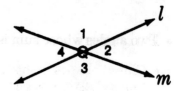

In the diagram, line *l* and line *m* intersect at point *Q*. ∠1, ∠2, ∠3, and ∠4 are formed.

$$\left.\begin{matrix} \angle 1 \text{ and } \angle 3 \\ \angle 2 \text{ and } \angle 4 \end{matrix}\right\} \text{ are vertical angles}$$

$$\left.\begin{matrix} \angle 1 \text{ and } \angle 2 \\ \angle 2 \text{ and } \angle 3 \\ \angle 3 \text{ and } \angle 4 \\ \angle 1 \text{ and } \angle 4 \end{matrix}\right\} \text{ are adjacent angles}$$

Therefore, $\begin{matrix} \angle 1 = \angle 3 \\ \angle 2 = \angle 4 \end{matrix}$

Types of Lines

• Two or more lines that cross each other at a point are called *intersecting lines*. That point would be on each of those lines.

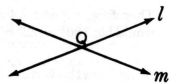

In the diagram, lines *l* and *m* intersect at *Q*.

• Two lines that meet to form right angles (90°) are called *perpendicular lines*. The symbol ⊥ is used to denote perpendicular lines.

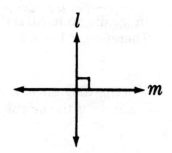

In the diagram, line *l* ⊥ line *m*.

- Two or more lines that remain the same distance apart at all times are called *parallel lines*. Parallel lines never meet. The symbol ‖ is used to denote parallel lines.

In the diagram, *l* ‖ *m*.

Polygons

- Closed shapes or figures with three or more sides are called *polygons*. (*Poly* means "many"; *gon* means "sides"; thus, *polygon* means "many sides.")

Triangles

- This section deals with those polygons having the fewest number of sides. A *triangle* is a three-sided polygon. It has three angles in its interior. The sum of these angles is *always* 180°. The symbol for triangle is △. A triangle is named by all three letters of its vertices.

This is △ *ABC*:

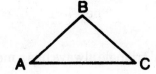

- Types of triangles:
  1. A triangle having all three sides equal (meaning all three sides have the same length) is called an *equilateral triangle*.
  2. A triangle having two sides equal is called an *isosceles triangle*.
  3. A triangle having none of its sides equal is called a *scalene triangle*.
  4. A triangle having a right (90°) angle in its interior is called a *right triangle*.

Facts about Triangles

- Every triangle has a base (bottom side) and a height (or altitude). Every height is the *perpendicular* (forms right angles) distance from a vertex to its opposite side (the base).

In this diagram of △ *ABC*, $\overline{BC}$ is the base, and $\overline{AE}$ is the height. $\overline{AE} \perp \overline{BC}$.

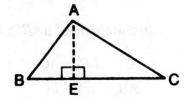

- Every triangle has a median. The median is the line segment drawn from a vertex to the midpoint of the opposite side.

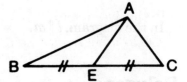

In this diagram of $\triangle ABC$, E is the midpoint of $\overline{BC}$.

Therefore, $BE = EC$. $\overline{AE}$ is the median of ABC.

- In an equilateral triangle, all three sides are equal, and all three angles are equal. If all three angles are equal and their sum is 180°, the following must be true:

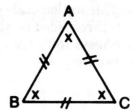

$$x + x + x = 180°$$
$$3x = 180°$$
$$x = 60°$$

Every angle of an equilateral triangle always has a measure of 60°.

- In any triangle, the longest side is always opposite from the largest angle. Likewise, the shortest side is always opposite from the smallest angle. In a right triangle, the longest side will always be opposite from the right angle, as the right angle will be the largest angle in the triangle.

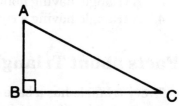

$\overline{AC}$ is the longest side of right $\triangle ABC$.

- The sum of the lengths of any two sides of a triangle must be larger than the length of the third side.

In the diagram of $\triangle ABC$:

$$AB + BC > AC$$
$$AB + AC > BC$$
$$AC + BC > AB$$

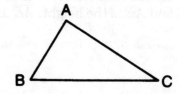

- If one side of a triangle is extended, the exterior angle formed by that extension is equal to the sum of the other two interior angles.

In the diagram of $\triangle ABC$, side BC is extended to D.

$\angle ACD$ is the exterior angle formed.

$\angle x = \angle y + \angle z$

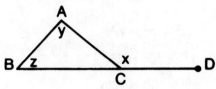

$x = 82° + 41°$

$x = 123°$

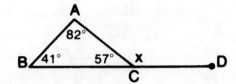

Pythagorean Theorem

- In any right triangle, the relationship between the lengths of the sides is stated by the Pythagorean theorem. The parts of a right triangle are:

$\angle C$ is the right angle.

The side opposite the right angle is called the *hypotenuse* (side c). (The hypotenuse will always be the longest side.)

The other two sides are called the *legs* (sides a and b).

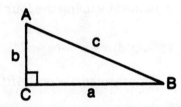

The three lengths a, b, and c will always be numbers such that:

$$a^2 + b^2 = c^2$$

For example:

If $a = 3$, $b = 4$, and $c = 5$,

$a^2 + b^2 = c^2$

$3^2 + 4^2 = 5^2$

$9 + 16 = 25$

$25 = 25$

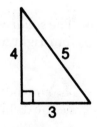

Therefore, 3-4-5 is called a Pythagorean triple. There are other values for a, b, and c that will always work. Some are: 1-1-$\sqrt{2}$, 5-12-13, and 8-15-17. Any multiple of one of these triples will also work. For example, using the 3-4-5: 6-8-10, 9-12-15, and 15-20-25 will also be Pythagorean triples.

- If perfect squares are known, the lengths of these sides can be determined easily. A knowledge of the use of algebraic equations can also be used to determine the lengths of the sides. *For example:*

$$a^2 + b^2 = c^2$$
$$x^2 + 10^2 = 15^2$$
$$x^2 + 100 = 225$$
$$x^2 = 125$$
$$x = \sqrt{125}$$
$$= \sqrt{25} \times \sqrt{5}$$
$$= 5\sqrt{5}$$

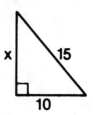

Quadrilaterals

- A polygon having four sides is called a *quadrilateral*. There are four angles in its interior. The sum of these interior angles will always be 360°. A quadrilateral is named by using the four letters of its vertices.

This is quadrilateral *ABCD*:

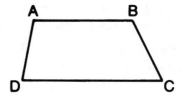

Types of Quadrilaterals

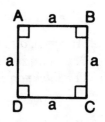

- The *square* has four equal sides and four right angles.

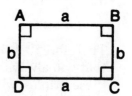

- The *rectangle* has opposite sides equal and four right angles.

- The *parallelogram* has opposite sides equal and parallel, opposite angles equal, and consecutive angles supplementary. Every parallelogram has a height.

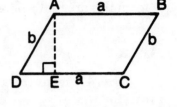

$\angle A = \angle C$

$\angle B = \angle D$

$\angle A + \angle B = 180°$

$\angle A + \angle D = 180°$

$\angle B + \angle C = 180°$

$\angle C + \angle D = 180°$

$\overline{AE}$ is the height of the parallelogram, $\overline{AB} \parallel \overline{CD}$, and $\overline{AD} \parallel \overline{BC}$.

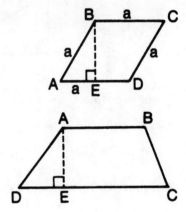

- The *rhombus* is a parallelogram with four equal sides. A rhombus has a height. $\overline{BE}$ is the height.

- The *trapezoid* has only one pair of parallel sides. A trapezoid has a height. $\overline{AE}$ is the height.

  $\overline{AB} \parallel \overline{DC}$

Other Polygons

- The *pentagon* is a five-sided polygon.
- The *hexagon* is a six-sided polygon.
- The *octagon* is an eight-sided polygon.
- The *nonagon* is a nine-sided polygon.
- The *decagon* is a ten-sided polygon.

Facts about Polygons

- *Regular* means all sides have the same length and all angles have the same measure. A regular three-sided polygon is the equilateral triangle. A regular four-sided polygon is the square. There are no other special names. Other polygons will just be described as regular, if they are. For example, a regular five-sided polygon is called a regular pentagon. A regular six-sided polygon is called a regular hexagon.

Perimeter

- *Perimeter* means the total distance all the way around the outside of any polygon. The perimeter of any polygon can be determined by adding up the lengths of all the sides. The total distance around will be the sum of all sides of the polygon. No special formulas are really necessary.

Area

Area (A) means the amount of space inside the polygon. The formulas for each area are as follows:

- Triangle: $A = \frac{1}{2}bh$

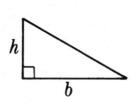   or

For example:

$A = \frac{1}{2}bh$

$A = \frac{1}{2}(24)(18) = 216$ sq in

- Square or rectangle: $A = lw$

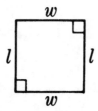   or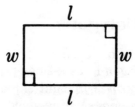

For example:

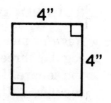

$A = l(w) = 4(4) = 16$ sq in

$A = l(w) = 12(5) = 60$ sq in

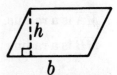

- Parallelogram: $A = bh$

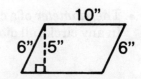

For example:

$A = b(h)$

$A = 10(5) = 50$ sq in

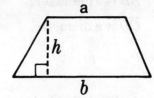

- Trapezoid: $A = \frac{1}{2}(a + b)h$

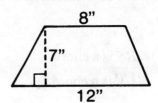

For example:

$A = \frac{1}{2}(a + b)h$

$A = \frac{1}{2}(8 + 12)7$

$\quad = \frac{1}{2}(20)7 = 70$ sq in

Circles

- A closed shape whose side is formed by one curved line all points of which are equidistant from the center point is called a *circle*. Circles are named by the letter of their center point.

This is circle M:

M is the center point, since it is the same distance away from any point on the circle.

Parts of a Circle

- The *radius* is the distance from the center to any point on the circle. In any circle, all radii (plural) are the same length.

$\overline{MA}$ is a radius.

$\overline{MB}$ is a radius.

- The *diameter* of a circle is the distance across the circle, through the center. In any circle, all diameters are the same length. Each diameter is two radii.

$\overline{AB}$ is a diameter.

$\overline{CD}$ is a diameter.

- A *chord* of a circle is a line segment whose end points lie on the circle itself.

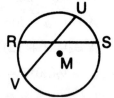

$\overline{RS}$ is a chord.

$\overline{UV}$ is a chord.

The diameter is the longest chord in any circle.

- An *arc* is the distance between any two points *on* the circle itself. An arc is a piece of the circle. The symbol ⌢ is used to denote an arc. It is written on top of the two endpoints that form the arc. Arcs are measured in degrees. There are 360° around the circle.

This is $\overset{\frown}{EF}$:

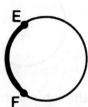

Minor $\overset{\frown}{EF}$ is the shorter distance between E and F.

Major $\overset{\frown}{EF}$ is the longer distance between E and F.

When $\overset{\frown}{EF}$ is written, the minor arc is assumed.

Area and Circumference

- *Circumference* is the distance around the circle. Since there are no sides to add up, a formula is needed. π (pi) is a Greek letter that represents a specific number. In fractional or decimal form, the commonly used approximations are: $\pi \cong 3.14$ or $\pi \cong$ $^{22}/_7$. The formula for circumference is: $C = \pi d$ or $C = 2\pi r$. *For example:*

In circle M, $d = 8$, since $r = 4$.

$C = \pi d$

   $= \pi(8)$

   $= 3.14(8)$

   $= 25.12$ inches

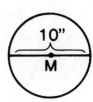

- The *area* of a circle can be determined by: $A = \pi r^2$. *For example:*

In circle M, $r = 5$, since $d = 10$.

$A = \pi(r^2)$

   $= \pi(5^2)$

   $= 3.14(25)$

   $= 78.5$ sq in

Volume

- In three dimensions there are different facts that can be determined about shapes. *Volume* is the capacity to hold. The formula for volume of each shape is different. The volume of any *prism* (a three-dimensional shape having many sides, but two bases) can be determined by: Volume $(V) =$ (area of base) (height of prism).

Specifically for a rectangular solid:

$V = (lw)(h)$

   $= lwh$

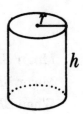

Specifically for a cylinder (circular bases):

$V = (\pi r^2)h$
   $= \pi r^2 h$

Volume is labeled "cubic" units.

Surface Area

- The *surface area* of a three-dimensional solid is the area of all of the surfaces that form the solid. Find the area of each surface, and then add up those areas. The surface area of a rectangular solid can be found by adding up the areas of all six surfaces. *For example:*

The surface area of this prism is:

top	$18 \times 6 =$	108
bottom	$18 \times 6 =$	108
left side	$6 \times 4 =$	24
right side	$6 \times 4 =$	24
front	$18 \times 4 =$	72
back	$18 \times 4 =$	72
		408 sq in

HISTORY/SOCIAL SCIENCES REVIEW

OUTLINES

The following outlines cover the eight major areas of U.S. history, world history, California history and geography, political science-government, the behavioral sciences, economics, and global geography. Each outline is an intensive review of the key points, facts, terms, and major concepts associated with each discipline.

U.S. HISTORY

I. EXPLORATION AND COLONIZATION (1450–1763)

A. The opening of new worlds was associated with the "Age of Discovery."

1. European explorers in search of Asia discovered a new continent.

2. The "Age of Discovery" resulted in renewed European rivalry.

3. Spain, France, England, Portugal, and the Netherlands competed for land.

B. England developed permanent colonies in North America.

1. Geographic diversity helped to create distinct economic regions.
   a. The New England colonies were associated with shipbuilding and commerce.
   b. The middle colonies were associated with farming and commerce.
   c. The southern colonies were associated with tobacco, cotton, and slavery.

2. The English colonies began to develop self-government.
   a. The Mayflower Compact (1620) was the basis for government by the consent of the governed.
   b. The House of Burgesses (1619) was an early colonial attempt at representative self-government.
   c. The colonists demanded their rights as Englishmen.

3. The population of the colonies steadily increased.
   a. Large families of ten or more were common.
   b. Steady immigration from abroad increased the overall population.
   c. Europeans and Africans were the major population groups.

4. The idea of free public education started in the colonies.

5. Class distinctions were less rigid than in England, and a strong middle class emerged.

6. The most prevalent religion in the colonies was Protestant.

   a. A single, established church was not practical in America.

   b. The decline of Puritanism led to greater religious tolerance.

II. THE FORMATION OF THE NEW NATION (1763–89)

A. The French and Indian War (1756–63) was a key turning point in England's domination over North America.

1. The English victory ended the French threat in America.

2. The English victory encouraged colonial America to seek a more active voice in its own affairs.

B. Background to the American Revolution (1763–76).

1. The English mercantile policy discouraged colonial economic independence.

2. Colonial concepts of political and economic freedom were key factors leading to the American Revolution.

3. Colonial opposition to British actions steadily increased during this period.

4. The colonies used a variety of methods to change British actions; petitions, boycotts, and other measures were used.

5. The Declaration of Independence stated the purposes for the colonies' break with England.

C. The American Revolution (1776–81) was fought to obtain independence.

1. Problems of military effectiveness hindered the early colonial effort.

   a. Colonial armies were underequipped.

   b. There was widespread opposition to fixed military terms.

2. Washington's leadership turned the tide of battle.

   a. The French alliance (1778) brought needed men, equipment, and money to the American cause.

   b. The defeat of Cornwallis at Yorktown (1781) brought victory to the colonies.

D. The Articles of Confederation (1781–89) proved inadequate as a central government.

1. The Articles held the nation together during the critical period.

2. The Articles were limited by major weaknesses.

   a. The national government did not have the power to regulate foreign trade.

   b. The national government did not have a court system.

   c. The national government did not have an independent taxing power.

E. The need for a strong central government led to the framing of the Constitution (1789).

F. The government under the Constitution solved many major problems.

1. A federal system was created which divided federal and state power.

2. Separation of powers and checks and balances were included to limit the power of the central government.

3. The legislative, executive, and judicial branches were established to divide the power of the new government.

4. The Bill of Rights was added to the Constitution to protect the rights of the people.

III. THE NEW NATION (1787–1823)

A. The early national period tested the new federal government.

1. Hamilton's financial plan placed the national government on a sound financial basis.

   a. The national government paid back the state, national, and foreign debts to demonstrate the credibility of the new government.

   b. The national government encouraged American business expansion by passing excise taxes and a tariff.

   c. The national government raised revenue by initiating a tax on domestic whiskey.

   d. The national government authorized the use of coins and paper money to encourage the growth of commerce.

   e. The national government encouraged the development of a national bank to facilitate the expansion of business.

2. Hamilton's financial plan led to the development of political parties.

   a. The Federalist Party believed in the concept of a strong central government ruled by the manufacturing interests of the country. (Hamilton)

   b. The Antifederalist Party believed in the concept of limited federal power based on the farming interests of the country. (Jefferson)

   c. The Federalist Party favored the rich and the wealthy.

   d. The Antifederalists developed a political philosophy that believed in the worth of the individual.

3. Foreign policy during the early national period was weak and ineffectual.

4. The Louisiana Purchase (1803) became the greatest real estate purchase in U.S. history.

B. The War of 1812 (1812–15) was fought between the United States and Great Britain.

1. Among the causes of the War of 1812 were violations of U.S. neutrality and impressment of U.S. sailors.

2. The U.S. victory resulted in national pride, self-sufficiency, and foreign credibility.

C. The new nationalism (1816–23) followed the War of 1812.

1. The scope and authority of the Supreme Court were established during this period.

2. The Era of Good Feelings characterized the political successes of the Republican Party.

3. The Monroe Doctrine defined American interests in the northern hemisphere.

4. The new nationalism led to the development of a new American culture.

IV. THE RISE OF DEMOCRACY AND THE WESTERN MOVEMENT

A. Jacksonian democracy (1826–36) symbolized the rise of the "common man."

1. Jackson's war against the bank and the tariff were key issues for the new Democratic Party.

2. Jackson initiated the spoils system in which political enemies are replaced by political friends.

3. Jackson pursued nationalistic policies.

B. The Whig Party opposed the Democratic Party's belief in states' rights and instead favored a strong national government.

C. The territorial expansion of the United States reached from the Mississippi River to the Pacific Ocean.

1. The rise of the new West created opportunities in transportation, education, politics, mining, and agriculture.

2. Manifest Destiny encouraged U.S. expansion to the Pacific.

   a. Texas was annexed to the United States in 1837.

   b. The Oregon Territory was added to the United States in 1846 and encouraged settlement of the Far West.

   c. The Mexican War (1848) added California and parts of the Southwest to the United States.

V. THE BACKGROUND OF THE CIVIL WAR AND RECONSTRUCTION (1800–76)

A. Geographic and economic factors contributed to the growth of slavery.

1. The dependence on slavery and cotton created a unique Southern economy.

2. The development of the "Cotton South" led to sectionalism.

B. The expansion of slavery was a political issue prior to the 1850s.

1. The Missouri Compromise of 1820 limited the spread of slavery.

2. The annexation of Texas (1837) added potential slave territory to the United States.

3. The Mexican War (1848) was criticized as a proslavery, expansionist war.

C. The failure of the politics of compromise led to war.

1. The Compromise of 1850 failed to hold the nation together.

2. In the 1850s, slavery and sectionalism continued to threaten the Union.

3. The failure of the Kansas-Nebraska Act (1854) led to bloodshed over the expansion of slavery.

4. The Dred Scott decision failed to solve the slavery question.

5. The election in 1860 of Lincoln, a sectional candidate, made secession inevitable.

D. The Civil War threatened the Union (1861–65).

1. The North and South prepared for war.

   a. The North had an overall superiority in manpower, firepower, and economic resources.

   b. The South had advantages in leadership and territory.

2. The Union strategy of isolating the South proved successful.

   a. The Union blockade economically strangled the South.

   b. The defeat at Gettysburg (1863) ended the Southern chances for foreign recognition.

   c. Economic and military weaknesses led to Lee's surrender at Appomattox (1865).

E. Reconstruction attempts to reunite the nation (1865–66).

1. Following the Civil War, the economic, political, social, and military reconstruction of the South was necessary.

2. The President and Congress differed on how to reconstruct the South.

   a. The presidential plan emphasized tolerance for the defeated South.

   b. The congressional (Radical) plan emphasized the use of military force in treating the South like a conquered territory.

3. Reconstruction was under Radical control from 1868 to 1876.

   a. The Fourteenth and Fifteenth Amendments were passed.

   b. Civil rights bills were passed.

   c. Military rule supported Radical Reconstruction.

   d. President Johnson was impeached for opposing Radical Reconstruction.

4. The disputed election of 1876 ended Radical Reconstruction.

   a. Social justice for blacks received a setback.

   b. The national commitment to equal opportunity was delayed a hundred years.

VI. A NEW ECONOMY (1876–1910)

A. The industrial development of the United States was encouraged by western expansion.

1. The settlement of the West was aided by the Homestead Act (1862) and the transcontinental railroad (1869).

2. Western industries were based on mining, cattle, and grain.

3. Farmers and ranchers settled the Great Plains.

B. The industrial growth of the United States was greatly expanded.

1. Inventions promoted industrial growth.

2. Raw materials and geographic factors contributed to regional economic diversity.

3. The development of communication and transportation aided the industrial growth of America.

4. New methods of production such as division of labor, standardized parts, the assembly line, and mass production fostered the expansion of industry.

5. Expanding markets at home and abroad encouraged industrial expansion.

6. The development of the steel, mining, electric, petroleum, textile, and food-processing industries characterized the period.

C. Industrialization reflected changing attitudes and conditions.

1. Mechanization and the factory system were introduced.

2. The growth of labor unions resulted from problems caused by industrialization.

3. Social, economic, and political changes became evident.

4. The rise of cities paralleled the industrial growth of America.

5. The need for government intervention increased.

   a. The Sherman (1890) and Clayton (1914) Anti-Trust Acts restricted the power of giant corporations.

   b. Workmen's compensation laws, child labor laws, and regulations on working conditions and minimum wages were part of the congressional reform movement to improve the plight of the working man.

   c. The National Labor Relations Act (1935) was passed by Congress to provide collective bargaining rights for employees.

6. The need for the conservation of natural resources was a result of the continued industrial growth of America.

VII. SOCIETY RESHAPED: THE TWENTIETH CENTURY

A. Immigrants were needed to work in an expanding industrial America.

1. The vast majority of the new immigrants came from eastern and southern Europe.

2. Immigrants came to America to escape religious, political, and economic persecution.

3. Immigrants retained much of their ethnic identity.

B. There were many common problems of urban life, such as sanitation, health, crime, and housing.

C. Reforms were initiated to enrich the lives of the American people.

1. Better treatment for the insane, the temperance movement, and the women's rights movement were important areas of reform.

2. The public school movement provided free public education.

D. **The development of democracy increased the opportunity for people to participate in civic and political life.**

VIII. THE DEVELOPMENT OF THE UNITED STATES AS A WORLD POWER: THE TWENTIETH CENTURY

A. **The new empire period was marked by territorial expansion.**

1. Alaska and Hawaii were purchased to provide increased national security.

2. The Spanish-American War (1898) resulted in the ceding of Puerto Rico, Guam, and the Phillipines to the United States.

3. The Panama Canal was built to protect the new global interests of the United States.

B. **U.S. foreign policy in Central America and South America was marked by new applications of the Monroe Doctrine.**

C. **U.S. relations with Japan and China were dictated by the need for trade and raw materials.**

D. **Events in Europe drew the United States into World War I.**

1. The U.S. entry into World War I (1917) ended U.S. neutrality and dictated new alliances.

2. The results of the war included Wilson's Fourteen Points and the failure of Congress to ratify the League of Nations.

E. **The end to the American economic boom period following World War I foreshadowed the Great Depression of 1929.**

1. Among the basic causes of the depression were the growth of monopolies, the unequal distribution of income, and overspeculation in the stock market.

2. President Franklin Roosevelt initiated the New Deal (1932–38).

   a. The New Deal was characterized by government programs to provide jobs for the unemployed.

   b. The New Deal broadened the scope of the federal government's activities.

   c. The New Deal permanently expanded the role of the presidency.

F. **Events in Europe and Asia foreshadowed World War II.**

1. Europe saw the rise of dictators in Russia, Germany, and Italy.

2. Japanese aggression in Manchuria encouraged further military activity.

3. The results of the war included the occupation of Japan and Germany by the Allies, the economic recovery of Europe (the Marshall Plan), the development of the United Nations, and the emergence of communism as a world threat.

IX. CRISIS IN THE FIFTIES

A. The Korean conflict (1950–52) was a controversial United Nations attempt to stop Communist aggression.

1. The concept of total victory was ruled out in Korea.

2. A search for scapegoats followed the Korean War.

B. The cold war dictated new foreign policy considerations.

1. Russia established an "iron curtain" in Eastern Europe.

2. The United States developed a foreign policy based on the containment of communism.

C. The cold war affected American domestic policy.

1. Senator Joseph McCarthy exploited the climate of fear following the Korean War.

2. The credibility of U.S. technological superiority was shattered by Sputnik.

3. The national frustration over Korea contributed to the nomination and election to the presidency of Dwight D. Eisenhower (1952).

4. The United States protected its global interests by joining the North Atlantic Treaty Organization (NATO).

D. The late 1950s was marked by a national concern with science, labor, and civil rights.

X. THE UNITED STATES SINCE 1960

A. President John F. Kennedy's New Frontier pledged to resolve domestic and cold war problems.

1. The Bay of Pigs invasion of Cuba (1961) proved to be a foreign policy fiasco.

2. The Cuban missile crisis (1962) almost led to a superpower conflict.

3. Russian-U.S. relations improved following the Cuban missile crisis.

4. The space program and civil rights legislation were both expanded.

5. The tragic circumstances of Kennedy's assassination left conflict and doubt.

B. President Lyndon Johnson's Great Society (1964) attempted to continue New Deal type programs.

1. Broad goals encompassed ending poverty, reducing pollution, regenerating urban life, and pursuing civil rights legislation.

2. The escalation in Vietnam shattered the dream of the Great Society.

3. Domestic turmoil and frustration over Vietnam contributed to the election of Richard Nixon as president (1968).

C. President Nixon attempted to unify the nation.

1. The tragedy of Vietnam ended in violence and disillusionment.

2. Inflation and recession became increasingly serious.

3. The Middle East became the second focus of diplomatic troubles.

   a. An Arab oil embargo followed the Arab-Israeli War (1974).

   b. Oil diplomacy redefined American global interests.

4. Nixon established better relations with Russia and China.

5. Watergate (1974), a national tragedy, destroyed the credibility of the American government.

D. The post-Watergate era began in an uncertain climate.

1. President Gerald Ford's political future was damaged by the pardon of Nixon.

2. President Jimmy Carter captured the imagination of the people, but his administration was plagued by serious problems.

   a. The energy crisis continued to affect the U.S. economy.

   b. Israel and Egypt signed a historic peace treaty, but key problems were left unsolved.

   c. The need for alternate sources of energy became a national priority.

   d. Detente with Russia suffered serious setbacks.

   e. Inflation continued to be a major problem affecting the U.S. economy.

E. The Iranian hostage crisis (1979–1981) and the Soviet invasion of Afghanistan (1979) increased the political uncertainties of the decade.

F. Ronald Reagan received an overwhelming electoral mandate from the American people (1980).

1. John Anderson represented a third-party challenge.

2. Double-digit inflation, Afghanistan, Iran, and continued domestic problems were major factors in Carter's defeat.

3. The perceived military and political threat of the Soviet Union influenced the confrontational direction of the Reagan presidency.

G. Reagan ushered in a new conservative approach to government.

1. Reaganomics attempted to dramatically reverse the economic direction of the nation.

   a. Massive federal budget cuts were passed by Congress.

   b. Welfare and traditional entitlement programs were reduced.

   c. Personal and corporate taxes were reduced.

   d. The tax plan was characterized as "trickle-down" economics.

2. The federal deficit escalated dramatically in the 1980s and threatened the economic stability of the United States.

   a. The trade gap widened.

   b. Domestic production in key industrial sectors (automobiles and airlines) was overshadowed by economic advances made by Japan and Germany.

3. The Reagan administration supported a massive build-up in the defense program.

   a. The "Strategic Defense Initiative" (Star Wars) developed a technologically advanced, but expensive, weapons system.

   b. The defense program was a response to the possibility of a Soviet challenge.

4. A pro-business emphasis and a reduction in government regulation of business and industry resulted in the dropping of antitrust suits against ITT and IBM.

   a. Deregulation led to a speculative merger craze.

   b. Multinational corporations influenced domestic government policy.

5. Libya (1981), Nicaragua (1982), and Grenada (1983) represented the aggressive anti-Communist Reagan approach to foreign policy.

   a. Support for the Contras in Nicaragua precipitated the Iran-Contra scandal (1986).

   b. The Sandinistas and Contras agreed to a cease-fire in Nicaragua (1987).

6. The Supreme Court was reshaped by conservative appointments (O'Connor, Scalia, and Kennedy).

H. The Bush presidency (1988–92).

1. Bush received a massive electoral mandate, winning 40 states and 426 electoral votes in defeating Dukakis.

2. Reaganomics was abandoned as Bush attempted to deal with the burgeoning deficit.

   a. The 1990 tax plan raised taxes on gasoline, tobacco, and Medicare; Bush backed away from his campaign promise not to raise taxes.

   b. Defense cuts and military base closings were implemented to reduce the growing deficit.

   c. The minimum wage was increased.

3. The savings and loan bankruptcies (largely due to bad real estate investments) resulted in massive federal intervention to cover the $300 billion debt.

4. The international economic slowdown (1988) affected the U.S. global economy.

   a. The gross domestic product (GDP) dropped significantly.

   b. Unemployment increased in key industrial sectors.

   c. The "Big Three" automakers posted record losses.

   d. Bankruptcies in key industries indicated the widespread economic problems facing the nation in the late 1980s.

   e. The Federal Reserve Board (Fed) lowered interest rates in an attempt to stimulate the economy (1991–92).

5. Bush continued the conservative Supreme Court appointments of the Reagan era by naming Souter and Thomas to the bench.

6. The Bush administration pursued an aggressive foreign policy.

   a. Noriega was removed from Panama through the use of direct U.S. military intervention (1989).

   b. The short-lived and violent Tiananmen Square pro-democracy movement in China (1989) resulted in limited U.S. sanctions against China.

   c. Economic sanctions were lifted against Nicaragua (1991).

   d. Economic sanctions were lifted against South Africa when it shifted away from apartheid (1990).

7. The collapse of Eastern European communism (1990) reduced cold war tensions.

   a. Poland, Czechoslovakia, East Germany, Hungary, and Yugoslavia gained independence.

   b. The change in cold war priorities affected the defense industry.

8. The dissolution of the Soviet Union (1991) resulted in a rethinking of Soviet-American diplomacy.

9. The Bush-Gorbachev summits (1990) officially ended the cold war.

10. The Persian Gulf War (1991) demonstrated the foreign policy resolve of the Bush administration.

   a. Saddam Hussein of Iraq invaded and occupied Kuwait (1990).

   b. The U.N. General Assembly condemned the invasion of Kuwait and authorized joint military contingency plans to liberate Kuwait.

   c. Bush mobilized the military in preparation for a possible invasion of Kuwait, called Operation Desert Shield (1990).

   d. Operation Desert Storm liberated Kuwait and destroyed the military and industrial war capacity of Iraq.

   e. Bush's political popularity was given a tremendous boost by the victory (1992); however, lingering economic and political problems undercut the success.

I. **The election of Bill Clinton (1992) was the result of many, diverse issues.**

   1. The third-party candidacy of Ross Perot provided a focus on the issues during the presidential debates.

   2. The conservative challenge from within the Republican Party polarized the political process over "right-to-life" and other sensitive issues.

   3. The depth of the economic recession and high unemployment, especially in urban areas, resulted in widespread dissatisfaction with the Reagan-Bush agenda.

   4. Bill Clinton's advocacy for change, coupled with the severe economic slowdown and huge deficit, provided the impetus for victory.

      a. Severe economic and social problems confronted the new administration.

      b. The Clinton administration proposed a program of tax cuts in government support programs, as well as tax increases, as a first step in reducing the deficit (1993).

      c. Further military base closings indicated the "new realities" of the defense industry.

WORLD HISTORY

I. EARLY CIVILIZATIONS

A. The Near East

1. The ancient Near East comprised the Tigris and Euphrates Valley, the Fertile Crescent, and the Nile Valley.

2. Cultural contributions associated with the ancient Near East.
   a. The first system of independent states.
   b. The first system of writing (cuneiform and hieroglyphics).
   c. The first massive architectural achievements (ziggurat and pyramid).
   d. The first lasting monotheism.
   e. The beginning of science, mathematics, and astronomy.
   f. The first codification of law.

B. Selected achievements of Mesopotamian civilizations.

1. The Sumerians were the creators of Mesopotamian civilization (3500–3000 B.C.).
   a. Material progress included large-scale irrigation projects, an advanced system of mathematics, and the invention of the wheel.
   b. The ziggurat was the center of community life and served as a temple, storehouse, and treasury.
   c. Sargon established the first empire (c. 2371 B.C.).

2. The Babylonians conquered Sumeria and established a "new empire" (2300–1750 B.C.).
   a. The Code of Hammurabi was the first universal written code that regulated society (1750s B.C.).
   b. Babylonian achievements included a centralized government and advancements in algebra and geometry.

3. The Hittites (2000–1200 B.C.) conquered much of Asia Minor and northern Mesopotamia; a major contribution included the invention of iron smelting, which revolutionized warfare.

4. The Assyrians created an empire based on military superiority, conquest, and terrorism (911–550 B.C.).
   a. Military techniques included siege warfare, intimidation, and the use of iron weapons.
   b. Assyria created a centralized government, a postal service, an extensive library, and a system of highways.

5. The Chaldeans established the "New Babylonian Empire" under Nebuchadnezzar (605–538 B.C.).

    a. They conquered Mesopotamia, Syria, and Palestine.

    b. They developed astrology, astronomy, advanced government bureaucracy, and architectural achievements such as the "Hanging Gardens."

6. The Persians attempted to unify the entire Near East under one rule (500s B.C.).

    a. Persia established an international government.

    b. Zoroastrianism was an ethical religion based on concepts of good and evil.

    c. Persia failed to conquer the Greeks; it was eventually conquered by Alexander the Great (334–331 B.C.).

C. Unique contributions of smaller civilizations of the Near East.

1. The Phoenicians became the first explorers, traders, and colonizers of the ancient world; their civilization reached its peak in 1000 B.C.

    a. They invented the first true alphabet.

    b. They dominated Mediterranean commerce and exported manufactured glass and purple dye (royal purple).

2. The Lydians occupied western Asia Minor (500s B.C.).

    a. Their culture reached its zenith under King Croesus (Golden King).

    b. They were responsible for the first coinage of money.

3. The Israelites established the first lasting monotheism.

    a. Saul established the first kingdom in Palestine (c. 1030–1010 B.C.).

    b. After the death of Solomon (922 B.C.), the Hebrews were divided into two kingdoms (Israel and Judah).

    c. Disunity and conquest resulted in the destruction of Israel (722 B.C.) and Judah (586 B.C.).

    d. The revolt of the Israelites against Rome resulted in the destruction of Jerusalem (A.D. 70) and the forced dispersal of the Jews from Palestine (Jewish Diaspora, c. A.D. 132–135).

D. Egypt established a civilization in the Nile Valley (3000 B.C.).

1. Defensible borders generally spared Egypt from the repeated political disruptions characteristic of Mesopotamia.

2. Egyptian history can be broadly outlined in specific time periods that reflect the changes taking place in Egypt over a 3000-year period.

3. Significant aspects of Egyptian civilization.

   a. Egyptian life was dominated by concerns for the afterlife, religion, and the pharaoh.

   b. Medical advances and specialized surgery were major contributions.

   c. The Egyptians invented a hieroglyphic writing system.

   d. Commerce flourished throughout Arabia, India, and part of Africa.

   e. Agriculture was the basis of the economy.

   f. Monumental architecture reflected remarkable building and engineering feats, as well as mathematical precision.

   g. Annual flooding of the Nile was the basis for the sustained economy; the Nile had an impact on all of Egyptian society.

II. THE GREEK WORLD

A. Greece is a land of mountains separated by deep valleys.

1. Scarcity of good agricultural land encouraged seafaring in eastern Greece.

2. Southern mainland with adequate agricultural resources relied on farming.

B. The Aegean background includes the Minoan and Mycenaean civilizations.

1. The Minoan civilization of Crete (c. 4000–1400 B.C.) based its prosperity on extensive commerce.

2. The Mycenaean civilization (c. 2000–1150 B.C.) developed heavily fortified cities and based prosperity on trade and warfare.

   a. Dorians conquered the Peloponnesus (peninsula of southern Greece) and ushered in a "dark age" characterized by violence and instability (c. 1150–800 B.C.).

   b. Ionia became the birthplace for the Hellenic civilization.

C. Greek civilization was dominated by Athens and Sparta.

1. Direct democracy was established in Athens (c. 507 B.C.).

2. The Age of Pericles (460–429 B.C.) represented the zenith of Athenian society and the height of its democracy.

3. Athens became a world commercial center and cosmopolitan city.

4. Sparta developed a totalitarian and militaristic state dependent on slave labor to sustain its agricultural system.

5. After defeating the Persians, conflict between Athens and Sparta dominated Greek politics.

D. **The Peleponnesian War (431–404 B.C.) devastated both Sparta and Athens (and their Greek city-state allies).**

1. Sparta was victorious but unable to unite the Greek city-states.

2. Greek individualism was a catalyst in the collapse of the Greek city-state alliances.

E. **Alexander the Great (336–323 B.C.) of Macedonia established the Hellenic Age (the fusion of Greek culture with the East).**

1. Alexander conquered Persia, Asia Minor, and Egypt and established a world empire.

2. Bureaucracy replaced the polis (city-state) as the form of government.

F. **Contributions of the Greek world.**

1. Greeks founded most of the major philosophical schools, established the systematic basis for the scientific method, and perfected advances in shipbuilding and commerce.

2. Greek civilization established democracy and a system of law to improve society.

3. In architecture, sculpture, art, literature, and the performing arts, the Greeks were dominant.

III. THE ROMAN WORLD

A. **The Roman Republic (509–27 B.C.) started after Etruscan control was overthrown.**

1. Roman society was divided into the patricians (propertied class), plebeians (main body of Roman citizens), and slaves.

2. Roman government was based on consuls, the Senate, and the Centurial Assembly.

3. The Roman army became the most powerful military organization in the world.

4. After the Punic Wars with Carthage (146 B.C.), Rome emerged as the dominant power in the Mediterranean.

   a. Rome incorporated Greek culture into its empire.

   b. Roman expansion resulted in a world republic.

5. Economic and political decline and repeated civil wars ravaged the Roman Republic.

   a. Caesar was assassinated in 44 B.C.

   b. Augustus became the first emperor of the Roman Empire (27 B.C.).

B. The Roman Empire lasted for five centuries.

1. The *Pax Romana* (Roman peace) was two centuries without a major war (27 B.C.–c. A.D. 180).

2. By the end of the second century A.D., Rome was in economic and political decline, which weakened the empire.

3. Constantine attempted to stem the tide.

   a. The empire split into the Western and Eastern Roman Empire.

   b. Barbarian invasions by the Goths, Vandals, and Huns devastated Rome, and it fell in A.D. 476.

   c. The Eastern Roman Empire at Constantinople remained intact; Byzantium survived until 1453.

4. Causes for the fall of Rome.

   a. The immediate cause was continuous barbaric invasion.

   b. Internal factors included political instability, decreasing farm production, inflation, excessive taxation, and the decline of the military, including the use of mercenaries.

   c. The rise of Christianity divided the empire.

C. Roman contributions to the western world.

1. Its greatest contribution was in the field of law.

2. Romans revolutionized building construction, engineering, and road construction (200,000 miles of roads).

3. Roman civilization passed on monumental architecture (the Colosseum, aqueducts, etc.)

4. The Romans continued the Greek tradition in literature, art, sculpture, and the humanities.

IV. THE RISE OF CHRISTIANITY

A. Basic doctrines.

1. Christianity began with the teachings of Jesus of Nazareth (compassion for the poor and downtrodden).

2. It emphasized the *Holy Bible* as the word of God, the sacraments as the instruments of God's grace, and the importance of a moral life for salvation.

3. Paul the Apostle was responsible for the spread of Christian theology and the resulting response from the Roman Empire.

4. St. Augustine (A.D. 354–430) became the first great Christian philosopher; he wrote *Confessions* and *City of God*.

B. Reasons for the spread of Christianity (the Roman period).

1. Individual conviction in one's beliefs (solidarity) had grown during the Roman persecution period.

2. The efficiency and organization of the early church administration.

3. Doctrines that stressed equality and and immortality.

4. The conversion of Constantine to Christianity (A.D. 313).

5. The establishment of Christianity as the official Roman religion (A.D. 380).

6. The establishment of the supremacy of the pope at the time imperial Rome was disintegrating.

V. THE EARLY BYZANTINE CIVILIZATION

A. Constantine established a "New Rome" at Constantinople in A.D. 330.

1. Constantinople was strategically located, had excellent defensible borders, and was a crossroads of world trade.

2. With the fall of Rome (A.D. 476), the Eastern Roman Empire became known as the Byzantine Empire.

B. Reasons for the Byzantine Empire's success (the empire lasted for 1000 years).

1. Economic prosperity was based on domination of the commercial trade routes controlled by Constantinople and a monopoly of the silk trade.

2. The Byzantines made excellent use of diplomacy to avoid invasions and they were geographically distant from the tribes who sacked Rome.

3. Codification of Roman law by Justinian (A.D. 528–565) strengthened the bureaucracy.

4. Constantinople was a fortress city with excellent defensible borders.

C. Reasons for the decline of the Byzantine Empire.

1. Its geographic proximity to the Arabs, Slavs, and Seljuk Turks, all of whom were becoming more powerful.

2. The loss of commercial dominance over the Italians.

3. Religious controversy with the west and a subsequent split with the Roman Catholic Church.

4. The sack of Constantinople during the fourth Crusade.

5. The fall of Constantinople (1453) marked the end of the Byzantine Empire.

D. Achievements of the Byzantine Empire.

1. It preserved the heritage of Greco-Roman civilization while the west was culturally stagnant.

2. It spread civilization to all of eastern Europe.

3. It preserved the Eastern Orthodox Church.

4. Its economic strength was based on the stability of its money economy.

VI. THE RISE OF ISLAM

A. Mohammed (A.D. 570–632) encouraged the expansion of the Islamic world; after Mohammed's death, Islam rapidly expanded and spread the word of Allah.

1. Expansion included most of the Byzantine Empire, Persia, North Africa, and Spain.

   a. The Battle of Tours (A.D. 732) resulted in Franks halting Moslem expansion in Europe.

   b. Moslem Spain lasted from A.D. 711 to 1031.

2. Military expansion also served as a vehicle for cultural exchange between the Arab and western worlds.

B. Moslem civilization.

1. Government was a theocracy based on Islamic law.

2. The economy was based on Moslem control of Near East trade routes.

3. Moslem culture excelled in mathematics, medicine, philosophy, literature and architecture; Europe at the same time was stagnant and backward.

4. The *Koran* became the center for Islamic moral and ethical conduct.

VII. THE EARLY MIDDLE AGES

A. The destruction of Rome resulted in a period of decline (500–800, the Dark Ages).

B. The Franks became the dominant Germanic tribe.

1. Clovis (481–511) was converted to Christianity.

2. Domestic feuds and civil war broke out among the Merovingians (561).

   a. Political power shifted away from the monarch.

   b. Charles Martel halted Moslem advance into Europe at the Battle of Tours (732), which had a lasting impact on the development of western civilization.

C. The Carolingians replaced the Franks as legitimate rulers.

1. Pepin the Short (747–768), appointed by the pope as king, established the Papal States on former Byzantine lands.

2. Charlemagne (768–814) dominated the political structure of the early Middle Ages.

    a. He was crowned "Emperor of the Romans" by Pope Leo in 800 and had a major impact on the history of Europe.

    b. He revived the concept of the Holy Roman Empire and established authority over secular rulers.

    c. His empire included most of the former Roman Empire and additional Germanic lands betwen the Rhine and Elbe Rivers.

    d. The Carolingian Renaissance resulted in the establishment of a palace academy with a prescribed academic curriculum.

3. The Frankish system of inheritance hastened the dissolution of the Frankish Empire.

    a. The Treaty of Verdun (843) divided Charlemagne's empire among his three grandsons.

    b. Carolingian rule ended in the tenth century because of the decline in central authority and the invasions of the Scandinavian tribes.

D. The Viking (Norse) invasions pillaged the coasts of Europe in the eighth century.

1. The Danes were responsible for the major invasions of England.

2. Alfred the Great (871–99) established the English kingdom after stemming the Danish invasions.

3. In France, the Carolingian king was forced to cede Normandy to the Vikings.

E. Society in the Middle Ages was based on the feudal system.

1. Under feudalism, political authority was dominated by the landed nobility.

    a. A feudal contract provided land in exchange for personal service to the king.

    b. The law of primogeniture gave all property to the eldest son.

    c. The church enjoyed a favorable position under feudalism and became a major landholder.

2. Manorialism was the agricultural organization and economic foundation of feudalism.

    a. Commerce was virtually nonexistent; a purely agricultural economy prevailed.

    b. The lord of the manor exercised full political, judicial, and economic control over the manor, including the serfs.

VIII. THE LATER MIDDLE AGES (c. 1000–1500)

A. The rise of feudal monarchs resulted in the development of the nation-states of France.

1. Hugh Capet (987–96) established Capetian rule in France that lasted for 300 years.

2. By the early thirteenth century, royal authority had expanded and France had become a European power.

3. Conflicts with the pope over the extent of religious rule resulted in an increase in the authority of the monarch.

4. The Hundred Years War (1138–1453) between England and France resulted in the English being driven out of most of France.

B. The Norman Conquest had a profound impact on the development of the culture, language, and judicial system of England.

1. The Battle of Hastings (1066) ended Anglo-Saxon rule in England.

2. By the twelfth century, English common law was firmly established.

3. The Magna Carta (1215) limited the power of the king. It is the most important document in English constitutional law.

4. By the fourteenth century, the English Parliament was firmly established.

   a. Parliament gained power at the expense of the king.

   b. The House of Lords (titled nobility) and the House of Commons (gentry and middle classes) composed Parliament.

5. The War of the Roses (1455–85) was fought over succession to the throne.

   a. The House of Lancaster crushed the House of York.

   b. Henry VII established the Tudor dynasty in England.

C. Spain and Portugal during the later Middle Ages.

1. The *Reconquista* reestablished Christian control over Moslem Spain in 1492.

   a. The Spanish state was marked by strong absolutist rule.

   b. The Catholic Church had a dominant role.

   c. The Jews were officially expelled from Spain (1492) and the Inquisition brutally crushed religious and political opposition.

2. The Portuguese monarch established royal authority at the expense of the nobility.

   a. The Catholic Church had a dominant role.

   b. The monarch instituted inquisitions and also expelled the Jews.

D. The Holy Roman Empire during the late Middle Ages.

1. The pope was dominant in religious matters and the king in secular matters.

    a. Germany consisted of kingdoms, dukedoms, and smaller princely states.

    b. Frederick Barbarossa (1152–90) called the union of Germany and Italy the Holy Roman Empire; he stated that the king's authority was higher than that of the pope.

2. A continuing power struggle with the pope resulted in the further decentralization of the Germanic states.

3. Conflict between the papacy and the secular ruler during the late Middle Ages.

    a. The papacy was dominated by a series of Holy Roman emperors from c. 962–1049.

    b. Under Pope Leo IX (1049–54), the independence of the papacy was established.

E. Characteristics of medieval civilization during the late Middle Ages.

1. Society was based on a strict class division: clergy and nobility were the privileged class, peasants and artisans were the work force, and serfs were tied to the land.

2. The decline of feudalism and manorialism was evident by the twelfth century and completed by the sixteenth century.

3. The commercial revival led to the rise of towns.

    a. A true middle class emerged.

    b. Economic activities in the towns were supervised by the guild system (merchant and craft guilds).

    c. Mediterranean commerce was dominated by the Venetians and Genoans.

    d. The Crusades led to the revival of international trade; money became the primary unit of exchange.

4. Education stressed the liberal arts.

    a. Theology was considered the "queen" of the sciences.

    b. Universities were created in Paris, Oxford, and Cambridge during the eleventh and twelfth centuries.

    c. Latin was the language of intellectual Europe; vernacular was used by the twelfth century.

5. Philosophy (Scholasticism) dealt with the consistency of faith and reason; realism and nominalism were rival points of view.

    a. Realism (Plato's view): reality consists of ideas (universals) which exist in the mind independent of sensory powers of perception.

    b. Nominalism: ideas (universals) are just symbols or names for objects; only perceived objects are real, and they exist independent of the mind.

6. Architecture was dominated by the Romanesque (eleventh to twelfth century) and Gothic (thirteenth to fifteenth century) styles.

F. Historical interpretations of the Middle Ages.

1. The Middle Ages were a period of transition between ancient and modern Europe.

2. The Middle Ages were unique with a distinctive culture.

IX. THE RENAISSANCE (c. 1350–1600)

A. The Renaissance began in Italy during the fourteenth century.

1. Conflicts between the papacy and the Holy Roman Empire in the thirteenth and fourteenth centuries resulted in regional autonomy for the Italian city-states.

2. The heritage of the Greek and Roman civilizations contributed to the development of the Italian Renaissance.

3. The Crusades focused attention eastward (on Greece and the Near East).

4. By the fourteenth century, the move toward secularization was predominant.

B. Literature and philosophy reflected the new secular trends.

1. Humanism stressed the importance of the individual.

2. Neoplatonism replaced Scholasticism as the dominant philosophy.

3. Machiavelli's *The Prince* stressed that "the ends justify the means" as a political philosophy.

4. The influence of the "classical" arts was strong, and a new emphasis was placed on science.

C. The Renaissance spread throughout Europe.

1. The Renaissance of northern Europe emphasized the teachings of Christianity and placed less reliance on humanism.

2. The French Renaissance reflected a democratic realism.

3. The English Renaissance did not flower until the Elizabethan Age.

D. **General characteristics of the Renaissance**

1. The emphasis was on man rather than God.

2. There was a reawakening or rebirth of classical models.

3. The ideal of the "universal man" was widely held.

X. THE REFORMATION

A. **The Protestant Reformation and the development of western civilization.**

1. Reasons for the Reformation.

   a. A dissatisfaction with church ritual and Latin overtones.

   b. Humanism emphasized man's needs and concerns.

   c. The printing press allowed mass communication.

2. Also, Martin Luther (1483–1546) and the right of the pope to grant indulgences was a primary cause.

   a. Luther's *Ninety-five Theses* served as a catalyst in starting the Reformation.

   b. Lutheranism allowed for a state church system controlled by individual German princes.

   c. The Peace of Augsburg (1555) officially recognized Lutheranism but allowed Catholic princes to support Catholicism.

3. Calvinism made Protestantism an international movement.

   a. The doctrine of predestination was central to Calvinistic belief.

   b. Calvinism became a revolutionary anti-Catholic movement.

4. The Act of Supremacy (1534) marked the beginning of the English Reformation.

   a. The king of England became the head of the church.

   b. The pope's refusal to annul the marriage of Henry VIII to Catherine of Aragon initiated the break.

   c. Elizabeth I (1558–1603) firmly established Protestantism in England and established the Anglican Church.

B. **The Counter Reformation (Catholic Reformation) attempted to halt the spread of Protestantism.**

1. The Jesuits (Society of Jesus) became the official Catholic response to the Reformation; Jesuits also initiated missionary and educational endeavors.

2. The Council of Trent (1545–63) defined the doctrines of Catholicism and reinforced papal authority.

C. Effects of the Reformation.

1. The medieval political unity of Europe was replaced by the spirit of modern nationalism.

2. The authority of the state was strengthened.

3. The middle class was strengthened.

4. Calvinism gave capitalism its psychological base.

5. Religious wars reflected the fervor of the times.

XI. THE SIXTEENTH AND SEVENTEENTH CENTURY RELIGIOUS AND DYNASTIC WARS

A. Spain and the Holy Roman Empire.

1. Spain was the leading nation in sixteenth century Europe.

2. Charles V in 1556 abdicated and divided the Spanish and Austrian Hapsburg dynasties.

3. The defeat of the Spanish Armada (1588) ended Spanish attempts to invade England.

   a. The defeat marked the beginning of Spain's decline in Europe.

   b. England became a dominant sea power.

   c. It ensured the success of the Dutch revolt against Spanish rule.

B. France as a world power in the sixteenth century.

1. The French religious wars (1562–98) were fought between the Catholics and the Huguenots for the control of France.

2. Henry IV (1589–1610), the first Bourbon ruler, reestablished royal authority.

3. The Edict of Nantes (1598) gave the Huguenots political and religious freedom.

C. England emerged as a dominant world power in the seventeenth century.

1. Henry VIII (1509–47) promoted the concept of a balanced Europe as England gained power in foreign affairs.

2. Under Elizabeth I (1558–1603), England emerged as a major European power.

3. James I (1603–25) began the colonization of North America in the seventeenth century.

4. Charles I (1625–49) failed to achieve internal stability; the Puritan revolution (1642–49) marked civil strife in England.

D. **The Thirty Years War (1618–48) marked the culmination of religious and political wars in Europe.**

1. The war involved most major European powers and resulted in the devastation of Germany.

2. The Peace of Westphalia (1648) provided new political boundaries and established Calvinism as a recognized religion.

   a. Germany was divided into Protestant and Catholic areas.

   b. The Holy Roman Empire was an empty shell of 300 autonomous states.

   c. Dutch independence was recognized.

3. France replaced Spain as the leading nation in Europe.

E. **The intellectual development of the early modern period.**

1. The scientific revolution was founded on the work of Copernicus, Galileo, and Newton.

2. The culture of the period was characterized by the Baroque style.

XII. **EUROPEAN ABSOLUTISM AND POWER POLITICS (1650–1715)**

A. **The philosophy of absolutism was based on the concept of total obedience to the sovereign and promoted the concept of the "divine right of kings."**

B. **Absolutism in France resulted in the restoration of royal power.**

1. Cardinal Richelieu was the "architect" of absolutist politics.

2. Louis XIV (1643–1715) was the quintessential example of absolutism.

   a. The palace of Versailles was a symbol of the classic age of France.

   b. Louis XIV revoked the Edict of Nantes.

   c. In foreign policy, Louis XIV attempted to end Hapsburg encirclement and secure "natural boundaries" for France.

   d. The French suffered territorial and political losses after being defeated by the English.

C. **The failure of absolutism in England.**

1. The power struggle between the Parliament and the crown dominated seventeenth century politics.

2. The English civil war (1642–49) was fought over religious and constitutional issues; the Royalists lost political power.

3. During the Commonwealth period (1649–60), England became a republic.

    a. Oliver Cromwell ruled as a dictator and abolished the monarchy and the House of Lords.

    b. Shortly after the death of Cromwell (1658), the monarchy was restored.

4. During the Restoration Era (1660–88), Stuart rule was restored, the Anglican Church regained power, and Puritanism was repressed.

5. The Glorious Revolution (1688–89) established both a constitutional monarchy in England and the supremacy of Parliament.

D. Absolutism in Russia began with Ivan the Terrible.

1. The Romanov dynasty (1613) provided a hereditary link to the monarchy until 1917.

2. Peter the Great (1689–1725) made the power of the czar absolute.

    a. Peter attempted to "westernize" Russia.

    b. Peter obtained a "window on the sea" by fighting a successful war with Sweden, but he failed in attempts to garner territory on the Black Sea from the Ottoman Turks.

E. Culture in the age of absolutism.

1. The Baroque style was dominant in architecture, sculpture, painting, and music.

2. Neoclassicism developed in literature.

3. The scientific revolution resulted in the invention of the thermostat, the barometer, and the reflecting telescope and microscope, as well as new ideas in science (Newton) and philosophy (Locke).

XIII. THE AGE OF ENLIGHTENMENT (1700–89)

A. Philosophy influenced by the Age of Reason.

1. Christianity and church dogma were questioned.

2. The proper function of government was defined by Voltaire, Montesquieu, Locke, and Rousseau. Their ideas led to the philosophical bases for the American and French Revolutions.

3. In economics, the doctrine of "laissez faire" stood in opposition to regulated trade.

4. Adam Smith wrote the *Wealth of Nations* (1776) and advocated manufacturing as the true source of a nation's wealth.

B. Enlightened despotism grew out of the earlier absolutism of Louis XIV and Peter the Great; it advocated limited responsibility to God and church.

C. The culture of the eighteenth century was dominated by Neoclassicism.

1. There was an attempt to revive the classic style and form of Greece and Rome.

2. In literature, the novel was the outcome; in architecture, the Rococo style was dominant.

3. In music, Bach, Handel, and Haydn emphasized the Baroque's religious themes.

XIV. THE FRENCH REVOLUTION AND NAPOLEON

A. Background to the French Revolution.

1. An inequitable class structure was the basic cause of the revolution.

2. A disorganized legal system and no representative assembly added to the problems of the government.

3. Enlightenment philosophy influenced the middle class.

4. The bankruptcy of the French treasury was the immediate cause of the revolution.

a. The nobility resisted expanded taxation plans.

b. The failure of the monarchy led to violent revolution.

5. The "Declaration of the Rights of Man and Citizen" defined enlightenment concepts of national law and the sovereignty of the people.

6. The first French Republic (1792–1804) was marked by the violence of the Reign of Terror (1793–94) and the rise of Napoleon.

B. Napoleon and the First Empire (1804–15).

1. Domestic reforms resulted in a more efficient government.

a. No tax exemptions were allowed for lineage, and government promotion was based on ability.

b. The Code of Napoleon modernized French law (equality before the law).

2. International relations placed France against Europe.

    a. Napoleon won territory from the Holy Roman Empire and forced Spain to cede the Louisiana territory to France.

    b. By 1807, the Holy Roman Empire was disbanded as France gained territory from Prussia and Poland.

    c. The "continental system" was a failed French attempt to close the continent to British trade in hopes of destroying the British economy.

    d. Napoleon's disastrous invasion of Russia (1812) marked the beginning of the end for Napoleon.

    e. The Battle of Waterloo (1815) ended in defeat for Napoleon and ended the French Empire. Napoleon was permanently exiled to St. Helena.

XV. REACTION, ROMANTICISM, AND REVOLUTION (1815–48)

A. The Congress of Vienna (1815) attempted to balance the powerful states of Europe.

1. The Congress ignored the legitimacy of the nationalistic aspirations of the European peoples.

2. Enforcement of the settlement was predicated on international agreements designed to preserve the status quo.

3. The Congress of Verona (1822) ended the congress system and allowed European powers to be guided by self-interest.

B. Romanticism raised basic questions about the nature of truth.

1. Unlike the Enlightenment, Romanticism encouraged a Gothic revival and rejected the rigid limitations of Neoclassicism.

2. Politically, Romanticism reinforced nationalistic philosophy and pursued the policy of self-determination.

C. The revolutionary movements of 1820, 1830, and 1848 resulted in territorial changes, liberal political reforms, and the abolition of serfdom.

1. The revolutions of 1848 were the precursor to future class warfare issues in Europe.

2. A consequence of the 1848 revolutions included the emergent voice of militant socialism. This would have profound effects on the political structure of Europe.

XVI. THE IMPACT OF THE INDUSTRIAL REVOLUTION ON EUROPE.

A. The causes of the industrial revolution.

1. The scientific revolution brought about new mechanical inventions.

2. The availability of investment capital and the rise of the middle class provided an economic base.

3. Conditions in England favored industrialization.

   a. The cotton textile industry was well established.

   b. Britain was a colonial and maritime power and was able to easily ship products.

   c. Coal, iron, and a plentiful supply of cheap labor were available.

B. The results of the industrial revolution.

1. A dramatic increase in productivity and the rise of the factory system.

2. Demographic changes (from rural to urban centers).

3. The division of society into defined classes (propertied and nonpropertied).

4. The development of modern capitalism (profits linked to the manufacturing of products).

C. The intellectual response to the industrial revolution.

1. The classical economists advanced the theory of laissez faire (limited government intervention in business affairs).

2. Thomas Malthus (1766–1834) theorized that population growth would far outstrip food production.

3. The revolutionary socialism of Karl Marx advocated a violent overthrow of the present economic system.

   a. History was seen as a class struggle between the exploiters (bourgeoisie) and the exploited (proletariat).

   b. *The Communist Manifesto* (1848), written by Marx and Friedrich Engels, advanced the theories of modern scientific socialism.

XVII. POLITICAL CHANGES IN EUROPE (1848–1917)

A. Great Britain passed a series of notable reforms to address some of the problems associated with a changing society.

1. Slavery was abolished throughout the British Empire (1836); the Corn Laws (high protective tariffs) were repealed (1846); and the middle class obtained voting rights.

2. By the 1850s, the Whig and Tory parties became the Liberal and Conservative parties.

3. The achievements of Disraeli (leader of Conservative Party).

   a. Political suffrage was extended (1867), and the first comprehensive public health act was passed (1875).

   b. In foreign policy, imperialistic practices enabled Britain to acquire the Suez Canal, control most of India and the surrounding areas of the Middle East, and maintain a dominant territorial position in Africa.

   c. The British imperial system was firmly established.

4. The achievements of Gladstone (leader of the Liberal Party).

   a. Political reforms continued in the areas of civil service (1870), secret balloting (1872), and universal manhood suffrage (1884).

   b. He supported an anti-imperialistic foreign policy.

   c. The Irish Question dominated the Gladstone period; Gladstone backed Irish home rule, which forced his resignation (1894).

5. During the period 1895–1904, the Conservatives were in power and were concerned with foreign affairs, primarily with the Boer War (1899–1902) in South Africa.

6. The Liberals regained power (1905–14).

   a. They continued with social reforms (unemployment insurance and old age pensions).

   b. The House of Commons was given authority in the new governmental structure.

B. **France pursued an aggressive, but ill-fated foreign policy during the latter part of the nineteenth century.**

1. The Second French Empire (1852–1870) placed Louis Napoleon on the throne; necessary social reforms were enacted.

   a. France pursued an aggressive foreign policy in the Crimea and Mexico.

   b. Costly intervention in Mexico resulted in the loss of international prestige.

   c. The Franco-Prussian War (1870–71) was a disaster for France and led to the collapse of the government.

2. The Third French Republic (1870–1940).

   a. France was forced to cede Alsace and part of Lorraine to Germany.

   b. The 1880s and 1890s were a time of crisis; the Dreyfus affair (1894–1906) characterized the internal problems of France.

C. **Italy became a kingdom in 1861 after Sicily, Naples, and the Papal States were annexed.**

1. Parliamentary government was established by 1878.

2. A lack of natural resources (coal and iron) restricted economic growth and led to depressed economic conditions.

3. By the turn of the twentieth century, Italy embarked on a policy of imperialism in northern Africa.

D. Germany embarked on a program of unification in the middle of the nineteenth century and expansion in the first half of the twentieth century.

1. Bismarck ended Austrian domination of the German Confederation of States.

2. The Franco-Prussian War (1870–71) resulted in territorial gains at the expense of France and led to German unification.

3. The German Empire (1871–1918), also called the government of the Second Reich, was dominated by Bismarck.

   a. Bismarck's foreign policy was aimed at isolating France as a European military power.

   b. Germany joined in a series of alliances to protect its territorial interests.

   c. By the beginning of the twentieth century, isolating France from Europe was reversed as France joined the Triple Entente (1907).

E. The dual monarchy of Austria-Hungary was established in 1867, but conflicting national groups vied for power.

1. The disastrous defeat during the Austro-Prussian War (1866), magnified the internal weakness of the Hapsburg monarchy.

2. By the end of the century, nationalist movements against German rule were evident.

3. By 1914, nationalism in Austria-Hungary would be an immediate cause of World War I.

F. Russian foreign policy during the last quarter of the nineteenth century was directed at reversing the negative results of the Crimean War.

1. The Russo-Turkish War (1877–78) was a decisive Russian victory, but the Congress of Berlin voided Russian gains.

2. The domestic policy of Alexander II resulted in the emancipation of the serfs, but growing opposition to his programs brought on radical terrorism.

   a. The position of the peasant masses in the late 1880s was becoming desperate because of high taxes and forced industrialization of the economy.

   b. Alexander III (1881–94) ruled on the basis of "autocracy, orthodoxy, and Russification."

3. Nicholas II (1894–1917), the last czar, attempted the rapid industrialization of the backward Russian state.

   a. Discontent and political opposition were crystallized in the formation of the Bolshevik Party led by Vladimir Lenin.

   b. The Russo-Japanese War (1904–05) resulted in a disastrous Russian defeat and the escalation of popular discontent on the domestic front.

   c. The Revolution of 1905 was a "dress rehearsal" for the 1917 revolution as violence erupted.

   d. General strikes paralyzed the government and forced Nicholas II to rely on a weak legislature for political survival (1906–16).

   e. The evil monk Rasputin exerted an undue influence on the monarchy and symbolized its political deterioration.

   f. As political and social unrest mounted, the onset of World War I temporarily united the Russian people behind Czar Nicholas II.

XVIII. WORLD WAR I

A. The background causes of World War I included an intricate alliance system at a time when international pressures were dangerously balanced.

1. The immediate cause was extreme nationalism.

   a. The desire for political independence was acute in the Balkans.

   b. France desired a war to avenge the loss of Alsace-Lorraine.

2. The colonial rivalry over raw materials between France and Germany heightened political tension.

3. Europe was divided into rival alliances.

   a. The Triple Alliance: Germany, Austria-Hungary, and Italy.

   b. The Triple Entente: France, Russia, and Great Britain.

4. The increased military preparedness of alliance countries was a significant factor.

5. Secret diplomacy and power politics created an atmosphere of suspicion, fear, and mutual mistrust.

B. The outbreak of World War I.

1. The assassination of Archduke Ferdinand, heir to the Austrian-Hungarian throne, by a Serbian terrorist (1914) triggered the alliance system.

2. The belligerents (as of 1914) in the war included the Allies (Great Britain, Italy, France, Russia, and Serbia) and the Central Powers (Germany, Austria-Hungary, Turkey, and Bulgaria).

3. The Allied strategy was to force Germany to fight a two-front war; the German plan was to defeat France before a two-front war was in place.

4. The United States entered the war as a result of German unrestricted submarine warfare (1917).

5. The Bolshevik Revolution (1917) resulted in a Russian armistice with Germany, the overthrow of the provisional government, and the death of Nicholas II and his family.

C. **The Paris Peace Conference (1919) was dominated by the Big Three (Wilson, Clemenceau, and George).**

1. Wilson's idealistic Fourteen Points incorporated a League of Nations.

2. The Treaty of Versailles resulted in a harsh peace for Germany.

   a. Germany lost all of its colonies and "spheres of influence."

   b. Demilitarization of the Rhineland restricted the German military.

   c. Germany was forced to pay huge reparations.

   d. Germany was forced to admit sole responsibility for starting World War I.

3. The failure of the United States to sign the Treaty of Versailles or join the League of Nations doomed the League to failure.

XIX. THE RISE OF COMMUNIST RUSSIA

A. **The Bolsheviks seized control of the central government (1917).**

1. Spontaneous food riots, a general strike of factory workers, and the mutiny of the armed forces forced Nicholas II to abdicate.

2. The Great Civil War (1918–20) consolidated Soviet rule and resulted in a victory for the Red Army.

B. **The early phase of Communist political domination, known as "war communism," resulted in the nationalization of banks, factories, and all private property.**

C. **The emergence of the Soviet Union under Joseph Stalin continued with forced industrialization and the collectivization of all farmland.**

1. In domestic policy, Stalin created a totalitarian society and purged all opposition.

2. In foreign policy, Stalin failed to obtain European collective security against emergent Nazi Germany and instead signed a neutrality pact with Hitler in 1939.

XX. THE RISE OF NAZI GERMANY

A. **The ideology of fascism used elaborate propaganda and complete censorship to maintain power; it also espoused racial intolerance and anti-Semitism as political philosophies.**

B. **Germany under the Weimar Republic (1918–33) was unable to maintain democratic institutions.**

   1. Economic hard times were caused by reparations and world inflation (1922–23) that resulted in the undermining of the middle class.

   2. Adolph Hitler used political, economic, and social unrest to attempt an unsuccessful takeover of the government (the Beer Hall Putsch).

      a. Hitler wrote *Mein Kampf* (1923) while in jail, which outlined the future course of the German Republic.

      b. Hitler based his appeal on the restoration of the German ego as well as a plan to end the severe economic conditions in Germany.

      c. Hitler's anti-Semitism and anticommunism appealed to the professional classes and the masses.

C. **The Nazi Party controlled the Reichstag (1932) and proceeded to strip the legislature of all political power (late 1930s).**

   1. Hitler established the Third Reich and began a policy of systematic destruction of all political enemies.

   2. Capitalism and private property were encouraged; unemployment was virtually eliminated.

   3. Socially, concepts of racial superiority and extreme anti-Semitism dominated Nazi dogma.

D. **Hitler attempted to reverse the restrictions imposed by the Treaty of Versailles.**

   1. Hitler's policies attempted to incorporate all German people into the Third Reich.

   2. Hitler pursued a program of obtaining territorial "living space" for the expanding German population.

   3. The Rome-Berlin Axis (1936) and the Rome-Berlin-Tokyo Axis (1940) were the bases for Hitler's military alliances.

XXI. THE RISE OF FASCIST ITALY

A. **Benito Mussolini's rise to power utilized squads of Black Shirts to attack Socialists and Communists.**

B. **The March on Rome established fascism in Italy, and by 1926 the Fascists constituted a one-party dictatorship.**

C. **The Mussolini government intensified militarism and attempted to make Italy a world power.**

   1. The policy of *Mare Nostrum* (Our Sea) attempted to make the Mediterranean an Italian sea.

   2. The policy of imperialistic expansion resulted in the invasion of Ethiopia (1935).

   3. The alliance with Germany was the key to foreign policy.

   4. Italy withdrew from the League of Nations (1937).

XXII. THE EUROPEAN DEMOCRACIES BETWEEN THE TWO WORLD WARS

A. **Great Britain's traditional prosperity, dependent on foreign trade, was undermined by the commercial ascendancy of the United States and Japan.**

   1. Unemployment became the most important problem in Britain prior to the outbreak of World War II.

   2. The partition of Ireland (1920) failed to resolve the Irish Question.

   3. British foreign policy was characterized by pacifism.

      a. Britain refused to intervene in preventing the Italian invasion of Ethiopia.

      b. Prime Minister Neville Chamberlain pursued a policy of appeasement with Hitler.

      c. Hitler's occuption of Czechoslovakia and Mussolini's occupation of Albania demonstrated the failed policy of appeasement.

B. **France's postwar problems were tied to the world economic crisis and the failure of Germany to pay reparations.**

   1. The world depression ended the slim chance of French prosperity and resulted in increased unemployment and a large national debt.

   2. The political instability of France was marked by the split between the extreme right and extreme left.

   3. The Popular Front (1936–38) initiated New Deal-type reforms and averted civil unrest.

   4. French foreign policy was predicated on an elaborate alliance system designed to maintain the status quo in Europe.

XXIII. THE CATACLYSM OF WORLD WAR II

A. The course of the war.

1. The Nazi Blitzkrieg (lightning war) devasted Europe (1939–40).

   a. By 1941, Poland, Denmark, Norway, the Netherlands, Belgium, Luxembourg, France, and Greece were defeated.

   b. The Battle of Britain (1940) was a critical early turning point in the war.

   c. Hitler's invasion of Russia was a military blunder (1941).

2. The U.S. became the "Arsenal of Democracy" of the western world.

   a. The U.S. Neutrality Act (1939) repealed the arms embargo and allowed the sale of war materiel on a "cash-and-carry" basis.

   b. The Lend-Lease Act (1941) marked the official abandonment of neutrality.

   c. The Japanese surprise attack on Pearl Harbor (December 7, 1941) resulted in a U.S. declaration of war against Japan; the allied Germany and Italy declared war on the United States (December 11, 1941).

   d. The industrial might of the United States turned the tide of the war against the Axis powers.

3. The Battle of Stalingrad and the Soviet counteroffensive marked the turning point of the war in Europe.

4. The Battle of Germany (1945), a combined Soviet offensive from the east and a U.S. and British offensive from the west, resulted in German surrender.

5. Japan was defeated in the Pacific.

   a. The Battle of Midway (1942) was the turning point in the Pacific.

   b. The U.S. policy of "island hopping" isolated the Japanese; the Battle of Okinawa (1945) prepared the way for the aerial onslaught on the mainland.

   c. President Truman ordered the atomic bombing of Hiroshima and Nagasaki; Japan surrenders, ending World War II.

B. Making peace.

1. The Yalta Conference accepted the principle of a divided Germany.

   a. Harsh criticism of the Yalta agreements centered on political charges that the United States allowed the Soviet Union to gain too much power in eastern Europe.

   b. Franklin Roosevelt considered concessions a necessary incentive to gain Russian support for the expected invasion of Japan.

2. The Potsdam Conference (1945) agreed to German disarmament, demilitarization, and the punishment of war criminals.

3. The peace settlement resulted in the revision of the territorial map of Europe.

   a. Italy, Romania, Hungary, Bulgaria, Finland, Germany, and Japan lost territory.

   b. Germany was divided into four occupation zones.

   c. Japan was reduced to its home islands.

   d. The United States and the Soviet Union emerged as major world powers.

XXIV. POLITICAL DEVELOPMENTS IN ENGLAND AND FRANCE (1945–92)

A. Britain following World War II.

1. The Labor and the Conservative Parties accepted sweeping social and political reforms.

   a. Major industries were nationalized (railroads, airlines, etc.)

   b. A comprehensive welfare state approach was established.

   c. The loss of colonial possessions reflected new world realities.
      (1) India (1947), Palestine (1948), and Burma (1947) gained political independence.
      (2) The Suez Crisis (1956) toppled the Conservative government.
      (3) The end to colonial rule in the 1960s resulted in increased immigration to Britain and a subsequent strain on the economic and social system.

   d. Continuing tension in Northern Ireland resulted in direct British rule (1972) and increased political problems.

   e. The OPEC oil embargo (1973) forced Britain to develop its oil and gas reserves, especially in the North Sea.

2. The return of the Conservative Party under Margaret Thatcher (1979–90) was marked by strong economic reforms and renewed political leadership in world affairs.

   a. New economic programs dramatically reduced the double-digit inflation of the 1970s.

   b. The Falklands Islands War (1982) with Argentina strengthened Britain's foreign policy position.

   c. A move away from the nationalization of the industrial complex changed the economic direction of Britain.

   d. Hong Kong was returned to China (actual transfer in 1997).

   e. NATO missile deployment in Europe was opposed.

   f. An economic austerity program was instituted to combat the effects of decolonization, slow economic growth, high unemployment, and a weak economy.

   g. Thatcher's economic revitalization produced long-term economic changes.

3. The economic slowdown of the 1980s, the uneven distribution of economic prosperity, and renewed inflation forced Thatcher from government (1990) as Britain faced the economic uncertainties of the early 1990s.

B. France following World War II.

1. The fall of the Fourth Republic (1946–58) was attributed to disastrous foreign policy decisions.

   a. The decisions involved Vietnam (1946–54), the Suez Crisis (1956), and Algeria.

   b. The Marshall Plan aided the postwar recovery of France.

2. Charles de Gaulle and the Fifth French Republic (1958–69).

   a. De Gaulle pursued a foreign policy independent of the United States and Great Britain and initiated closer ties with the Third World and communist countries.

   b. The colonial policy allowed for independence of French colonial possessions; Algerian independence (1962) was obtained through war and pressure on the French government.

   c. France refused to sign a nuclear test ban treaty; France withdrew from NATO as a military partner (1965).

   d. Political reversals and student protest riots forced de Gaulle from office (1969).

3. France continued a program of Gaullist reforms (1969–81).

   a. France maintained a leadership role in the European Economic Community (EEC).

   b. The economic impact of the Arab oil embargo (1973) forced France to pursue an aggressive domestic economic program; France provided government support for the Concorde aircraft and nuclear technology programs.

   c. Independent direction in foreign policy was continued.

4. Post-Gaullist period (1981–92).

   a. Socialist Mitterand established a Socialist-Communist coalition.
      (1) Nationalization programs were directed at major industries.
      (2) Economic problems of the 1980s and loss of popular support changed the direction of the Mitterand government.

   b. The coalition government (1986–92) split control of the foreign and domestic policies.
      (1) France pursued a cooperative stance with NATO.
      (2) Nationalization programs in the industrial sector were modified.
      (3) The world economic crisis in the 1990s had a negative "ripple effect" on France's international trade picture and domestic economy.
      (4) Closer European cooperation was fostered by the completion of the tunnel project connecting France and England (1986–93).

XXV. THE CONTEMPORARY WORLD (1945–92)

A. Key developments following World War II.

1. The United Nations (1945) reestablished the dream of a world organization designed to preserve the peace.

    a. The Big Five (United States, Soviet Union, United Kingdom, France, and China) were given a predominant political position.

    b. Communist China replaced Taiwan in 1971.

    c. The United Nations became an association of sovereign states.

2. The structure of the United Nations included the Security Council (each permanent member had veto power) and the General Assembly.

3. Specialized agencies of the United Nations include the UN Educational, Scientific, and Cultural Organization (UNESCO), the World Health Organization (WHO), the World Bank, and the International Monetary Fund.

4. A balance sheet of UN intervention for peace.

    a. Successes include the Kashmir disputes, the Korean conflict, and the Persian Gulf War.

    b. Partial successes include the Arab-Israeli conflicts.

    c. Failures include events in Lebanon, Nigeria, the Congo, Afghanistan, and the former Yugoslavia.

    d. The Persian Gulf War (1991) demonstrated international cooperation to prevent the takeover of Kuwait by Saddam Hussein.

    (1) Hussein's military and industrial complex was crushed by international forces led by the United States.

    (2) Military no-fly zones restricted Hussein's movement on the Kurdish border.

    (3) The threat of further military intervention forced Iraq to dismantle all of its nuclear, chemical, and biological war-related industries.

B. The cold war: the ideological and economic struggle between the United States and the Soviet Union (1947–1992).

1. The basic causes of the conflict included Soviet attempts for territorial expansion and its desire for permanent, defensible borders.

2. Churchill coined the term Iron Curtain to characterize the Soviet control of Eastern Europe.

3. The official beginning of the cold war included:

    a. The U.S. policy of containment of communism (1947).

    b. The Truman Doctrine (1947) provided U.S. aid to Greece and Turkey; signaled start of anti-Communist foreign policy.

    c. The Marshall Plan (1947) resulted in massive economic aid for the postwar recovery of Western Europe.

4. The Soviet reaction to Western Europe heightened postwar tensions.

   a. Communists seized power in Czechoslovakia (1948).

   b. The Berlin Blockade (1948) and the Berlin Airlift (1949) threatened world peace.

5. The military alliance system divided Europe.

   a. The North Atlantic Treaty Organization (NATO) became the cornerstone of U.S. policy in Europe.

   b. The Warsaw Pact (1955) was the Soviet response to NATO.

   c. The United States established a policy of "massive retaliation" against the Soviet Union and Communist China, policy backed up by a ring of air bases in Europe and Asia.

6. The Cuban Missile Crisis threatened the world with thermonuclear war.

   a. The crisis was precipitated by Russian attempts to construct offensive missile bases in Cuba.

   b. President Kennedy ordered a naval blockade of the Cuban coast.

   c. Khrushchev backed down in the face of the U.S. challenge.
      (1) The Soviets removed all offensive missiles from Cuba.
      (2) Khrushchev was ousted by the Soviet leadership and became the scapegoat for the crisis.

7. The end to the cold war was precipitated by the collapse of communism in Eastern Europe (1989–90) and the dissolution of the Soviet Union into entities (1992).

C. The Korean War (1950–52) tested U.S. resolve in Asia.

1. The UN Security Council authorized the use of force to support the preservation of the South Korean government.

2. The results of the UN peacekeeping mission.

   a. The containment of communism.

   b. Communist China was recognized as an emergent world power.

3. One hundred fifty thousand casualties marked the U.S. commitment in Korea.

D. The four Arab-Israeli wars underscored the instability of the Middle East.

1. The first war started immediately after Israel's proclamation of independence (1948) and resulted in an Israeli victory.

2. The Suez Crisis (1956) was precipitated by Nasser's nationalization of the Suez Canal.

3. The Six-Day War (1967) changed the balance of power in the Middle East and established buffer zones in captured Arab territory in Gaza, the Golan Heights, and the Sinai Peninsula.

4. The Yom Kippur War (1973) was a military setback but a psychological victory for the Arabs. In defeat, the Arab oil embargo threatened to sabotage the economies of the West.

5. In 1978, Egypt and Israel signed a "Framework for Peace" after spending thirteen days at Camp David with President Carter. A formal peace treaty was signed in 1979.

6. The Persian Gulf War (1990–91) united Egypt, Syria, Saudi Arabia, and a number of western nations to halt Iraqi aggression. (Israel was subjected to Scud missile attacks but refrained from direct retaliation against Iraq.)

E. The crisis in Vietnam (1946–75).

1. Following World War II, the French unsuccessfully attempted to restore colonial rule in Indochina. France was forced to withdraw from the area in the First Indochinese War (1946–54).

2. Encouraged by Ho Chi Minh, the Vietcong started a civil war in South Vietnam (1961) with aid from the North Vietnamese and Chinese Communists.

3. The initial U.S. involvement was limited to an advisory role (1961–63). As the conflict escalated, U.S. troop presence was dramatically increased, reaching a peak of 545,000 in 1968.

    a. The Tet Offensive (1968), a massive Vietcong military operation, had a dramatic psychological impact on the United States.

    b. President Nixon ordered a policy of unilateral withdrawal of U.S. troops (1969) and the training of South Vietnamese to replace the Americans.

4. The South Vietnamese government collapsed (1975), and after a century of western domination, Vietnam was reunified.

F. The Persian Gulf War (1991).

1. Saddam Hussein of Iraq invaded and occupied Kuwait (1990) as part of a historic "territorial imperative plan." An additional reason for the invasion was based on the premise that Kuwait and the United States conspired to flood the oil market to keep prices low.

2. The UN Security Council condemned the Iraqi invasion and member nations pledged military and economic support.

3. President Bush mobilized the military in preparation for military intervention in the Persian Gulf (Operation Desert Shield, 1990).

4. Operation Desert Storm (1991) was an international effort headed by the United States to force Iraqi withdrawal from Kuwait.

   a. The Iraqi military and industrial complex was destroyed.

   b. Kuwait was liberated.

   c. Permanent cease-fire zones were established.

   d. Kurdish rebellions and Iraqi retaliation resulted in the placement of no-fly zones in northern Iraq.

   e. Iraq was forced to submit to United Nations inspection and destruction of its nuclear, chemical, and biological warfare potential.

   f. The Persian Gulf suffered dramatic environmental damage resulting from Iraqi sabotage of Kuwait's oil fields.

G. The economic and political collapse of communism in Eastern Europe (1990–92).

1. Communist satellite nations in Eastern Europe were under varying degrees of Soviet domination from 1948–80.

   a. The Polish solidarity movement in the 1980s forced the liberalization of its economic and political structure.

   b. The Hungarian Revolt (1956) demonstrated the total domination of Soviet power in Eastern Europe.

   c. Czechoslovakia failed in its liberalization attempts in 1968.

   d. East Germany was firmly under Soviet control, serving as a buffer against possible western attempts to undermine the Soviet position in Eastern Europe.

2. Soviet detente with the United States in the 1970s and 1980s.

   a. Detente was evidenced by Soviet and U.S. cooperation in the space program.

   b. The Strategic Arms Limitation Treaty (SALT II) was a significant attempt to ease postwar tensions.

3. The strong anti-Soviet stance of President Reagan (1980s) resulted in a European rethinking of permitting NATO missile placement on European soil.

4. The Russian invasion of Afghanistan (1979) led to a decade of "Vietnam-style" economic, political, and military setbacks for the Soviet Union.

5. The changing power structure evident in the Soviet Union encouraged the independence movement in Eastern Europe.

   a. Gorbachev initiated sweeping economic, political, and social reforms (1985).

   b. *Perestroika* (the restructuring of Russian society) and *glasnost* (increased free expression and travel) led to closer ties with the West and political reforms at home.

   c. World economic problems affected the massive Soviet military and the foreign aid program.

6. The dismantling of the Berlin Wall (1989) symbolized the political end to Communist control over Eastern Europe.

   a. The total collapse of Communist governments (1989–90) in Hungary, East Germany, Czechoslovakia, Poland, and Yugoslavia resulted in independent economic and political restructuring.

   b. East and West German reunification (1990) resulted in profound political, economic, and social changes.

   c. The breakup of Yugoslavia (1990) unleashed historic hatreds and ethnic fighting between Moslems and Christian Serbs and Croatians.

   d. "Ethnic cleansing" directed at the Moslems in Bosnia threatened the peace of the entire Eastern European region.

7. The end of the Soviet Union as a political entity (1992) resulted in a redrawing of the political and economic map of Europe.

   a. The Baltic republics of Latvia, Estonia, and Lithuania acted as a catalyst (1989–90) for the eventual dissolution of the Soviet empire.

   b. Gorbachev pursued drastic western-style capitalistic changes (1987–91).

   c. Early attempts at creating a market economy resulted in severe economic hardships.

   d. The unsuccessful coup against Gorbachev to return Russia to its previous status failed (1991).

   e. Boris Yeltsin (elected in 1991) continued Gorbachev's reform plans, but continuing economic uncertainty and political turmoil encouraged an independence movement in the former fifteen Soviet republics (1992).

CALIFORNIA HISTORY

I. PREHISTORIC PERIOD

A. First humans to enter North America crossed the Bering Strait land bridge at the end of the Pleistocene Period, or the last Ice Age, approximately 15,000 to 30,000 years ago.

1. They migrated southward from Alaska and populated North and South America.

2. They entered California approximately 15,000 years ago; evidence from the early man archaeological site at Calico could push the date back to 50,000 years ago.

B. Indian occupation of California.

1. General characteristics of California Indians prior to European contact.

   a. They spoke a great diversity of dialects.

   b. They represented the largest concentration of Indians in North America (estimated 150,000 to 300,000).

c. They had similar physical traits and features.

d. The groups showed general uniformity in economy, material goods, religious practices, and social organization.

e. They were primarily hunter/gatherer societies.

f. Local subsistence was based almost exclusively on available resources.

g. Dwellings reflected the groups' climatic and geographic locations: frame and plank houses in the north, brush shelters in the southern deserts, and earth houses along the coastal areas.

h. Crafts were limited; basketmaking was generally universal with distinct local variations (twined in north, coiled in south).

i. The groups were not generally warlike and weapons were not sophisticated (in comparison to those of the Plains Indians). They used the atlatl, bow and arrow, obsidian points, hunting blades, spears, harpoons, clubs, and throwing sticks. Hunting technology was linked to geographic factors.

j. Acorns were extensively used as a food source where oak trees were plentiful. This involved drying, storing, cracking, and leaching.

k. Their transportation reflected geographic factors: balsa and raft-type boats were used in the south, and plank canoes were used in the north.

2. The shared heritage of the various tribes.

a. Lineage was traced on the paternal side.

b. Native tobacco and jimsonweed were widely used in ceremonial activities.

c. Sweathouses were used (by men only).

d. Functional musical instruments were played, and they sang and danced.

e. The groups' religions were similar in myths, creation stories, shamanism, and the influence of nature.

f. Ceremonies dealt with birth, death, puberty, marriage, hunting, etc.

g. Their cultures integrated with and reflected the environment; nature provided for them.

h. Fables dealt with animals and other natural phenomena of the region (coyote, raven, bear, snake, thunder, etc.).

i. Roles were sex differentiated: the men hunted and fished, and the women gathered food and materials and killed small game.

j. The oral story tradition was used by all California Indians.

3. Geographic factors isolated many tribes. Desert and mountain barriers restricted contact.

a. Northern California tribes included the Yurok, Hupa, Modoc, and Pomo.

b. Central California tribes included the Maidu and Miwok.

c. Coastal tribes included the coastal Miwok, Esselen, and Chumash.

d. Desert tribes included the Mojave and Serrano.

e. Sierra Nevada tribes included the Miwok and Mono.

4. Their material belongings were similar.

a. Body garments and dress.

b. Subsistence agricultural implements: mortar and pestle, metate, grinding slab, and digging sticks.

c. Houses (earth, bark, plank, thatch) and ceremonial houses (sweat, dance, menstrual).

d. Weapons and tools: knife, adz, ax, maul, scraper, awl, and drill.

e. Textiles (bags, wallets, beadwork and other designs).

f. Receptacles: baskets (most famous), pottery, wood and stone bowls.

g. Musical instruments: drum, rattle, flute, rasp, and bow.

h. Money: clam disks and olivella shells.

II. SPANISH CONQUEST

A. The search for the Seven Cities of Cibola by Cortez in the 1530s resulted in Spanish exploration of the Baja peninsula.

1. Spain was interested in conquest and wealth.

2. Exploration centered on a search for an island inhabited by Amazon-like women who used golden weapons.

B. Cabrillo discovered San Diego Bay, the Santa Barbara Islands, Point Conception, and Point Reyes in 1542–43.

1. He searched for a water passage between the Pacific and Atlantic oceans.

2. Future voyages traveled the entire coast of California.

C. Drake, an English explorer, sailed up the California coast in 1579 and claimed the area for England.

1. The threat from England compelled Spain to colonize California.

2. Spanish explorations discovered safe harbors at Monterey and San Francisco.

3. For the next 100 years, Spanish colonization of California was minimal.

D. Russian excursions along the northern American coast (1800s) resulted in renewed Spanish efforts to colonize California.

1. Russian fur interests in Alaska pushed southward.

2. Russians established Fort Ross eighty miles north of San Francisco Bay in 1812 as a trading post.

3. The American government also viewed Russian exploration of the California coast as a threat.

a. The Monroe Doctrine (1823) restricted European colonization of the Americas.

b. The Spanish reacted to potential Russian, British, and American presences by establishing presidios (military forts) and pueblos (small settlements) in valleys around San Francisco Bay.

E. The Spanish established the California missions.

1. Jesuits established five permanent settlements in Baja California in the early 1700s.

2. Franciscan friars established 21 Spanish missions along the California coast from San Diego to Sonoma (one day's journey apart at completion in 1823).

   a. The purpose was to convert the Indians to Christianity, establish cultural and agricultural centers, and populate Alta California for Spain.

   (1) Both the "sword" and the "cross" were used to subdue the Indians.

3. Father Serra is credited with the development of the mission system.

   a. Serra's lasting contributions are controversial.

4. Positive aspects of the mission system.

   a. It spread Christianity.

   b. It colonized California.

   c. It spread the cultural and technological advances of Spain.

5. Negative aspects of the mission system.

   a. The dehumanization of the Indians.

   b. The high infant mortality and suicide rates among the Indians.

   c. The forced labor and virtual slavelike conditions.

   d. Indian self-sufficiency never developed.

6. In about 1830, the mission system began a secularization process. By 1836, most mission property was privately owned.

III. MEXICAN RULE IN CALIFORNIA

A. After Mexican independence from Spain in 1822, California residents exerted increased control in local political matters.

B. The land grant system and the ranchos fueled independent action.

C. The Mexican government failed in its attempts to dominate California.

D. By 1845, the Californios (provincial Californians) expelled the last of the Mexican governors.

E. **American trappers (including Jedediah Smith), explorers (including Kit Carson and Joseph Walker), and a variety of wagon masters opened California to American settlement.**

IV. CALIFORNIAN INDEPENDENCE FROM MEXICO (1846–48)

A. **Migrations of American pioneer families in the 1840s swelled the American population in California.**

1. Americans settled in the San Joaquin and Sacramento valleys.

2. They increased the demand that California become part of the United States.

B. **President Polk indirectly supported the annexation of California.**

1. John C. Frémont, possibly acting on presidential orders, raised the U.S. flag near Monterey, then retreated from the area.

2. War was declared on Mexico in 1846 (the Mexican American War).
   a. The Bear Flag Revolt prematurely captured California (1846).
   b. Commander Sloat captured Monterey Bay and claimed the area for the United States.
   c. General Stockton captured Los Angeles; Governor Pico and General Castro retook the area for Mexico.
   d. Stockton and Kearny defeated Pico and raised the American flag over Los Angeles in 1847.

3. The Treaty of Guadalupe Hidalgo (1848) transferred California from Mexican to American control.

V. GOLD DISCOVERED IN CALIFORNIA

A. **The discovery of gold by James W. Marshall in 1848 changed the political, social, and economic history of the state.**

1. "Gold fever" became a national phenomenon; the California population increased tremendously from 15,000 in 1847 to 92,000 in 1850, and 380,000 in 1860.

2. The population growth led to statehood (thirty-first).

B. **The Compromise of 1850 allowed California to be a free state.**

1. Slavery was prohibited, which upset the balance of free and slave states.

2. California statehood became a background issue to the Civil War.

VI. CALIFORNIA FROM THE CIVIL WAR TO THE TURN OF THE CENTURY

A. The completion of the transcontinental railroad in 1869 made the dream of Manifest Destiny come true.

1. The Central Pacific met the Union Pacific at Promontory, Utah. Immigrant labor was used: Chinese on the Central Pacific and Irish on the Union Pacific.

2. The Big Four (Hopkins, Crocker, Huntington, and Stanford) controlled the railroad industry and most of the California political scene.

B. Economic depression hit California in the 1870s; a cycle of boom and bust was begun.

1. The depression was characterized by low wages, high unemployment, railroad abuses (unfair pricing and rebates), and the restriction of water rights by land monopolies.

2. The collapse of the Bank of California in 1875 (and other financial institutions) further weakened the California economy.

C. Open hostility toward the Chinese erupted.

1. They were blamed for most of the economic problems (backlash from the mining and railroad frontier).

2. The Chinese Exclusion Act was passed by Congress in 1882.

3. By 1877, politicians, newspapers, and citizens urged open agitation against the Chinese in California.

4. The Workingmen's Party was established. It was nativist, anti-Chinese, and anti-big-business (1877).

    a. It demanded a constitutional convention and populist-type reforms.

    b. The California Constitution (1879) codified anti-Chinese legislation.

D. The California land boom of the 1880s swelled the population again.

1. The ensuing bank collapse in 1887 devastated the economy.

2. Hard times and economic retrenchment followed.

VII. EARLY TWENTIETH CENTURY CALIFORNIA

A. New immigration (mainly from the Midwest) led to a dramatic population increase.

B. Fears of the "yellow peril" were raised again.

1. Japanese were imported in large numbers to work in agriculture. They displaced Anglo workers and resentment grew.

2. Orientals had been restricted from naturalization at the turn of the century.

3. The San Francisco Board of Education segregated Caucasians and Orientals in 1905.

4. The resentment led to an international "Gentlemen's Agreement" (1907).

   a. Japanese immigration to the United States was voluntarily restricted (but the measure was ineffective in reducing tension).

   b. Integrated schools were permitted.

   c. Agitation against Asians continued.

C. Populist reforms aimed to bring government closer to the people.

1. The Lincoln-Roosevelt League (a coalition party) pushed through reforms and controlled the Republican Party.

2. Hiram Johnson (a progressive) was elected governor, and a reform program was initiated.

   a. Twenty-three amendments were added to the California Constitution (1911).

   b. The provisions included women's suffrage; initiative, referendum, and recall; workmen's compensation; a new railroad commission, and others.

3. California supported the Bull Moose Party (progressive) in 1912.

4. Anti-Japanese agitation continued.

   a. The Japanese were ineligible for citizenship (national law), they could not own land (the California Alien Land Act), and more restrictive federal legislation was passed against them in 1913 and 1924.

   b. The U.S. Supreme Court upheld anti-Japanese legislation.

5. The labor movement lost political power after an anarchist bombing in Los Angeles (1910).

VIII. CALIFORNIA FROM WORLD WAR I TO 1930

A. World War I produced a new economic boom.

1. Wages, production, manufacturing, and commerce expanded rapidly.

2. The Panama Canal was opened in 1914, which extended international links.

3. An influx of immigrants arrived in the 1920s.

   a. Economic advances were tied to movie, oil, and agricultural production.

   b. A real estate boom fueled the housing industry.

   c. By 1930, the California population had grown to six million, an increase of 65 percent during one decade. It was the sixth most populous state.

B. **California politics was characterized as a power struggle between the north and south and between rural and urban areas.**

IX. CALIFORNIA FROM 1930 TO 1960

A. **The economic collapse of 1930 resulted in large-scale unemployment, bank failures, and foreclosures.**

B. **The economic downturn renewed the call for political reform.**

1. Upton Sinclair (a reform candidate) ran unsuccessfully for governor on a platform for political change.

2. The Utopian Society promoted economic and social reform.

3. The Townsend Plan favored pensions for the aged and a graduated income tax.

C. **Depression-era California.**

1. Dust Bowl migrants added more than 350,000 to the population.

2. Economic and social problems, including homelessness, confronted the state.

D. **The U.S. entry into World War II brought economic revitalization to California.**

1. California's manufacturing base was greatly increased (airplanes, ships, and other war products).

2. California became the "defense center" of the nation.

E. **Japanese-Americans were relocated from coastal areas to inland detention camps (1942).**

1. Constitutional and moral questions were raised.

2. The Japanese were forced to sell their homes and businesses on short notice at huge losses.

F. **Huge defense contracts following the war fueled economic prosperity.**

1. Hundreds of thousands of armed forces personnel migrated to California.

2. The need for public services increased.

3. Pollution and water became political issues.

X. RECENT DEVELOPMENTS IN CALIFORNIA HISTORY

A. The California public education system was greatly expanded in the 1960s, including a low-cost college and university system.

B. Regulating water resources became a fundamental political issue.

1. A series of canals, dams, and reservoirs was established.

2. Northern California water was relocated to burgeoning population centers in the south.

C. California became the most populous state in the nation (1964).

D. California cities reflected new urban problems.

1. Minorities were generally left out of the economic prosperity.

2. The Watts Riot (1965) focused national attention on the economic and political status of minorities.

3. African-Americans and Mexican-Americans continued to experience discrimination in the housing and job markets.

   a. Reforms in housing, education, and employment provided new opportunities for minorities.

   b. Federal affirmative action programs provided a legal basis for changing discrimination in hiring practices.

4. Cesar Chavez organized the first farm workers' union in 1962.

   a. The United Farm Workers (UFW) struck the table grape growers in Delano and the San Joaquin Valley (1965).

   b. In 1970, the UFW signed a historic contract with the grape growers.

E. Recession in the 1970s followed cutbacks in California defense contracts. The housing and aerospace industries were affected.

F. Californians passed Proposition 13 (1978).

1. Proposition 13 restructured local control over property taxes.

2. It led to cutbacks in property taxes and a decrease in the tax base available to fund social programs.

G. The 1980s were a period of fragile prosperity.

1. Santa Clara County (Silicon Valley) led the nation in the computer industries.

2. Defense contracts and the agricultural industries continued to bolster the California economy.

3. Land prices escalated and housing prices soared.

4. The impact of Proposition 13 led to further cutbacks in social services.

5. Economic, political, and social problems threatened prosperity (late 1980s).

   a. Immigration (both legal and illegal) from Mexico and Asian countries swelled the population and affected the social service system.

   b. Increased crime, gangs, pollution, and other urban problems affected the state.

   c. The cost of public higher education escalated dramatically.

   d. An economic downturn emerged.

H. California in the early 1990s.

1. Urban violence, restricted funding for social welfare programs, high taxes, and a prolonged economic recession affected the state.

2. Unemployment (at approximately ten percent) exceeded the national average.

3. Severe cutbacks in the California defense industry exacerbated economic problems.

   a. This followed the breakup of the Soviet Union.

   b. The cutbacks had a ripple effect in the housing, auto, and computer industries, among others.

   c. Major industrial plant closings further weakened the economy.

   d. The cost of public higher education continued to escalate.

4. The acquittal of police officers in the Rodney King trial led to the worst civil disturbance in U.S. history (1992).

   a. National attention again was centered on California.

   b. Destruction in the Los Angeles area ran into the billions of dollars.

   c. The result was new calls for economic and political opportunity for minorities.

XI. CALIFORNIA APPROACHES THE TWENTY-FIRST CENTURY

A. Guilty verdicts in the federal Rodney King trial (1993) reduced racial tensions.

B. Diversification holds the key to economic growth in the 1990s.

C. Ethnic diversity, minority population growth, and increased minority political presence represent new directions in the state.

D. Economic advantages of California.

1. The gross domestic product (GDP) ranks California number one in the nation.

2. The California GDP ranks it among the top ten *countries* in the world.

3. Vast natural resources (oil, timber, minerals, etc.) and abundant fertile land allow for future growth.

4. California leads the nation in manufacturing and agricultural production.

5. The higher education system (junior colleges, state colleges, and universities) is among the finest in the nation.

CALIFORNIA GEOGRAPHY

I. THE PHYSICAL GEOGRAPHY AND TOPOGRAPHY OF CALIFORNIA REPRESENT GREAT DIVERSITY

A. California extends approximately 800 miles from north to south and ranges from 150 to 350 miles east to west.

B. It borders Oregon, Nevada, Arizona, and Mexico.

C. Mount Whitney, at 14,495 feet, is the highest peak in the continental United States. Death Valley is the lowest point at 282 feet below sea level.

D. California shows dramatic changes in topography across the state: rugged mountain peaks, fertile valleys, dense forests, ocean boundaries, and extensive deserts.

E. California geology evidences faulting, folding, alluvial and sedimentary deposition, and volcanic activity.

F. California is a region of frequent seismic activity. The San Andreas fault system extends for 500 miles. Its movement is largely horizontal, with the west side of the fault moving northward and the east side moving southward.

G. Growing seasons extend throughout the year. In many areas of the state, there are just two distinct seasons: a mild, wet winter and a relatively dry, long summer.

H. Southern California's climate is characterized as Mediterranean and is unique in the United States. The state has many diverse microclimates, though generally the coastal climate is mild and the interior is much more extreme. The interior basins have the most extreme temperatures.

I. Few California rivers are navigable. Notable rivers are the San Joaquin and the Sacramento and their tributaries, and the Colorado.

J. The coastline extends approximately 1200 miles.

K. Rainfall varies greatly: the extreme north receives more than 110 inches per year, and the southern desert regions receive less than two inches per year.

II. CALIFORNIA ENCOMPASSES SEVEN DISTINCT REGIONS.

A. The Coast Ranges.

1. These are mountains along the western coast of California, extending from the Klamath Mountains in the north (Oregon border region) to the southwestern section of the Sierra Nevada (southern California).

2. The San Andreas fault system divides this region along a north/south axis.

3. The range is approximately 550 miles long.

4. The plant diversity ranges from giant redwoods in the north to chaparral in the south.

5. The mountains are a series of parallel ranges formed by sedimentary deposition uplifted by faulting and folding.

6. The climate of the Coast Ranges varies from low-pressure areas that produce fog and rain in the northern sections to a Mediterranean-type condition in the south.

B. The Klamath Mountains.

1. The Klamath Mountains are located in the northwestern corner of the state.

2. They are an extension of the Coast Ranges.

3. The mountains are rugged, steep, and in the 6,000- to 8,000-foot range.

4. The area receives heavy precipitation, and dense forests cover the mountains.

C. The Sierra Nevada (The Snowy Range).

1. The Sierra Nevada range is about 400 miles long and follows the eastern border of the state, forming the eastern wall of the Central Valley.

2. The mountains were formed through extensive uplifting and subsidence and are characterized as fault-block mountains. The backbone of the range is igneous rock.

3. They are the highest mountains in California, with many serrated peaks around 13,000 feet. Mount Whitney is located at the southern end.

4. The peaks have sharp drop-offs on the eastern side and have been a barrier to east/west transportation. The mountains have gentle slopes on the western side, which has trapped water to the benefit of Central Valley agriculture.

5. Sierra Nevada streams cut deep valleys. Gold was discovered in these streams where it was eroded from veins in the rocks.

6. The Sierra Nevada cause a rain-shadow effect: clouds rise against the high mountain peaks, causing them to drop their moisture. This has created fertile valleys on the west and a dry landscape on the east.

7. Ice Age glaciers have created the current mountain profiles. Yosemite National Park's U-shaped valleys were carved by glacial action.

8. Southern California is dependent upon the average annual seventy inches of rain and snow that fall on the Sierra Nevada for its water supply.

D. The Central Valley.

1. The Central Valley separates the Sierra Nevada and the Coast Range.

2. The valley extends from the northwest to the southeast for 400 miles and is an average of 50 miles wide.

3. The valley is a flat, sedimentary plain. The soil is fertile and makes the valley the major agricultural region of the state.

4. Sixty percent of California's farmland is located in the Central Valley.

5. A majority of the state's water supply is caught in the Central Valley as runoff from the Sierra Nevada.

6. The Sacramento Delta, encompassing 1200 square miles of waterways, is located where the Sacramento (south-flowing) and San Joaquin (north-flowing) rivers meet.

E. The Basin and Range.

1. This extreme landscape of short parallel mountain ranges and desert basins extends along the eastern border of California.
   a. The northern section is part of a lava plateau.
   b. The southern section is generally dry. The Mojave Desert is the major geographical feature in the south.

2. The Northwest and Southwest Great Basin, the Northwestern Sonoran Desert, and the Salton Sea Trough are significant areas in this region.

3. Death Valley (in the Mojave Desert), the lowest point in the United States, was formed by faulting (not erosion).

4. The system extends into Nevada and Utah.

5. Irrigation with water from the Colorado River has allowed large-scale farming in the Imperial and Coachella valleys.

F. The Cascade Range and Modoc Plateau.

1. The southern extreme of the Cascade Range is located in the northeastern corner of California. It extends 550 miles northward into Canada.

2. The area is separate from the Sierra Nevada and is about 25 miles wide.

3. The Cascade Range mountains were formed exclusively by volcanic activity. Many, like Mt. Shasta (14,162 feet), are dormant or extinct volcanoes.

4. Lassen Peak is the largest plug dome (filled with magma) volcano in the world.

5. The Modoc Plateau is a level tableland of volcanic origin.

G. The Transverse and Peninsular ranges.

1. This area extends from Santa Barbara to San Diego.

2. The Transverse/Los Angeles ranges extend in an easterly (transverse) direction from the coast (all other California ranges extend north and south).

3. These ranges include the Santa Ynez, Santa Monica, San Gabriel, and San Bernardino Mountains.

4. The Los Angeles Basin in the state's largest coastal basin and was formed by the alluvial deposition of soil from the surrounding mountain ranges.

5. The Peninsular ranges extend south from the San Bernardino Mountains in Baja California and from the Pacific Ocean east to the Salton Sea Trough.

6. The faulted eastern sections of the Peninsular ranges are characterized by sharp drop-offs. It is a complex region of active fault zones. Significant faults include the San Jacinto (near Palm Springs) and the Elsinore.

POLITICAL SCIENCE-GOVERNMENT

I. SOME BASIC THEORIES OF GOVERNMENT AND THE STATE

A. The theory of divine right.

1. The right of the ruler to rule was inherited from his or her ancestors, who were believed to have been appointed by a supreme being.

2. It is identified with absolutist governments.

3. It was accepted as the justification for the rule of kings in much of the western world from the fifteenth through the eighteenth centuries.

4. This theory was weakened and replaced by the new contract theory, which held that a ruler's power was granted to him not by God, but by the sovereign people.

B. The economic interest theory.

1. The primary role of government and of the state is to develop, promote, and protect economic interests such as trade, markets, commerce, and wealth.

2. Economic interests which thrive under the protection of the state are powerful in determining the direction of governmental policy.

C. The force theory.

1. This theory holds that the state is a product of force and conquest.

2. Like other theories, it cannot be proved and is generally considered inadequate as an explanation of the origin of the state.

II. CLASSIFICATION ACCORDING TO THE RELATIONSHIP BETWEEN THE EXECUTIVE AND THE LEGISLATURE

A. Presidential government.

1. A distinctive feature of the executive is that he or she is elected independently of the legislature and holds office for a fixed period. Also, the executive has extensive power not subject to control by the legislature.

2. The term *presidential government* is descriptive of the system employed by the United States.

B. Cabinet or parliamentary government.

1. Policy-making executives are the prime minister and the members of the cabinet, all of whom are members of the legislature and dependent on support of the legislature for continuance in office.

2. Parliamentary government differs from the American system of *separation of powers* in that executive authority is dependent on the legislature.

III. CLASSIFICATION ACCORDING TO THE LOCATION OF POWER IN GOVERNMENT

A. Confederation.

1. A loose union of states in which the principal powers of government (perhaps *all* the real power) are retained by the individual member states.

2. Central government exists to perform a limited number of functions, such as national defense.

3. The United States was a confederation for eight years under the Articles of Confederation.

B. Federation.

1. A federation, such as the United States, is a union of two or more local governments under one central government, *with both the central and the local governments exercising independent spheres of authority, either in theory or in practice.*

2. It encourages unity in matters of general concern, but autonomy (independent authority) in matters of local concern.

IV. **CLASSIFICATION ACCORDING TO THE DEGREE OF GOVERNMENTAL REGULATION OF THE LIVES OF INDIVIDUALS**

    A. **Anarchism holds that all government is evil, unnecessary, and undesirable.**

    B. **Individualism advocates the restriction of governmental activities within narrow limits, leaving a broad area of freedom to the individual.**

    C. **Socialism stands for relatively rapid and sweeping economic collectivism (government ownership).**

V. **CLASSIFICATION ACCORDING TO LIMITATION ON GOVERNMENTAL POWER**

    A. **Dictatorship.**

        1. Government resting on the will of a single person or a small group of persons is a dictatorship.

        2. The welfare of the state is often held above the welfare of the individual.

    B. **Democracy.**

        1. The primary meaning is *government by the people.*

        2. *Indirect* democracy implies government by the people's representatives, as in the United States.

VI. **THE CONSTITUTION OF THE UNITED STATES AS A RESTRAINT ON GOVERNMENTAL POWER**

    A. **National power: the separation principle.**

        1. Powers are carefully separated and balanced among executive, legislative, and judicial branches to avoid centralization of powers and resultant tyranny.

        2. The presidential veto is an example of an executive check on the legislative branch.

        3. Control of expenditures is an example of a legislative check on the executive branch.

        4. The power to interpret the Constitution and laws is an example of a check the judiciary holds over the president and Congress.

        5. The power of enforcement of court decisions is a check of the executive over the judicial branch.

B. Restraints on state power.

1. Article I, Section 10.

   a. This forbids the states to enter treaties, coin money, subvert the national currency, or pass any law impairing the obligation of contracts, etc.

   b. It outlaws tariffs by states.

2. The supremacy of the Constitution, laws, and treaties of the United States.

3. The Fourteenth Amendment.

   a. It defines citizenship, providing supremacy of national citizenship over state citizenship.

   b. It restrains the states from depriving persons of life, liberty, or property without due process of law or denying persons the equal protection of laws.

4. The Fifteenth Amendment intended to give blacks the right to vote.

5. The Nineteenth Amendment forbids states to deny women the right to vote.

6. The Twenty-fourth Amendment forbids states to collect a poll tax as a prerequisite to voting in national elections.

7. The Twenty-sixth Amendment allows eighteen-year-olds to vote in national elections.

VII. THE TWO-PARTY SYSTEM

A. Traditions in American politics.

1. During most of U.S. history, power has alternated between two major parties.

2. Minor parties do arise and influence national politics.

3. No minor party has ever had a president elected.

4. Major parties sometimes disappear, but the development of a new second party is the traditional pattern.

5. Minor parties have sometimes had senators and representatives elected.

6. Minor parties have occasionally dominated state and local politics.

B. Advantages of a two-party system.

1. Voters can be confronted with an either-or choice, thus simplifying decisions and political processes.

2. Electoral decisions are usually majority decisions, encouraging majority support for governmental policies.

3. Governmental stability is enhanced by a two-party system as opposed to a multiparty system.

BEHAVIORAL SCIENCES

I. ANTHROPOLOGY

A. **The scope of anthropology is concerned with all varieties of humans, and it considers humans of all periods, beginning with the emergence of humanity and tracing its development until the present. Anthropology is comparative (comparing differing cultures) and historical.**

B. **The subfields of anthropology relate to each other.**

1. Physical anthropology studies humans as biological organisms.

2. Cultural anthropology studies humans' cultures.

3. Ethnology studies humans and why cultures differ.

4. Archaeology and prehistory study the ways of life of peoples of the past.

5. Anthropological linguistics studies the cultural development of language and communication.

C. **The concept of culture.**

1. Culture is the sum total of humanity's customs, practices, and beliefs.

2. An item of behavior is referred to as a cultural trait.

3. A group of related cultural traits is called a culture complex.

4. Culture is not static and therefore is always changing.

D. **The evolution of culture traces the technological development of humans.**

1. Technology is the study of ways that a society employs to achieve a successful adaptation to the environment.

2. Subsistence technology is the study of the techniques of obtaining food.

3. Food producing, or domestication, includes the cultivation of plants and the keeping and breeding of animals.

4. Stock breeding combined with farming is called mixed subsistence.

E. **Economic systems were developed to distribute goods and services.**

1. Reciprocity refers to giving and taking without the use of money.

2. Redistribution is the accumulation of goods for the purpose of subsequent distribution.

3. The development of market exchange occurs when surpluses of food are regularly produced.

F. The development of social systems.

1. Egalitarian societies occur where there are as many positions of prestige in any given age-sex group as there are persons capable of filling them.

2. Stratified societies are characterized by socially structured, unequal access to economic resources.

G. Kinship is based on descent, and it is associated with a set of privileges and obligations.

1. In most societies, culture is transmitted through the kin group.

2. Lineage is a kinship group whose members trace their descent from a common ancestor.

3. Patterns of marital residence are often determined by kinship.

4. Members of a society are bound together into ascending ranks through kinship.

H. Political organizations are usually classified according to degree of centralization of authority and include tribes, states, and nations.

I. Religion is a universal phenomenon present in all cultures.

J. Culture dynamics in the modern world.

1. Culture borrowing results from the direct or indirect exposure to another culture.

2. Diffusion is the process of borrowing.

II. SOCIOLOGY

A. Sociologists study societies to obtain data, develop concepts, and formulate theories about human interaction.

1. A society is a group of persons who are organized in an orderly manner, share a distinct lifestyle, and think of themselves as united.

2. Society consists of a network or system of social relationships among individuals.

3. Status is a position an individual occupies in a group or society.

4. A role is the expectation of behavior (norms) for those who occupy a given status.

5. Societies can be basically divided into folk or modern.

   a. A folk society is small, generally based on agriculture, and today is found only in isolated areas.

   b. A modern society is large, generally based on advanced division of labor, and is rapidly changing.

B. Sociologists, as well as anthropologists, study culture, since culture depends on human interaction.

1. There is a culture for every society.

2. Culture can be classified as learned, taught, adaptive, shared, etc.

3. Only humans are considered to have culture, since they are the only species known capable of creating a language.

4. Values, attitudes, and norms of behavior are defined by the culture.

C. The individual learns about the culture through the process of socialization.

1. Disciplines, aspirations, skills, and roles are learned by the individual through socialization.

2. Socialization is deliberately carried out by such institutions as the school or family.

3. Socialization encourages a mold for personality development reflecting that culture's values.

4. Social deviance is behavior that differs a great deal from the given norm.

5. Social movements are deliberate efforts to produce change in society.

6. Groups are fundamental to the socialization process.

   a. Groups may be classified from primary (in which members feel close to one another) to secondary (in which members feel no strong ties to one another).

   b. The family is the most important primary group.

   c. Cooperation, competition, and conflict are part of group processes.

   d. The social nature of minority classification.

      (1) Racial and ethnic group differences are closely related to respective class and status positions.

      (2) A variety of groups can be classified as a minority in any given society.

      (3) A group becomes a minority when it is defined as such.

      (4) Prejudice and discrimination are learned behaviors and have limited the social and economic mobility of minorities.

7. Religion, government, and the economy are fundamental to the socialization process.

ECONOMICS

I. THE BACKGROUND OF ECONOMICS

A. All civilized societies are organized to fulfill basic social needs.

1. The institution of the family fulfills primary and basic needs.

2. Educational and religious institutions transmit the ideals and values of society.

3. Political institutions provide the means for enforcing rules and regulations.

4. Economic institutions provide a method to analyze the goods and services in a society.

B. There are four basic universals of economics that are present in all types of economic organizations.

1. How to allocate resources among competing and alternative uses.

2. How to distribute goods and services among the population.

3. How to provide economic stability and security.

4. How to provide continued economic growth.

C. The basis of economics is that society must make choices.

1. Since there are not enough resources to satisfy all wants, there is a conflict between unlimited wants and limited resources.

2. Societal choice: what to produce, how to produce, and for whom to produce.

D. Some basic economic principles that are fundamental to an understanding of economics.

1. Marginal costs: the costs of producing additional units of a good.

2. Law of diminishing returns: the point at which the production of extra units results in decreased returns.

3. Markets: bringing together persons who wish to exchange goods.

II. ECONOMIC ORGANIZATION

A. The U.S. economy is based on concepts of modern capitalism.

1. Private ownership of property is fundamental to a capitalistic society.

2. A competitive, free-market, free-price system is necessary for capitalism to function efficiently.

3. Modern capitalism can be divided into basic sectors.

   a. Consumption: characterized by freedom of consumer choice.

   b. Production: characterized by freedom of enterprise.

   c. Financial: composed of all banking and financial institutions.

   d. Government: performs task of stabilizing the economy through monetary and fiscal policies.

4. Measuring economic variables provides a means of analyzing the economy.

   a. Wealth is a measurement of assets on hand at a given point in time.

   b. Income is the monetary return or other material benefits from currently produced goods and services.

   c. The purchasing power of the dollar has to do with its ability to command goods and services. Measuring changes in the value of the dollar is a key economic concept.

5. Production is a source of wealth and income and involves the inflow and outflow of goods and services. The economic growth of the U.S. is measured by the Gross National Product (GNP) which is the value of all goods and services produced in a particular year.

B. The underdeveloped areas of the world have shown limited economic growth.

1. Two-thirds of the world's population is economically deprived.

2. Restricted growth is the result of a combination of many factors.

   a. The quality of land, labor, and capital are key factors that determine economic growth.

   b. Less-developed countries usually have high population densities.

   c. Low incomes retard economies by restricting the opportunity to consume goods.

III. THE ROLE OF GOVERNMENT IN THE U.S. ECONOMY

A. The degree of government control and influence in our economy has steadily grown throughout history.

1. Industrialization has created problems in labor-management relations that government seems to be able to handle best.

2. Urbanization has created problems in providing essential public services such as police and fire protection and sewage disposal.

3. Foreign policy commitments and military expenditures have had lasting effects on the role of government in the economy.

4. In our modern society, people have simply demanded more of government.

B. The major types of government activities in the economy include direct controls over the economy, ownership of production (for example, Hoover Dam), and welfare expenditures.

C. **The major economic impact of government activity comes from its spending, taxing, and public debt policies.**

    1. The various types of taxes include direct, indirect, proportional, progressive, and regressive.

        a. Federal personal and corporate taxes are progressive.

        b. Most state and local taxes are proportional.

        c. Nearly all excise, sales, and property taxes are regressive.

    2. "Ability to pay" and "benefits received" are the cornerstones of the U.S. tax system.

        a. "Ability to pay" is a theory that bases taxation in accordance with income and wealth position.

        b. "Benefits received" is a theory that bases taxation in accordance with the benefits received by the taxpayer; hunting and fishing fees are examples.

IV. CONSUMER CHOICE AND THE PRICE SYSTEM

A. **In the United States, economic production is aimed at satisfying the desires of the consumer.**

    1. The utility of a product is the satisfaction one receives from consuming goods.

    2. Consumer behavior is determined by available money, priorities, and utilities.

B. **Basic to the price system are demand, supply, and equilibrium.**

C. **The government's role in the marketplace includes the enforcement of regulations, imposing taxes, and controlling prices.**

    1. Government actions can create shortages or surpluses.

    2. Government actions can restrict the price system.

V. THE LABOR MARKET

A. **The demand for labor is largely determined by the demand for the final product and the price of substitute factors.**

B. **The supply of labor is largely determined by population growth, immigration, and alternative lifestyles.**

C. **Changes in the labor market have brought about the formation and growth of large firms and labor unions.**

    1. Management usually seeks to maximize long-term profits.

2. Labor unions attempt to obtain high wages, full employment, and job security.

3. The conflict of goals between labor and management is usually resolved through collective bargaining.

VI. INTERNATIONAL TRADE AND FINANCE

A. **International economic relations involve the movement of goods, services, people, and capital across national political boundaries.**

B. **The United States is the world's largest single exporter and importer.**

1. The volume of U.S. imports is of vital significance to other countries' economies.

2. The volume of U.S. imports is closely related to the level of its national income; the higher the income, the greater its imports.

C. **The balance of payments includes all the economic and financial transactions between one country and the rest of the world over a given period of time.**

1. A favorable balance of trade results when exports are greater than imports.

2. An unfavorable balance of trade results when imports are greater than exports.

GLOBAL GEOGRAPHY

I. THE IMPORTANCE OF TODAY'S GEOGRAPHY

A. **Peoples of the world are brought closer together by improved means of transportation and communication.**

B. **The division of the earth into separate nations has influenced the lives of people and the way in which they use the land.**

C. **The effects of geography on world conditions are readily seen in the political and social arena.**

1. Russia's desire for defensible borders encouraged the domination of Eastern Europe following World War II.

2. The emergence of the Middle East as a political force was a result of the world's dependence on oil.

II. THE EFFECTS OF THE INCLINATION OF THE EARTH'S AXIS (SEASONAL CHANGES)

A. The number of growing seasons a country has is influenced by both geography and climate.

B. The Tropics of Cancer and Capricorn are generally areas of warmer temperatures and climates.

C. The Arctic Circle and Antarctic Circle are areas of generally colder temperatures and climates.

III. GLOBES AND MAPS ARE ESSENTIAL TOOLS OF GEOGRAPHY AND DEPICT HUMANITY'S KNOWLEDGE OF THE EARTH AND ITS FEATURES

A. Maps are drawings which show where places are in relation to each other.

1. Information given on maps consists of the title, legend, scale, direction, longitude and latitude, etc.

2. Longitude is an angular distance east and west of a given meridian measured in degrees.

3. Latitude is distance measured in degrees north and south of the equator.

4. The prime meridian is the reference point for measuring longitude.

5. The time of the day or night at any place in the world is measured from the prime meridian.

B. Map projections (Mercator, polar, azimuthal, cylindrical, conic, mathematical, etc.) show some distortion of the earth's surface.

C. There are many types of maps, including political (political divisions), physical (geographic features), relief (elevations and depressions), and special-purpose (products, vegetation, mining, population, etc.).

D. Globes are accurate representations of the earth and show relative size, shape, and distance.

IV. WEATHER AND CLIMATE

A. Weather is the day-by-day change in the earth's atmosphere, and climate is weather conditions over a long period of time.

B. **Weather and climate are affected by many factors.**

1. Air movements, such as prevailing winds (westerlies and trade winds), affect climate.

2. Local air movements, such as land-sea breezes and valley-mountain breezes, affect climate.

3. Marine (sea) and continental (land) air masses affect weather and climate.

4. Ocean currents and mountain barriers affect weather and climate.

V. **GEOGRAPHERS DIVIDE THE EARTH INTO REGIONS IN ORDER TO STUDY IT MORE ADEQUATELY**

A. **The topography of land masses includes mountains, deserts, plains, plateaus, and valleys.**

B. **The major bodies of water include oceans, seas, lakes, rivers, and gulfs.**

C. **Vegetation is affected by land forms and water distribution.**

VI. **THE STUDY OF GEOGRAPHY ATTEMPTS TO ANALYZE THE INTERRELATIONSHIP BETWEEN HUMANS AND THEIR ENVIRONMENT**

A. **The distribution of the world's population is determined by such things as climatic regions, vegetation regions, soils, water systems, and other resources.**

B. **Unfavorable regions are generally those with extreme climatic conditions or limited natural resources.**

C. **The relationship of humans' environment to land use determines occupations, political organizations, economic prosperity, etc.**

D. **Physical features often determine political boundaries.**

E. **A knowledge of climate and topography are important in understanding land-use patterns.**

F. **Environment influences economic, cultural, and political development.**

VII. **U.S. GEOGRAPHY: AN OVERVIEW**

A. **The Gulf Stream, an Atlantic warm water current, warms the East Coast in winter and is responsible for excellent fishing.**

B. **The southeastern Coastal Plain extends along the coast from New Jersey to Texas and is generally low land.**

C. **The Piedmont (the foothills at the base of Appalachian Mountains), the Appalachian Mountains, and the Cumberland and Allegheny plateaus are in the eastern region of the United States.**

D. **In the northeast, the Appalachians meet the ocean, forming a rough, rocky coast.**

E. **West of the Appalachians, the wind (prevailing westerlies) is an important influence on climate.**

   1. In the winter, cold air from the northwest produces freezing temperatures.

   2. In summer, warm, moist southwesterly winds cause hot, humid weather.

F. **Most of the interior is generally flat land.**

   1. The eastern half is called the interior lowlands.

   2. The western half is called the Great Plains.

G. **The Mississippi River drains the interior of the United States.**

H. **The crest of the Rocky Mountains is called the Continental Divide.**

   1. Rivers that begin east of the Continental Divide flow toward the Atlantic Ocean.

   2. Western rivers flow toward the Pacific Ocean.

I. **The land between the Rockies and the Sierra Nevada is called the Great Basin.**

J. **The Sierra Nevada and the Cascade Range form the western mountain ranges.**

   1. The western slope of the Sierra Nevada borders the Central Valley of California.

   2. The Coast Ranges are the western wall of the Central Valley.

SCIENCE REVIEW

INTRODUCTION TO THE SCIENCE REVIEW

This section is designed to give you an intensive summary of some of the material covered by the Science section of the MSAT. The material includes reviews of the natural sciences and glossaries of important terms.

The reviews of biology, geology and meteorology, chemistry, physics, and astronomy provide explanations of the major ideas in those fields. Read them slowly and carefully, underlining key words and phrases. The main purpose of your study should be to understand the central concepts (like evolution and energy), not to memorize the technical vocabulary. Don't spend excessive time on any one section. If you have difficulty with a concept, write a question mark in the margin and return later. Further reading frequently clarifies a difficulty.

The glossaries define the principal scientific terms of the five natural sciences. Don't attempt to memorize the lists. Their utility is to increase your understanding of technical ideas. When studying the glossaries, it is helpful to mentally compare terms that are related (like atom and molecule). Write your own comments after some of the definitions. If you don't understand a term, write a question mark and return later.

BASIC CONCEPTS

- **Biology** is the science of life. Life has astonishing variety, embracing bacteria and baboons, whales and walnuts, algae and alligators—yet all those life forms share some similar materials and processes. The complexity of life compels biologists to specialize in certain levels of life: organic molecules, cells, organs, individuals, species, and communities. Here are some important characteristics of most life forms. A living organism has a very complicated *organization* in which a series of *processes* takes place. Life *responds* to its environment, often with *movement*. An organism must *maintain* itself and *grow*. Finally, a plant or animal will produce new organisms much like itself; *reproduction* is the most universal process of life, explaining its survival and variety.

- **The cell** is the smallest amount of living matter, a bit of organic material that is the unit of structure and function for all organisms. Cells range in size from the smallest speck visible through an excellent microscope to the yolk of the largest egg. Some tiny organisms (like bacteria) are one-celled, but all larger organisms are composed of many cells arrayed in tissues. Although an isolated cell may be spherical, the cells packed together in plant or animal tissues have flattened walls. The essential subdivisions of a cell are the cell membrane, the cytoplasm, and the cell nucleus. (See Figure 1.) The cell membrane is semipermeable, allowing some substances to pass while excluding others. The main material within a cell, the cytoplasm, varies in consistency from a fluid to a semisolid. Embedded in the cytoplasm are functional bodies: the centrosome that participates in cell division, ribosomes for constructing proteins, mitochondria that conduct metabolism, Golgi bodies involved in secretion, and vacuoles used in digestion. The cytoplasm of plant cells also contains plastids, bodies with chlorophyll which carry out photosynthesis. The cell nucleus is a separate mass containing nucleoli and chromosomes, the genetic material.

THE CELL

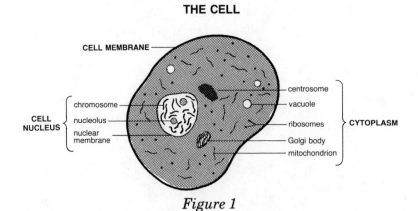

Figure 1

- **Metabolism** is the set of chemical reactions within protoplasm, the living material of the cell. The chemical constituents of protoplasm include water as well as organic and inorganic compounds. The organic molecules are proteins, carbohydrates, lipids, and nucleic acids. Proteins are both structural components and enzymes, organic catalysts that enable particular metabolic reactions to proceed; all proteins are built from simpler amino acids. Carbohydrates (starches and sugars) and lipids (fats) are energy sources for cellular processes. The two nucleic acids, deoxyribose nucleic acid (DNA) and ribose nucleic acid (RNA), are complex chained molecules with encoded instructions for metabolism; the chromosomes of the cell nucleus contain the DNA. Metabolic reactions involve assimilation, photosynthesis, digestion, and respiration. The result is to store chemical energy as adenosine triphosphate (ATP). During cellular work the ATP decomposes and yields energy.

- **Mitosis** is the process of cell division in which the nuclear material of the original cell is divided equally between the newer cells. Such multiplication of cells permits growth of an organism, whether it occurs in the core of a tree or the muscle of a human. (See Figure 2.)

MITOSIS

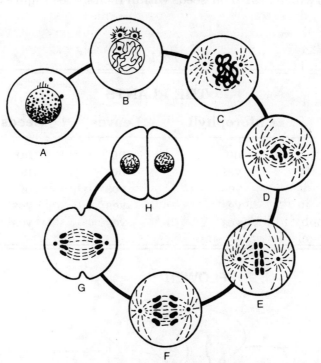

A, resting cell; B, C, and D, prophase;
E, metaphase; F, anaphase; G and H, telophase.

Figure 2

Mitosis begins as the chromosomes thicken and the centrosome divides (prophase). Then the nuclear membrane disappears and a spindle develops between the two parts of the centrosome. The chromosomes gather on that spindle (metaphase). The spindle divides, splitting each chromosome apart (anaphase). Finally, the nuclear membranes form and two new cells result (telophase). The chromosomes carry a genetic message enabling the cell to make proteins, so mitosis provides a complex mechanism for a new cell to obtain the genetic instructions it needs.

- **Plants** may be divided into five broad groups. The more primitive groups are *algae* and *fungi;* these plants lack true roots, stems, and leaves. Algae range from a single cell to huge seaweeds; mostly they inhabit lakes and oceans. The fungi include molds, yeasts, and mushrooms. Fungi lack chlorophyll and thus are incapable of manufacturing food, so they are either parasites, preying on other living organisms, or saprophytes, existing on waste products and decaying organisms. A lichen is actually two organisms, a fungus and an alga, living together symbiotically. The more advanced plants possess roots, stems, and leaves. The *ferns* lack seeds and reproduce by means of spores, each of which may develop into a new plant without fertilization. Unlike the ferns, the seed plants require fertilization, and male pollen grains are carried to the female ovule by vectors like the wind and insects. The *gymnosperms* are cone-bearing plants (including pines) with seeds exposed on cone scales. The *angiosperms* are flowering plants which bear their seeds within fruits. (See Figure 3.)

Table 1

THE PLANTS

Plant Group	Chlorophyll	Leaves	Seeds	Flowers
Fungi	no	no	no	no
Algae	yes	no	no	no
Ferns	yes	yes	no	no
Gymnosperms	yes	yes	yes	no
Angiosperms	yes	yes	yes	yes

FLOWER

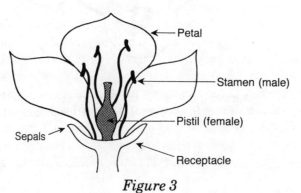

Figure 3

- **Photosynthesis** is the process by which plants convert light into the chemical energy stored in foods. Chlorophyll, the green pigment within the leaf, is necessary to trap light energy for the photosynthetic reaction. In photosynthesis, carbon dioxide and water react to form sugar and oxygen:

$$6CO_2 + 6H_2O + \underset{energy}{Light} \xrightarrow{\text{chlorophyll}} C_6H_{12}O_6 + 6O_2$$

$$\underset{\substack{carbon \\ dioxide}}{} \quad \underset{water}{} \quad \quad \quad \quad \underset{sugar}{} \quad \underset{oxygen}{}$$

Thus plants absorb carbon dioxide and give off oxygen. The sugar made by plants can be oxidized later in a process that releases energy. The oxidation can be in the plant itself or in an animal that eats the plant. The release of energy by oxidation of sugar is respiration:

$$C_6H_{12}O_6 + 6O_2 \xrightarrow{\text{Krebs cycle}} 6CO_2 + 6H_2O + Energy$$

$$\underset{sugar}{} \quad \underset{oxygen}{} \quad \quad \quad \underset{\substack{carbon \\ dioxide}}{} \quad \underset{water}{}$$

Table 2

ENERGY GENERATION

Photosynthesis	Respiration
Carbon dioxide and water are raw materials	Sugar and oxygen are raw materials
Sugar and oxygen are produced	Carbon dioxide and water are produced
Reduction reaction	Oxidation reaction
Occurs only in light	Occurs in light or darkness
Occurs only in chlorophyll-containing cells	Occurs in all living cells
Occurs in chloroplasts	Occurs in mitochondria

- **Animals** cannot perform photosynthesis and, therefore, derive their food from other organisms. Herbivores eat plants directly. Carnivores prey on other animals, but this food chain, too, ends in plants. Plants and animals are classified into *phyla* on the basis of their cells, tissues, organs, and overall organization. Each phylum is a major group of organisms. There are about six phyla of protists (one-celled organisms), eight phyla of plants, and twenty-one phyla of animals. Table 3 lists the most important animal phyla. For the last three advanced phyla, the main classes of animals are also given. There are some small marine chordates of primitive form, but those chordates listed are the vertebrates, characterized by a backbone, a definite head, well-developed brain and eyes, a central heart, red blood cells, and two pairs of limbs. Let's take a closer look at the organs within the vertebrates, using a human as our example.

Table 3

THE ANIMALS

Phylum	Members and Description
Porifera	Sponges; ingest microscopic food from currents
Coelenterata	Corals; capture food with stinging tentacles
Platyhelminthes	Flatworms, tapeworms; most are parasitic
Nematoda	Roundworms, hookworms; some are parasitic
Annelida	Segmented worms, including earthworms
Bryozoa	Colonial animals in ocean
Brachiopoda	Lampshells; bivalves with tentacles inside shell
Echinodermata	Starfish, sea urchins, crinoids; 5-rayed symmetry
Mollusca	Pelecypoda: clam, oyster, mussel; bivalves Gastropoda: snail; often with coiled shell Cephalopoda: octopus, squid
Arthropoda	Crustacea: crab, crayfish, lobster Insecta: ant, bee, fly, grasshopper; 6 legs Arachnida: spider, tick, scorpion; 8 legs
Chordata	Agnatha: lamprey; primitive fishes with round mouths Chondrichthyes: shark, ray; skeleton of cartilage Osteichthyes: cod, perch, trout; bony fishes Amphibia: frog, toad, salamander; lay eggs in water Reptilia: snake, turtle, alligator; lay eggs on land Aves: sparrow, pigeon, chicken; birds with feathers Mammalia: cat, man, whale; females have mammary glands for milk

- **The sensory system** includes those specialized structures which initiate a nerve impulse after being affected by the environment. The eyes are the organs of vision. Light rays are refracted as they pass through the cornea, lens, and vitreous body to focus on the retina, where an image is formed. The optic nerve then carries impulses from the light-sensitive cells of the retina to the brain. (See Figure 4.)

THE EYE

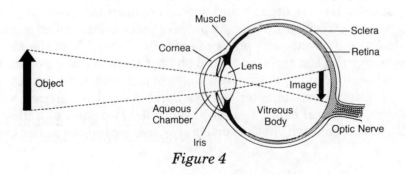

Figure 4

The ear is the receptor of sound and the organ of balance. When sound waves cause the tympanum (eardrum) to vibrate, three tiny bones transmit the motion to the cochlea and the organ of Corti, which initiates a nerve impulse. The seat of balance is in the semicircular canals within the inner ear. The receptors of taste are distributed on the upper surface of the tongue. Each taste bud detects one of the four primary tastes (salty, sweet, sour, and bitter); other taste sensations are combinations of the primary tastes.

- **The nervous system** is composed of the brain, spinal cord, and peripheral nerves which extend throughout the body. The functional unit of the nervous system is the neuron, a nerve cell with short dendrites that carry electrical impulses to the cell body, and a long axon, the outgoing fiber along which the impulse is transmitted further. (See Figure 5.) Sensory neurons conduct signals from sense organs to the central nervous system, the spinal cord, and brain. Motor neurons transmit signals from the central nervous system to muscles. Figure 6 shows several major parts of the human brain. The hindbrain (cerebellum and medulla oblongata) operates unconsciously and automatically to regulate vital functions like circulation, respiration, excretion, and muscle tension. The cerebrum is the largest part of the brain; it receives information from the senses and makes conscious decisions.

NEURON

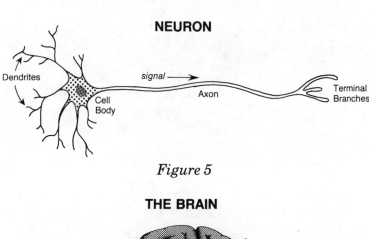

Figure 5

THE BRAIN

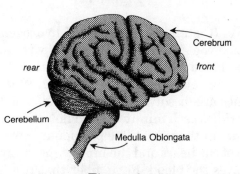

Figure 6

- **The digestive system** includes the mouth, pharynx (throat), esophagus, stomach, small intestine, and large intestine. Other organs in this system are the salivary glands, liver, gallbladder, and pancreas. The enzymes contained in saliva, gastric juice, pancreatic juice, and intestinal fluids convert carbohydrates, fats, and proteins into molecules small enough to be absorbed into the blood. Simple sugars are absorbed as such and do not require digestion. Carbohydrates are converted to various sugars by the action of several enzymes, including ptyalin from saliva. Fats are transformed to glycerol and fatty acids by the combined action of bile from the liver and the enzyme lipase from the pancreas. Proteins are broken apart to their constituent amino acids. The final products of digestion—sugars, glycerol, fatty acids, and amino acids—are absorbed into the bloodstream through the millions of projections (villi) lining the small intestine. Once in the blood, these molecules are metabolized in the various body tissues.

- **The circulatory system** consists of the blood, the heart, and the blood vessels. (See Figure 7.) The blood is composed of red cells, white cells, and platelets suspended in a watery medium called plasma. Red cells transport oxygen in combination with the iron pigment, hemoglobin. Human hemoglobin is a protein with the formula

THE CIRCULATORY SYSTEM

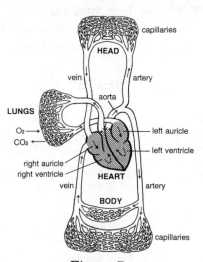

Figure 7

$C_{3032}H_{4816}O_{872}N_{780}S_8Fe_4$ (C stands for carbon, H hydrogen, O oxygen, N nitrogen, S sulfur, and Fe iron), and that giant molecule transports just four oxygen molecules. The function of white blood cells is to fight infection, while platelets initiate the clotting necessary to stop bleeding after a wound. Nutrients, wastes, hormones, antibodies, and enzymes are dissolved in the plasma. The heart is a muscular pump, beating about seventy times each minute. Blood flows from the heart through arteries and returns to the heart in the veins. The pulmonary circulation is the flow of blood between the right side of the heart and the lungs, where oxygen diffuses into the blood and carbon dioxide leaves the blood. Remember that respiration enables the body to oxidize food, consuming oxygen and producing carbon dioxide. From the lungs, the oxygenated blood returns to the left side of the heart, where the powerful left ventricle pumps it through the aorta into general circulation. Arteries lead into smaller vessels called capillaries, where oxygen and nutrients diffuse into tissue cells. Wastes diffuse back into the capillaries, which lead into veins and, ultimately, back to the right side of the heart.

- **Reproduction** in organisms may occur by either sexual or asexual processes. In asexual reproduction there is only one parent and simple mitotic division produces the offspring; most protists, many plants, and a few primitive animals follow this reproductive strategy. Sexual reproduction involves two parents, as in all higher animals, except in the cases of self-fertilization in many flowering plants. The advanced plants and animals produce male and female sex cells by a special mode of cell division called meiosis. The normal adult organism has a double set of chromosomes within each cell, a condition described as diploid. A haploid cell has only half the normal number of chromosomes. Figure 8 shows the four pairs of chromosomes within the diploid cells of the fruit fly, *Drosophila*. The meiotic division employs the same spindle machinery as used in mitosis, but the consequence is not diploid daughter cells identical to the parent (as in mitosis) but haploid sex cells, the gametes. Gametes from a male are sperm cells, while gametes from a female are egg cells (ova). A haploid sperm must unite with a haploid egg to form a diploid zygote, which develops into a mature organism through the process of embryogeny. Meiotic production of gametes provides the means of mixing genetic information through the sexually reproducing population, and the spread of useful information allows successful evolutionary adaptation.

MEIOSIS

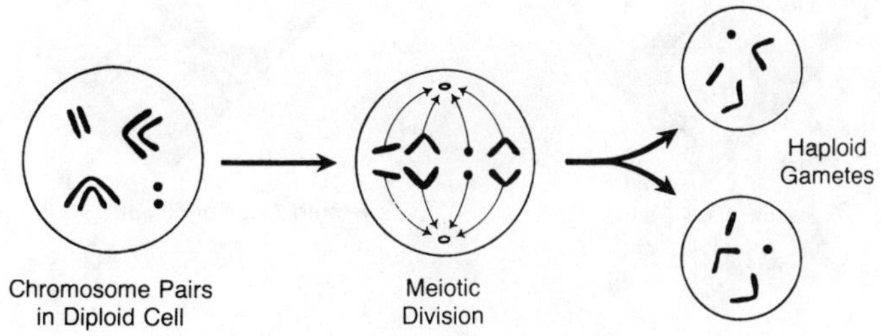

Chromosome Pairs in Diploid Cell

Meiotic Division

Haploid Gametes

(cell components besides chromosomes not shown)

Figure 8

- **Nucleic acids** store genetic messages and instruct the cell how to make the many proteins needed for life. Heredity has an elegant molecular basis. Nucleic acids are truly the secret of life. DNA in the chromosomes of the cell nucleus is a long molecule of two chains twisted into a double spiral, or helix. Nitrogenous bases are attached to the chains in a special sequence that is a coded message, the instructions for life. The double chain permits the DNA to duplicate itself exactly during reproduction, retaining the original genetic message. The message contains the instructions necessary to build various proteins, many of which function as enzymes. Some RNA molecules carry the message from the DNA in the cell nucleus to the ribosomes in the cytoplasm, where protein assembly occurs.

- **Genes** are the functional message units along the DNA chains within the chromosomes. One chromosome is composed of many genes, each of which determines or influences an inheritable trait. In diploid organisms, chromosomes occur in pairs and so must genes. The first to study such pairs of genetic traits was the Austrian monk Gregor Mendel (1865) who cultivated garden peas, the seeds of which were either round or wrinkled. He discovered that when he crossed purebred round peas with wrinkled peas, the first hybrid generation was all round peas. Mendel inferred that the round characteristic (*R*) was dominant over the wrinkled characteristic (*w*) in the hybrid plants (*Rw*). In Figure 9, each adult pea plant has two genetic characteristics (alleles), while the gametes have only one allele apiece. Then the hybrid peas were crossed and the next generation was 75 percent round and 25 percent wrinkled. (See Figure 10.) Notice that the recessive wrinkled trait can manifest itself only in a plant with two wrinkled alleles (*ww*), but round pea seeds occur with either (*RR*) or (*Rw*). Mendelian genetics permits understanding of the frequencies of various genetic traits in populations. New alleles arise by mutations, errors during copying of the DNA code.

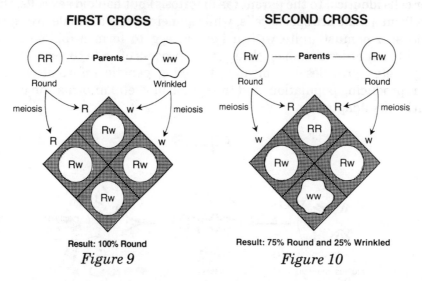

Figure 9

Figure 10

- **Evolution** of life is indicated by the fact that fossil organisms in rock strata are different from modern organisms. As we go back in time, searching lower and older strata, the organisms diverge more and more from those living today. Yet the variation in life forms appears to be relatively continuous. For example, 60 million years ago horses were quite small and had four toes on each foot. As time passed, horses evolved through a series of larger sizes and fewer toes to today's large, single-toed creature. Other evidence for the evolution of life comes from the study of biogeography (the distribution of present-day species), embryology (the similarities among early developmental stages of animals), homology (structural similarities in various organisms), and biochemistry (chemical similarities in various organisms). Charles Darwin listed evidences for the progression of life in his book *The Origin of Species* (1859) and proposed that evolution proceeded by natural selection. Within a variable population those organisms able to adapt to the environment most successfully would tend to have more offspring than their less successful rivals, and so the genetic characteristics of the entire population would slowly shift toward better adaptation. In this manner, given the immensity of geologic time, entire new organic structures, systems, and species could arise. Modern evolutionary biologists emphasize the central role of mutation in providing the genetic variation necessary for nature's trial-and-error selection.

- **Taxonomy** is the classification and naming of organisms. Over 1,300,000 different species have been described, so it is essential to sort them systematically. The binomial nomenclature devised by the Swede Linnaeus (1735) gives each organism two names, the genus and species. For example, the dog is *Canis familiaris*. Genera are grouped into higher taxonomic levels, arranged in a hierarchy as shown in Table 4. At the highest level are the three kingdoms: protists, plants, and animals. Organisms are classified into taxonomic groups by morphological similarities and genetic affinities.

Table 4

THE TAXONOMIC GROUPS

Kingdom
  Phylum
    Class
      Order
        Family
          Genus
            Species

- **Ecology** is the study of the relationship of organisms to their environment. The major habitats are the oceans, fresh water, and land. The oceans have the greatest proportion of living things. The upper layers of the oceans contain microscopic plants collectively called phytoplankton. Through photosynthesis, phytoplankton produce food for the marine life of the depths. Because ocean conditions are relatively uniform, most marine species are broadly distributed. Rivers, brooks, lakes, and swamps house different species of organisms. Fresh water shows greater variation in currents, composition, and temperature than seawater, so many freshwater species are quite restricted in distribution. Land habitats show the greatest extremes in temperature and moisture, with a corresponding diversity in life. In any habitat the various organisms compete for food. The ultimate source of food is photosynthetic plant life.

GLOSSARY

Adrenaline—A hormone secreted by the adrenal medulla; also called epinephrine.

Algae—Simple plants containing chlorophyll.

Amino acid—An organic compound containing an amino and a carboxyl group; the building blocks of proteins.

Amphibians—A class of vertebrates capable of living both in water and on land. The larval forms have gills and the adults have lungs; includes frogs and toads.

Angiosperms—The class of flowering plants, with seeds enclosed in fruits.

Antibiotic—A substance that destroys a microorganism or inhibits its growth.

Antibody—A substance produced by the body to combat the injurious effect of a foreign substance (antigen).

Aorta—The main artery leaving the heart.

Arachnids—A class of arthropods with no antennae and four pairs of legs; includes spiders, scorpions, ticks, mites, and king crabs.

Artery—A blood vessel which carries blood away from the heart.

Arthropods—The phylum of segmented invertebrates with jointed appendages and a chitinous exoskeleton; includes arachnids, crustaceans, and insects.

Asexual—Reproduction in one individual, without the union of gametes.

Bacteria—Unicellular organisms without a distinct nucleus and usually without chlorophyll.

BACTERIA

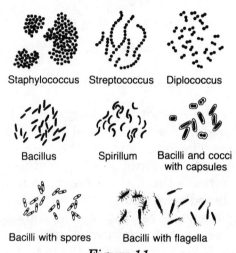

Staphylococcus   Streptococcus   Diplococcus

Bacillus   Spirillum   Bacilli and cocci with capsules

Bacilli with spores   Bacilli with flagella

Figure 11

Bile—A yellowish-green fluid secreted by the liver that aids in the digestion of fats.

Budding—Asexual reproduction by splitting of a new organism from the parent.

Capillary—The smallest blood vessel which carries blood between an artery and a vein.

Carbon cycle—The exchange of carbon between living things and their environment.

Carnivore—A flesh-eating animal.

Cell—The basic unit of organic structure and function.

Cellulose—The woody tissue of plants.

Chlorophyll—The green coloring matter in a plant that facilitates photosynthesis.

Chordates—The phylum characterized by a spinal cord; includes the vertebrates.

Chromosome—A body in the cell nucleus that is the bearer of genetic information.

Cold-blooded—An animal whose body temperature varies with the surroundings.

Cross-pollination—The transfer of pollen from one plant to a flower on another plant.

Crustaceans—The class of arthropods with gills and two pairs of antennae; includes lobsters, crabs, barnacles, and crayfish.

Cytoplasm—The substance of the cell outside the nucleus.

Deoxyribose nucleic acid (DNA)—The compound in the chromosomes that stores genetic information as a molecular code.

Dominant—The one of the two alternative genetic traits which is displayed in a heterozygous individual.

Ecology—The study of relations between organisms and their environment.

Embryo—An organism in the early stages of development.

Enzyme—A protein that serves as an organic catalyst for metabolic reactions.

Evolution—The modification of life forms with the passage of time.

Exoskeleton—A hard, jointed case outside the fleshy tissues of an animal.

Fertilization—The union of gametes to form a zygote.

Fossil—Any naturally preserved remains of ancient life.

Fungi—Plants that lack chlorophyll; molds, mushrooms, and yeasts.

Gamete—A sex cell; an egg or sperm.

Gene—A unit of heredity located on the chromosome.

Germination—The sprouting of a seed.

Gymnosperms—A class of vascular plants bearing seeds in cones.

Herbivore—A plant-eating animal.

Homology—The similarity of body structures of different organisms, due to common ancestry; the structures may not have the same function. A bat's wing is homologous to a squirrel's foreleg.

Hormone—A chemical substance that regulates body processes.

Insulin—A hormone produced by the pancreas, which regulates the body's utilization of sugar.

Mammals—A class of warm-blooded vertebrates possessing hair and feeding their young milk by means of mammary glands.

Meiosis—The mode of cell division that produces gametes, each with one-half the number of chromosomes of the parent cell.

Metabolism—The chemical processes within an organism.

Mitosis—Cell division with chromosome duplication, forming offspring cells with the same number of chromosomes as the parent cell; cell splitting.

Mutation—An inheritable change in a gene.

Natural selection—The survival of the best-adapted organism.

Nucleus—The central part of a cell, containing the chromosomes and controlling cellular activities.

Organ—A group of cells or tissues functioning as a whole.

Ovum—An egg; a female gamete.

Parasite—An organism that lives in or on another organism, deriving food at the expense of its host.

Pasteurization—The killing of microorganisms in milk by heating it to 145°F for thirty minutes.

Photosynthesis—The production of carbohydrates by green plants in the presence of light.

Phylum—A major group of animals or plants; the main division of a kingdom.

Plasma—The liquid part of the blood.

Pollination—Fertilization by the transfer of pollen from an anther to a stigma.

Protein—An organic compound made up of amino acids.

Protoplasm—A general term for the living matter of the cell.

Recessive—The one of two alternative genetic traits which is masked in a heterozygous individual.

Respiration—Biological oxidation.

Ribose nucleic acid (RNA)—A substance in the cell with the function of making proteins.

Sexual—Reproduction involving the union of an egg and sperm.

Symbiosis—The close living association of organisms of different species in which both benefit.

Taxonomy—The classification of organisms.

Trait—An inherited characteristic.

Transpiration—The evaporation of water from plants.

Tropism—A growth movement in a plant in response to an environmental stimulus.

Vaccine—A fluid containing dead disease germs injected into an animal to produce immunity.

Vertebrates—Chordates characterized by a well-developed brain, a backbone, and usually two pairs of limbs; includes the fishes, amphibians, reptiles, birds, and mammals.

Virus—A simple form of matter, on the borderline between inorganic chemicals and life; often infects higher organisms.

GEOLOGY/METEOROLOGY

BASIC CONCEPTS

- **Geology** is the science that describes and interprets the earth. It classifies the materials that make up the earth, observes their shapes and distribution, and tries to discover the processes that caused the materials to be formed in that manner. Some major geological fields are geomorphology (landforms), petrology (rocks), stratigraphy (layered rocks), and paleontology (fossils). All fields contribute to historical geology, the ambitious attempt to list the specific events which have produced the present earth. Processes occurring today are observed carefully and their effects are measured. Then geologists assume that similar effects in ancient rocks were caused by processes similar to those of the present. This method of using the present to interpret the past is called uniformitarianism. For example, glaciation in early eras is indicated by ancient deposits with features very similar to those produced by present-day glaciers.

- **The earth's structure** (see Figure 12) has been inferred from its astronomical properties and seismic records of earthquake waves which traveled through the interior of the earth. Temperature rises from the surface (20°C) to the center (3000°C) of the earth; this fact is essential to understanding geological processes. About 31

STRUCTURE OF THE EARTH

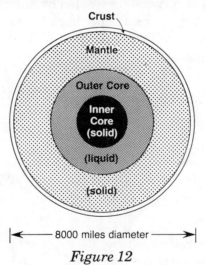

Figure 12

percent of the earth's mass is a dense core of iron and nickel metals, melted by the extremely high temperature of the center of the earth. Around that liquid core is the largest zone of the planet (68 percent), the mantle of crystalline silicates rich in magnesium, calcium, and iron. The very hot mantle is mainly solid, but local melting to magma (molten rock) is the source of volcanic eruptions. Above the mantle is the crust, which makes up less than one percent of the earth. This relatively thin zone (5–25 miles) contains the only rocks we can study, even in the deepest mines or drillholes. Table 5 shows the average chemical composition of crustal rocks.

Table 5

AVERAGE COMPOSITION OF CRUSTAL ROCKS

Element		Percent
Oxygen	O	62.6
Silicon	Si	21.2
Aluminum	Al	6.5
Sodium	Na	2.6
Calcium	Ca	1.9
Iron	Fe	1.9
Magnesium	Mg	1.8
Potassium	K	1.4

- **The rock cycle** (see Figure 13) displays the linkage of processes within the crust. The earth's internal heat from radioactivity fuses (melts) solid rock to liquid magma, which has a temperature of about 1000°C. The magma is of lower density than the overlying rocks, so it tends to squeeze its way upward. Plutonic rocks form when the magma cools and crystallizes beneath the surface, but volcanic rocks form when the magma erupts at the surface. Exposure of any rock type at the surface leads to fragmentation by weathering and erosion of the particles. Sand and mud are deposited as soft sediments, which may be compacted by burial or cemented by subsurface solutions to form sedimentary rocks. Deeper burial of sedimentary and volcanic rocks to zones of higher temperature forces recrystallization to metamorphic rocks and, eventually, melting to magma.

THE ROCK CYCLE

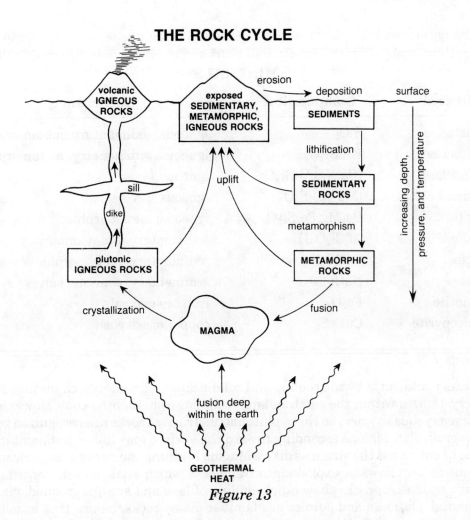

Figure 13

- **Minerals** are natural chemical compounds which are the crystals that make up rocks. Each mineral has a specific composition or narrow range of composition. In Table 6 showing common rock-forming minerals, two chemical elements which may substitute for each other are enclosed by parentheses; thus the mineral olivine—$(Mg,Fe)_2SiO_4$—varies in composition from Mg_2SiO_4 to Fe_2SiO_4. The most abundant minerals in the crust are the two feldspars (orthoclase and plagioclase), quartz, olivine, and augite. Note that these five minerals are silicates, built from interlocking silicon and oxygen atoms.

Table 6

MINERALS

Mineral	Composition	Occurrence
Quartz	SiO_2	igneous, sedimentary, metamorphic
Orthoclase	$KAlSi_3O_8$	igneous, sedimentary, metamorphic
Plagioclase	$(Ca,Na)Al_2Si_2O_8$	igneous
Olivine	$(Mg,Fe)_2SiO_4$	igneous
Augite	$Ca(Mg,Fe)Si_2O_6$	igneous, metamorphic
Kaolin	$Al_2Si_2O_9H_4$	sedimentary: a clay mineral
Calcite	$CaCO_3$	sedimentary, metamorphic
Halite	$NaCl$	sedimentary: common salt
Hematite	Fe_2O_3	iron ore deposit
Chalcopyrite	$CuFeS_2$	copper ore deposit

- **Igneous rocks** form by the cooling and solidification of molten rock matter. Magma that crystallizes within the earth in large volumes as batholiths cools slowly enough for large crystals to grow, so these plutonic (instrusive) rocks are recognized by their coarse grain size. Magma ascending toward the surface may follow sedimentary beds as sills or cut across the strata as dikes. Magma reaching the surface as a volcano may spill out as lava flows or explode into fragments which settle as ash deposits. Such volcanic (extrusive) rocks show quick chilling of lava and are fine-grained, glassy, or fragmental. Obsidian and pumice are familiar glassy rocks. Notice that basalt is the volcanic equivalent of gabbro, and rhyolite is the volcanic equivalent of granite.

Table 7

COMMON IGNEOUS ROCKS

Occurrence	Rock Name	Grain Size	Minerals
Plutonic	Gabbro	coarse	plagioclase, augite, olivine
	Granite	coarse	quartz, orthoclase, plagioclase
Volcanic	Basalt	fine	plagioclase, augite, olivine
	Rhyolite	fine	quartz, orthoclase, plagioclase

- **Sedimentary rocks** form by deposition at the earth's surface, usually in a body of water. Clastic sediments are accumulations of mud, sand, and pebbles from erosion of preexisting rocks. Chemical sediments are salts precipitated from seawater or a salt lake. Organic sediments were formed by life, usually by an aquatic creature extracting material from the water to form its shell; millions of shells may form a large bed or reef.

Table 8

COMMON SEDIMENTARY ROCKS

Process	Rock Name	Description	Minerals
Clastic	Conglomerate	cemented pebbles	rock fragments
	Sandstone	cemented sand	quartz and orthoclase
	Shale	hardened mud	clays, like kaolin
Chemical	Salt	crystalline	halite
Organic	Limestone	shelly	calcite

- **Metamorphic rocks** are produced when sedimentary or igneous rocks are transformed by high temperature or pressure. The extreme conditions force chemical reactions and recrystallization to new minerals and textures. Texture describes the size, shape, and orientation of mineral grains in a rock. Contact metamorphism is baking adjacent to an igneous intrusion. Regional metamorphism occurred where an entire area was buried and deformed during mountain building; such rocks have crystals with parallel orientations from the pressure of deformation.

Table 9

COMMON METAMORPHIC ROCKS

Rock Name	Texture	Minerals	Parent Rock
Gneiss	coarse oriented	quartz, orthoclase	shale, sandstone
Schist	medium oriented	quartz, micas	shale, sandstone
Slate	fine oriented	micas	shale
Marble	coarse granular	calcite	limestone
Quartzite	medium granular	quartz	sandstone

- **Weathering** is the destruction of bedrock by atmospheric action, with the generation of soil and loose, erodible debris. Most weathering involves chemical action by the air and water, which attack the minerals of the rocks. Iron-bearing minerals are oxidized, while common feldspar grains undergo hydrolysis to kaolin and other clays. Carbon dioxide in aqueous solution is a weak acid capable of slowly dissolving carbonates, like limestone; such limestone solution can yield a karst terrain pitted with small lakes and caverns. Weathering may involve only mechanical action, as in the shattering of rock by alternate freezing and thawing. The soil formed atop bedrock tends toward a profile of several layers, which may be inspected along highway roadcuts.

- **Erosion** carries away the debris from weathering, moving it downslope to a more stable site of deposition. The most important erosional agent is running water. The water carries some salts in solution while particles are transported in suspension. Stream erosion of an uplifted highland leads to a characteristic time-series of landforms, from youthful terrain with V-shaped valleys to mature terrain with rounded hills and broad valleys. Wind is a significant means of erosion in arid regions; fine particles are blown away to be deposited downwind as sand dunes. At high elevations and polar latitudes ice is present throughout the year, so glacial erosion may occur. Snow accumulates and its weight transforms it to ice, which oozes slowly downslope under the pressure of its own weight. Glacial ice is a remarkably effective agent of erosion, capable of carving out U-shaped valleys in mountains. During the Pleistocene Ice Age, which ended only about 12,000 years ago, great glacial sheets covered much of North America and deposited an irregular blanket of till (mud and boulder debris).

- **Strata** are the layers of sediment deposited in a quiet environment. Common sites of deposition are lakes, deltas at the mouths of rivers, beaches and sandbars along the coast, and (most important) the marine environment. Strata are commonly very extensive laterally and relatively thin vertically, like a blanket. An important geological rule is the law of original horizontality, which states that most sediments are deposited in beds which were originally horizontal, and any tilting is due to later earth movements. A second stratigraphic principle is the law of superposition: younger beds were originally deposited above older beds.

- **Fossils** are traces of ancient life preserved in the strata as shells, footprints, and the like. Because life has evolved (changed) continually through geological history, the fossils in older strata differ from those found in more recent deposits. In fact, strata deposited during one geological period contain characteristic life forms different from those of any other period. For example, the earliest fossil-rich beds have many trilobites, early crablike creatures which have been extinct for hundreds of millions of years; discovery of fossil trilobites in a formation permits assignment of that bed to an early period.

- **The geological time scale** was a major achievement of stratigraphers, who used fossils to arrange strata in a standard order. More recently, geochemists have measured the amount of radioactive decay in minerals and calculated the time at which the rock formed. So the geological time scale in Table 10 represents interpretations from fossils and radioactivity. The earth is believed to be about 5.6 billion years old. The fossiliferous strata record only the last 11 percent of earth's history. And human civilization has lasted only 10,000 years, a brief moment on the geological time scale. The immensity of geological time is the major discovery of geology. There has been ample time for very slow processes to produce large consequences.

Table 10

THE GEOLOGICAL TIME SCALE

Geological Era	Beginning (years before present)	Duration (years)	Characteristic Life Forms
Cenozoic	70,000,000	70,000,000	mammals
Mesozoic	225,000,000	155,000,000	reptiles
Paleozoic	600,000,000	375,000,000	invertebrates
Precambrian	5,600,000,000	5,000,000,000	no life except algae

- **Oceans** cover 70 percent of the earth's surface. The salts in seawater were dissolved during the weathering of bedrock. The major ions in seawater are shown in Table 11. During one period or another, every portion of the continents has been depressed beneath sea level, and most of the strata seen in roadcuts throughout the United States are marine deposits. A typical cross section for the Atlantic Ocean would look like Figure 14. The broad, shallow continental shelf collects much sediment from the continents. The mid-ocean ridge has frequent earthquakes and volcanic eruptions, so it is thought to be the site of upwelling of material from within the mantle.

Table 11

MAJOR IONS IN SEAWATER

Ion		Percent
Chloride	Cl^{-1}	55.1
Sodium	Na^{+1}	30.6
Sulfate	SO_4^{-2}	7.7
Magnesium	Mg^{+2}	3.7
Calcium	Ca^{+2}	1.2
Potassium	K^{+1}	1.1
Bicarbonate	HCO_3^{-1}	0.4

CROSS SECTION OF THE ATLANTIC OCEAN

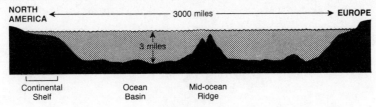

Figure 14

- **Continents** may be divided into two zones. A shield area is a broad plain of Precambrian-age granite and gneiss, providing a stable core for the continent. Most of Canada is such a shield area. The second type of zone is one of recent upheaval, an orogenic (mountain-building) zone. Mountains occur in long, narrow belts, mostly along the edges of continents. On a map or globe, look at the western margins of South and North America to realize the edge-of-continent location of mountain ranges. Orogenic belts are sites of many earthquakes and volcanoes.

- **Earth movements** are the result of forces within the earth, where temperature and pressure differences lead to instability. The stress is particularly severe in orogenic zones, which are characterized by volcanism, metamorphism, deformation, and uplift. Two styles of rock deformation are faulting and folding. Today many geologists attribute edge-of-continent deformation to plate tectonics, a modern theory that suggests that oceanic crust emerges from the mantle along the oceanic ridges. Broad plates of oceanic crust may spread outward from the ridges until they crush against the margins of continental crust, the oceanic plate being forced under the continental plate back into the mantle.

- **Natural resources** obtained from the earth may be classed as metal and fuel deposits. Most metals are obtained by mining ore minerals in open-pit or underground mines. Gold is the only metal to occur commonly in its native, metallic state. Precambrian strata rich in chemically precipitated iron oxides are mined in northern Minnesota. Copper sulfides were deposited in veins by hydrothermal (hot water) solutions following igneous intrusions in Arizona, New Mexico, and Utah. By contrast, the fuel deposits (except uranium) are of organic origin. Plant debris that accumulated in ancient swamps has been transformed by heat and pressure to coal beds. Other plant and animal remains yielded oil and natural gas, which have accumulated in porous reservoir rocks. Uranium deposits are inorganic chemical precipitates from groundwater.

- **Meteorology** is the science of the atmosphere and weather. The composition of air is shown in Table 12. The amount of water vapor in the air depends on the prevailing temperature and the availability of water. The hydrologic cycle links the processes. Water in the ocean is evaporated by the sun's energy. As the warm, moist air rises to altitudes of lower pressure, the air expands and cools. The cooling results in condensation of water vapor to minute droplets of liquid water, which make up visible clouds. The clouds may be blown inland and cool further, leading to precipitation of rain or snow. Much of such precipitation is drained by rivers (the process is termed *runoff*) into the ocean, but an important fraction seeps into porous soil and rocks. That groundwater percolates laterally through permeable materials until it too ultimately reaches the ocean.

Table 12

THE COMPOSITION OF AIR

Gas		Percent
Nitrogen	N_2	78.08
Oxygen	O_2	20.95
Argon	Ar	0.93
Carbon dioxide	CO_2	0.03
Water vapor	H_2O	varies

GLOSSARY

Alluvium—Loose sediment deposited by a stream.

Aquifer—A bed of rock permeable to underground water.

Atmospheric pressure—The pressure exerted by the weight of the air lying directly above the area; at sea level, about fifteen pounds per square inch.

Basalt—An igneous rock formed from lava.

Cloud—A collection of tiny water or ice droplets sufficiently numerous to be seen.

Coal—A rock composed of partly decayed and compressed plant material.

Conglomerate—A sedimentary rock consisting of pebbles cemented together.

Continental drift—The hypothesis of continents moving laterally.

Crust—The thin outer zone of the earth above the mantle.

Cyclone—A low-pressure area around which winds blow counterclockwise in the Northern Hemisphere.

Delta—A triangular deposit of sediment at the mouth of a river.

Erosion—The removal of rock debris by water, ice, and wind.

Evaporation—The process by which a liquid changes to a gas; specifically, when water changes to water vapor.

Extrusive—Igneous rock of volcanic origin.

Fault—A planar break in rock along which displacement has occurred.

Fold—Bent or warped rock layers.

Front—The boundary between two air masses of different temperature; a common site for cloud formation and precipitation.

Geothermal energy—Heat obtained from hot water or steam within the earth.

Igneous—Rock formed by the solidification of molten rock material.

Intrusive—Igneous rock crystallized beneath the surface of the earth.

Karst—Pitted topography due to solution of limestone.

Laterite—Iron-rich soil caused by tropical weathering.

Lava—Molten rock extruded from a volcano.

Limestone—Sedimentary rock composed of calcium carbonate.

Lithification—The consolidation of loose sediment.

Lithology—Rock type.

Magma—Molten rock within the earth.

Mantle—The zone of the earth between the core and the crust.

Metamorphic—Rock formed by the transformation, under high temperature and pressure, of older sedimentary or igneous rock.

Mineral—A naturally occurring inorganic chemical compound.

Paleontology—The science of fossil life.

Permafrost—Ground that is frozen throughout the year.

Petroleum—A liquid fuel from the transformation of plant and animal remains.

Plutonic—Igneous rock that has crystallized beneath the earth's surface, as opposed to *volcanic* rock.

Precipitation—Any form of water, whether liquid or solid particles, that falls from the atmosphere; rain, sleet, snow, or hail.

Rainbow—A circular arc of colored bands produced by the refraction and reflection of sunlight by a sheet of raindrops. The sun must be behind the observer.

Sedimentary—Rock formed by deposition at the earth's surface.

Specific gravity—Relative density; the density of a substance divided by the density of water, which therefore has a specific gravity of 1.

Stalactite—A cone of calcareous rock hanging from the roof of a cavern.

Stalagmite—A pillar of calcareous rock rising from the floor of a cavern.

Strata—Layers of sedimentary rock; singular is *stratum*.

Stratosphere—The atmospheric shell above the troposphere; the stratosphere extends from six to thirty miles above the earth's surface.

Syncline—The trough of a rock fold.

Tectonic—Refers to movements of the earth's crust.

Troposphere—The lowest six miles of the atmosphere, characterized by temperature decreasing with height.

Water table—The upper limit of groundwater, below which all pores in the rocks are filled with water.

Weathering—The physical and chemical destruction of rock by the atmosphere.

CHEMISTRY

BASIC CONCEPTS

- **Chemistry** is the science of the substances which make up our world. Any tangible matter is chemical in its nature. Chemists study substances by measuring their properties and observing the changes they undergo. Matter is anything which occupies space and has mass. Matter may exist in the state of solid, liquid, or gas, depending on the prevailing temperature and pressure. Modern chemistry began when the Frenchman Lavoisier stated (1780) the law of conservation of mass: there is no gain or loss of mass in a chemical change. For example, when hydrogen reacts with oxygen to yield water, the water produced has precisely the same weight as the gases that reacted. Consequently, water can be considered to be built from the *elements* hydrogen and oxygen. Elements are the simplest chemical substances. Compounds (like water) are homogeneous substances of constant composition that have formed by chemical union of elements.

- **Atoms** are the smallest particles of chemical elements. The experimental fact that chemical compounds have fixed compositions led the Englishman John Dalton to propose (1805) that substances consist of small particles of matter, which he called atoms from the Greek word for indivisible. Later it was realized that chemical compounds must likewise have a smallest particle, the molecule. Water, for example, is made up of many molecules with the composition H_2O and the structure (arrangement) shown in Figure 15. The straight lines denote bonds between atoms. One water

WATER MOLECULE

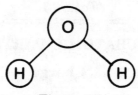

Figure 15

molecule is built from two atoms of hydrogen and one atom of oxygen. The molecules of the gaseous elements hydrogen and oxygen are shown in Figure 16. Each of these molecules is itself diatomic, with two atoms bonded together. Finally, we can diagram the reaction that produces water molecules. (See Figure 17.) The size of each box portrays the fact that the volume of gas is proportional to the number of molecules, rather than atoms. The chemical reaction is seen to be primarily a change in the bonding of atoms.

303

HYDROGEN MOLECULE   **OXYGEN MOLECULE**

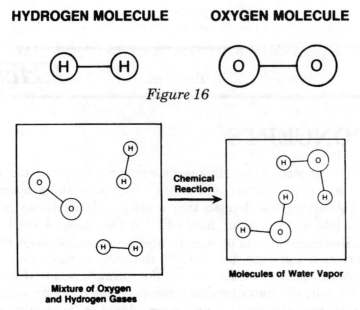

Figure 16

Mixture of Oxygen
and Hydrogen Gases

Chemical
Reaction

Molecules of Water Vapor

Figure 17

- **Subatomic particles** have been discovered as physicists learned how to split the supposedly indivisible atom. The three principal particles are listed in Table 13. The masses are in international atomic mass units (amu). Protons and neutrons have masses of approximately 1 amu, while the electron is much lighter, zero for chemical purposes. An atom has a small, dense nucleus composed of protons and neutrons packed together. The nucleus is surrounded by a much larger cloud of electrons. Thus atomic weight is determined by the nucleus, but the size of the atom is fixed by the electrons. *The number of protons establishes the chemical nature of an atom.* The number of neutrons is approximately equal to the number of protons, and the function of neutrons appears to be to stabilize the nucleus. The number of electrons precisely equals the number of protons for an electrically neutral atom.

Table 13

THE SUBATOMIC PARTICLES

Particle	Charge	Mass
Proton	+1	1.007
Neutron	0	1.009
Electron	−1	0.001

Table 14

SOME ELEMENTS AND THEIR SUBATOMIC MAKEUP

Element	Symbol	Protons	Neutrons	Mass
Hydrogen	H	1	0	1
Helium	He	2	2	4
Carbon	C	6	6	12
Oxygen	O	8	8	16
Iron	Fe	26	30	56
Uranium	U	92	146	238

• **Chemical elements** may be assigned atomic numbers equal to the protons in their atoms. When elements are charted in order of increasing atomic number, a pattern of recurring physical and chemical properties is displayed. This periodic table of the chemical elements was first devised by the Russian Mendeleev (1869). Ninety-one elements occur naturally and another twelve have been made in the laboratory. Of these 103 elements, only the first twenty are shown in Table 15. The elements increase in atomic number and atomic weight horizontally. Each vertical column contains a group of elements with similar chemical properties. Element behavior repeats every eight atomic numbers, the octet rule. Lithium, sodium, and potassium are alkali metals that are very reactive and form caustic bases in solution. (Hydrogen has unique properties and is grouped with the alkali metals only because they have the same valence number, to be discussed later.) Beryllium, magnesium, and calcium are less reactive metals. Moving to the right, we leave the metallic elements and meet the nonmetals. Interconnected carbon atoms are the skeleton for organic molecules, while silicon atoms link into a similar framework within natural crystals. Nitrogen and phosphorous are slightly reactive nonmetals. Fluorine and chlorine are highly reactive gases that form strong acids in solution. Finally, the elements in the right-hand column—helium, neon, and argon—are inert, "noble" gases that form no chemical compounds.

Table 15

ABRIDGED PERIODIC TABLE OF THE CHEMICAL ELEMENTS

1 hydrogen H							2 helium He
3 lithium Li	4 beryllium Be	5 boron B	6 carbon C	7 nitrogen N	8 oxygen O	9 fluorine F	10 neon Ne
11 sodium Na	12 magnesium Mg	13 aluminum Al	14 silicon Si	15 phosphorous P	16 sulfur S	17 chlorine Cl	18 argon Ar
19 potassium K	20 calcium Ca						
+1	+2	+3	+4, −4	+5, −3	−2	−1	0

valence for each column

- **Compounds** are written as formulas with standard symbols for the chemical elements. The subscript following each symbol shows the number of atoms of that type in one molecule or formula unit of the compound; absence of a subscript implies one atom. Therefore a molecule of the gas ethylene (C_2H_4) has two atoms of carbon and four of hydrogen. The common mineral calcite ($CaCO_3$) has one calcium, one carbon, and three oxygen atoms per formula unit. Most compounds contain metallic and nonmetallic elements in proportions so that their valences sum to zero. Check again the abridged periodic table and note that hydrogen has a valence of +1 while oxygen is −2; consequently they combine in the proportion 2:1 as the formula H_2O denotes. Sodium (+1) combines with chlorine (−1) to yield NaCl, common table salt. The valence number summarizes the chemical behavior of each element. Metals have positive valences, while nonmetals are negative. Note that in a formula the metallic symbol is written first. Now you should try to write the chemical formula for magnesium fluoride; the answer is printed as a footnote.

- **Bonds** between atoms are electronic in origin. Electrically neutral atoms may share electrons to form a covalent bond, as in a hydrogen molecule. (See Figure 18.) The electrons are in shells around the nuclear protons. Atoms which have an electrical charge are called *ions*. A positive ion has lost electrons (which have a charge of −1, remember) and a negative ion has gained electrons. Ions of different charges have a strong electrostatic attraction, or ionic bond.

Magnesium fluoride is MgF_2.

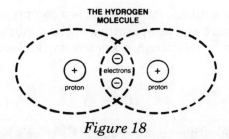

Figure 18

- **Solids** are characterized by their ability to retain their shape. They are relatively incompressible. Solids melt when heated and vaporize only slightly. All substances become solid if cooled sufficiently. Solids may be either crystalline or amorphous, depending on whether the arrangement of the atoms is regular or irregular. Figure 19 shows the crystalline structure of sodium chloride. Note that the positive sodium ions and the negative chlorine ions alternate in both the rows and columns, so that differently charged ions are closest neighbors. Ionic bonding holds the atoms in this rigid, stable arrangement.

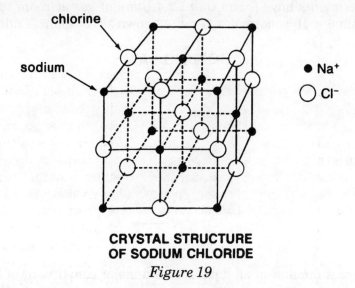

**CRYSTAL STRUCTURE
OF SODIUM CHLORIDE**
Figure 19

- **Liquids** take on the shape of their containers, yet cannot be compressed to any significant extent. The volume of a liquid is constant unless evaporation is occurring. Liquids crystallize when chilled sufficiently, while heat causes liquids to vaporize; boiling is very rapid vaporization. When evaporation occurs, some molecules in the liquid have gained enough energy to overcome the attractive forces exerted by the neighboring molecules and escape from the surface of the liquid to become gas. Thus the liquid state is intermediate between the solid and gaseous states, with regard to molecular motion and attractive forces between molecules.

- **Gases** expand to fill any available space. A gas is a compressible fluid, with its volume determined by the pressure and temperature of the environment. The volume varies inversely with pressure, a relationship known as Boyle's law (see Figure 20) and written

$$PV = k_1$$

where k_1 is a constant. Another relationship is Charles's law, that gas volume varies directly with temperature:

$$V = k_2 T$$

where k_2 is another constant, not equal to k_1. According to the kinetic molecular theory, gases are swarms of tiny molecules moving at a speed dependent on the temperature. Pressure is due to the molecular impacts on the walls of the container. The Italian physicist Avogadro proposed that equal numbers of molecules are contained in equal volumes of all gases, providing the pressure and temperature are identical. Experiments have found that 22.4 liters of gas at room temperature and pressure contain 6×10^{23} molecules, a value known as Avogadro's number.

BOYLE'S LAW

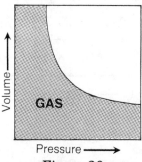

Figure 20

- **Water** is the most familiar of all liquids. It is a major constituent of living creatures and our environment. Ordinary water, even rainwater, is impure, with dissolved salts and gases. It may be purified by distillation, where the water is boiled to vapor, which is condensed and collected. The particular *state* of water—liquid, solid, or gas—is determined by the pressure and temperature. (See Figure 21.) The dashed line shows the behavior of water at room pressure (1 atmosphere), freezing at 0°C, and boiling at 100°C. At other pressures, the freezing and boiling temperatures for liquid water differ from the familiar values.

STATES OF H₂O

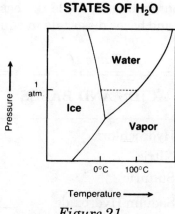

Figure 21

- **A solution** is a mixture of two or more substances, the proportions variable between wide limits. Most solutions have a liquid solvent containing a lesser amount of dissolved solute, either a solid, a gas, or another liquid. An aqueous solution has water as the solvent. The concentration of a solution expresses the amount of solute dissolved in a standard unit (usually 1 liter) of the solvent. The solubility of a substance is the maximum concentration of solute which a solution can hold. The solubility of solids commonly increases with higher temperature, while the solubility of gases decreases with higher temperature. Precipitation of a salt occurs when the solution becomes supersaturated in that salt, the concentration exceeding the solubility.

- **Ions** form when compounds dissociate in solution to positive and negative particles. For example, magnesium fluoride (MgF_2) separates in solution to magnesium and fluorine ions:

$$MgF_2 \xrightarrow{H_2O} Mg^{+2} + 2F^{-1}$$
$$\text{\textit{salt}} \qquad\qquad \text{\textit{ions in solution}}$$

In many cases, at least one ion is complex, containing several atoms. An example where two complex ions are present is the dissociation of ammonium nitrate:

$$NH_4NO_3 \xrightarrow{H_2O} NH_4{}^{+1} + NO_3{}^{-1}$$

The strong, covalent nitrogen-hydrogen and nitrogen-oxygen bonds were not disrupted by the water. However, the solution did break the ionic bond between the ammonium group of atoms and the nitrate group. The most important complex ion is the hydroxyl ion (OH^{-1}) which may be formed by the dissociation of water molecules:

$$H_2O \longrightarrow H^{+1} + OH^{-1}$$

- **Acids and bases** are solutions with unusual concentrations of either hydrogen or hydroxyl ions, such a solution being acidic or alkaline (basic). The familiar acids contain hydrogen which is loosely bound, while the bases are hydroxides of alkaline metals. (See Table 16.) Acids and bases dissociate in aqueous solution and modify the

Table 16

ACIDS AND BASES

Acids	Hydrochloric	HCl
	Nitric	HNO_3
	Sulfuric	H_2SO_4
Bases	Sodium Hydroxide	NaOH
	Potassium Hydroxide	KOH
	Ammonium Hydroxide	NH_4OH

concentration of hydrogen ions, which is measured as pH by litmus paper or other indicators. (See Table 17.) The reaction of an acid with a base is called neutralization and releases some heat.

Table 17

pH OF SOLUTIONS

Solution	pH
strong acid	1
weak acid	4
neutral	7
weak base	10
strong base	13

- **Electrolysis** occurs as an ionic melt or solution conducts electricity. Pure water is a fine insulator, but may be made a conductor by adding an electrolyte, a substance that dissociates to many ions capable of transporting electric charge. Figure 22 shows the electrolysis of a dilute solution of sodium chloride. The positive sodium ions (cations) move toward the negative electrode (cathode), while the negative chlorine ions (anions) are attracted to the positive electrode (anode). At the electrodes the electrical charges react with water to yield oxygen and hydrogen gases, the volume of hydrogen being twice that of oxygen. So the dissolved salt enables a current to decompose water.

ELECTROLYSIS

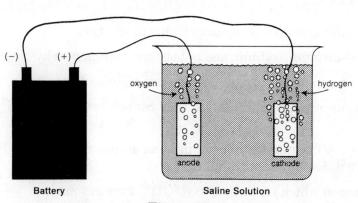

Figure 22

Very pure oxygen and hydrogen may be obtained by electrolysis of aqueous solutions. Other chemical elements may be obtained by passing a current through a molten salt. Electrolysis of fused sodium chloride (of course, no water is present) produces a layer of sodium metal on the cathode and bubbles of chlorine gas at the anode.

- **Chemical reactions** show the number of molecules or formula units of the reactants and products. For example, nitrous oxide is a colorless, odorless gas which causes mild hysteria when breathed, hence the name *laughing gas;* it is prepared by heating ammonium nitrate crystals:

$$\underset{\substack{ammonium \\ nitrate}}{\underset{Reactant}{NH_4NO_3}} \xrightarrow{heat} \underset{\substack{water \\ vapor}}{2H_2O} + \underset{\substack{nitrous \\ oxide}}{\overset{Products}{N_2O}}$$

Conditions necessary for the reaction to proceed—like heat, light, or a catalyst—are shown alongside the reaction arrow, which always points from reactants to products. In our example, one molecule of ammonium nitrate yielded two molecules of water and one of nitrous oxide. Now let's consider the atomic weights involved as shown in Table 18. Adding up the atoms in the molecules, you find that the reaction states that, say, 80 grams of NH_4NO_3 yields 36 grams of H_2O and 44 grams of N_2O. Here we've returned to the conservation of mass, the great discovery of Lavoisier.

Table 18

ATOMIC WEIGHTS OF SOME ELEMENTS

Chemical Element		Atomic Number	Atomic Weight
Hydrogen	H	1	1
Nitrogen	N	7	14
Oxygen	O	8	16

GLOSSARY

Acid—A compound which yields hydrogen ions in solution.

Alkali metals—Lithium, sodium, and potassium; common as hydroxides.

Alloy—A metal composed of two or more metallic elements.

Atom—The smallest particle of matter that cannot be subdivided by chemical reactions.

Atomic number—The number of protons in an atomic nucleus; the different chemical elements have different atomic numbers.

Base—A compound which yields hydroxyl (OH^-) ions in solution.

Boyle's law—The volume of a gas varies inversely with pressure.

Carbon dioxide—CO_2 is a colorless, noncombustible gas under normal conditions.

Catalyst—A substance which accelerates a chemical reaction, without itself being a reactant.

Charles's law—The volume of a gas varies directly with temperature.

Combustion—Rapid oxidation that releases heat and light.

Compound—A substance formed by the chemical union of several chemical elements.

Decomposition—A chemical reaction in which a compound is broken down into simpler compounds or elements.

Density—Mass per unit volume of a substance.

Diffusion—The mixing of different substances, commonly in a liquid or gas.

Distillation—The process of purification in which an impure substance is heated to vapors, which are collected and condensed.

Electron—A negatively charged, subatomic particle; electrons form a cloud around the atomic nucleus. Electron movement constitutes electrical current.

Electrolysis—A chemical change brought about by an electric current; used to separate chemical elements.

Element—A substance which cannot be decomposed to simpler substances.

Evaporation—A change of state from a solid or liquid to a gas.

Freezing point—The temperature at which a liquid changes to a solid.

Hydrocarbons—Compounds of carbon and hydrogen.

Hydrolysis—Chemical decomposition of a compound by reaction with water.

Ion—A charged atom or group of atoms formed by the gain or loss of electrons.

Isotope—Isotopes of an element have the same number of protons and show the same chemical behavior, but they differ in the number of nuclear neutrons and thus in atomic weight; isotopes may be stable or radioactive.

Litmus—Paper that turns red in acid and blue in alkaline solution.

Mixture—Substances mixed without a chemical reaction; the substances can be in any proportion.

Molecule—The smallest particle of a compound, composed of several bonded atoms.

Neutron—A subatomic particle of zero charge which occurs in the atomic nucleus.

Organic compound—A compound with interconnected carbon atoms.

Oxidation—The addition of oxygen to a substance.

pH—A number indicating the concentration of hydrogen ions in a solution. A pH of 7 is neutral, less than 7 is acidic, and greater than 7 is alkaline.

Proton—A subatomic particle with a positive charge, occuring in the atomic nucleus.

Saturated—Describes a solution which contains as much solute as possible.

Solute—The substance dissolved in a solution.

Solvent—The pure liquid within a solution.

Sublimation—The change from a solid to a gas, without an intermediate liquid.

Synthesis—The formation of a compound by combining elements or simpler compounds.

PHYSICS

BASIC CONCEPTS

- **Physics** is the most basic and most general of the natural sciences. It covers subjects from matter to energy in the most general way. Physicists try to provide orderly explanations for natural events by formulating laws broad enough to explain all particular situations. Such laws are often suggested by regularities in experiments, but the clear logic and advanced mathematics used to construct physical formulas make physics the supremely theoretical science. The scientific method requires observation, conjecture, calculation, prediction, and testing. Successive scientific revolutions have taught us that today's laws are not certain, only more accurate than yesterday's laws.

- **Measurement** is the beginning of scientific wisdom. The physicist's first reaction to a new idea is: Can it be measured? Can I describe it with numbers? Numerical data can be manipulated with many powerful mathematical tools, from arithmetic and geometry to statistics and differential equations. Physical quantities range from subatomic smallness to astronomic hugeness, so the numbers are conveniently expressed in *scientific notation,* in which any number is written in the form

$$N \times 10^P$$

where N is a number between 1 and 10, and P is a power of 10. The population of Brazil is about 130,000,000, and that number could be written as

$$1.3 \times 10^8$$

You should also be aware of the three basic units of the metric system. (See Table 19.) A unit 1000 times the basic unit has the prefix *kilo,* so a kilometer equals 1000 meters. The prefix *milli* (as in millimeter) denotes a unit 1/1000 the basic unit.

Table 19

BASIC UNITS OF THE METRIC SYSTEM

Quantity	Unit	Symbol	Approximation
Length	meter	m	1.1 yard
Volume	liter	l	1.1 quart
Mass	gram	g	1/30 ounce

- **Motion** is described by stating an object's position, velocity, and acceleration. Velocity is the rate of change of position with time. For example, an automobile that is 100 miles farther along a highway at 3 P.M. than at 1 P.M. has an average velocity during the interval of

$$v = \frac{\Delta d}{\Delta t} = \frac{100}{2} = 50 \text{ miles/hour}$$

where the Δd represents change of distance and Δt is the change of time. Acceleration is the rate of change of velocity with time. If the automobile in our example had an initial velocity of 40 mph and a final velocity of 60 mph, then its average acceleration would be

$$a = \frac{\Delta v}{\Delta t} = \frac{20}{2} = 10 \text{ miles/hour/hour}$$

- **Newton's laws** relate the motion of an object to the forces acting upon it. The *law of inertia* asserts that, in the absence of any force, a body at rest will continue at rest, while another body moving in a straight line will continue to move in that direction with uniform speed. Any change of speed or direction must be due to a force. The *law of acceleration* states that a body acted on by a force will undergo acceleration proportional to the force:

$$f = m \cdot a$$

where m is the mass of the object, the quantity of matter for that object. Table 20 lists masses for a range of objects. Newton's *law of reaction* says that for every action there is an equal and opposite reaction.

Table 20

MASSES OF SOME OBJECTS

Representative Object	Mass in Grams
Electron	10^{-27}
Atom	10^{-23}
Amoeba	10^{-5}
Ant	10^{-2}
Human	10^5
Whale	10^8
Earth	10^{28}
Sun	10^{33}

- **Gravitation** is familiar to us through weight, which is directly proportional to mass:

$$w = m \cdot g$$

where g is the acceleration due to gravity. The mass of an object is constant throughout the universe, but its weight varies with the object's position. Because the moon has a weaker gravitational field than the earth, an astronaut weighing 180 pounds here would weigh only 30 pounds there. Gravitational forces exist between all pairs of tangible objects, with the force being directly proportional to the product of their masses and inversely proportional to the square of the distance separating them. An astronaut weighs less on the moon because its mass is less than that of the earth. A balloon rising from the surface decreases in weight as it ascends and the distance from the earth increases.

- **Energy** is the ability to perform work, to move objects. That ability can take several forms. The energy possessed by a moving object is called *kinetic* energy. An object in an unstable position has *potential* energy, for the position could be converted into movement. Consider a baseball thrown vertically upward. Its speed decreases upward because the acceleration of gravity is acting downward. The rising ball loses kinetic energy (slows down) as it gains potential energy (rises higher). At the peak of the ball's flight, the ball is instantaneously at rest, with no kinetic energy but maximum stored potential energy. As the ball falls, the potential energy is transformed into kinetic energy and the ball accelerates. *Thermal* energy also exists, for it has been shown that heat can be converted to motion, and motion can produce heat. Electricity and magnetism are still other forms of energy, for they can be converted into heat and motion. Notice that this key concept of energy is the abstract idea that there is something identical in motion, heat, and electricity, which appear so different to our senses. It is possible to define the various forms of energy so that their mathematical sum is constant. The law of conservation of energy states that energy can be neither created nor destroyed.

- **Temperature** is a measure of the movement of the molecules in a substance. Heat is nothing else than kinetic energy on an atomic level. The basic temperature scale of science is the centrigrade (or Celsius) scale (see Table 21), on which water freezes at 0°C and boils at 100°C. At absolute zero, all molecular motion would cease. You should be able to convert our familiar Fahrenheit temperatures to centrigrade or vice versa:

$$C = \tfrac{5}{9}(F - 32)$$
$$F = \tfrac{9}{5}C + 32$$

Just for practice, try to calculate the centigrade temperature equivalent to 50°F, then look at the answer in the footnote. The quantity of heat contained in a substance is measured in calories and must not be confused with temperature. At one temperature, a large mass of lead contains more heat than a smaller mass of lead. If those two pieces of lead had equal heat contents, the small mass would have a higher temperature than the larger mass.

$C = \tfrac{5}{9}(F - 32) = \tfrac{5}{9}(50 - 32) = \tfrac{5}{9}(18) = 10°C$

Table 21

TEMPERATURE OF OBJECTS IN °C

Absolute zero	−273
Oxygen freezes	−218
Oxygen liquifies	−183
Water freezes	0
Human body	37
Water boils	100
Wood fire	830
Iron melts	1535
Iron boils	3000

- **Sound** is produced by the mechanical disturbance of a gas, liquid, or solid. The disturbance consists of alternating zones of abundant and scarce molecules, and such zones travel as waves. (See Figure 23.) In such waves, the molecules vibrate and collide with each other, thus passing on their kinetic energy without changing their average position. The speed of sound depends on the physical properties of the medium through which it travels. In air, sound travels at 740 miles per hour, while steel transmits sound fifteen times faster. The intensity level of sound is commonly reported in decibels.

**SOUND WAVES
IN A PIPE**

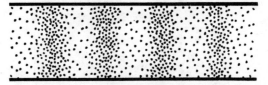

Figure 23

- **Electricity** exists where the number of negative electrons does not precisely equal the number of positive protons. If we suspend small charged balls on nonconducting threads (see Figure 24), we find that there are forces of repulsion between similar charges and attraction between unlike charges. One type of electricity can neutralize the effect of the other type, so we regard the opposite charges as being due to an excess (−) or deficit (+) of *negative* electrons. Two bodies of opposite charge are said to have a difference of electrical potential, which is measured in volts. The chemical reaction in a battery produces a potential difference, and connecting the two poles through a conducting wire leads to the passage of an electric current, which is simply a flow of electrons.

ELECTRIC FORCES

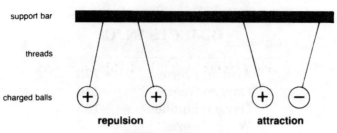

Figure 24

- **Magnetism** is displayed by permanent magnets and around electric currents. All of us have had the opportunity to study the interesting properties of permanent magnets, small bars or horseshoes of iron which have aligned internal structures induced by other magnets. The north pole of one magnet attracts the south pole of another, but like poles repel each other. Either pole can attract unmagnetized iron objects. Iron filings spread on a piece of paper above a bar magnet become arranged in a pattern which maps a magnetic *field* in the space around the magnet. (See Figure 25.) The earth's magnetic field orients the iron needles of navigational compasses. An electric current also generates a magnetic field, demonstrating an intimate connection between electricity and magnetism. Later work has united these phenomena and light, too, into electromagnetic radiation.

MAGNETIC FIELD
ABOVE A BAR MAGNET

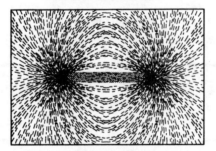

Figure 25

- **Light** seems to travel in perfectly straight lines as rays. The direction of a ray changes at the interface between two transparent materials, like air and water. Some of the light is reflected, the angle of reflection being equal to the angle of incidence. The portion of the light that crosses the boundary is, however, deflected in another direction, and the angle of refraction does not equal the angle of incidence. Other optical experiments are inconsistent with a simple ray theory and require that light travels as waves of electromagnetic energy. When white light (including sunlight) is refracted by a glass prism, it is separated into its component colors as a beautiful spectrum. Experiments have shown that the various colors travel at the uniform speed c:

$$c = 186,000 \text{ miles/second} = 3 \times 10^8 \text{ meters/second}$$

The colors differ in wavelength, and Table 22 displays the relative wavelengths for all forms of electromagnetic energy.

Table 22

ELECTROMAGNETIC RADIATION

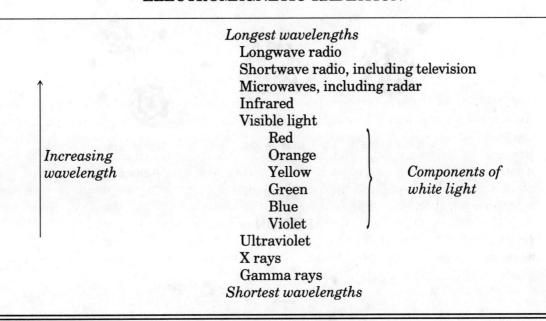

Longest wavelengths
Longwave radio
Shortwave radio, including television
Microwaves, including radar
Infrared
Visible light
   Red
   Orange
   Yellow — *Components of white light*
   Green
   Blue
   Violet
Ultraviolet
X rays
Gamma rays
Shortest wavelengths

Increasing wavelength

- **Relativity** of basic physical concepts like mass, distance, and time was postulated by Einstein (1905) to explain the experimental discovery that the speed of light in a vacuum was a universal constant. The principle of relativity states that all the laws of physics have the same form despite the movement of the observer. An observer performing an experiment on an object moving relative to the observer finds that the object's measured mass is greater and length is less than if the object were at rest relative to the observer. These curious effects are significant only at incredibly high velocities and may be neglected for most purposes. Einstein's famous law for the conversion of mass to energy

$$E = mc^2$$

suggested that atomic reactions could release unprecedented quantities of energy.

- **Nuclear energy** has been obtained by two different means, fission and fusion. Nuclear fission releases energy when a heavy nucleus splits into smaller fragments. (See Figure 26. Black balls show neutrons, and white balls show protons.) Bombarding uranium with a neutron produces an unstable intermediate, which disintegrates to lighter nuclei with the conversion of 0.1 percent of the mass into energy. Nuclear fission is used in power plants and atomic bombs. The opposite process of nuclear fusion yields energy when very light nuclei unite to a heavier nucleus. (See Figure 27.) A hydrogen bomb contains the two heavy isotopes of hydrogen, deuterium (H^2) and tritium (H^3), which unite to form helium nuclei and neutrons, with a conversion of 0.4 percent of the initial mass into energy. Stars (including the sun) derive their energy from nuclear fusion.

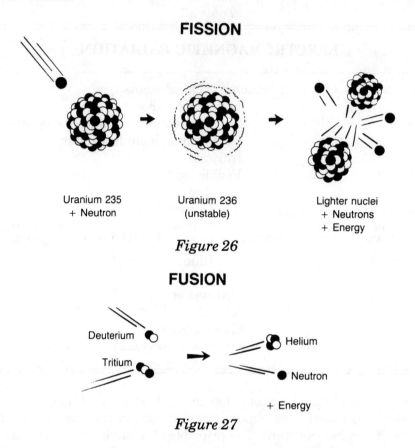

FISSION

Uranium 235	Uranium 236	Lighter nuclei
+ Neutron	(unstable)	+ Neutrons
		+ Energy

Figure 26

FUSION

Deuterium

Tritium

Helium

Neutron

+ Energy

Figure 27

- **Quantum theory** originated when Max Planck discovered that the radiation of energy from a heated body occurs only in integral multiples of a small quantity (1901). That *quantum* is the product of the frequency of radiation f and the universal constant h, now known as Planck's constant. The hypothesis of discrete quantities of energy explains many features of atomic physics. The photoelectric effect, in which light induces an electric current in metals, suggests that light acts as particles of energy called *photons*. Line spectra of energy emitted from atoms reveal that the electrons in each atom are restricted to several specific energy levels. The radiation of energy seems to occur both as waves and as particles, and that wave/particle duality applies to matter also. One fascinating deduction of quantum theory is the *uncertainty principle:* it is impossible to determine the exact position and momentum of a particle.

GLOSSARY

Absolute zero—The lowest possible temperature, equal to 0°K, −273°C, or −459°F.

Buoyancy—The upward force on an object immersed in a fluid.

Calorie—A unit of measurement of energy; the amount of heat required to raise the temperature of one gram of water by 1°C.

Capillarity—The ability of liquids to rise in very thin tubes.

Centrifugal—Toward the perimeter.

Centripetal—Toward the center.

Chain reaction—Occurs when the fission of one atom causes the fission of other atoms.

Conduction—Transfer of heat or electricity.

Conservation of energy—Energy may be changed from one form to another, but it cannot be created or destroyed.

Density—Mass per unit volume.

Doppler effect—The apparent change of pitch due to differing motions of the sounding source and a listener.

Electric current—The flow of electrons; a *direct current* (DC) flows in one direction, while an *alternating current* (AC) periodically reverses the direction of flow.

Energy—The ability to perform work; *kinetic energy* is due to a body's motion, whereas *potential energy* is due to a body's position.

Fission—The splitting of an atomic nucleus into several lighter nuclei.

Fusion—Nuclear fusion is the union of atomic nuclei to a heavier nucleus.

Gravitation—The attraction of bodies because of their masses.

Half-life—The time required for the radioactivity of a substance to drop to half its original level.

Heat—Kinetic energy of molecular motion.

Hypothesis—A tentative explanation of a phenomenon.

Inertia—The ability of a body to resist acceleration and continue at rest or moving with uniform velocity.

Mass—The quantity of matter; the measure of inertia.

Momentum—The product of mass and velocity; the conservation of momentum is a fundamental law of nature.

Photon—A particle of light energy.

Pitch—The frequency of a sound wave.

Prism—A triangular piece of glass used to disperse white light into a spectrum.

Radioactivity—The spontaneous decay of an atomic nucleus with the emission of alpha particles, beta particles, or gamma rays.

Refraction—The bending of a light wave at the boundary between two substances.

Relativity—The principle that the laws of physics are the same for any two observers, whatever their relative motion.

Spectrum—The *visible spectrum* is the band of colors from the dispersal of white light; the *electromagnetic spectrum* is the total range of frequencies for electromagnetic waves, including radio and light waves.

Temperature—The average kinetic energy of a group of molecules; it determines the direction of heat flow.

Thermodynamics—The study of heat energy.

Volt—A unit of measurement of electric potential; the amount of work necessary to move the charge.

Watt—A unit of measurement of electrical power, the rate at which electrical energy is dissipated.

Weightlessness—A condition where accelerating forces precisely offset one another.

Work—The product of force and distance; it measures the action performed on an object.

ASTRONOMY

BASIC CONCEPTS

- **Astronomy** is the science of the heavens, from the nearby moon to remote galaxies. In past cultures, humans spent much more time outdoors than do we, and the recurring patterns of day and night, seasons, eclipses, and paths of planets across the background of stars led to the birth of science, an attempt to find order rather than mystery in the world. Aristotle (340 B.C.) conjectured that the heavenly bodies were affixed to crystalline spheres concentric about the earth. Then Ptolemy (A.D. 151) in his great *Almagest* presented a detailed mathematical description of celestial orbits about the earth, the circular orbits being made to fit observations by a complicated mechanism with arbitrary eccentrics and epicycles. The first great triumph of modern science was when Copernicus (1543) realized that the earth was not at the center of the universe, but that it revolved around the sun yearly and rotated on its axis daily.

- **The earth** travels in an orbit that is slightly elliptical (oval), so the distance from the sun ranges from 91.5 to 94.5 million miles. Its daily rotation deforms the earth to a flattened spheroid, with a polar radius slightly less than the equatorial radius. Locations on the surface are described by a grid of latitude and longitude lines. Latitude is the degrees north or south of the equator, while longitude is the degrees east or west of the prime meridian through Greenwich, England. For example the location of New York City is 41°N, 74°W. The seasons of the year are the consequence of the earth's equatorial plane being tilted about 23° from the orbital plane (see Figure 28). In each hemisphere at noontime, the sun is near the zenith during summer and low in the sky during winter.

THE SEASONS OF THE YEAR

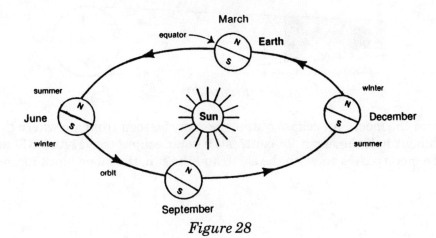

Figure 28

323

• **The moon** travels around the earth each month. Its distance from the earth averages 237,000 miles. The phases of illumination through which the moon passes each month (see Figure 29) can be understood by contemplating its position relative to those of the earth and the sun. A new moon occurs when the moon sets at sunset; then the moon is between the earth and the sun, so we see only the dark half of the moon. Each night the moon sets a few minutes later and we perceive more of its illuminated half. After the moon has waxed through crescent, quarter, and gibbous phases, a full moon appears. At that time the moon rises at sunset, so we see all of its illuminated side. Then the phase wanes gradually to another new moon. The moon itself has rugged topography formed billions of years ago by volcanic eruptions and meteorite impacts.

LUNAR PHASES

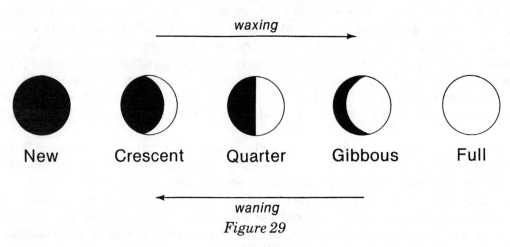

Figure 29

• **Eclipses** of the moon and the sun are quite spectacular. Ancient astronomers found that eclipses occur periodically and learned to predict them accurately. A lunar eclipse (see Figure 30) darkens the moon as the earth passes between it and the sun, casting a

LUNAR ECLIPSE

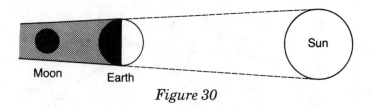

Figure 30

shadow on the moon. An eclipse of the moon my be seen from anywhere the moon is visible, about half the earth. In contrast, a solar eclipse (see Figure 31) takes place when the moon passes between the earth and the sun, the moon blocking the sunlight

SOLAR ECLIPSE

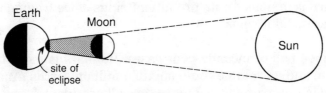

Figure 31

for about two minutes. A total eclipse of the sun may be seen only from a small zone on the earth.

- **Planets** appear brighter than almost all stars, and they move across the background of fixed stars. Actually, such bodies travel around the sun in elliptical orbits within the plane called the ecliptic. Of the nine major planets, ancient astronomers were aware of the inner six, Mercury through Saturn. Uranus was discovered telescopically by William Herschel in 1781, Neptune was found at the position predicted mathematically by Urbain Leverrier in 1846, and Pluto was discovered after a painstaking photographic search by Clyde Tombaugh in 1930. Between the orbits of Mars and Jupiter are thousands of asteroids, small planetary fragments. Table 23 has current data on the solar system. The values are all relative to the earth's. The earth is 93

Table 23

THE SOLAR SYSTEM

Planet	Distance from Sun*	Sidereal Period*	Radius*	Mass*	Satellites
Mercury	0.39	0.24	0.38	0.05	0
Venus	0.72	0.62	0.96	0.82	0
Earth	1.00	1.00	1.00	1.00	1
Mars	1.52	1.88	0.53	0.11	2
Asteroids	2.8		(thousands of small bodies)		
Jupiter	5.2	11.9	11.0	317.8	16
Saturn	9.5	29.5	9.2	95.1	17
Uranus	19.2	84.0	3.7	14.5	5
Neptune	30.1	164.8	3.5	17.2	2
Pluto	39.5	248.4	0.5	0.002	1

*relative to Earth = 1

million miles from the sun, has a sidereal period (the time for one revolution) of 365 days, has a radius of 4000 miles, and has a mass of 7×10^{21} metric tons. Notice from the column of sidereal periods that planets complete their orbits more quickly the closer they are to the sun. The columns of radii and masses reveal that the inner four planets (Mercury to Mars) are much smaller than the four giant planets (Jupiter to Neptune). Saturn is famous for its prominent rings of ice fragments, but Jupiter and Uranus also possess faint rings.

- **The sun** is a huge ball of incandescent gases. Its mass is more than 300,000 times that of the earth, and its volume could engulf a million earths. Analysis of absorption lines in the solar spectrum (see Figure 32) allows identification of the chemical elements present and measurement of the surface temperature. The principal constituents of the sun are the lightest elements, hydrogen and helium. Under solar conditions, those gases are undergoing nuclear fusion to heavier elements with the release of prodigious quantities of energy. The center of the sun may have a temperature of millions of degrees; the visible surface, the *photosphere,* is about 6000°C. Sunspots are somewhat cooler disturbances in the photosphere. The sun's atmosphere is divided into the inner *chromosphere* with explosive prominences and the outer *corona,* a glowing halo visible only during a total eclipse. The sun is constantly emitting particles as a solar wind.

SOLAR SPECTRUM

Fraunhofer Lines (lettered)

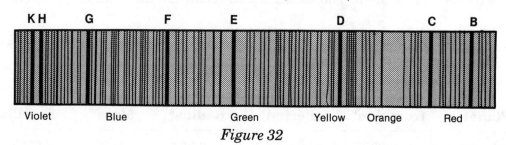

Figure 32

- **Stars** are bodies similar to the sun but immensely distant. Astronomers have calculated the distance to many of the closest stars by measuring the parallax, a slight shift in apparent position against the background of more distant stars as the earth travels around the sun. Interstellar distances are described in light-years, one light-year being the distance light travels in one year. Remember, the velocity of light is 186,000 miles *per second!* The nearest stars are four light-years away. The apparent brightness of stars is measured by a scale of *magnitudes,* from −1 (the brightest) through +6 (just visible with the unaided eye) to +23 (the limit of the largest telescope). The intrinsic brightness of stars, as if each were seen from a standard distance of thirty-three light-years, is reported as *absolute magnitude.* The color or spectral class of stars is a function of surface temperature, from blue-white (hottest) through yellow (like the sun) to red (coolest). Ejnar Hertzsprung and Norris Russell plotted absolute magnitudes versus spectral class in a famous diagram (see Figure 33). Notice that the sun is an average star in the middle of the main sequence. The giant stars are unstable and will evolve toward the main sequence. A star that explodes as a spectacular nova may end up as a depleted dwarf star.

HERTZSPRUNG-RUSSELL DIAGRAM

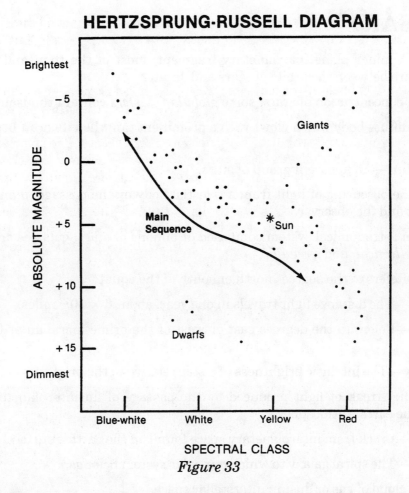

Figure 33

- **Galaxies** are huge systems of stars. Our own Milky Way galaxy is estimated to have 100 billion stars arranged in a great disk. The sun is not at the center of the disk, but out toward the perimeter, and is revolving around the galactic center. Some of the faint nebulae beyond the Milky Way have been resolved into myriads of individual stars—galaxies like our own. From studies of Cepheids, stars of variable luminosity that serve as distance indicators, the neighboring Andromeda galaxy is about 20 million light-years away. Galaxies of spiral, elliptical, and irregular form are speckled throughout the visible universe. The largest telescope has detected galaxies to its limit of several billion light-years. The spectra of distant objects display a *red shift,* which is interpreted as meaning they are rapidly receding from us. This apparent expansion of the universe has given rise to the *big bang theory* of cosmology, in which one primeval mass exploded about 12 billion years ago.

GLOSSARY

Asteroid—A minor planet or planetary fragment; most of the thousands of known asteroids are between the orbits of Mars and Jupiter.

Cluster—A concentration of stars; some *globular clusters* contain thousands of stars.

Comet—A diffuse body which glows with a prominent tail when its orbit brings it near the sun.

Constellation—An apparent group of stars.

Eclipse—The obscuring of light from a celestial body by the passage of another body between it and the observer.

Galaxy—An astronomical system composed of billions of stars; galaxies are classified as *spiral, elliptical,* and *irregular.*

Latitude—Refers to the degrees north or south of the equator.

Light-year—The distance light travels in one year, about 6×10^{12} miles.

Longitude—Refers to the degrees east or west of the prime meridian at Greenwich, England.

Luminosity—The intrinsic brightness of a star relative to the brightness of the sun.

Meteor—The streak of light produced by the passage of an interplanetary particle through the earth's atmosphere.

Meteorite—A rock from interplanetary space found on the earth's surface.

Milky Way—The spiral galaxy to which our solar system belongs.

Nebula—A cloud of gas or dust in interstellar space.

Nova—A star which suddenly becomes many times brighter than usual.

Quasar—Quasi-stellar radio source; a distant object with extraordinary luminosity.

Star—A large, hot, glowing body of gases.

Sunspot—A darker patch observed on the surface of the sun.

Tide—The rise and fall of the ocean due to gravitational attraction by the moon and sun.

VISUAL AND PERFORMING ARTS REVIEW

MUSIC

OUTLINE

I. AESTHETIC PERCEPTION

A. The educational goals of aesthetic perception are:

1. To develop sensitivity to music's expressive qualities.

2. To increase aural awareness.

3. To encourage musical responsiveness, involvement, and discrimination.

B. Elements of music.

1. Pitch.
   a. May be high or low and may repeat.
   b. Creates melody.
   c. Progression of pitches creates melodic contour.
   d. Progressive pitches create scales.
   e. Melodic meaning is affected by range, register, length of groupings, and size of intervals.

2. Rhythm.
   a. Measured by units of time.
   b. These pulses, or "beats," can be organized in sets (meters).
   c. Patterns can be repeated.

3. Harmony.
   a. Consists of two or more simultaneous tones.
   b. Three or more simultaneous tones make a chord.
   c. Chords can be modified.

4. Form.
   a. The "design" of music is created by the interaction of its elements.
   b. Sections of music ("phrases") can be similar or different depending upon amount of repetition of elements.
   c. Repetition of elements creates unity.
   d. Contrasting elements create variety.

5. Texture.
   a. Total sound may have differing "textures," such as thick, thin, opaque, and transparent.

    b. Motifs may have textures, such as legato (smooth sounding) and staccato (clipped sounding).

6. Tempo.

    a. The speed of a section or composition.

    b. Affects the music's character.

    c. Provides contrast when tempos differ.

    d. Adds to expressiveness.

    e. Is referred to by specific terms, for example lento (slow) and presto (quick).

7. Dynamics.

    a. The comparative loudness and softness of music.

    b. Changes the expressive effect.

    c. Is referred to by specific terms, for example piano (soft), pianissimo (very soft), forte (loud), and fortissimo (very loud).

8. Timbre.

    a. The unique tonal quality produced by an instrument or voice.

    b. Each instrument family (such as woodwinds, percussion, strings, and brass) has its characteristic sound (timbre).

    c. Instruments of different cultures produce different timbres.

9. Notation.

    a. The written form of music.

    b. Composed of a variety of symbols for notes, rests, pitch, etc.

II. CREATIVE EXPRESSION

A. Development of musical skills.

1. A basis for complete musical understanding.

2. Skill development leads to:

    a. Sensitivity to music's expressive qualities.

    b. Development of musical responsiveness, involvement, and discrimination.

B. Types of musical skills.

1. Auditory skills—hearing music.

    a. Attentive listening is the basic activity of music education.

    b. Aural acuity is a requirement of musical growth.

    c. Students must be able to hear tones in the mind when no sound is actually being produced.

2. Translative skills—reading and writing

a. For notation to have meaning, experience with sounds must precede contact with visual symbols.

b. Drill on key signatures, meter signatures, names of isolated notes, and intervals is unlikely to promote growth unless taught in conjunction with singing and playing.

3. Creative skills—creating music.

a. Creating music should parallel other musical activities.

b. Performing both improvised and written music should be encouraged.

4. Performance skills.

a. Singing.
   (1) Musical selections should be chosen based on the physical development of students' voices.
   (2) Listening while singing should be encouraged to develop interpretive skills and understanding of the structure and elements of music.

b. Playing instruments.
   (1) Instrument playing aids in understanding the concepts of sound, pitch, rhythm, etc.
   (2) Can be used to accompany singing to produce harmony.
   (3) Students should have access to class instruction and, at a certain level, to playing in orchestras and band ensembles.

c. Body movement.
   (1) Moving to music is a learned skill which promotes acuity of perception.
   (2) A wide range of music and modes should be used.

d. Conducting.
   (1) Even young children can experience elements of music through conducting speech chants, involving changes in tempo, dynamics, pitch, and so forth.
   (2) Conducting fosters sensitivity to musical expression.

e. Musical analysis.
   (1) Students should compare their listening and playing experiences.
   (2) Students should be encouraged to verbalize their musical analysis.

III. MUSIC HERITAGE

A. Fosters understanding and skills within a historical/cultural context.

B. Develops understanding of the styles, idioms, performance media, and purposes of types of music which are part of our multicultural heritage.

C. Reveals the relationships between people and their music.

D. Communicates to students that:

1. Music is a part of living and can communicate feelings, lighten labors, and satisfy emotional needs.

2. Music as therapy has power to satisfy emotional needs.

3. Social influences affect choices in music.

4. Present-day musical instruments have evolved from simple beginnings.

5. Musical instruments were created from material from people's environments.

6. Music has its own forms, periods, and cultural characteristics.

IV. AESTHETIC VALUING

A. Extends beyond knowledge and skills.

B. Is the comprehension of beauty and the expression of feeling in music.

C. Has as its goal to provide a basis on which students can make intelligent judgments of musical value.

1. Music is a unique medium for human expression.

2. Knowledge about music can increase one's ability to choose music that is meaningful to the individual.

3. The ability to make aesthetic judgments can heighten personal pleasure derived from music.

GLOSSARY

Allegro—Fast tempo.

Bar lines—The vertical lines on the staff used to mark off the grouping of beats.

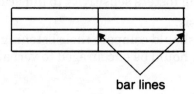

bar lines

Beat—The underlying pulse present in most music.

Brasses—Wind instruments made of metal, including the trumpet, French horn, trombone, and tuba.

Chamber music—One to twenty performers.

Chord—Several notes sounded together.

Clavichord—A small predecessor of the piano.

Clef—The symbol indicating the pitch of the notes.

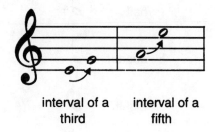

treble clef (high)   bass clef (low)

Consonance—The combination of tones that produces a quality of relaxation.

Dissonance—The combination of tones that produces a quality of tension.

Dynamics—The loudness of music.

Fugue—A fugue is based upon a short theme called a *subject*. The fugue subject contains both rhythmic and melodic motifs. The opening of the fugue is announced by one voice alone. A second voice then restates the subject, usually on a different scale. A third and then a fourth voice enter, each carrying the subject.

Harmony—Refers to the chordal aspect of music.

Harpsichord—Another predecessor of the piano, sounded by plucking the strings.

Interval—The distance between notes.

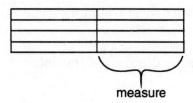

interval of a third   interval of a fifth

Largo—Very slow tempo.

Lento—Slow tempo.

Lied—German song.

Lyre—An ancient harp.

Mass—Music for a Catholic service.

Measure—The space on a staff between two bar lines.

measure

Melody—Concerns the sequence of notes.

Meter—The organization of beats into groups.

Meter signature—The numerical symbol at the beginning of a composition to indicate the meter—for example, 2/4, 3/4, 6/8, 4/4.

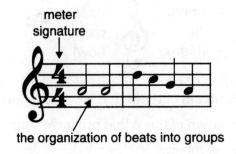

meter
signature

the organization of beats into groups

Moderato—Intermediate tempo.

Motif—A recurring group of notes, as the four in Beethoven's Fifth Symphony.

Movement—A large section of a lengthy composition.

Note—A musical sound of specific pitch, as middle C.

whole

half

quarter

eighth

sixteenth

Opus—Work, usually identified by a number.

Oratorio—A major orchestral piece with solo voices and chorus.

Orchestra—A large group of instrument players, usually seventy-five to ninety.

Percussion—Instruments sounded by striking, as drums, cymbals, and chimes.

Pitch—The frequency of a sound wave.

Polyphony—Choral music with several simultaneous voice-lines.

Presto—Very fast tempo.

Rhythm—Concerns the relative duration of the notes.

Rondo—The main feature of a rondo is the return of the main theme, which alternates with secondary themes. For example,

simple rondo: ABABA
second round: ABACA
third round: ABACABA

Scale—The succession of notes arranged in an ascending order.

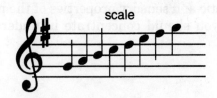

Sonata—A work for one or two instruments.

Song form—When the first section of a simple ternary form is repeated—for example, AABA. (A simple ternary form is music in three sections, with the third generally an exact repetition of the first, ABA.)

Staff—The five lines on which musical notes are written.

Strings—Violin, viola, cello, and double bass (bass viol).

Subject—The principal melodic motif or phrase, especially in a fugue.

Symphony—A major orchestral composition.

Syncopation—A rhythmic effect produced when the expected rhythm pattern is deliberately upset.

Tempo—The pace of the music.

Timbre—The characteristic sound of a voice or instrument.

Tone—A musical sound of a specific pitch.

Woodwinds—Instruments originally made of wood, including the piccolo, flute, clarinet, oboe, English horn, bassoon, and saxophone.

VISUAL ARTS

An educated analysis of an art composition should be systematic and should emphasize both the aesthetic and sensory properties of the piece. The following outline suggests areas on which you should concentrate in understanding and evaluating a piece of art.

OUTLINE

I. ELEMENTS OF ART

A. Line.

1. Can take many forms, such as thick or thin and wavy or straight.

2. Operates in terms of the visual field (for example, as an edge, as the meeting of areas, or to suggest space).

3. Can hold emotional qualities.

    a. Straight lines suggest rigidity.

    b. Diagonal lines suggest opposition.

    c. Vertical lines suggest strength.

    d. Horizontal lines suggest stability and repose.

    e. Curved lines suggest movement.

    f. Sweeping curved lines suggest calm.

    g. Sharp, short curved lines suggest agitation.

B. Color.

1. Depends on the reflection and absorption of light (hue, value, and intensity).

2. Affects the emotions directly.

3. Is dependent on derived light (for example, night light appears as shades of gray and bright daylight casts strong shadows).

4. Includes these types:

    a. Primary: red, yellow, and blue.

    b. Secondary: orange, green, and violet; produced by mixing equal amounts of two primary colors.

    c. Tertiary: produced by mixing unequal amounts of two primary colors.

5. Is used to:
   a. Define certain spatial qualities of a composition.
   b. Provide organization and unity.
   c. Create balance.
   d. Convey emotion and symbolize ideas, such as hope and despair.

C. Value.

1. Is defined as the amount of light and dark areas in a composition; can range from black to white.

2. Allows for contrasts, creating the appearance of form on a flat surface.

3. Can:
   a. Be created by the placement of lines.
   b. Produce textures.
   c. Create form by depicting shadows and highlights caused by direct light.

4. Allows for expressive qualities and moods by using:
   a. Primarily dark areas to suggest melancholy or uneasiness.
   b. Primarily light areas to suggest happiness or freedom.

D. Shape (form).

1. Is based on the use of contours.

2. Can be defined by the use of value, color, and texture.

3. Can range from purely representational to completely abstract, allowing for creativity and individualism.

4. May suggest two dimensions or three dimensions.

E. Texture.

1. Is the suggestion of how something feels to the touch, ranging from silky smooth to rough.

2. Is sometimes unique to the medium (such as pencil, crayon, ink, watercolor, or oil paint).

3. Can be simulated by:
   a. The application of line (thin to thick).
   b. The shading effect that helps define space.

F. Space.

1. Is defined as the representation of depth and the relative positions of objects.

2. Is manipulated through the use of such elements as color, line, value, and perspective.

3. Techniques include:
   a. Indistinct drawing: suggests distant objects.
   b. Overlapping objects: establishes their relative positions.
   c. Gradation of color: creates depth.
   d. Linear perspective: creates depth by using parallel lines that converge on a vanishing point.

II. PRINCIPLES OF DESIGN

A. Balance.

1. Is defined as the harmonious arrangement of elements in a composition.
2. Is dependent on object placement, size, and direction.
   a. Placement: the area occupied by shapes, chosen to create harmony or lack of it.
   b. Size: variation of object size to balance or unbalance a composition (for example, a large circular shape may be balanced by three smaller circular shapes, while a large circular shape and a single small circular shape may be unbalanced).
   c. Direction: drawing of the viewer's eye to elements in a composition by use of object position to represent directional forces.

B. Symmetry.

1. May be achieved by mirrorlike repetition.
2. May be achieved by symmetrical balance; things/objects are approximately the same on each side.

C. Asymmetry.

1. Achieved through the use of unequal elements, with no axis or central point.
2. Associated with dynamic, expressive qualities.

D. Repetition.

1. Is defined as the recurring elements in a composition.
2. Creates rhythm (flow), unity, and balance.

E. Contrast.

1. Is defined as differences in form, line, texture, and color.
2. Adds variety and increases viewer interest in and attention to a work.

    F. Dominance.

       1. Is defined as the emphasis of a featured point.

       2. Uses contrast between featured point and other elements.

III. QUESTIONS TO ASK WHEN ANALYZING ART

  A. How are the lines in the composition arranged (horizontally, vertically, diagonally)?

  B. How do the lines in the composition create action, mood, interest, shading, and the like?

  C. How is color used to show contrast, highlight an area, or create a mood?

  D. How does color create spatial relationships?

  E. Where are the light and dark areas in a composition? How does light enhance the directionality? Does it "lead" the viewer?

  F. What types of shapes are used? Geometric? How do the various shapes affect the composition as a whole?

  G. What textures are used in the pictures? What feelings do the textures convey?

  H. Is there controlled space in the picture?

  I. Are the elements in the picture in perspective?

  J. Is the composition balanced (symmetrical or asymmetrical)? How is the balance achieved?

  K. What elements are repeated? Do the various elements contrast with or complement each other?

  L. Is one area or element dominant? What does this indicate about the picture?

  M. What is the overall effect of the composition (busy, cluttered, etc.)? How does the total composition affect your feelings? Why? What is the artist attempting to convey? How can you determine this?

GLOSSARY

Abstract—A nonrepresentational composition created through the use of form, line, and color.

Accent—The emphasis in a picture, set off by the use of value, shape, or contrasting color.

Advancing colors—Colors that appear to "come forward," usually red, orange, and yellow.

Analogous colors—Colors that are closely related to one another (for example, blue, blue-green, and green).

Area—The flat surface within the borders of a picture.

Asymmetrical—Unequal; not identical on both sides of a central line.

Balance—A harmonious arrangement of the elements of a composition.

Blending—A device used to allow one color or tone to merge with another.

Center of interest—The area of focus; the part of a picture that attracts the most attention.

Chroma—The strength or purity of a color.

Collage—An artwork made by gluing pieces of paper, photographs, cloth, and other materials together in an overlapping design.

Color—Light waves of different lengths create colors to the eye. Color also includes hue, value, and intensity.

Color harmony—An effect that is unified and aesthetically pleasing. Color harmony is produced by combining colors that are similar in one or more aspects.

Color scheme—The dominant color arrangement in a picture used to create color unity.

Complementary colors—Colors opposite each other on the color wheel complement each other (for example, red and green, purple and yellow, and orange and blue).

Composition—The particular arrangement of forms, colors, lines, and other elements used in a drawing or painting.

Contour—An outline or profile of an object.

Contrast—Strong differences in form, line, texture, and/or color create contrast.

Cool colors—Green, blue-green, blue, and violet are cool colors, often used to suggest wet objects.

Crosshatch—Parallel lines crossing other parallel lines, creating value and texture.

Delineation—Representing an object by using lines instead of mass.

Depth—The illusion of distance on a flat surface.

Design—A planned arrangement of the composition elements.

Distortion—Arranging art elements to suggest other than a natural shape. Distortion is used to create emotion in the viewer.

Dominant—The most significant element of a composition.

Edge—The outline or border of a form or shape. A sharp or distinct border is called a hard edge. A blurred or diffused border is called a soft edge.

Ellipse—The shape of a circle when viewed at an angle, used to obtain perspective.

Emphasis—The stress or accent on a particular element of composition.

Eye level—(1) The horizontal plane depicted by the artist in a composition, also called the *horizon line;* (2) the eye level of the artist.

Focal point—The center of interest in a composition.

Foreshorten—Using the laws of perspective to shorten forms, objects, or figures.

Form—The actual three-dimensional shape and structure of a composition object.

Gradation—The gradual change in value, tint, or color as rendered in a picture.

Harmony—The pleasing arrangement of picture elements based on using similar qualities of shape, size, and color.

Horizon line—An imaginary horizontal line which represents the height or actual direction of the observer's vision.

Hue—The name used to distinguish a color, such as red, blue, or blue-green.

Intensity—The strength, saturation, or purity of a color.

Line—Any continuous unbroken mark.

Negative space—The area or space in a composition not represented by the principal focus point.

Opaque—The limitation of light; not transparent or translucent.

Outline—The outside edge of a figure or object; a sketch using only line, without shading.

Perspective—A geometric method for representing three-dimensional relations on a flat surface and for indicating depth.

Primary colors—Blue, red, and yellow are the primary colors, and other hues can be prepared by combining these three.

Proportion—The relationship (size) of one part of a composition to another or of one part to the whole.

Realism—The depiction of a form in a realistic, or true-to-life, manner; re-creating the semblance of an object.

Relief—Sculpted figures projecting from a background.

Rhythm—The repetition of similar elements in a composition, such as colors, forms, values, and lines.

Secondary colors—Orange, green, and violet are the secondary colors. They are prepared by mixing equal amounts of two primary colors.

Shade—(1) The result of mixing a pure color and a quantity of black; (2) surface shadows on an object used to indicate form.

Shape—The flat, two-dimensional form of an object.

Spectrum—The arrangement of colors as they are refracted into a rainbow by a prism.

Still life—The pictorial arrangement of inanimate objects.

Symmetry—Arrangement of objects so there is a similarity in size, shape, and relative positioning on opposite sides of a composition; mirror-image or equal balance in a composition.

Technique—(1) The characteristics of a particular medium; (2) the style of a particular artist.

Tertiary colors—Intermediate colors prepared by mixing unequal amounts of two primary colors.

Texture—The appearance or suggested feel of a flat surface.

Three-dimensional—Possessing the qualities of height, width, and depth.

Tint—A mixture of white and a pure color.

Translucent—A material or representation that transmits light, but not so well that an object can be clearly seen through it.

Transparent—A material or representation through which objects can be clearly seen.

Two-dimensional—Representing only the dimensions of width and height without delineating depth, thickness, or solid form.

Value—The lightness or darkness of a color or hue.

Vanishing point—The point at which receding parallel lines converge.

Warm colors—Colors that are associated with heat or dry objects, generally red, orange, and yellow.

DANCE

OUTLINE

I. CURRENT PHILOSOPHY OF CALIFORNIA DANCE EDUCATORS

A. Dance instruction:

1. Offers an alternative mode of expression, particularly emphasizing the personal interpretation of movement through dance.

2. Provides diversity by involving both physical and mental properties.

3. Serves the interests of good health by encouraging physical fitness.

4. Contributes to one's sense of self.

5. Aids in the internalization of one's own culture and in the understanding of other cultures.

6. Enhances the study of other academic areas.

B. Basic dance programs should include:

1. Creative dance.

2. Modern dance.

3. Social dance.

4. Dance of other cultures.

5. Ballet, jazz, and tap if appropriate resources are available.

II. COMPONENTS OF DANCE

A. Aesthetic perception.

1. Develops awareness of the body and its communicative potential.

2. Increases motor efficiency and kinesthetic sensitivity.

B. Creative expression.

1. Develops ability to express feelings, images, and thoughts through movement.

2. Develops respect for originality in dance.

C. Dance heritage.

    1. Develops knowledge and appreciation of multicultural dance heritage.

D. Aesthetic valuing.

    1. Develops a sense of involvement and capacity to enjoy expression in dance.

    2. Encourages a cultivation of a critical understanding of dance.

GLOSSARY

Abstraction—The essence of an idea applied to the art of movement.

Adagio—As in music, the opposite of *allegro,* or a slower tempo. Adagio is also a set of practice exercises in class consisting of extensions and balances.

Alignment—The way in which various parts of the dancer's body are in line with one another while the dancer is moving.

Allegro—From the musical term, this refers to quick or lively movements.

Arabesque—A pose in which the working leg is extended with a straight knee directly behind the body (both height of the leg and position of the arms are variable).

Attitude—A pose modeled after the statue of the winged Mercury by Bologna in which the working leg is extended behind the body with the knee bent. Can also be held in front of the body.

Barre—A round rail attached to the wall horizontally, about 3½ feet above the floor, for dancers to hold during the first half of technique class; also used for stretching the legs by placing the feet or legs on it.

Basic positions—The five positions of the arms and feet, so called because they are the basis for all steps in the vocabulary of the classic dance.

Body movement—Includes *locomotor* (moving from one place to another) and *axial* (contained movement around an axis of the body).

Choreography—The steps of a dance as put together for performance or the art of composing dances.

Classical—Refers to the lexicon of dance as taught in the original academies; also used in reference to ballets as created during the Imperial Russian days, such as *The Sleeping Beauty, Nutcracker,* and *Swan Lake;* also refers to a style of performing that was developed over the years from France, Italy, Denmark, and Russia or the kind of dancing that comes from that style.

Corps de ballet—Literally, the "body of the ballet," or the chorus; the dancers who stand behind the principals, forming a stage picture with their poses; also, all those members of a dance company who are not designated as soloists or principals.

Creative movement—Dance movement which is primary and nonfunctional, with emphasis on body mastery for expressive and communicative purposes.

Dance—All-inclusive term meaning the aesthetics of movement. (*A* dance is the organization of moves with a beginning, middle, and end in sequential form.)

Dance form—Structure which embodies a choreographed dance.

Dance style—Specific manner of performing, characteristic of a period, culture, individual, etc.

Dance type—Category such as tap, jazz, modern, or ethnic.

Dance work—A dance choreographed and presented in performance.

Demi-pointe—On the ball of the foot, or half toe.

Elevation—The ability to get up into the air and remain there long enough to perform various movements or poses.

En bas—Low, usually in reference to an arm position.

En haut—High; used to indicate when the arms are raised over the head.

En l'air—Refers to steps performed in the air or to a leg that is in the air.

Entrechat—A "beating" movement in which the feet criss-cross one another around the ankles in the air with the legs straight.

Exploration—Experimentation with the uses of movement in human responses.

Extension—Raising the leg to a straightened position with the foot very high above the ground; the ability to lift and hold the leg in position off the ground.

Force—Release of potential energy into kinetic energy.

Grand jeté—A leap from one leg to the other in which the working leg is kicked or thrown away from the body and into the air; the pose achieved in the air differs as does the direction the leap takes.

Grand jeté en tournan (tour jeté)—In this leap, the dancer turns halfway in midair to land facing the direction in which the movement started.

Improvisation—Movement without previous planning.

Kinesthetic awareness—Feeling the dance movements of others in one's own muscles.

Lifts—A part of *pas de deux* in which one dancer is lifted off the ground by another.

Line—The arrangement of head, shoulders, arms, torso, and legs while dancing.

Modern dance—Type of creative dance involving specialized movement techniques; emphasis is on expression and communication.

Movement materials—Sequences, motifs, and phrases developed as the choreographed dance.

Muscle memory—The way in which most choreography is remembered by dancers.

Neoclassicism—A term coined to denote that form and technique of dancing which came after classicism; often used in reference to George Balanchine, although he never used this expression to describe his work.

Pas de deux—Literally, "a step for two"; referring to a specific codified form which is choreographed in many classical ballets; also used to refer to any section of a dance performed by two dancers together.

Passé—A "passing" position in which the foot passes by the knee of the supporting leg. When this position is held, as in pirouettes, with the foot of the working leg resting against the knee of the supporting leg, it is known as *retiré*.

Pirouette—French, "to whirl or spin"; a turn on one foot that can be executed outward, away from the body, or inward, toward the body.

Pointe—Dancing on the toes.

Postmodern dance—A term coined in the 1960s by those who wished to create movement outside the influences of any of the then-traditional modern dance pioneers, such as Cunningham, Graham, Humphrey, Limón, and Taylor.

Promenade—An adagio movement in which the dancer pivots completely around on one foot while maintaining a pose with the working leg.

Romantic era—A period from about 1820 to 1870 in which ballet was characterized primarily by supernatural subject matter, long white tutus, dancing on the toes, and theatrical innovations that permitted the dimming of the house lights for theatrical illusion.

Space—Immediate area surrounding the body; the area in which bodies can move at all levels.

Spotting—Focusing the eyes on one point in the distance in order to keep balance while turning.

Stasis—The state of being at rest.

Supporting leg—The leg upon which the dancer is balancing.

Time—The duration of a dance; can be divided into the rate of speed (fast, moderate, or slow); metric time (beat, pulse, accent, tempo, and duration).

Turnout—Rotating the leg outward from the hip such that the feet form a straight line on the floor, toes facing away from each other; a way of holding the body, developed in ballet, that allows the dancer more articulation, speed, and variety of movement.

Working leg—The leg that is delineating movement.

Because drama uses both language and body movement, it helps students develop poise, confidence, ease, and versatility both verbally and physically. Drama develops creative, critical, and communication skills and should be a regular offering at all grade levels.

This outline provides an overview of the elements of drama with which students can be involved. The following glossary suggests terms with which you should be familiar for the MSAT.

OUTLINE

I. ELEMENTS OF DRAMA IN THE CURRICULUM

A. Acting.

1. Involves sensory awareness, rhythm and movement, pantomime, oral communication, and playmaking.

2. Often requires preparation and rehearsal of scripted literature and may lead to a performance before an audience.

3. Suggested for secure students under the guidance of a specifically trained teacher-director.

B. Drama.

1. Involves the reenactment of life situations for entertainment and human understanding.

2. Does not necessarily require a formal audience.

C. Improvisation.

1. Involves creative, cooperative, spontaneous, and flexible response to changing and unexpected dramatic stimuli.

2. Embraces problem solving without preconception of how to perform and allows anything within the environment to to used during the experience.

D. Playmaking.

1. Involves the consciously planned and structured activity of creation of an original script.

2. No formal audience is required.

E. Theater.

1. Involves the formal presentation of a scripted play.

2. Incorporates elements such as acting, directing, designing, and managing.

II. CRITERIA FOR DRAMA EVALUATION

A. Intent.

1. Involves the objective, purpose, theme, or basic idea of a work of drama.

B. Structure.

1. Involves the interaction of all elements.

2. Includes, but is not limited to, design, rhythm, climax, conflict, balance, and sequence.

C. Effectiveness.

1. Involves the degree to which a dramatic work succeeds.

2. Includes the evaluation of the work's success in such things as entertaining, informing, illuminating, persuading, inspiring, amusing, engaging, shocking, and awing.

D. Worth.

1. Involves a value judgment.

2. Includes assessment of the knowledge, insight, wisdom, or feeling imparted by a work.

GLOSSARY

Action—In a character-character interaction, the total array of purposeful activity, both external (physical) and internal (psychological), by which characters attempt to achieve their objectives.

Antagonist—In traditional dramatic theory, an element, usually a character, that resists the protagonist. Conflict results from the efforts of the protagonist to achieve his or her objectives in spite of the obstacles introduced by the antagonist.

Arena staging—The physical configuration of audience and actor in which the audience essentially surrounds the playing area.

Aristotelian theater—In general, the traditional theater thought to be espoused by Aristotle. It includes clear, simple plotting; strong (but not necessarily complicated) characters; high levels of intellectual content; and a minimum of spectacle. In the Renaissance, other criteria were added to these, some native to Aristotle, some imposed through fancied symmetry: plays should display the three unities, be written in five acts, avoid violence, and not mix comedy and tragedy.

Block—(verb) Deciding upon the gross movement of actors upon the stage; assigning the physical relationship of actors and the location of entrances and exits; creating stage "pictures." Frequently, early rehearsals ("blocking rehearsals") are devoted to this task.

Broadway theater—The commercial model which dominated the American theater from the end of the nineteenth century until shortly after World War II. Named after the New York boulevard which runs through the Manhattan theater district, this kind of theater is essentially a profit-making enterprise in which shares in a production are sold to investors with the expectation that, after meeting the initial expenses of production, they will receive a substantial return on their investment. To enhance these profits, Broadway theater aspires to very long runs of a single play, frequently using star performers appearing in vehicles with the widest possible audience appeal.

Center stage—The exact center of the floor of the stage.

Character—A figure portrayed in the play; the sum total of the actions which define a person so portrayed.

Chorus—In Greek and Roman drama of the classical period, a group of characters in a play who comment on the action, frequently speaking directly to the audience. The function of the chorus is usually that of an intermediary between the audience and the major characters in the play. Although they are often given a collective role, the individual members of the chorus seldom have separate names or characters. Instead the group as a whole serves as a surrogate "audience" to the degree that it is detached from the dramatic action and can view with horror or amusement the action of the major characters; at the same time, the chorus can participate directly in the action, advising the protagonist, arguing with the antagonist, and praying to the gods for guidance.

Chronological time—Time as a linear experience of events related by cause and effect. Most history is written in chronological order, but much theater chooses to take liberties with the chronological presentation of facts. The earliest modification was to leave out long and unimportant passages of time in order to present scenes which capture the essence of the story in an episodic plot. Later developments include the flashback and the flashforward.

Climax—In traditional dramatic structure, the point in the play that completes the rising action. The contending forces, having raised the conflict to the highest point possible, face one another in a confrontation so inescapable that only one can emerge victorious. At this point, frequently a new piece of information is made public which tips the balance one way or another. The climax is followed by the dénouement.

Comedy—Historically, comedy is any play which ends happily. More specifically, it is the genre of dramatic literature which is lighter in tone than drama but more serious than farce. Comedy differs from drama in that the characters are less well developed, the theme less weighty, the language usually wittier, and the ending invariably happy. Comedy is often difficult to distinguish from farce; in the latter, the humor is more physical, the characters are more broadly drawn, and the plots are more contrived.

Company—In the broadest sense, all of the people associated with producing a play, including the designers, technicians, director, stage managers, and actors. In the narrowest sense, the concept of "the company" is confined to the actors alone.

Conflict—The central feature of dramatic action; the arrangement of the objectives of two or more strong characters in such a way that those objectives are competing and mutually exclusive.

Connotative meaning—The meaning conveyed by connotative symbols, symbols which are vague in terms of strict definition, but rich in poetic meaning. Much connotative meaning evokes an emotional rather than intellectual response.

Content—What is portrayed in theater; namely, the interaction of at least one character with some aspect of his or her environment. Since the portrayed interaction is normally with another person (or an aspect of the natural environment endowed with human qualities), the content of theater is character-character interaction.

Conventions—The temporary "rules" of the performance. The conventions of the theater are specific to particular cultures, styles of theater, and even individual productions.

Creative drama—A form of enactment in which students improvise scenes for their own growth and edification, not that of an audience. In some cases, the aim of creative drama is to learn subjects other than theater (history, psychology, literature, etc.); in others, it is to learn about theater itself.

Dénouement—In traditional dramatic theory, the portion of action which immediately follows the climax of a play. In the dénouement, the last remaining loose ends are "tied up," including the disposition of any unresolved conflicts and the reestablishment of stasis (a condition of balance or harmony).

Director—In the modern theater, the major interpretive figure, whose job it is to bring to life the vision of the playwright or otherwise provide artistic meaning to the theater experience.

Downstage—The portion of the proscenium stage which is closest to the audience.

Drama—The category of literature intended for the stage. Also, in general usage, the perception that a series of real-life events have the kind of meaning commonly experienced in the theater or films, as in "a dramatic rescue" or the "drama of a summit meeting."

Dramatic criticism—The work of a drama critic. Commentary on play or script intended to enrich the experience of seeing the play or reading the script by others. Dramatic criticism can appear in written form in periodicals, as media presentations, or in public talks.

Dramatic question—The first and most important element in rising action. As soon as conflict has been established, the next question must be "How will this turn out?" The dramatic question then raises the issue of which of the conflicting parties will prevail and, in doing so, begins to develop suspense.

Environmental staging—The form of physical relationship between audience and performers in which there is little or no clear definition between the space dedicated to each. The conventions of environmental staging dictate that audience and performers use the same space during the course of the experience.

Exposition—The playwriting device of providing information to the audience. Retrospective exposition usually occurs early in the action and gives the audience important information about what has occurred *before* the play begins; current exposition provides information about events offstage happening *during* the play.

Flashback—A manipulation of time in plot in which a scene from earlier in the story is shown *after* those which occur later. Rather rare in traditional playwriting, flashbacks are common in films.

Form—The relationship of all the parts of plays of a certain type considered apart from any single example of that type, as in the *form* of farce and the *form* of the well-made play. What emerges is a model or ideal of a theatrical experience which can be used to describe specific examples.

Full-length play—A single play which typically fulfills the expectation for a complete theatrical experience. In the Western tradition, this means one play of three to five acts, usually filling two to four hours.

Gallery—In the Elizabethan theater, one of a tier of alcoves surrounding the interior of the "yard" where, in enclosed boxes and on benches, those who could afford the greatest comfort could sit. Comparable galleries are found in most Renaissance theaters; they continue today in the tiers of balconies and boxes found in most opera houses.

Illumination—The act of casting light upon an otherwise darkened stage.

Improvisation—Acting without a script or prepared text.

Inciting incident—In traditional dramatic structure, the first incident in the chain of events called rising action. It is the inciting incident which throws the world of the play into disequilibrium (destroying stasis); the remainder of the play is an attempt to reestablish that balance. The inciting incident may be deceptively simple: the arrival of a new person in the community, the delivery of a letter, a piece of news emerging in casual conversation, and the like.

Kabuki—A classical Japanese theater form which combines colorful song and dance, flamboyant characters, and extravagant plots in a popular art which has retained its wide popularity since the early seventeenth century.

Lighting plot—A plan of the stage showing the location of each lighting instrument, its size and character, and the area of the stage where its light will fall.

Melodrama—The genre of theater which is normally placed between tragedy and drama and which shares some characteristics with each. It is largely serious in tone, placing its major figures in great jeopardy, but unlike tragedy, saves them from destruction at the end. The moral stance of melodrama is always clear: The good characters are *very* good, the bad ones *very* bad.

Mood—In lighting, the use of elements of stage lighting to evoke or support particular emotional states in the audience of a play. As an element of theater, the place on the humorous-serious scale which a play is expected to occupy.

Multiple plots—The traditional element of theater plotting in which more than one story line is presented, usually simultaneously. Frequently, the plots are kept separate until late in the play, at which point they intersect in some ingenious way. Multiple plots work best when each separate plot is somehow a treatment of the same theme or in some other way shares an important theatrical element with the others.

Neoclassic drama—Plays of the neoclassic period or plays modeled after them in which Renaissance writers attempted to recapture the glory of theater in ancient Greece and Rome. Particularly in seventeenth- and eighteenth-century France, this effort was aided by the application of certain rules of playwriting, such as the unities, the enforced use of rigid verse forms, and the general concern for "decorum" on the stage.

One-act play—A play of short duration (usually less than an hour) which can be presented without an intermission and without major changes in scenery.

Orchestra—In an ancient Greek theater, the open dancing area in front of the stagehouse. In modern usage, the orchestra is the lowest and usually most expansive array of seats directly in front of the stage. Should not be confused with the orchestra pit.

Pastoral play—An extinct genre of play, popular during the Italian Renaissance, which is set in a countryside populated by nymphs, satyrs, shepherds, shepherdesses, and wandering knights. Persistently upbeat in tone, the pastoral play existed chiefly to give courtiers a chance to indulge a taste for dressing up as peasants, singing, and dancing. The pastoral play may have been the Renaissance attempt to recapture the Greek satyr play.

Pit—In the Elizabethan theater, the portion of the theater immediately in front of the stage. This area was occupied by patrons who had paid the lowest admission fee and were willing to stand for the duration of the production. Over time, this area was filled, first with benches and later with chairs. Today it is called the orchestra.

Playscript—"Script" for short. A detailed, written description of a play intended to give the reader as clear a sense of the produced work as possible. When it is first written by a playwright, the playscript refers to an imagined production; later, the playscript may describe an actual production. In either case, the aim is to provide enough information so that a group of performers can mount a production of the play in question.

Plot—The series of incidents which make up the action of a play. These incidents are selected from a series of events which, when described chronologically, make up a story.

Proscenium arch—The major architectural feature of Western theaters since the Renaissance, the proscenium arch is essentially an opening in the wall between two rooms. In one room (the stagehouse), the actors perform; in the other (the auditorium), the audience is located. The arch itself can range from extremely elaborate and intrusive to nearly undetectable.

Proscenium staging—The form of physical configuration bewtween actor and audience encouraged by (some would say demanded by) the proscenium arch. It consists of a fairly narrow array of audience gathered on one side of the stage only. There is a clear distinction between the areas occupied by the actors and the audience area; in traditional proscenium theaters, there is also an effort to keep the audience directly in front of the center of the proscenium arch.

Protagonist—Literally, the "first person to enter a contest." The major figure in traditional theater; the person around whom the action of the play turns. The antagonist is the person or force which resists the protagonist, thus forming the conflict of a play.

Restoration comedy—Characteristic comedy of the period known as the English Restoration (1660–1700). Restoration comedy is known for its glittering language, salacious plots, and frequently debauched characters.

Revolving stage—A portion of the stage which is so constructed that it rotates around a pivot. Such a stage can be used in a number of ways, the most frequent being to change settings; the downstage scenery rotates out of sight, revealing scenery which had previously been set upstage.

Rising action—In traditional dramatic structure, the portion of the plot which begins with the inciting incident and continues until the climax. The incidents which make up rising action are expected to build in intensity and frequency, often alternating good and bad news, in such a way as to increase suspense.

Satyr play—A form of Greek drama which coexisted with tragedy in the classic period. Little is know of the satyr play except that it seems to have been a burlesque of the same ideas presented in tragedies, ridiculing the gods and heroic legends, using the bawdiest language, dance, and song to do so.

Stage left—In a proscenium arch configuration, the side of the stage to the left of an actor facing the audience; sometimes called "audience right."

Stage right—In a proscenium arch configuration, the side of the stage to the right of an actor facing the audience; sometimes called "audience left."

Stereotyped character—One based on the assumption that all members of a given group possess certain simple behavioral traits. Hence, a few swift strokes of character development (a dialect, a distinctive walk, a costume, etc.) suffice to communicate the stereotype to the audience. Contrasted with the unique character, who shares nothing of consequence with any other person, whose life experiences have created a character which is, taken as a whole, entirely distinct from all others.

Stock company—In the eighteenth, nineteenth, and early twentieth centuries, a form of resident company in which actors were hired according to lines of work and large numbers of plays were prepared, usually with very short rehearsal periods and for relatively short runs. The practice and the term continue to live in the experience of "summer stock."

Storyboard—A visual display of the plot of a play or film in which each scene (or shot) is represented by a single picture or short description. The pictures or notecards are then arranged on a wall or bulletin board in such a way as to depict the flow of the plot.

Tempo—The speed with which incidents that make up action take place.

Thrust staging—The physical configuration of audience and performers in which at least some part of the stage extends into, and is surrounded by, the audience. In thrust staging, the audience surrounds the acting area to no more than 270 degrees; beyond that, the configuration is called arena staging.

Upstage—In proscenium staging, the portion of an acting area which is farthest from the audience.

Vomitoria—In Roman theater, the vomitoria were the tunnels which allowed the audience to enter and exit the large theaters with ease. In contemporary theaters, the vomitoria ("voms" for short) are the tunnels which allow the *actors* to reach the downstage portions of a thrust stage by passing through the audience.

HUMAN
DEVELOPMENT
REVIEW

OUTLINE

This section on human development reviews educational psychology, or how a child learns.

I. STIMULUS-RESPONSE (S-R) LEARNING

A. John B. Watson: behaviorism (behavior is shaped by one's environment).

1. Analysis of S-R learning.
   a. If a stimulus is present (bright sunlight), then a response will follow (pupil contraction).
   b. S-R experiments yield objective data.
   c. S-R connections are shaped through repeated experiences and influence all behavior.
   d. All complex behaviors are reducible to conditioned, reflexive, S-R connections.
2. Behavior is a function of experience.
   a. Behavior is totally dependent on learning.
   b. Conditioned responses are the basis of emotional responses.
   c. A child's learned experiences can account for later behavioral patterning.
3. Educational implications.
   a. A child's behavior can be shaped by the teacher by arranging learning experiences to meet educational objectives.

B. B.F. Skinner: goal-directed acts (learned acts depend on desired environmental outcomes/results).

1. Operant conditioning involves reinforcement.
   a. A behavior trait that is reinforced (rewarded) will tend to be strengthened.
   b. A behavior that is not reinforced will tend to be eliminated or extinguished.
   c. Interval or intermittent reinforcement will tend to strengthen a behavior (partial reinforcement).
   d. Responses are characterized by *respondents* (automatic reflexes) and *operants* (all other responses).
2. Behavior modification is a classroom procedure that uses operant conditioning techniques.

3. Educational implications.

    a. The teacher should consciously attempt to reinforce desirable behaviors (for example, introducing positive comments, praise, or gold stars) and not reinforce behaviors that are undesirable.

    b. Behavior can be altered by changing the environment (physical and emotional).

    c. A teacher should reinforce positive behavior in a child as soon as the positive behavior is evidenced.

C. Albert Bandura: how child-rearing techniques influence personality development.

1. Children imitate behavior. Role models, both peers and adults, and outside stimuli, such as television and movies, influence how children respond to feelings like frustration and aggression.

2. Children learn by observing behavior. Aggressive models encourage aggressiveness. Viewing violence can increase the probability that violent behavior will be imitated.

3. Educational implications.

    a. Teachers need to recognize how to model appropriate behavior.

    b. Teachers need to know how to counteract the negative influences of media presentations (cartoons that show violence and commercials that deal with frustration in an unacceptable manner).

    c. Teachers need to reward calm, nonaggressive behavior.

II. COGNITIVE DEVELOPMENT: INTELLECTUAL GROWTH AND AGE-RELATED CHANGES IN COGNITIVE SKILLS

A. Kurt Lewin: cognitive field theory (focuses on perception, motivation, learning, and "life space").

1. The influence of the Gestalt school.

    a. Perception is an abstract theoretical event which intervenes between the sensation of internal or external stimuli and the production of a response.

    b. Perceptual organization contributes to perception.

    c. Personal experience (reality) is involved in formulating basic perceptions—for example, reversible figures (vase with two profiles), simultaneous contrast (four squares on gray backgrounds), and linear perspective (identical boxes on receding surface).

2. Lewin analyzed authoritarian, democratic, and laissez faire types of leaders.

3. Lewin analyzed motivational conflicts as conflicts between positive and negative goals.

4. Educational implications.

a. A child's behavior is not simply the result of the external stimuli presented.

b. Internal stimuli, such as anxiety or fear, affect each child differently and determine how external stimuli are interpreted.

c. Individual differences in children should be recognized, and educational opportunities to address those differences should be provided.

B. J.L. Bruner: learning based on structure has meaning and leads to real understanding.

1. Theory of instruction (the individual processes information and builds increasingly complex models of the world).

a. Motivation is based on intrinsic value, curiosity, and cooperation/reciprocity.

b. Structures must address a child's intellectual development and maturation.

   (1) The way problems are structured creates an organizational pattern that yields understanding; structuring is purposeful.

   (2) The three modes of how things are represented.

      (a) Enactive: rests on motor responses (touch, feel, manipulation of objects, etc.).

      (b) Iconic (image): uses images to stand for perceptual events (pictures, drawings, etc.).

      (c) Symbolic representation: language provides the means for representing experience and for transforming thought processes into words which stand for ideas.

c. Sequencing is based on a hierarchy of learning and interaction among the enactive, iconic, and symbolic modes of representation.

d. Reinforcement is based on the use of appropriate rewards and feedback to influence the direction of learning.

2. Educational implications.

a. Teachers should structure their room environments to encourage exploration and increase motivation.

b. A child should know the expected learning goals.

c. The stages of cognitive development must be incorporated into a presentation of cognitive concepts.

d. Children who "discover" solutions to problems will be able to better retain the material.

C. Jean Piaget: theories of cognitive development (the learning processes by which children arrive at answers to problems).

1. Piaget's developmental theory (concept-learning processes).

a. Assimilation: how a child adds information to existing concepts.

(1) An individual assimilates only that part of the environment from which he or she can make sense.

(2) Concepts are formed by assimilating new information.

b. Accommodation: how a child adjusts a concept to contradictory information.

(1) "New" material is understood in the context of previous material that is "almost" understood.

(2) Accommodation adapts existing schemata (cognitive structures) to allow unassimilated stimuli to be assimilated.

c. Adaptation: how a child adjusts the combined processes of assimilation and accommodation to the environment.

(1) The interaction between an infant and his or her environment results in continuous cognitive development.

(2) The child learns the consequences of specific actions.

d. Organization: how a child integrates or systematizes cognitive structures.

(1) The increasing interrelation of cognitive structures (schemata) allows a child to understand increasingly complex logic.

(2) Children learn to modify experiences.

2. Piaget's stages of cognitive (intellectual) growth.

a. Sensorimotor stage (from birth to approximately 2 years).

(1) A child's intelligence is manifested in action.

(2) A child proceeds to the acquisition of language.

(3) Generalized responses are used to "solve" problems.

(4) A child begins to manipulate his or her environment.

(5) The emphasis is on egocentric play (purely self-gratifying).

(6) By the end of the sensorimotor stage, a child understands that objects have separate identities.

b. Preoperational stage (approximately age 2 to 7 years).

(1) A child makes the transition from self-centered behaviors to the beginnings of socialization.

(2) A child gains language.

(3) Actions are now related to understanding the meaning of objects and events. (The thought processes become organized and understandable systems.)

(4) The period is characterized by the mastery of symbols (pretending and playing are significant).

(5) A sense of morality begins.

c. Concrete operations stage (approximately age 7 to 11 years).

(1) A child is able to form mental representations of a series of actions.

(2) A child demonstrates an inability to deal with abstractions accurately.

(3) A child begins to understand *reversibility* and *conservation* (the ability to judge space and volume relationships accurately).

(4) Operational thought appears. A child can order and relate experiences into an organized whole.

      (5) A child is capable of exploring alternate outcomes and solutions.

      (6) The notion of time assumes an abstract quality.

      (7) An emphasis on the peer group defines a new level of morality.

  d. Formal operations stage (approximately age 11 and older).

      (1) A child is capable of complex abstract reasoning.

      (2) A child can contemplate the "future".

      (3) A child does not need concrete operations to solve problems and can symbolize complex mental operations (for example, algebraic equations).

      (4) A child's personality becomes more solidified.

      (5) Absolute morality is replaced by relative morality.

3. Educational implications.

  a. Piaget's stages of cognitive development provided an alternative to the classical conditioning belief that the child is only a passive learner.

  b. Piaget quantified the conceptual-learning process—there are predictable stages of cognitive development.

  c. A child learns how to make adjustments to his or her environment.

  d. A child cannot skip stages of cognitive growth.

  e. A child can be tested for his or her level of cognitive understanding (for example, understanding the conservation of liquids—the ability to differentiate equal volumes of water in a glass and saucer).

  f. Educational practice should be based on a child's cognitive stages of development.

  g. Educational practice should facilitate spontaneous discovery.

III. AFFECTIVE DOMAIN: ATTITUDES AND INTERESTS OF CHILDREN

A. Lawrence Kohlberg: the level of a child's moral development is sequential and dependent on both age and maturation.

1. Kohlberg's three levels of moral reasoning (a child's thought process in the development of moral thinking).

  a. Preconventional: cultural rules, labels (good and bad), and consequences (reward and punishment) determine behavior, *not* moral convictions.

  b. Conventional: a child conforms to the expectations of the group, family, and society; conforming is seen as valuable or as doing one's duty.

  c. Postconventional: a child's behavior is tied to moral choices; the highest level of moral judgment.

2. Educational implications.

  a. Teachers need to recognize the moral stages inherent in a child's development—for example, that at a particular stage, a child needs to understand that certain behaviors will result in specific consequences.

  b. Teachers need to recognize the sequential foundation upon which higher moral principles are based.

B. Abraham Maslow: the theory of self-actualization (expression of one's potentialities).

1. Maslow identifies five steps—from biological needs to self-actualization—that humans need to meet.

    a. Physiological needs, such as hunger and thirst.

    b. Safety needs, such as security and support.

    c. Affiliation needs, such as affection and friendship.

    d. Esteem needs, such as self-respect and self-confidence.

    e. Self-actualization needs, such as self-motivation and independence.

2. Lower needs must be satisfied before higher needs can be met.

3. Educational implications.

    a. Teachers must understand that motivation and personality are linked to achieving the hierarchy of needs.

    b. A child who feels "loved" will perform at higher levels; a child will "meet" a teacher's expectations.

C. Carl Rogers: a basic drive of human nature is to fulfill one's potential (self-actualization).

1. Aggressive, anxious, or selfish behavior occurs because one's actualization tendencies have been distorted or blocked.

2. Reinforcement and satisfaction come from continuous growth experiences.

3. Eventually one develops a need for positive self-regard; one will behave only in ways consistent with one's self-concept.

4. Development is a continuous evolution of self-fulfillment. Parent-child interaction is the basis for a "developed" self-concept.

5. Goals for individuals should be based on self-direction (being able to accept personal shortcomings and to avoid simplicity in explaining human behavior).

6. Educational implications.

    a. Every child is an individual. Education must emphasize the growth potential of all children.

    b. Children benefit from learner-centered teaching that encourages the development of socialization skills.

    c. A child who sees himself or herself as successful will opt for success.

GLOSSARY

Accommodation—In Piaget's theory, the forming of new schemata, or the modification of old ones, to create a more complex cognitive organization.

Acquisition—The insertion of new information into long-term memory.

Algorithms—A problem-solving method in which every possibility of a solution is considered.

All-or-none learning theory—Material is either completely learned or not learned at all.

Antecedent condition—Cause; that which precedes another event and without which the event will not occur.

Anticipatory error—An intrusion error in serial learning; when a subject responds too soon with a correct answer (responding with Item 5 immediately after Item 2).

Anxiety reaction—Long-standing and moderately severe anxiety or tension without accompanying causes; in acute form often is accompanied by somatic disturbances.

Aphasia—Disturbed language behavior resulting from brain damage; an inability to understand verbal or written material (sensory aphasia) or an inability to articulate certain words (motor aphasia).

Aptitude test—A test that predicts how successfully an individual may learn a new skill.

Assimilation—In Piaget's theory, the tendency to take in from the external world only that information that current cognitive structures can process.

Associationism—An empirical belief that complex psychological processes emerge from very simple processes.

Attitude—The basic psychological unit of interpersonal experience; a learned predisposition to behave in certain ways toward certain persons, objects, or experiences.

Attitude scales—Common techniques for assessing presence and strength of attitudes and beliefs.

Attribution—A process whereby one attempts to assign behavioral dispositions to another by noting certain important behaviors.

Autonomic nervous system—The part of the nervous system that regulates functioning of smooth muscles and endocrine glands; consists of the sympathetic and the parasympathetic branches.

Behaviorism—A kind of psychology associated with John Watson; belief that the only data appropriate for psychologists are observations of behavior.

Case-history approach—A clinical approach to discover important variables associated with the behavior of a single individual.

Cause and effect—A basic relationship wherein a particular cause is always followed by a particular effect.

Central tendency—In a frequency distribution, a single value representing the average of an entire distribution of scores; the three most common measures of central tendency are *mean, median,* and *mode.*

Classical conditioning—Learning to respond to a conditioned stimulus when that response was made previously only to an unconditioned stimulus.

Class intervals—When the range of scores in a frequency distribution is so large that it is inefficient to record a score for each subject, the range is broken into intervals with a frequency score for each interval.

Clustering—In learning, recalling items from a list in meaningful organization.

Concept—A grouping of ideas or perceptions related by some common element.

Conditioned discrimination—Following conditioned-response training, responding differently to different stimuli; for example, after conditioned-response training, if a monkey begins trembling (anticipating a shock, for instance) when presented with a red light, but not with a blue light, the monkey is manifesting conditioned discrimination.

Conditioned response (CR)—Any response that is elicited by a conditioned stimulus after conditioning has occurred.

Conditioned stimulus (CS)—That stimulus to which a new response becomes associated through conditioning.

Conduct disorders—A loose collection of behavior patterns, all of which are found offensive to society.

Confabulation—A memory error made whenever a particular item cannot be remembered and a substitute is manufactured.

Conformity—The disposition to accept the group's attitude, judgment, or perception.

Conservation—In Piaget's theory, one part of mental development in which a child understands that certain properties of an object do not change (for example, volume or weight).

Constructionism—An empirical belief that the knowledge of the world is a construction of the mind, each to his or her own, based on his or her unique experience.

Control group—A group that is as identical as possible to an experimental group but that is not exposed to the experimental variable being studied.

Correlation approach—In psychological research, the basic aim of the correlation approach is to determine if a relationship exists between two or more psychological variables without active manipulation of independent variables.

Correlation coefficient—A statistical index ranging from +1 through 0 to −1 which describes the relationship between two variables by giving both the sign and the magnitude of a correlation.

Covert behavior—A response that is not directly observable by an observer without the aid of instrumental readings or through introspection by the individual doing the behaving.

Creative problem solving—Involves producing new and original solutions through concentrated thinking by an individual.

Critical period—Certain periods in development when the environment has greatest impact on shaping particular behaviors.

Culture—The learned pattern of behaviors (including art, science, politics, religion, child-rearing, technology, food habits) that are transmitted in their entirety from generation to generation.

Data—The "facts" of psychology that are reducible to observable, quantifiable (measurable) events.

Delusion—A personal belief that is mistaken or unreal; in psychotic disorders, delusions are often associated with grandiose ideas or feelings of persecution.

Denial—The outright ignoring of events or messages that are too painful.

Dependent variable—Those variables over which the experimenter has no control, like behavior; the dependent variable changes as the result of changes in the independent variable.

Depersonalization—A feeling that "things are not real"; a state in which a person doubts his or her own reality; reality appears dreamlike.

Discrimination—Responding differentially to stimuli according to their dissimilarity.

Dizygotic twins (fraternal twins)—Twins having no more similar genetic structures than any siblings.

Double-blind procedure—In psychological research, neither subjects nor the experimenter know which subjects are in the control group to ensure against experimental bias.

Drive—A drive consists of an organismic state that activates behavior and is brought about by an unsatisfied need.

Ecological approach—A special use of the correlation approach; the basic aim is to observe behavior in natural settings without interfering with the interaction between individuals and environmental variables in order to find a relationship among many variables; also called *field technique* or *naturalistic study*.

Emotion—A complex response pattern characterized by arousal, physiological changes, and feelings.

Experimenter-expectancy confound—Experimenter bias, in which the experimenter perceives or records data incorrectly or unintentionally treats one group of subjects differently, based on prior expectancy of the experimental results.

Extinction—In classical conditioning, the repeated presentation of a conditioned stimulus alone leads to the reduction and eventual elimination of the conditioned response; in operant conditioning, the reduction and eventual elimination of a behavior by removing the reinforcement that maintained the behavior.

Free-recall task—A task in which a subject is presented with some material to learn and later must recall as much of the material as possible in any order.

Frequency distribution—A distribution of scores, arranged in order of magnitude, showing the number of times each score occurred.

Functionalism—An early school in psychology that believed that the function and not the structure of conscious experience be studied; emphasized perception, adaptation, and the application of psychological principles.

Generalization—Giving the same response to similar but not identical stimuli.

Gestalt therapy—A system of therapy founded by Fritz Perls in which principles of Gestalt psychology (especially the concepts of figure-ground and of closure) are used. Original Gestaltists were largely concerned with perception and patterns of organization.

Halo effect—The primacy effect leads to stereotyped impressions of "goodness" or "badness" of a person's qualities.

Homeostasis—The status-quo preserving tendencies within an organism through which the physiological balance is ideally maintained without the voluntary awareness of the organism.

Hypothesis—An unproved explanation of complex data.

Identification—A way in which certain social roles are acquired; a defense mechanism in which a person behaves in a way suggesting his or her desire to be another person.

Imprinting—Species-specific and rapidly learned behavior occurring during a critical early stage in development; includes so-called following or attachment responses.

Incremental learning theory—All learning is done by small steps, and any part of the material may be partially learned (also called *continuity theory*).

Incubation—A stage in problem-solving behavior during which time rapid progress toward a solution occurs after a "rest" period; many believe unconscious problem-solving continues during the incubation period.

Independent variable—A variable that is under the control of the experimenter (one that he or she actively manipulates).

Insight—That moment at which the solution is recognized; also called the "aha!" experience (also called the *illumination stage* in creative thinking).

Instincts—Rigidly patterned behavior that is presumably unlearned and observable in all members of a species.

Instrumental (operant) conditioning—Conditioning overt behavior by requiring the specific overt behavior to occur before reinforcement is given.

Intelligence quotient (IQ)—A description of an individual's relative ability in general intelligence.

Interference—Incompatibility between learned responses; a theory of forgetting emphasizing competition between related responses acquired at different times.

Isolation effect—In verbal learning, when a list contains a few items that are different from the majority of items, those different items are learned more quickly.

Kinesthetic sensations—Sensations from muscles and joints conveying information about bodily position by recording the contraction and stretching of muscles.

Learning—A change in behavior caused by experience or practice.

Long-term memory—Involves complex processes by which new information is acquired; memory of information acquired long ago.

Massed practice—Continuous practice of a motor skill.

Mean (M)—A central-tendency measurement; a common average (arithmetical average) obtained by dividing the sum of all the scores by the number of scores (assuming you have interval or ratio data).

Measurement—The process of extracting from the array of data certain clear, representative, quantifiable events in scientific investigation.

Measures of variability—The amount of dispersion (scatter) in a distribution.

Median—A central-tendency measurement; the score that falls in the middle of a distribution when the scores are arranged from the lowest to the highest values.

Mnemonics—A means for remembering involving a series of memorized symbols that serve as cue words for new stimuli (*"i* before *e* except after *c* . . .*"*).

Mode—Central-tendency measurement; the score that occurs most frequently in a distribution (only central-tendency measure that can be used with nominal data).

Monozygotic twins (identical twins)—Twins having identical genetic structures.

Motivation—General term referring to all the conditions that energize and direct behavior, including instincts, drives, needs, wants, arousal, motives (learned or "secondary" drives).

Motive—A learned drive based in emotional arousal.

Negative transfer—In learning, when the acquisition of one item directly hampers the acquisition of a second item.

Nonsense syllable—A sequence of letters, usually consonant-vowel-consonant, used in verbal-learning experiments to minimize previous associations connected with meaningful words.

Null hypothesis—An assumption in statistical tests; a belief that there is no difference between different conditions.

Overlearning—Continued practice after having mastered the material.

Overt behavior—A response that is easily observable.

Paired-associate task—A verbal-learning task in which a subject is presented with a list of pairs of items (usually nonsense syllables) and must learn to associate one item with another; presented with one item, the subject must recall the pair.

Percentile score—A kind of converted score giving a person's score in relation to his or her group in percentile scores; the percentage of scores a particular score equals or excels.

Perception—The organization of basic sensory data into meaningful interpretations of reality by the nervous system.

Personality—A relatively stable subset of characteristics and tendencies that determine one's uniquely organized and changing psychological behavior (thoughts, feelings, and actions) as one attempts to adapt to one's environment.

Placebo—Some physiologically inert compound that is sometimes given as a control in studies of the effects of drugs; useful to control for "suggestability" in subjects.

Prediction—A formulation of precise statements about the effects of certain conditions on certain behaviors.

Primacy effect—(1) Reflects the superiority in learning of the first part of the list: a serial-learning effect; (2) in persuasive communication and impression formation, the tendency for the first-received information to dominate in attitude development.

Projection—The attributing of an unacceptable impulse to others.

Projective test—A test that requires an individual to respond in various ways to ambiguous stimuli (inkblots, pictures, etc.). Psychologists believe that an individual's response to ambiguous material reflects that person's motives and other personality components.

Psychological variables—A class of events of interest to psychologists to which values may be assigned, such as overt behavior, covert behavior, population, individual differences, environment, etc.

Psychosomatic disorders—The deterioration or malfunction of bodily organs due in part to emotional causes.

Punishment—Any painful or unpleasant event that serves to suppress unwanted responses or to produce avoidance responses.

Random sample—Within the limitations imposed by collecting a representative sample, each member of the population has an equal chance to be selected from the sample. Opposite of *biased sample*.

Range—The total distance between the highest and the lowest scores in a frequency distribution; a simple numerical measure of dispersion.

Recall—Retrieving an item from memory; a way in which stored information may be measured.

Recency effect—(1) Reflects the superiority in learning the last part of the list: a serial-learning effect; (2) in attitude formation, the tendency, under special circumstances, for the most recently processed information to dominate the organized impression.

Reconditioning—Reintroduction of the unconditioned stimulus with the conditioned stimulus for even one trial after extinction has occurred.

Regression—A person drifts backward to childhood experiences and feelings.

Reinforcement—That stimulus needed to ensure the performance of any learned behavior.

Replicability—In the scientific method, a requisite that demands all experiments to be reported so that another investigator can reproduce the experimental procedure and thus can test the results.

Response—Any physical process as a consequence of stimulation.

Retention—The process of something previously learned being available for use on later occasions.

Reversibility—In Piaget's theory, one part of mental development in which a child understands that certain properties of an object are changeable.

Rorschach test—A personality test devised in the 1920s in which a subject is presented with inkblots; his or her response to the inkblots is a means whereby psychologists may assess the subject's needs and style of looking at the world.

Rote learning—The memorization of material without the need to understand that which is learned.

Scapegoat—The displacement of one's own feelings of incompetence or guilt onto another (person, nationality, idea, etc.).

Scatter plot—A graphic representation of the association between two variables, with Variable 1 arranged along the abscissa and Variable 2 arranged along the ordinate.

Schemata—A term used by Piaget to illustrate how a human begins cognitive development by using inborn motor equipment and how each sequence of experience leads to the building of ever more complicated experiences and eventually the ability to form mental representations of such experience.

Second-order conditioning—After conditioned training, the conditioned connection can be used as a foundation for further conditioning; for example, a youngster conditioned to cry when hearing a bell ring can be conditioned to cry when seeing a cat if the cat and ringing bell are paired.

Serial-learning task—A verbal-learning task in which a subject is presented with a list of material, one at a time. Later, one syllable or word is presented; the subject must recall the succeeding syllables or words in order.

Serial-position effect—Those items that appear either first or last on a list are learned best; items appearing in the middle of the list are learned most slowly.

Skinner box—An apparatus devised by Skinner that provides rich data on instrumental conditioning.

Sociogram—A graphic representation of interpersonal patterns.

Spontaneous recovery—Reappearance of previously learned material without additional learning.

Standard deviation—A sensitive measure of variability that is a function of each score's deviation (distance) from the mean; obtained by squaring the deviations of each score from the mean, adding the squared deviations, dividing by their number, and computing the square root; sometimes called the root mean square.

Standardization—The process by which items are finally selected and average scores (norms) are established in psychological tests.

Stereotype—A rigid or biased perception of reality.

Stimulus—Any object, event, or energy that arouses a receptor and produces some effect on an organism.

Superego—One of the three personality structures suggested by Freud and consisting of one's internal standards and rules.

Syllogistic reasoning—The process of evaluating conclusions for logical validity; for example, if $A = B$, and $A = C$, then $B = C$.

Thematic Apperception Test (TAT)—A personality test consisting of a series of pictures of people in various settings sufficiently ambiguous so that the subject may create his or her own "story" for each picture.

Theory—A general principle stated to explain a group of phenomena; *theory* is more firmly supported by evidence than is *hypothesis* but is less firmly supported than is *law*.

Thorndike's law of effect—The response that is followed by some positive consequence is the most likely to be retained, while responses not reinforced will drop out eventually from the subject's response repertoire.

Thorndike's law of exercise—The response that is performed most frequently and most recently during a trial is the response most likely to be elicited in the future under similar stimulus conditions.

Trait—A label for a closely knit group of behaviors.

Unconditioned response (UCR)—An involuntary response to a stimulus that usually involves feelings or expectancies.

Unconditioned stimulus (UCS)—A stimulus that is able to elicit a particular response without training.

Variables—Causes; actual quantities that are data.

PHYSICAL
EDUCATION REVIEW

OUTLINE

This section reviews basic physical education concepts.

I. MOVEMENT CONCEPTS AND FORMS

A. Basic skills: skills involved in movement actions and motor patterns.

1. Locomotor skills.

   a. Skills used to move the body from one location to another.

   b. Skills include jumping, hopping, skipping, leaping, sliding, galloping, walking, etc.

2. Nonlocomotor skills.

   a. Skills in which the individual does not have to change location in order to practice an activity.

   b. Skills include stretching, pushing, pulling, twisting, circling, and most calisthenic activities (movements toward and away from the center of the body, raising and lowering body parts).

3. Manipulative skills.

   a. Skills used to handle or manipulate play objects, such as bats, balls, wands, and hoops.

   b. Skills include movements that increase hand-eye and hand-foot coordination, tracking skills, and dexterity and propulsion skills (such as throwing, kicking, and batting).

4. Specialized skills.

   a. Skills related to specific sports, games, and apparatus.

   b. Skills are structured (specific rules, guidelines, and techniques) rather than unstructured.

B. Basic movement: skills related to the possibilities of the body and the ability to express, explore, and interpret the physical environment.

1. Program applications.

   a. Structure the learning environment; provide a variety of movement expressions; individualize the activities; build confidence in efficiently moving one's body.

   b. Provide both gross-motor (big-muscle) activities and fine-motor (manipulative) movement possibilities.

   c. Develop awareness for a variety of concepts including space, time, force, and qualities of movement and flow.

2. Basic movement processes.

a. Traits considered as a whole (not isolated actions).

b. Development of body mechanics.
   (1) Broad movement competencies.
   (2) Freedom to explore the physical environment.
       (a) Spatial factors include both general and personal space in performing locomotor activities.
       (b) Movements include direction, patterns, and size and angle of movement (such as horizontal, vertical, diagonal, and circular).

3. Movement considerations.

a. Variation in speed, acceleration, deceleration, rhythm, etc.

b. Quality of movement.
   (1) Force and effort: How fast can you stop? What body mechanics improve force?
   (2) Flow: direction of the movement.
       (a) Sustained movement (free flow; continuity of movement).
       (b) Interrupted movement and interval activities.
   (3) Body factors: the body and its parts in relation to specific movement activities.
       (a) Unilateral: one-sided activities.
       (b) Bilateral: two-sided activities.
       (c) Cross-lateral: each side working independently.
   (4) Body zones: anterior, posterior, etc.

4. Classifying movement patterns.

a. Unstructured movement: movement exploration that involves choices related to response, experimentation, exploration, and balance.
   (1) Movements, patterns, and sequences can involve knowledge of special skills but do not require them.
   (2) Exploring general space, moving in any direction; free expression.

b. Structured movement: involves a specific skill that can be quantified.

c. Combinations of movement patterns (includes both structured and unstructured movement): stretch like a rubber band, recoil, jump and hop, squat, twist, gallop.

5. Perceptual-motor competencies: used to diagnose perceptual-motor deficiencies.

a. General coordination: ability to move in rhythm and with muscular control.

b. Balance: control of the center of gravity and laterality (sideward movement).
   (1) Static balance.
   (2) Dynamic balance.
   (3) Rotational balance.

    c. Body image: knowledge of body parts and body in space.
      (1) Hand-eye and foot-eye coordination: tracking objects while throwing, kicking, catching, etc.
      (2) Hearing discrimination: ability to respond to auditory signals; listening; attention to rhythmic movements.
      (3) Form perception: recognizing different spaces, shapes, and sizes.

6. Rhythmic activities: basic movements using the medium of rhythm; includes locomotor, nonlocomotor, and manipulative skills.

    a. Integral component of a comprehensive physical education program.

    b. Involves gross body movements while keeping time with rhythm of music.

C. Principles of learning associated with movement education: to develop efficient and effective movement skills and to understand movement principles.

1. Readiness: the ability to learn and understand movement patterns is influenced by such things as maturation, coordination, physique, and experiences.

2. Motivation: the desire to learn is influenced by intrinsic and extrinsic rewards.

3. Form and technique: establish the basis for sound mechanical principles in learning a skill.

    a. Throwing: principle of opposition.
      (1) Arm swings back in preparation for throw; elbow moves forward.
      (2) Trunk rotates toward throwing side of body.
      (3) Weight of foot shifted to nonthrowing side during follow-through.

    b. Catching.
      (1) Eyes follow ball; elimination of avoidance reaction (fear).
      (2) Arms bend at elbows; relaxed; object brought toward body.
      (3) Nonrigid catching style; hands brought together as catch is made.

    c. Batting.
      (1) Eyes follow the ball; elbow cocked in a horizontal position (somewhat parallel with upper chest); noncross grip; bat held above head.
      (2) Weight shifted to front foot upon contact with ball.
      (3) Hit "through the ball"; continuity of movement.

4. Progression: logical progression of motor skills based on an increasing and decreasing degree of difficulty.

5. Feedback and reinforcement: ability to critique an activity and to provide a sound basis for future activity.

6. Transfer of learning: ability to transfer previous learning of a movement technique to a new skill area.

II. FITNESS

A. Exercise and health.

1. Conditioning: a purposeful exercise program to counteract heart disease and related circulatory problems.

    a. Factors include a sound diet and regular exercise.

    b. Body conditioning: ability of the body to meet the demands put upon it.

    c. Poor physical conditioning contributes to coronary heart disease (about forty percent of all deaths) and blood circulatory problems (stroke, arteriosclerosis, hypertension).

2. Elements of conditioned fitness: blood circulation is the major factor in a well-conditioned individual.

    a. Bloodstream carries nutrients and oxygen to every cell in the body.

    b. Fitness tests include oxygen intake and oxygen consumption; air exchange in the lungs; blood pressure.

    c. Fitness tests measure:
    (1) Body conformation (appearance of body fitness, excess fat around waistline).
    (2) Body balance (how muscles react in a coordinated manner).
    (3) Agility (controlled motor fitness).
    (4) Muscular power (ability to exert force with a sudden motion).
    (5) Endurance (ability to sustain an effort).
    (6) Flexibility (ability to move the body to handle a wide range of movements).
    (7) Strength (ability of specific muscle groups to perform specific functions—back, buttocks, chest, etc.)

3. Proper nutrition.

    a. Daily caloric requirement: depends on age, size, and activity (older people require fewer calories).
    (1) Maintenance diet (weight balance).
    (2) Reducing diet: physical exercise "burns" excess calories; reduce fat in diet (concentrated calories); total food intake must be decreased (all nutrients produce calories).

    b. Proteins: includes essential amino acids; sources include lean meat, dairy products, fish, nuts, whole grains, and beans.

    c. Carbohydrates: body synthesizes and breaks down carbohydrates from sources such as breads, cereals, rice, potatoes, and beets.

    d. Fats: some fatty acids cannot be synthesized in the body.
    (1) Saturated fats: solid at room temperature; mainly from animal products, linked to elevated cholesterol counts.
    (2) Unsaturated fats: from sources such as corn oil and soybean oil.
    (3) Blood-fat levels: indicate amount of cholesterol in the body.
    (a) Cholesterol: natural fatty substance in the body; found only in animal products.

        (b) Excess levels (above 200 mg/dl) can indicate symptoms of arteriosclerosis.

        (c) Cholesterol reduction programs must limit intake of animal products and products with large amounts of saturated fats (such as avocados and palm oil).

e. Vitamins: organic substances needed in small amounts to enable the body to complete chemical reactions.

f. Minerals: inorganic compounds needed in small amounts; sources include milk (for calcium), red meats (for iron), and leafy vegetables (for phosphorus).

g. Sodium: found naturally in many foods; linked to elevated blood pressure.

B. Health-related fitness.

1. General conditioning: maintaining proper health by following a sensible exercise and diet program.

   a. Consult a physician prior to beginning vigorous exercise program; determine risk factors.

   b. Use a proper exercise program.
      (1) Warm-up (preparing for vigorous exercise).
      (2) Peak exertion (achieving exercise goals).
      (3) Cool-down (returning body to normal condition).

   c. Provide basic fitness opportunities in a nonsports atmosphere.
      (1) Maintain proper body mechanics while sitting, standing, picking up items, etc.
      (2) Provide opportunities for daily exercise such as walking, jogging, swimming, calisthenics, aerobic dancing, and backpacking.
      (3) Use any environment for isometric exercise.

2. Individual exercise program.

   a. Duration: brisk walking (three times per week for thirty minutes); vigorous aerobic exercise (three times per week for twenty minutes).

   b. Aerobic capacity: to achieve your target heart rate.

   c. Fitness activities: based on progression and general health fitness.

   d. Proper warm-up.
      (1) Approximately ten to fifteen minutes in duration; consists of bending, stretching, rotating, abduction, and adduction.
      (2) Purpose is to elevate the heart rate.

3. Calisthenics (anaerobic).

   a. Exercise for muscular strength, flexibility (range of motion), endurance (repetitions), cardiorespiratory fitness.

   b. Examples of muscular and flexibility exercises include leg raises, alternate knee bends, push-ups and modified push-ups, and sit-ups and modified sit-ups.

4. Typical physical-fitness testing battery: includes measurement of standing height, weight, resting heart rate, resting blood pressure, skinfold tests, and timed sit-ups.

C. Skill-related fitness.

1. Competencies.
   a. Agility: ability to change direction quickly while controlling body.
   b. Reaction time: ability to recognize a stimulus, react to it, and complete a response.
   c. Balance: ability to maintain body equilibrium.
   d. Coordination: ability to complete hand-eye and foot-eye activities.
   e. Speed: ability to change direction/location.
2. Skill-related fitness activities include the shuttle run, fifty-yard dash, softball throw, and standing long jump.

D. Movement forms: games and sports are culturally defined.

1. Games: integrate fundamental motor skills as in bowling, dodging, kicking, running, striking, throwing, and catching.
2. Team sports (in the United States).
   a. Traditional: basketball, baseball, soccer, volleyball, football.
   b. Nontraditional: field hockey, lacrosse, badminton, water polo.
3. Individual sports (in the United States).
   a. Traditional: track, swimming, tennis, golf, skiing.
   b. Nontraditional: fencing, table tennis, cross-country skiing, weightlifting.

III. PHYSICAL AND BIOLOGICAL SCIENCE FOUNDATIONS

A. Exercise physiology: changes in body chemistry related to exercise.

1. Heart and circulation (cardiorespiratory).
   a. Oxygen uptake.
      (1) Respiratory system: oxygen transported through circulatory system.
      (2) Cardiovascular system: distributes oxygen throughout the body.
      (3) Musculoskeletal system: uses oxygen and converts into energy.
   b. Blood pressure (BP) (force of blood pushing against walls of the arteries under pumping action of the heart).
      (1) Resting BP: normal diastolic under 85, normal systolic under 140.
      (2) Resting heart rate: normal range forty to ninety beats per minute (training will decrease this rate).
      (3) Maximum desirable heart rate: formula, 220 minus your age equals maximum desirable heart rate during exercise.

(4) Desirable heart rate during exercise: sixty percent of maximum desirable rate.

c. Recovery: indicates efficiency of circulatory system.

d. Strength-building exercises (isometric or static): not designed for heart-related fitness.

e. Risk factors of heart disease: cigarette smoking, high cholesterol, family history of heart disease, obesity.

2. Breathing and lungs.

a. Aerobics: oxygen-based exercises that stimulate the heart and lungs, such as running, walking, and swimming.

b. Aerobic efficiency: involves the lungs during performance.
   (1) Exercise intensity increases body's demand for oxygen.
   (2) Fitness tests (step-test, ergometer, treadmill) measure lung capacity.

c. Anaerobics: exercises for short periods of time at high power levels (football, basketball, sprints).

3. Body composition.

a. Height and weight tables: dependent on frame size.

b. Skinfold measurements (chest, abdomen, thigh, triceps).

c. Percentage of body fat: lean (less than eight percent in males, less than thirteen percent in females), fat (greater than twenty-one to twenty-four percent in males, greater than twenty-six to thirty-two percent in females).

4. Musculoskeletal fitness: focuses on abdominal strength, lower-back and hamstring flexibility, and endurance.

5. Physical fitness conditioning based on:

a. Duration, repetition, and intensity of exercise.

b. Nutrition and diet.

B. Motor learning: methodologies and instructional design.

1. Motor skills: gross- and fine-motor skills and locomotor and nonlocomotor skills.

2. Movement qualities: body movement and adjustment to various elements of movement.

3. Learning concepts.

a. Perceptual adjustments: for example, a child makes a basket, completing a lay-up.

b. Kinesthetic awareness: for example, a child controls movements while completing a tumbling routine.

c. Understanding movement qualities: force, time, space, flow.

d. Development of skills: for example, a child progressively increases distance while throwing a football through a hoop.

e. Transfer and feedback: for example, a child transfers skills learned in catching a basketball to catching a football.

C. Kinesiology: effects of internal and external forces that act on the body.

1. Kinesiology.

   a. Kinesiology is concerned with understanding how the joints and muscles cause movement of the skeletal structure of the body.

   b. Biomechanics is considered mechanical kinesiology and is concerned with the human body as a mechanical system; it is concerned with the physics of motion.

   c. Physical principles can be applied to biomechanics.
      (1) Motion: linear displacement, velocity, and acceleration.
      (2) Force: Newton's laws of motion.
      (3) Energy: potential and kinetic.
      (4) Aerodynamics: projection angles and flight velocity.
      (5) Landing and striking: elasticity and dissipation of force.

2. Applications of kinesiology and biomechanics.

   a. Balance: ability to maintain body position and equilibrium in stationary and movement activities.
      (1) Static balance: center of gravity is directly over base of support.
      (2) Dynamic balance: center of gravity is raised and base of support is narrowed—for example, in the movements progressing from walking to running.

   b. Friction: effects of traction on an activity.

   c. Force: application to pushing, pulling, or striking an object.

3. Principles of physics applied to sports.

   a. Prediction of the movement of a ball in flight; prediction of various angles.

   b. Mechanics of extending the arms while hitting a baseball (concept of levers).

   c. Mechanics of throwing a ball with velocity involves wrist movement and range of motion.

   d. Blocking position in football involves stability.

4. Computer-enhanced performance images and high-speed photography: used to analyze basic movement.

CURRICULUM OBJECTIVES BY GRADE

KINDERGARTEN

Motor Development

The student will be able to

- *Locomotor Skills*

1. gallop ten steps forward using either foot as the lead foot
2. run in a cross extension pattern, forward and backward
3. jump in place (simultaneously landing on both feet) three consecutive times
4. hop a distance of ten feet on the preferred foot
5. slide ten feet to each side without crossing feet

- *Perceptual-Motor Skills*

Fine motor:

1. cut out eight-inch by ten-inch shapes, cutting on the line
2. put together puzzles with large, simple pieces
3. copy simple mosaic patterns
4. keep pencil within the lines on ¼-inch-wide maze

Balance:

1. walk a four-inch-wide balance beam forward, stepping over a six-inch-high obstacle
2. stand on preferred foot for ten seconds

Ball skills:

1. catch a playground ball with hands only from ten feet (no bounce)

Physical Fitness

The student will be able to

- *Cardiovascular Endurance*

1. run/walk ¼ mile
2. run ⅛ mile without walking

- *Muscle Strength Development*

1. perform sit-ups at the ____ percentile or above for age and sex according to the AAHPERD (American Association of Health, Physical Education, Recreation, and Dance) Health Related Fitness Test.
2. develop upper body strength

- *Flexibility*

1. perform the sit-and-reach at the ____ percentile or above for age and sex according to the AAHPERD Health Related Fitness Test.

- *Fitness Concepts*

1. identify aerobic activities
2. identify major muscle groups
3. maintain percent body fat within the limits set for age and sex in the AAHPERD *Health Related Fitness Manual*

Health Enhancement

The student will be able to

- *Nutrition*

1. identify nutritious foods and junk foods

- *Relaxation*

1. lie down and remain still for one minute

Self-image

The student will be able to

- *Responsibility*

1. lead a small-group activity

- *Confidence*

1. try an unfamiliar activity

Social Development

The student will be able to

- *Self-control*

1. follow class procedures

- *Cooperation*

1. work with one other student in a self-directed activity
2. share playground equipment

- *Respect for Others*

1. show consideration for others when lining up
2. accept individual differences among classmates
3. express a positive attribute of classmates

Recreation

The student will be able to

- *Playground Activities*

1. participate in self-directed play on the playground equipment

- *Games*

1. demonstrate a knowledge of tag games through active participation

- *Safety*

1. demonstrate the correct use of playground equipment
2. follow school playground rules

- *Leisure Time*

1. re-create games learned during physical education class during a leisure time situation

THIRD GRADE

Motor Development

The student will be able to

- *Perceptual-Motor Skills*

Balance:

1. jump rope held by self a minimum of twenty consecutive times
2. hop on either foot in a game or relay situation

Ball skills:

1. catch a tennis ball with one hand from a distance of fifteen feet
2. throw a softball thirty feet with a step/throw opposition pattern
3. absorb force while catching a ball

Spatial awareness:

1. be aware of other equipment and children in order to prevent injuries

- *Tumbling/Gymnastics*

1. perform a headstand with assistance
2. compose a tumbling routine including variations of forward and backward rolls
3. perform a cartwheel
4. v-sit on a balance beam for five seconds

- *Rhythmic Activities*

1. recognize and perform the basic steps to a variety of dances

Physical Fitness

The student will be able to

- *Cardiovascular Endurance*

1. run ½ mile without walking
2. perform a variety of aerobic activities

- *Muscle Strength*

1. perform sit-ups at the _____ percentile or above for age and sex according to the AAHPERD Health Related Fitness Test
2. develop upper-body strength

- *Flexibility*

1. perform the sit-and-reach at the _____ percentile or above for age and sex according to the AAHPERD Health Related Fitness Test
2. perform basic stretching exercises

- *Fitness Concepts*

1. identify aerobic activities
2. identify major muscle groups
3. maintain percent body fat within the limits set for age and sex in the AAHPERD *Health Related Fitness Manual*
4. locate pulses
5. identify flexibility exercises
6. discuss the effects of exercise on the body
7. identify strength-building activities
8. understand the importance of warm-up and cool-down exercises

Health Enhancement

The student will be able to

- *Nutrition*

1. relate information learned about nutrition and calories to physical activities

- *Relaxation*

1. understand the importance of stress reduction on the body

Self-image

The student will be able to

- *Responsibility*

1. act as a team captain
2. be responsible for the care of equipment
3. organize a game with a small group
4. demonstrate a skill for the class
5. make repeated attempts to improve performance

- *Confidence*

1. demonstrate a positive attitude when learning new skills

- *Self-evaluation*

1. identify areas of needed improvement
2. identify areas of skill

Social Development

The student will be able to

- *Self-control*

1. take turns when participating in a group
2. obey class rules
3. respect authority
4. take direction from peers when appropriate

- *Cooperation*

1. share equipment and play areas
2. conform to a group decision

- *Respect for Others*

1. accept individual differences among classmates
2. encourage and praise others

- *Sportsmanship*

1. obey game rules
2. accept the judgment of the teacher or responsible individual
3. win graciously and lose honorably
4. refrain from criticizing classmates

Recreation

The student will be able to

- *Sports*

Net sports:

1. throw and catch a playground ball over a five-foot net
2. demonstrate knowledge of modified positioning and rotation

Soccer:

1. dribble in a controlled fashion twenty yards at a slow pace
2. receive and trap a soccer ball
3. pass a ball accurately to a student fifteen feet away
4. understand general positioning

Softball:

1. stand in correct batting position with correct grip
2. use correct finger placement when catching balls
3. understand where to field a ball with assistance

Basketball:

1. understand and perform proper dribbling technique
2. identify person-to-person guarding techniques

- *Games*

1. understand the concept of dodging balls in dodgeball and bombardment
2. demonstrate a knowledge of rules by more active participation in advanced games of tag, relays, base games, and handball
3. perform a drop kick

- *Safety*

1. demonstrate safe use of playground equipment and explain the potential hazard associated with its misuse
2. demonstrate the correct care of sports equipment

- *Leisure Time*

1. identify specific exercises that can be performed during leisure time

SIXTH GRADE

Motor Development

The student will be able to

- *Tumbling/Gymnastics*

1. perform a dive roll
2. perform a hand-spring with assistance
3. perform a variety of turns on the balance beam
4. demonstrate a simple routine on the uneven bars consisting of a mount, dismount, and use of both high and low bars
5. demonstrate a simple routine on the balance beam consisting of a mount, dismount, and various walks and poses

- *Rhythmic Activities*

1. recognize and perform a variety of steps to various dances and learn about other cultures through dance

Physical Fitness

The student will be able to

- *Cardiovascular Endurance*

1. run one mile without walking
2. perform a variety of aerobic activities

- *Muscle Strength*

1. perform sit-ups at the _____ percentile or above for age and sex according to the AAHPERD Health Related Fitness Test
2. develop upper-body strength

- *Flexibility*

1. perform the sit-and-reach at the _____ percentile or above for age and sex according to the AAHPERD Health Related Fitness Test
2. perform flexibility exercises

- *Fitness Concepts*

1. identify the difference between aerobic and anaerobic activities
2. identify exercises that affect specific muscles
3. maintain percent body fat within the limits set for age and sex in the AAHPERD *Health Related Fitness Manual*
4. compare recovery pulse rate with resting and exercise pulse rates
5. identify exercises which develop cardiovascular endurance, muscular strength, and flexibility

Health Enhancement

The student will be able to

- *Nutrition*

1. understand the difference between simple and complex carbohydrates

- *Relaxation*

1. identify the areas of stress in one's life
2. understand the relationship between stress reduction and exercise

Self-image

The student will be able to

- *Responsibility*

1. act as a team captain
2. be responsible for the care of equipment
3. lead the class in an exercise
4. demonstrate a skill

- *Confidence*

1. demonstrate a positive attitude when learning a new skill

- *Self-evaluation*

1. evaluate one's own performance
2. work independently to improve performance

Social Development

The student will be able to

- *Self-control*

1. take turns when participating in a group or team
2. obey class rules
3. understand and respect authority
4. take direction from peers

- *Cooperation*

1. share equpiment and play areas
2. conform to group decisions

- *Respect for Others*

1. accept individual differences among classmates
2. encourage and praise others
3. use only acceptable language

- *Sportsmanship*

1. obey game/sport rules
2. accept judgment of teacher or responsible individual
3. win graciously and lose honorably
4. refrain from criticizing

Recreation

The student will be able to

- *Sports*

Volleyball:

1. demonstrate a knowledge of the six-player game and proper rotation
2. demonstrate a knowledge of when to use bump and set passes
3. identify the name of each position

Soccer:

1. dribble a ball in a controlled manner while jogging
2. pass a ball using the inside and outside of the foot
3. demonstrate a knowledge of offensive and defensive positions

Softball:

1. demonstrate a knowledge of correct positioning when fielding
2. explain the difference between tag-outs and force-outs
3. demonstrate accuracy in throwing overhand to a baseperson

Basketball:

1. demonstrate a lay-up shot
2. pass accurately to a partner using a variety of passes
3. attempt to shoot a basket in a game situation

Football:

1. understand basic rules and scoring
2. show proper kick-off and punt positions
3. demonstrate proper ball-carrying and hand-off skills

- *Safety*

1. use common sense and take safety precautions when handling equipment

- *Leisure Time*

1. use knowledge and skills acquired in physical education class to pursue game and sport activities outside school

Part IV:
Two Full-Length
Practice Tests

PRACTICE TEST 1

Answer Sheet for Practice Test 1

1. Ⓐ Ⓑ Ⓒ Ⓓ	35. Ⓐ Ⓑ Ⓒ Ⓓ	69. Ⓐ Ⓑ Ⓒ Ⓓ	103. Ⓐ Ⓑ Ⓒ Ⓓ
2. Ⓐ Ⓑ Ⓒ Ⓓ	36. Ⓐ Ⓑ Ⓒ Ⓓ	70. Ⓐ Ⓑ Ⓒ Ⓓ	104. Ⓐ Ⓑ Ⓒ Ⓓ
3. Ⓐ Ⓑ Ⓒ Ⓓ	37. Ⓐ Ⓑ Ⓒ Ⓓ	71. Ⓐ Ⓑ Ⓒ Ⓓ	105. Ⓐ Ⓑ Ⓒ Ⓓ
4. Ⓐ Ⓑ Ⓒ Ⓓ	38. Ⓐ Ⓑ Ⓒ Ⓓ	72. Ⓐ Ⓑ Ⓒ Ⓓ	106. Ⓐ Ⓑ Ⓒ Ⓓ
5. Ⓐ Ⓑ Ⓒ Ⓓ	39. Ⓐ Ⓑ Ⓒ Ⓓ	73. Ⓐ Ⓑ Ⓒ Ⓓ	107. Ⓐ Ⓑ Ⓒ Ⓓ
6. Ⓐ Ⓑ Ⓒ Ⓓ	40. Ⓐ Ⓑ Ⓒ Ⓓ	74. Ⓐ Ⓑ Ⓒ Ⓓ	108. Ⓐ Ⓑ Ⓒ Ⓓ
7. Ⓐ Ⓑ Ⓒ Ⓓ	41. Ⓐ Ⓑ Ⓒ Ⓓ	75. Ⓐ Ⓑ Ⓒ Ⓓ	109. Ⓐ Ⓑ Ⓒ Ⓓ
8. Ⓐ Ⓑ Ⓒ Ⓓ	42. Ⓐ Ⓑ Ⓒ Ⓓ	76. Ⓐ Ⓑ Ⓒ Ⓓ	110. Ⓐ Ⓑ Ⓒ Ⓓ
9. Ⓐ Ⓑ Ⓒ Ⓓ	43. Ⓐ Ⓑ Ⓒ Ⓓ	77. Ⓐ Ⓑ Ⓒ Ⓓ	111. Ⓐ Ⓑ Ⓒ Ⓓ
10. Ⓐ Ⓑ Ⓒ Ⓓ	44. Ⓐ Ⓑ Ⓒ Ⓓ	78. Ⓐ Ⓑ Ⓒ Ⓓ	112. Ⓐ Ⓑ Ⓒ Ⓓ
11. Ⓐ Ⓑ Ⓒ Ⓓ	45. Ⓐ Ⓑ Ⓒ Ⓓ	79. Ⓐ Ⓑ Ⓒ Ⓓ	113. Ⓐ Ⓑ Ⓒ Ⓓ
12. Ⓐ Ⓑ Ⓒ Ⓓ	46. Ⓐ Ⓑ Ⓒ Ⓓ	80. Ⓐ Ⓑ Ⓒ Ⓓ	114. Ⓐ Ⓑ Ⓒ Ⓓ
13. Ⓐ Ⓑ Ⓒ Ⓓ	47. Ⓐ Ⓑ Ⓒ Ⓓ	81. Ⓐ Ⓑ Ⓒ Ⓓ	115. Ⓐ Ⓑ Ⓒ Ⓓ
14. Ⓐ Ⓑ Ⓒ Ⓓ	48. Ⓐ Ⓑ Ⓒ Ⓓ	82. Ⓐ Ⓑ Ⓒ Ⓓ	116. Ⓐ Ⓑ Ⓒ Ⓓ
15. Ⓐ Ⓑ Ⓒ Ⓓ	49. Ⓐ Ⓑ Ⓒ Ⓓ	83. Ⓐ Ⓑ Ⓒ Ⓓ	117. Ⓐ Ⓑ Ⓒ Ⓓ
16. Ⓐ Ⓑ Ⓒ Ⓓ	50. Ⓐ Ⓑ Ⓒ Ⓓ	84. Ⓐ Ⓑ Ⓒ Ⓓ	118. Ⓐ Ⓑ Ⓒ Ⓓ
17. Ⓐ Ⓑ Ⓒ Ⓓ	51. Ⓐ Ⓑ Ⓒ Ⓓ	85. Ⓐ Ⓑ Ⓒ Ⓓ	119. Ⓐ Ⓑ Ⓒ Ⓓ
18. Ⓐ Ⓑ Ⓒ Ⓓ	52. Ⓐ Ⓑ Ⓒ Ⓓ	86. Ⓐ Ⓑ Ⓒ Ⓓ	120. Ⓐ Ⓑ Ⓒ Ⓓ
19. Ⓐ Ⓑ Ⓒ Ⓓ	53. Ⓐ Ⓑ Ⓒ Ⓓ	87. Ⓐ Ⓑ Ⓒ Ⓓ	121. Ⓐ Ⓑ Ⓒ Ⓓ
20. Ⓐ Ⓑ Ⓒ Ⓓ	54. Ⓐ Ⓑ Ⓒ Ⓓ	88. Ⓐ Ⓑ Ⓒ Ⓓ	122. Ⓐ Ⓑ Ⓒ Ⓓ
21. Ⓐ Ⓑ Ⓒ Ⓓ	55. Ⓐ Ⓑ Ⓒ Ⓓ	89. Ⓐ Ⓑ Ⓒ Ⓓ	123. Ⓐ Ⓑ Ⓒ Ⓓ
22. Ⓐ Ⓑ Ⓒ Ⓓ	56. Ⓐ Ⓑ Ⓒ Ⓓ	90. Ⓐ Ⓑ Ⓒ Ⓓ	124. Ⓐ Ⓑ Ⓒ Ⓓ
23. Ⓐ Ⓑ Ⓒ Ⓓ	57. Ⓐ Ⓑ Ⓒ Ⓓ	91. Ⓐ Ⓑ Ⓒ Ⓓ	125. Ⓐ Ⓑ Ⓒ Ⓓ
24. Ⓐ Ⓑ Ⓒ Ⓓ	58. Ⓐ Ⓑ Ⓒ Ⓓ	92. Ⓐ Ⓑ Ⓒ Ⓓ	126. Ⓐ Ⓑ Ⓒ Ⓓ
25. Ⓐ Ⓑ Ⓒ Ⓓ	59. Ⓐ Ⓑ Ⓒ Ⓓ	93. Ⓐ Ⓑ Ⓒ Ⓓ	127. Ⓐ Ⓑ Ⓒ Ⓓ
26. Ⓐ Ⓑ Ⓒ Ⓓ	60. Ⓐ Ⓑ Ⓒ Ⓓ	94. Ⓐ Ⓑ Ⓒ Ⓓ	128. Ⓐ Ⓑ Ⓒ Ⓓ
27. Ⓐ Ⓑ Ⓒ Ⓓ	61. Ⓐ Ⓑ Ⓒ Ⓓ	95. Ⓐ Ⓑ Ⓒ Ⓓ	129. Ⓐ Ⓑ Ⓒ Ⓓ
28. Ⓐ Ⓑ Ⓒ Ⓓ	62. Ⓐ Ⓑ Ⓒ Ⓓ	96. Ⓐ Ⓑ Ⓒ Ⓓ	130. Ⓐ Ⓑ Ⓒ Ⓓ
29. Ⓐ Ⓑ Ⓒ Ⓓ	63. Ⓐ Ⓑ Ⓒ Ⓓ	97. Ⓐ Ⓑ Ⓒ Ⓓ	131. Ⓐ Ⓑ Ⓒ Ⓓ
30. Ⓐ Ⓑ Ⓒ Ⓓ	64. Ⓐ Ⓑ Ⓒ Ⓓ	98. Ⓐ Ⓑ Ⓒ Ⓓ	132. Ⓐ Ⓑ Ⓒ Ⓓ
31. Ⓐ Ⓑ Ⓒ Ⓓ	65. Ⓐ Ⓑ Ⓒ Ⓓ	99. Ⓐ Ⓑ Ⓒ Ⓓ	133. Ⓐ Ⓑ Ⓒ Ⓓ
32. Ⓐ Ⓑ Ⓒ Ⓓ	66. Ⓐ Ⓑ Ⓒ Ⓓ	100. Ⓐ Ⓑ Ⓒ Ⓓ	134. Ⓐ Ⓑ Ⓒ Ⓓ
33. Ⓐ Ⓑ Ⓒ Ⓓ	67. Ⓐ Ⓑ Ⓒ Ⓓ	101. Ⓐ Ⓑ Ⓒ Ⓓ	
34. Ⓐ Ⓑ Ⓒ Ⓓ	68. Ⓐ Ⓑ Ⓒ Ⓓ	102. Ⓐ Ⓑ Ⓒ Ⓓ	

CONTENT KNOWLEDGE

Time: 2 Hours
134 Questions

Directions:Each of the following questions or incomplete statements is followed by four possible answers or completions. Choose the answer or completion that is best in each case.

I. Literature and Language Studies

Questions 1–3 refer to the following poem by Tennyson.

The Eagle

The wrinkled sea beneath him crawls;
He watches from his mountain walls,
And like a thunderbolt he falls.

1. The first line of the poem uses a
    (A) metaphor
    (B) simile
    (C) antithesis
    (D) paradox

2. The figure in the last line is a simile, not a metaphor, because it
    (A) compares two unlike objects
    (B) uses "like"
    (C) compares the eagle to a thunderbolt
    (D) is an example of figurative language

3. The rhyme scheme of the poem is best described as
    (A) ballad stanza
    (B) blank verse
    (C) couplet
    (D) triplet

4. In which of the following is there a mixed metaphor?
    (A) "Take arms against a sea of troubles"
    (B) "Hair falling in cascades of ringlets"
    (C) "Out of the frying pan and into the fire"
    (D) "Opportunity knocks on every door"

5. Which of the following is the best example of an aphorism?
   (A) "Fools rush in where angels fear to tread."
   (B) "I fear thee, ancient mariner."
   (C) "My mistress' eyes are nothing like the sun."
   (D) "That is no country for old men."

6. In the discussion of what literary form would the terms "point of view," "turning point," and "flashback" most likely be used?
   (A) An essay
   (B) A novel
   (C) A lyric poem
   (D) A comedy

7. With which of the following is a psychological approach likely to be most useful?
   (A) An essay
   (B) A satiric comedy
   (C) A novel
   (D) A lyric

8. In the word "constellation," the part of the word that means "star" is
   (A) con
   (B) stella
   (C) la
   (D) tion

Questions 9–11 refer to the following poem, from *Essay on Criticism* by Alexander Pope.

> 'Tis with our judgments as our watches, none
> Go just alike, yet each believes his own.
> In poets as true genius is but rare,
> True taste as seldom is the critic's share.

9. The poet expresses his meaning in lines 1–2 by using
   (A) a literary allusion
   (B) a metaphor
   (C) a personification
   (D) an analogy

10. In lines 3–4, which of the following pairs are parallel?
    (A) Poets–genius
    (B) Poets–taste
    (C) Genius–taste
    (D) Taste–critics

11. With which of the following would the author of these lines agree?
    (A) We should not trust our own conclusions.
    (B) Great poets are rarely appreciated.
    (C) Most criticism is inadequate.
    (D) Most poets are better critics than are professional critics.

Questions 12–14 refer to the following passage by Thomas Macaulay.

Nations, like individuals, first perceive, and then abstract. They advance from particular images to general terms. Hence the vocabulary of an enlightened society is philosophical, that of a half-civilized people is poetical. Generalization is necessary to the advancement of knowledge; but particularity is indispensable to the creations of the imagination. In proportion as men know more and think more, they look less at individuals and more at classes. They therefore make better theories and worse poems.

12. The passage opposes all of the following EXCEPT
    (A) particular–general
    (B) individual–nations
    (C) philosophy–poetry
    (D) knowledge–imagination

13. According to the argument of this passage, of the following, at which period in the development of English would the poetry be best?
    (A) In the earliest periods of Old English poetry
    (B) In the sixteenth century of Queen Elizabeth
    (C) In the Romantic period of the early nineteenth century
    (D) In the contemporary era

14. Of the following, which would be the most logical consequence of the ideas of Macaulay's paragraph?
    (A) Shakespeare's plays are no longer produced more than those of any other playwright.
    (B) Poetry books outsell nonfiction works in some bookstores.
    (C) Many colleges now require English students to take more classes in literary theory than in modern poetry.
    (D) There is a surplus of lawyers in America today.

15. All of the following words or expressions could be used to introduce conditional sentences EXCEPT
    (A) if
    (B) yet
    (C) supposing
    (D) in case that

16. If the dictionary described the pronunciation of a word as bāt, of the following, the word that rhymes with it is
   (A) rat
   (B) rate
   (C) rot
   (D) write

17. Read the following paragraph carefully and arrange the sentences in the most coherent order.

   (1) More than half of this time is necessary to allow the rising or the resting of the dough. (2) Or you will have to bake them earlier and freeze them. (3) To make a good croissant takes eleven hours. (4) So if you want fresh croissants for breakfast, you will have to stay up all night.

   (A) 1–3–2–4
   (B) 3–4–1–2
   (C) 3–1–4–2
   (D) 2–1–4–3

18. A fourteen-line poem with the last six lines rhymed efefgg is
   (A) an ode
   (B) a sonnet
   (C) a ballad
   (D) a lyric

19. Of the following, which does not belong in this group of terms and definitions: reasoning from the general to the particular, paradox, deductive logic, syllogism?
   (A) Reasoning from the general to the particular
   (B) Paradox
   (C) Deductive logic
   (D) Syllogism

20. Which of the following is a proper major premise for a syllogism that concludes with "Alligators are reptiles; therefore alligators are cold-blooded"?
   (A) Some reptiles are warm-blooded.
   (B) All reptiles are alligators.
   (C) Some reptiles are cold-blooded.
   (D) All reptiles are cold-blooded.

21. Which of the following does not affect language acquisition?
   (A) Mental and emotional growth
   (B) Social growth
   (C) Retention
   (D) Physical growth

22. Manuel drank his brandy. He felt sleepy himself. It was too hot to go out into the town. Besides there was nothing to do. He wanted to see Zurito. He would go to sleep while he waited.

Which of the following terms best describes the style of the passage above?
(A) Ornate
(B) Complex
(C) Foreign
(D) Simple

23. For the beginner, learning to read mainly involves
(A) learning to recognize printed symbols associated with sounds or words
(B) shifting the focus of one's information-gathering process from the spoken to the printed form
(C) reasoning
(D) a sensitizing of the visual process

Questions 24–25 are based on the following conversation.

Boy: How do you spell *alfalfa*? Is it a-l-f-a-l-f-a?
Girl: Well, I just learned that *ph* sounds like *f*, so you'd better spell it a-l-p-h-a-l-p-h-a.
Boy: That can't be right. Too many letters.

24. Which of the following assumptions is the girl making?
(A) Certain *f* sounds are spelled with *f*.
(B) No *ph* sounds are spelled with *f*.
(C) All *f* sounds are spelled with *ph*.
(D) She knows nothing about spelling.

25. Which of the following assumptions is the boy making?
(A) The spelling of a word is related to how long it takes to pronounce it.
(B) The girl's knowledge of spelling must be right.
(C) Any spelling of "alfalfa" will do.
(D) Correct spelling is a mystery.

26. The pronunciation guide for the word shown below does not contain the accent mark.

in tim i date

Of the following, the proper pronunciation of the word "intimidate" by the proper placement of the accent mark is shown by
(A) iń tim i date
(B) in tiḿ i date
(C) in tim í date
(D) in tim i daté

27. Which one of the following words indicates a comparison?
    (A) Therefore
    (B) And
    (C) Analogous
    (D) Furthermore

II. Mathematics

28. If 10 kilometers equal 6.2 miles, how many miles are in 45 kilometers?
    (A) 4.5
    (B) 7.25
    (C) 27.9
    (D) 29.7

29. Which of the following times gives approximately a 90° angle between the two hands of the clock?
    (A) 5:15
    (B) 7:30
    (C) 8:35
    (D) 12:15

30. Rossana knows that a geometric figure is a rectangle and that it has sides of 18 and 22. How can Rossana compute the area of a square that has the same perimeter as this rectangle?
    (A) Add 18 and 22, double this sum, divide by 4, and then multiply by 2.
    (B) Add 18 and 22, double this sum, divide by 4, and then multiply by 4.
    (C) Add 18 and 22, double this sum, divide by 4, and then square the quotient.
    (D) Add 18 and 22, double this sum, and then multiply by 4.

31. Arnold purchases one pair of slacks a dress shirt, a tie, and a sports coat. The shirt and slacks each cost three times what the tie cost. The sports coat cost twice what the shirt cost. If Arnold paid a total of $156 for all four items, what was the price of the pair of slacks?
    (A) $12
    (B) $36
    (C) $48
    (D) $78

32.

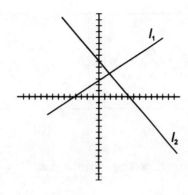

In the graph above, what is the solution of the equations of the two lines l_1 and l_2?
(A) $x = 4; y = 2$
(B) $x = 0; y = 2$
(C) $x = 2; y = 0$
(D) $x = 2; y = 4$

33. Tom is just four years older than Fran. The total of their ages is twenty-four. What is the equation for finding Fran's age?
(A) $x + 4x = 24$
(B) $x + 4 = 24$
(C) $4x + x = 24$
(D) $x + (x + 4) = 24$

34.

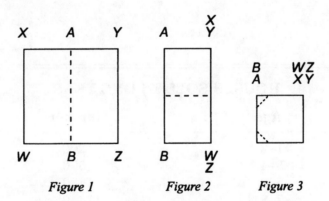

Figure 1   Figure 2   Figure 3

In Figure 1 above, a square piece of paper is folded along dotted line AB so that X is on top of Y and W is on top of Z (Figure 2). The paper is then folded again so that B is on top of A and WZ is on top of XY (Figure 3). Two small corners are cut out of the folded paper as shown in Figure 3. If the paper is unfolded, which of the following could be the result?

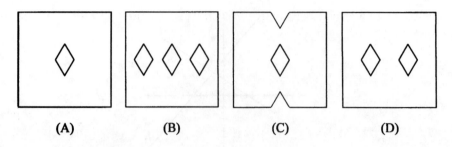

(A)   (B)   (C)   (D)

35. All of the following are equal to the equation $2x + 4 = 3x + 3$ EXCEPT
    (A) $4 = x + 3$
    (B) $-x + 4 = 3$
    (C) $2x + 1 = 3x$
    (D) $x = -1$

36. Which of the following is the smallest?
    (A) $\frac{3}{5}$
    (B) $\frac{4}{9}$
    (C) $\frac{7}{13}$
    (D) $\frac{23}{44}$

37. How many integers between 1 and 100 are divisible by both 5 and 3?
    (A) 4
    (B) 5
    (C) 6
    (D) 7

38.

HOUSES SOLD IN ONE YEAR

Age	Number
1–2	1200
3–4	1570
5–6	1630
7–8	1440
9–10	1720

According to the chart, how many more houses from five to ten years old were sold than those four to eight years old?
(A) 2455
(B) 1570
(C) 150
(D) Cannot be determined

39. The product of two numbers is greater than zero and equals one of the numbers. Which of the following must be one of the numbers?
    (A) -1
    (B) 0
    (C) 1
    (D) A prime number

40. Holiday bouquets cost the Key Club $2.00 each. The Key Club sells them for $4.75 each.

    Based on the above information, how could Clark determine how many bouquets must be sold (Q) to make a profit of $82.50?
    (A) $Q = \$82.50 \div \$2.75$
    (B) $Q = \$82.50 - \$2.00$
    (C) $Q = \$4.75 - \$2.00(Q)$
    (D) $Q = \$82.50 \div \$4.75 - \$2.00$

41.

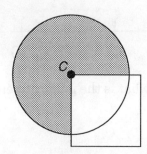

In the diagram above, a square and a circle intersect as shown. If C is the center of the circle, what percent of the circle remains unshaded?
    (A) 25%
    (B) 35%
    (C) 45%
    (D) 50%

42.

The large square above consists of squares and isosceles right triangles. If the large square has side 4 cm, the area of the shaded portion in square cm is
    (A) 2
    (B) 4
    (C) 6
    (D) 8

43. Juan approximated 35×45 as 40×50, but the answer was much too high. To get the best approximation, he should multiply
   (A) 50×50
   (B) 45×50
   (C) 30×50
   (D) 30×40

44. Teachers will be assigned special camp duty one day of the week during a seven-day camping trip. If all the days of the week (Monday through Sunday) are tossed into a cap and each teacher chooses one day of the week, what is the probability that the first teacher will randomly select a weekday (Monday through Friday)?
   (A) 1/7
   (B) 1/5
   (C) 2/7
   (D) 5/7

45.
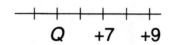

On the number line above, what is the point fifteen units to the left of point Q
   (A) -10
   (B) -9
   (C) 0
   (D) 5

46. If the product of two numbers is five more than the sum of two numbers, which of the following equations could represent the relationship?
   (A) $AB + 5 = A + B$
   (B) $5AB = A + B$
   (C) $AB = A + B + 5$
   (D) $A/B = 5 + A + B$

47.
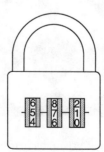

On the combination lock above, each of the three slots has ten possible numbers 0 through 9. How many possible combinations are there for this lock?
   (A)   100
   (B)   999
   (C)   1000
   (D) 10,000

48. Brenda's new sports car averages 35 miles per each gallon of gasoline. Assuming Brenda is able to maintain her average miles per gallon, how far can she drive on 12 gallons of gas?
    (A) Almost 3 miles
    (B) 42 miles
    (C) 350 miles
    (D) 420 miles

49. How many paintings were displayed at the County Museum of Art if 30% of them were by Monet and Monet was represented by 24 paintings?
    (A) 80
    (B) 76
    (C) 60
    (D) 50

50. It is estimated that at a picnic each adult will drink a fifth of a gallon of lemonade. How many gallons of lemonade should be brought to the picnic if twenty-eight people, all adults, are expected to attend?
    (A) 3
    (B) Between 3 and 4
    (C) 5
    (D) Between 5 and 6

51. $a < b < c < d < 0$

    Using the information above, which of the following has the LEAST value?
    (A) $1/a$
    (B) $1/d$
    (C) 0
    (D) Cannot be determined

52.

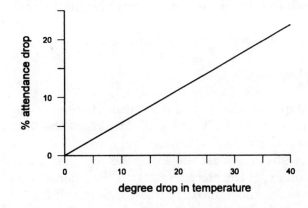

    According to the graph, if the temperature falls 35 degrees, what percentage will school attendance drop?
    (A) 10
    (B) 20
    (C) 30
    (D) 40

53. Which of the following is an example of only the associative property of addition?
    (A) $a + (b + c) = (a + b) + c$
    (B) $a + (b + c) = (a + c) + b$
    (C) $(a + b) + c = (b + a) + c$
    (D) $(a + c) + b = b + (c + a)$

54.

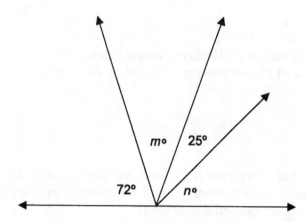

In the figure above, what is the number of degrees in the sum of $m + n$?
    (A) 83
    (B) 93
    (C) 97
    (D) 103

III. History/Social Sciences

55. Which of the following measures would have the greatest effect in making California a bellwether in national political affairs?
    (A) Holding California presidential primaries in March
    (B) Holding both the Democratic and Republican national conventions in California
    (C) Adding two additional members from California to the House of Representatives
    (D) Electing a Democratic Congress

56. In 1942, both Japanese aliens and American citizens of Japanese ancestry were interned in detention camps. Historically, which of the following constituted the most serious objection to the relocation program?
    (A) The mass hysteria against the Japanese and the threat of violence following the attack on Pearl Harbor necessitated the relocation of Japanese aliens and Americans of Japanese ancestry to detention facilities.
    (B) The Japanese in Hawaii, following the attack on Pearl Harbor, were not relocated or removed in an arbitrary or encompassing manner.
    (C) The mass internment of the Japanese without evidence of disloyalty demonstrated that constitutional safeguards could be rendered ineffective in wartime.
    (D) The Japanese in the agricultural industry were interned at a time when agricultural production for the war effort was most needed.

57. Alexis de Tocqueville, in *Democracy in America,* described the American scene in a manner that romanticized the new nation and subsequently led to increased European immigration to America. Which of the following publications most closely followed the de Tocqueville tradition by romanticizing the California scene and therefore encouraged eastern migration to the Pacific Coast?
   (A) *The Grapes of Wrath* by John Steinbeck
   (B) *Two Years before the Mast* by Richard Henry Dana
   (C) "The Celebrated Jumping Frog of Calaveras County" by Samuel Clemens
   (D) *The Call of the Wild* by Jack London

58.

The symbolic representation of the picture above is most frequently associated with
   (A) Roman worship of animal fertility figures
   (B) Mesopotamian cult figures offering food to a deity
   (C) Egyptian subservience to a deity
   (D) Greek statues of naturalistic design

59. The U.S. federal government has used protective tariffs since the early 1800s as part of a comprehensive fiscal program. Which of the following is the best reason to eliminate a protective tariff?
   (A) To strengthen the national government
   (B) To protect the auto industry
   (C) To encourage manufacturing
   (D) To encourage free trade

60. If the dollar were to rise sharply against other world currencies, the probable effect on the U.S. economy would be to
   (A) make imports cheaper
   (B) make exports cheaper
   (C) increase the price of products made in the United States
   (D) encourage foreign tourism in the United States

61. The Vietnam War provided the impetus for the passage of the Twenty-sixth Amendment—the right to vote for eighteen-year-olds. According to sociological studies of recent U.S. elections, the young voter (18–26) in comparison to the middle-aged voter (44–60) is likely to be
    (A) less mobile
    (B) less familiar with candidates for public office
    (C) more likely to vote
    (D) more familiar with political terminology

62. The Hellenistic Age began with the death of Alexander the Great. Which of the following is not considered a characteristic of the Hellenistic Age?
    (A) The fusion of Greek and Eastern cultures
    (B) Economic centralization in Athens
    (C) An increase in international trade and commerce
    (D) An end to the Greek city-state system as a major political entity

63.

Date	Issue Polled	Percent in Agreement
March 1936	The manufacture and sale of munitions for private profit should be limited.	82
November 1936	The United States should not take part in another conflict like World War I.	95
April 1937	The United States made a mistake in 1917.	70

At the time of this survey, which of the following statements is the most logical conclusion based on the information presented?
(A) The United States will continue to pursue a policy of strict isolationism.
(B) The United States made a mistake by not joining the League of Nations in 1919.
(C) The United States should sell munitions to any democracy fighting against dictatorships.
(D) The United States should honor its global commitments.

64.

The map above best represents conditions on which of the following dates?
(A) 100 B.C.
(B) A.D. 200
(C) A.D. 500
(D) A.D. 800

65. In the twentieth century, which of the following forces of social change had the greatest impact upon the traditional American family?
(A) Socialization and stratification
(B) Immigration and migration
(C) Specialization and assimilation
(D) Industrialization and urbanization

66. The Central Powers were defeated in 1919. From a German point of view, what was the most serious objection to the Treaty of Versailles at the time the treaty was ratified?
(A) Relinquishing art treasures to the Allies
(B) Inclusion of a war-guilt clause
(C) Demilitarization of the Rhineland
(D) Loss of colonial "spheres of influence"

67. Which of the following statements is (are) accurate regarding economic advances made by black Americans during World War I?

  I. War jobs produced the first major black migration to northern cities in the twentieth century.
  II. Job discrimination was temporarily reduced by wartime needs.
  III. The revival of the Ku Klux Klan symbolized an emerging white backlash to black economic gains.

  (A) I only
  (B) III only
  (C) II and III only
  (D) I, II, and III

68. The Gulf of Tonkin Resolution in 1964 led to an escalation of the war in Vietnam because
  (A) it permitted American soldiers to be under the direct control of U.S. military commanders
  (B) it gave President Johnson authority to extend the war into Cambodia
  (C) it authorized Congress to increase the number of individuals eligible for the draft
  (D) it permitted the bombing of military targets in North Vietnam

69.

Primitive Logic

Which is the most logical extension of the philosophy implied in the preceding cartoon?
  (A) Slogans are effective in controlling public opinion.
  (B) Gun-control legislation is supported by radical elements in society.
  (C) Obvious truths can be obscured for centuries.
  (D) Liberal elements of society are responsible for gun-control legislation.

70. "It is important to consider that the world population problem cannot be adequately resolved by simply producing more food. Increased food production cannot keep pace with current increases in world population."

From the quotation, it can be concluded that the author
(A) favors a drastic reduction in the birth rate
(B) favors a policy that allows food production to keep pace with population growth
(C) opposes cooperative sharing of the world's food resources
(D) opposes economic sanctions against countries that encourage overproduction of food

71. Deferred gratification best characterizes which of the following?
(A) The lower class
(B) The middle class
(C) The upper class
(D) Minority groups

72.

Election of 1868

CANDIDATES: 1868	ELECTORAL VOTE	POPULAR VOTE
REPUBLICAN Ulysses S. Grant	214	3,013,421
DEMOCRATIC Horatio Seymour	80	2,706,829
NOT VOTED	23	
	317	5,720,250

According to the chart above, which of the following paired states had the largest number of electoral votes in the 1868 election?
(A) California and Massachusetts
(B) Illinois and Tennessee
(C) Pennsylvania and Ohio
(D) New York and Kentucky

73.

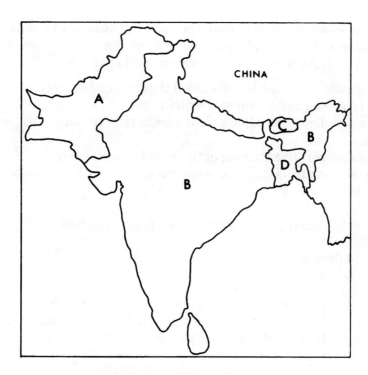

In the map of the subcontinent of India shown above, the letters A through D represent countries in the region.

Which country does not have a Moslem or Buddhist majority?
(A) Country A
(B) Country B
(C) Country C
(D) Country D

74. John Foster Dulles was secretary of state during the Eisenhower administration. Dulles altered the foreign-policy approach of the preceding Truman administration in dealing with the Soviet Union in which of the following areas?
(A) Detente with the Soviet Union
(B) The containment of communism
(C) The liberation of Eastern Europe
(D) Repudiating the New Deal

75. The "remission of temporal punishment for a sin through the sale of indulgences" was an immediate cause of the
(A) Protestant Reformation
(B) Renaissance
(C) English Reformation initiated by Henry the Eighth
(D) Age of Exploration

76. Place the following items in chronological order based on the emergence of each as a national party.

    I. Republican Party
   II. Whig Party
  III. Federalist Party
  IV. Democratic Party

   (A) II, I, IV, III
   (B) III, II, IV, I
   (C) III, IV, II, I
   (D) IV, III, I, II

77. Stratified sampling techniques are used in polling primarily to ensure that
   (A) if twelve percent of the population comes from one area, then twelve percent of all interviews will be from that area
   (B) the educational level of the sample is homogeneous
   (C) variables such as sex, geographic location, and economic status are distributed in the sample in the same proportion as in the general population
   (D) the sample includes variables that have a high correlation with the behavior being studied

78.

Wheatland (acres)	Input of Labor and Capital	Output of Wheat (bushels)	Output per Unit of Input
10	1	10	10
10	2	40	20
10	3	150	50
10	4	280	70
10	5	400	80
10	6	360	60
10	7	280	40

Based on the information in the chart above, after what point will adding additional units of labor no longer be profitable?
   (A) 2
   (B) 3
   (C) 4
   (D) 5

IV. Science

79. Key environmental factors seem to indicate that the greenhouse effect is increasing. A dramatic increase in which of the following would have the most serious long-range impact in intensifying the greenhouse effect?
    (A) The size of the polar icecaps
    (B) Burning of organic material
    (C) Chlorofluorocarbons (CFCs) released into the stratosphere
    (D) Ultraviolet rays in the atmosphere

80. Pure nitrogen is obtained commercially by first liquefying air, which is seventy-eight percent nitrogen. Which of the following is the best method to condense air to a liquid?
    (A) Lowering the temperature very quickly
    (B) Lowering the pressure very quickly
    (C) Lowering the temperature while raising the pressure
    (D) Lowering the pressure while leaving the temperature constant

81. A car is abandoned on a cliff overlooking the ocean; over a period of time, the car begins to rust. Which of the following most closely explains why the car is subject to the rusting process?
    (A) Water molecules at the beach combine with the iron in the car to form iron oxide.
    (B) The oxygen in the air combines with the iron in the car to form iron oxide.
    (C) The oxygen in the air combines with sulfur dioxide to form acid rain.
    (D) The paint on the car inhibits oxidation.

82. In which of the following life zones would the appearance of plants change the most during the seasons of the year?
    (A) Coniferous forest
    (B) Deciduous forest
    (C) Desert
    (D) Prairie

83. Which of the following processes causes the contents of an aerosol can to spray out when the top button is depressed?
    (A) The change from a gaseous to a liquid state
    (B) The expansion of a gas after being heated
    (C) The movement of molecules toward a lower pressure area
    (D) The change in temperature from the can to the atmosphere

84. Most lakes have been formed in recent geological time. Which of the following natural processes is destroying many existing lakes?
    (A) Chemical fertilizers entering the lake through water runoff
    (B) Constant evaporation
    (C) Pollution of the outlet streams
    (D) Sedimentation

85.

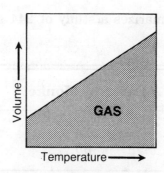

Which of the following is (are) true based on the information presented in the diagram above?

   I. Higher temperature causes molecules to move more slowly and hit the walls of the container.
  II. As the temperature of the gas increases, the volume of the gas increases.
 III. As the pressure of the gas increases, the volume decreases.

    (A) I only
    (B) II only
    (C) I and III only
    (D) II and III only

86. What would best explain the former shorelines in the hills along the western coast of North America?
    (A) The coast has gradually increased in elevation as a result of the accumulation of organic shells.
    (B) Deposits in the ocean basin have caused the sea level to rise.
    (C) Earth movements have lifted up the land along the coast.
    (D) Former wave action deposited huge volumes of material along the coast.

87. Which of the following sources of air pollution probably contributes most to the sulfur dioxide problem?
    (A) Automobile exhaust
    (B) Electric power plants
    (C) Burning of the tropical rain forest
    (D) Compaction of garbage dumps

88. Two items are dropped simultaneously from a ten-story building. The items are shaped similarly and are relatively close in weight. Which of the following statements is correct concerning the falling rate of the objects?
    (A) The weight of the objects has no effect on the falling rate.
    (B) The resistance of the air has no effect on the falling rate.
    (C) The shape of the objects has a minor effect on the falling rate.
    (D) The distance of the fall has a minor effect on the falling rate.

89. The following chart summarizes a study of 244 species of insects offered to a monkey as food.

	Eaten by Monkey	Rejected by Monkey
Insects of Bright Colors	23	120
Insects of Dull Colors	83	18

Which of the following is/are the most likely interpretation(s) of the results of the study in terms of animals adapting to their environment?

   I. Insects have adapted to have dull colors to avoid being eaten.
  II. Some insects of bright colors have likely adapted to have bitter tastes.
 III. Many insect species have adapted to have bright colors for protection.
 IV. Monkeys have adapted to eat most species of insects.

(A) I and II only
(B) I and IV only
(C) II and III only
(D) III and IV only

90. The following diagram shows the dispersion of sunlight.

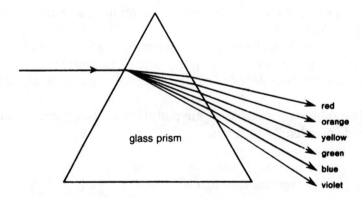

Which of the following is demonstrated by the experiment shown above?
(A) The deflection of light rays is due to reflection.
(B) Light is always deflected when passing through glass.
(C) The reflection of white light yields many colors.
(D) White light is a mixture of many colors.

91. An experiment was conducted to purify water using a solar still as the scientific model. The following items were used.

    A large plastic tarp

    A five-inch-deep pan of sufficient size to hold a large turkey

    Muddy water

    A small rock

    A small plastic bowl

    The muddy water was placed in the five-inch-deep pan. The plastic bowl was placed in the middle of the muddy water. The plastic tarp was placed over the five-inch-deep pan, and the sides of the tarp were taped to the pan. The small rock was placed in the middle and on top of the plastic tarp. The tarp did not touch the bowl. The materials were not interfered with for three hours.

    The results of this experiment would include all of the following EXCEPT:
    (A) Solar rays heated the water making it evaporate.
    (B) The dirt that made the water muddy evaporated at the same temperature as did the water.
    (C) The water would be purified through distillation.
    (D) The water vapor that touched the cooler plastic condensed back into water droplets.

92. Which of the following biological processes is most helpful in explaining the metabolism of an amoeba?
    (A) Photosynthesis
    (B) Reproduction
    (C) Respiration
    (D) Secretion

93. Which of the following properties is the best evidence for considering viruses a life form?
    (A) They have a crystalline structure.
    (B) They are found inside animals, plants, and one-celled organisms.
    (C) They produce nucleic acids to reproduce themselves.
    (D) They possess the ability to become larger.

94. If a flower depends on bees to carry the pollen from one flower to another, the pollen would most likely be on the
    (A) stamen
    (B) pistil
    (C) sepals
    (D) petals

95. Table salt is a compound made up of sodium and chlorine atoms. What type of bonding exists between these atoms?
    (A) Covalent
    (B) Ionic
    (C) Metallic
    (D) Molecular

96. As a covered kettle of vegetable soup continues to boil gently on the stove, what happens to the temperature of the soup?
    (A) It falls very slowly.
    (B) It remains the same.
    (C) It rises very slowly.
    (D) It rises rapidly.

97. An experiment is conducted in which five circular holes of equal size are cut into a large plastic bottle. The holes are arranged from top to bottom, with each hole exactly one inch from the next. The holes are covered with tape, and the bottle is filled with water. The tape is then removed. Which of the following is a true statement based on the information above?
    (A) Water from each hole will squirt out the same distance from the bottle.
    (B) Water from the top hole will squirt out farther than that from the bottom hole.
    (C) Water from the bottom hole will squirt out farther than that from any other hole.
    (D) Water from all five holes rapidly being released will cause the bottle to collapse.

98. The following diagram shows the decomposition of water by an electric current.

ELECTROLYSIS

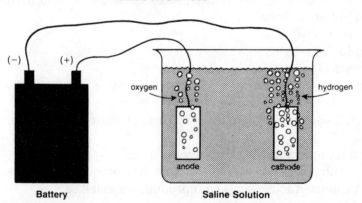

If you examine the diagram carefully, you will see more bubbles of hydrogen than of oxygen. What is the best explanation for this reaction?
    (A) The cathode material is considerably more porous than the anode material.
    (B) Hydrogen gas is less dense than oxygen gas, so hydrogen bubbles rise faster.
    (C) Some oxygen is dissolved into the solution, while all the insoluble hydrogen escapes.
    (D) The water which is being decomposed has twice as much hydrogen as oxygen.

99. Rock samples taken from the moon are estimated to be approximately five billion years old. How was the age of these rocks accurately determined?
   (A) By the size of the crystals found in the samples
   (B) By the ratio of radioactive potassium to argon
   (C) By the half-life of carbon 14 atoms
   (D) By the temperature of the rocks after heating

100. Which of the following LEAST involves inertia?
   (A) Passengers in a car move forward when a car stops suddenly.
   (B) A hockey puck accelerates as it slides in a straight line.
   (C) The great Egyptian pyramids have not moved for thousands of years.
   (D) Each day is precisely the same length as the previous day.

101. The moon at night appears to be a white object in the night sky. At the same time, the planet Mars appears to be reddish. What is the best explanation for the difference in color between the two objects?
   (A) The fact that the moon revolves around Earth and Mars revolves around the sun
   (B) The radioactive dust on the moon's surface
   (C) The mineral compositions of the cores of the planetary objects
   (D) The light that is reflected by each

102. All of the following pairs are examples of symbiosis, whether beneficial, neutral, or harmful, EXCEPT
   (A) ants and beetles
   (B) egrets and rhinoceroses
   (C) foxes and chickens
   (D) whales and barnacles

V. Visual and Performing Arts

103. Which of the following is not directly associated with modern dance as advocated by Isadora Duncan?
   (A) Expressive dance should attempt to imitate nature.
   (B) Expressive dance should incorporate classical techniques if grace and effortless movement are desired dance outcomes.
   (C) Expressive dance should release an individual's spirit in movements that involve the whole body.
   (D) Expressive dance should seek inspiration from the music of the great classical composers.

104. Agnes de Mille's *Rodeo* broke with American ballet tradition because the choreography
   (A) used a mythical setting in order to tell a story
   (B) romanticized a tragic theme
   (C) incorporated a folk tradition in the story line
   (D) relied on the technical skill of the dancer to develop the story line

105. An arabesque is a fundamental ballet pose. By definition, an arabesque is a pose in which
    (A) one leg is extended with a straight knee and pointed foot directly behind the body
    (B) one leg is raised and bent either behind or in front of the dancer
    (C) a dancer jumps straight up and rapidly crosses his or her legs before and behind each other
    (D) a dancer completes a full turn on one foot

106. Which of the following is an incorrect association?
    (A) The tango: France
    (B) The flamenco: Spain
    (C) The samba: Brazil
    (D) The cha-cha: West Indies

107. Traditional Kabuki theater developed in Japan in the seventeenth century. It still remains popular in modern Japan. Which of the following is not associated with this theater form?
    (A) All roles played by male actors
    (B) Elaborately choreographed struggles in which the hero maintains a "freeze" during the action segments
    (C) Plots which often place the hero in an impossible moral dilemma but in which good wins out over evil in the end
    (D) Actors not elaborately costumed

108. Elizabethan theater in sixteenth-century England was marked by a tradition established by the playwrights William Shakespeare, Ben Johnson, and Christopher Marlowe. Which of the following is an atypical stage setting for a production of one of their works during this period?
    (A) Modifying the structure of the Elizabethan stage to accommodate variations in scripts
    (B) Using the thrust stage as a neutral space without necessitating a change in scenery
    (C) Incorporating stage left and stage right doors to allow entrances and exits for the actors
    (D) Incorporating balconies and second-story windows to allow the extension of a scene

109. Following which of these plays is an incorrect thematic association?
    (A) *King Lear:* The relationship of parents and children
    (B) *Hamlet:* Survival against all odds
    (C) *Oedipus the King:* Hubris resulting in retribution
    (D) *Macbeth:* Corruption as a result of power

110. Blocking is a fundamental technique used by directors in staging a play. Which of the following is LEAST associated with the initial stages of blocking?
   (A) The frame-by-frame placement of the characters on the stage
   (B) The gross movement of actors in a stage space
   (C) The speed in which specific scenes take place
   (D) The positioning of actors so that perspective is achieved by both upstage and downstage placement

111. A string quartet most typically consists of which of the following combinations of instruments?
   (A) Violin, viola, cello
   (B) Clarinet, viola, double bass, violin
   (C) Violin, cello, harp, oboe
   (D) Viola, cello, bass, double bass

112. A waltz is best represented by which of the following meter signatures?
   (A) 3/4
   (B) 4/4
   (C) 6/8
   (D) 4/4 or 6/8

113. In music, when a central theme alternates with subordinate themes (for example, ABACA), the form is referred to as
   (A) binary
   (B) theme and variation
   (C) rondo
   (D) canon

114. When complementary colors are mixed together in equal amounts, the resulting color is
   (A) black
   (B) brown
   (C) gray
   (D) white

115. All of the following are characteristic of Byzantine art EXCEPT
   (A) the extensive use of mosaics
   (B) the realistic depiction of religious figures
   (C) using art to help people understand their faith
   (D) portraying figures as flat objects and with little reliance on perspective

116. Which of the following best characterizes an asymmetrical composition?
   (A) Unity is easily attained through the repetition of similar elements.
   (B) A featured point is shown in contrast with its surrounding area.
   (C) Balance can be achieved through the use of unequal elements.
   (D) The eye of the viewer is not focused on any particular feature.

VI. Human Development

117. A young child consistently calls out answers without raising her hand. When the child raises her hand, the teacher immediately calls upon the child. Which of the following terms most closely identifies the technique used to change behavior?
    (A) Operant conditioning
    (B) Negative practice
    (C) Intrinsic reward
    (D) Symbolic representation

118. According to "child-oriented" play theorists, which of the following is <u>not</u> a factual statement regarding childhood play?
    (A) Play is children's means of interpreting the world around them.
    (B) Play activities emphasize the ends rather than the means.
    (C) Play has its own intrinsic value and is not done to satisfy social demands.
    (D) Play activities in older children are more likely to be structured, while younger children are more likely to be involved in solitary play activities.

119. An educational psychologist determined that students who achieve high academic marks in English have a more positive self-image than do students who are below grade level in English.

    In the above case, the independent variable is
    (A) level of achievement in English
    (B) a more positive self-image
    (C) positive self-image and high academic achievement
    (D) students who show learning readiness

120. Cultural bias in testing refers to the fact that
    (A) the sample that was the norm for the test was randomly selected and therefore the test items lack validity
    (B) test items are more familiar to some cultures than to others
    (C) teachers may vary the curriculum by teaching to the test
    (D) standardized tests are unreliable

121. According to Piaget's stages of development, the sensorimotor period is characterized by

    I. mental combinations and problem solving
    II. goal-directed behavior
    III. emergence of symbolic functions

    (A) I only
    (B) II only
    (C) I and II only
    (D) II and III only

122. A child observes a series of violent cartoons. Soon after viewing the cartoons, the child is observed displaying aggressive behavior. According to Albert Bandura, what is the best explanation for this behavior?
   (A) Children are naturally aggressive.
   (B) The rapid eye movements associated with watching cartoons accelerates psychomotor aggressiveness.
   (C) Imitative behavior is a powerful social learning tool.
   (D) Intense television viewing is directly associated with stereotypical sex-role behavior.

123. Which of the following is not characteristic of a criterion-referenced test?
   (A) Pass or fail reporting
   (B) National norming
   (C) Comparing a child's score against a goal the child must reach
   (D) Hierarchy of question types

124. According to Lawrence Kohlberg's stages of moral development, moral development in children begins with preconventional thinking. Which of the following is the best example of Kohlberg's preconventional-thinking stage?
   (A) Stealing is bad.
   (B) Stealing is bad because I might get caught.
   (C) Stealing can be justified if higher moral principles are involved.
   (D) Stealing is neither justified nor bad.

125. This question is based on the chart below and your knowledge of classical conditioning.

Stimulus	Response
Ring a bell	No response
Presentation of food	Salivation
Ring a bell with the presentation of food	Salivation
Ring a bell without the presentation of food	Salivation

After a series of conditioning attempts, if a bell is rung without the presentation of food, which of the following statements is most closely correlated to the information above?
   (A) No response
   (B) An unconditioned stimulus and an unconditioned response of salivation
   (C) A conditioned stimulus and a conditioned response of salivation
   (D) A conditioned stimulus and an unconditioned response of salivation

VII. Physical Education

126. To practice catching skills, a child should reach out for an object and then draw the arms toward the body as the catch is made. The purpose of this catching technique is to
    (A) combine appropriate techniques to facilitate twisting and rotating motions
    (B) bend the ankles, knees, and hips while visually tracking the object
    (C) allow the force of the object to be absorbed over a longer period of time
    (D) model behaviors that are consistently used by professional athletes

127. Which of the following examples best describes a structured movement activity?
    (A) Rolling a ball around a room, alternating the pace you choose to traverse the room
    (B) Crawling over and under a series of poles supported by cones
    (C) Throwing a ball with your right hand while stepping forward with your left foot
    (D) Demonstrating how many different ways you can imitate flight

128. Which of the following is not considered a side effect of a prolonged use of anabolic steroids?
    (A) Reproductive abnormalities associated with infertility, including atrophy of the testicles
    (B) Increase in the incidence of adult acne
    (C) Adverse psychological effects
    (D) Elevated levels of high-density lipoproteins (HDL)

129. If a third-grade student cannot sustain the locomotor movement of skipping for a distance of fifty feet, the best method to improve this skill is to
    (A) require the student to practice the skill until it is mastered
    (B) isolate the student from the class so that, when practicing skipping, the child's self-esteem will not suffer
    (C) offer a reward to the student for any attempts to improve on skipping skills
    (D) individualize the instruction by breaking down the pattern and reinforcing the components

130. In a well-designed elementary physical education program, at what grade level should rhythmic activities be introduced?
    (A) Kindergarten
    (B) First grade
    (C) Second grade
    (D) Third grade

131. Which of the following is the best example of aerobic conditioning?
    (A) Lifting weights for one hour in a four-station cycle consisting of leg curls, arm curls, bench press, and chest extension
    (B) Running intensely until a target heart rate is reached
    (C) Walking briskly for a half-hour
    (D) Doing flexion exercises for a half-hour

132. Of the following, beneficial effects of warm-up activities before starting strenuous exercises include

    I. greater delivery of oxygen to working muscles
    II. decrease in muscle viscosity
    III. earlier onset of sweating, which reduces the risk of high body temperature during exercise

    (A) I only
    (B) II only
    (C) II and III only
    (D) I, II, and III

133. Improper posture can be the result of a weakness in the abdominal wall as well as in the musculature of the upper back and neck. Identifying and correcting improper posture is a goal of all elementary physical education programs. Of the following, what is the best evidence that a lateral deviation in posture exists?
    (A) The back curves slightly.
    (B) The pelvis is noticeably tilted forward.
    (C) One shoulder is higher than the other.
    (D) The body is symmetrical in relation to the spinal column.

134. Mimetics is used as an important approach in teaching the basic concepts of a new motor skill. Which of the following is the best example of using mimetics to teach a new skill?
    (A) Increasing the length of practice sessions so that skills can be mastered
    (B) Practicing the rudiments of a skill without using an implement such as a ball, bat, or physical object
    (C) Organizing an activity geared to the interest level of the children involved
    (D) Developing a sequential lesson based on gross-motor skills

CONTENT AREA EXERCISES 1

Time: 2 Hours
14 Questions

<u>Directions</u>: On the actual MSAT, you will have a page and a half to two pages of 8½ × 11 paper on which to write each answer. For the following questions, use no more than two pages to write each response.

I. Literature and Language Studies

1.   THE MAN HE KILLED

                    "Had he and I but met
                    By some old ancient inn,
                We should have sat us down to wet
                    Right many a nipperkin!

      (5)   "But ranged as infantry,
                    And staring face to face,
                I shot at him as he at me,
                    And killed him in his place.

                    "I shot him dead because—
      (10)   Because he was my foe,
                Just so: my foe of course he was;
                    That's clear enough; although

                    "He thought he'd 'list, perhaps,
                    Off-hand like—just as I;
      (15)   Was out of work, had sold his traps—
                    No other reason why.

                    "Yes; quaint and curious war is!
                    You shoot a fellow down
                You'd treat if met where any bar is,
      (20)   Or help to half-a-crown."

                                          THOMAS HARDY

Discuss the meaning of the third stanza of the poem above and how it functions in the structure of the poem.

2. Name and discuss three major elements of the novel.

3. Discuss the differences between analytical and descriptive writing.

4. The Inuit language has many different words for snow, while the English language has only a few. Explain why the Inuits would have so many ways to refer to snow.

II. Mathematics

5.

Total: 40 Hours of Office Work

10 hours typing
4 hours clerical
20 hours computer data entry
6 hours telephone answering

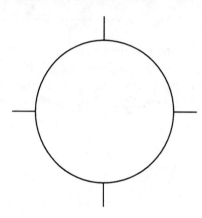

Use the circle above to construct a pie chart showing percentages to reflect the office work. Explain the reason for the size of each of the sections.

6. If x is an even integer, then $x(x + 1)(x + 2)$ is also an even integer. How do you know that this is true? Show and explain two methods.

7.

+	2			
3				
3		7	9	
	9	11		15

The chart above contains squares with 16 sums which result from the addition of positive integers located in the margins along the top row and the left side of the chart. These integers in each margin increase in a consistent pattern.

Using the information given in the chart, complete the chart, including the margins, and explain your methods.

8.

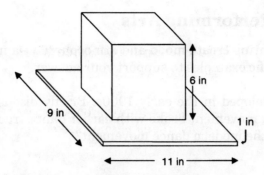

The cube above is glued onto a rectangular piece of wood one inch thick, which is sitting on a table. If you wanted to paint the complete surface that is exposed, except the one-inch edge of the rectangular piece of wood, what is the measure of the surface area that needs to be painted? Show your work and explain your steps.

III. Visual and Performing Arts

9. How can stage lighting create mood and atmosphere in a modern theater production? Include specific examples to support your answer.

10. Modern dance developed in the early 1900s. Briefly discuss specific reasons that leaders of this new movement broke with earlier dance tradition. How did Isadora Duncan influence the modern dance movement?

IV. Human Development

11. Piaget discovered that there are developmental learning processes by which children arrive at answers to problems. How would Piagetian levels explain the following observation?

    A child thinks the following two rows have a total of eight objects

    OOOO
    OOOO

    but thinks that the following rows have a different total number of objects.

    OO
    OOO
    OO
    O

12. List the dominant abilities of the left and right hemispheres of the brain. What implications does this research hold for teachers?

V. Physical Education

13. List six health-related risk factors for cardiovascular disease. How can a comprehensive health-related physical fitness program reduce health-risk factors? What does current research indicate about this subject?

14. Briefly discuss two motor-development patterns that are prerequisites for a fourteen-year-old to efficiently throw a forward pass during a football game. Include in your answer the body mechanics necessary to throw a forward pass.

CONTENT AREA EXERCISES 2

Time: 1 Hour
8 Questions

Directions: On the actual MSAT, you will have a page and a half to two pages of 8½ × 11 paper on which to write each answer. For the following questions, use no more than two pages to write each response.

I. History/Social Sciences

1. In the 1988 presidential election, only fifty-three percent of eligible U.S. citizens voted. Briefly discuss four key factors to explain limited voter participation in national elections.

2. Describe how the geography of Egypt influenced the area's historical growth.

3. The progressive reform movement swept America in the early twentieth century. Why was the presidential election of 1912 a bench mark for progressivism? Discuss three important progressive reforms at the national level implemented by the Democratic and Republican parties.

4. Discuss how the triangular trade connected New England, Africa, and the West Indies in the seventeenth century. Include in your answer the products exchanged and the significance of the "middle passage" as an example of inhumane practices.

II. Science

5. Discuss three key characteristics of asexual reproduction. Give examples from the plant and animal kingdoms and include regeneration in your answer.

6. List and discuss four reasons that can be cited as evidence for the continental drift theory.

7. Which of the following diagrams shows a situation in which more force would be needed, and which shows one in which less force would be needed? Discuss the lifting principles involved in the diagrams.

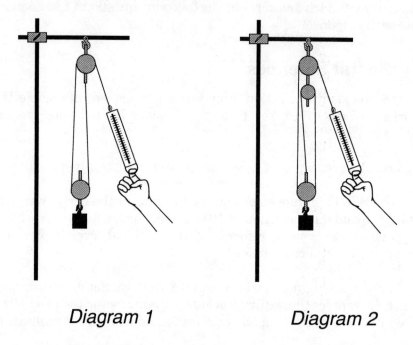

Diagram 1   Diagram 2

8. The two structures below show changes in the earth's crust. Briefly discuss the forces present in each structure.

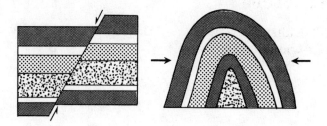

ANSWER KEY FOR PRACTICE TEST 1

Content Knowledge

1. A	28. C	55. A	82. B	109. B
2. B	29. D	56. C	83. C	110. C
3. D	30. C	57. B	84. D	111. A
4. A	31. B	58. C	85. B	112. A
5. A	32. D	59. D	86. C	113. C
6. B	33. D	60. A	87. B	114. B
7. C	34. C	61. B	88. A	115. B
8. B	35. D	62. B	89. C	116. C
9. D	36. B	63. A	90. D	117. A
10. C	37. C	64. C	91. B	118. B
11. C	38. D	65. D	92. C	119. A
12. B	39. C	66. B	93. C	120. B
13. A	40. A	67. D	94. A	121. C
14. C	41. A	68. D	95. B	122. C
15. B	42. D	69. C	96. B	123. B
16. B	43. C	70. A	97. C	124. B
17. C	44. D	71. B	98. D	125. C
18. B	45. A	72. C	99. B	126. C
19. B	46. C	73. B	100. D	127. C
20. D	47. C	74. C	101. D	128. D
21. D	48. D	75. A	102. C	129. D
22. D	49. A	76. C	103. B	130. A
23. A	50. D	77. C	104. C	131. C
24. C	51. B	78. D	105. A	132. D
25. A	52. B	79. B	106. A	133. C
26. B	53. A	80. C	107. D	134. B
27. C	54. A	81. B	108. A	

Content Area Exercises

See the Essay Checklist on page 442 and the discussion of essay scoring beginning on page 16 to evaluate your short essays.

ANALYZING YOUR TEST RESULTS

Use the following charts to carefully analyze your results and spot your strengths and weaknesses. Complete the process of analyzing each subject area and each individual question for Practice Test 1. Examine your results for trends in types of error (repeated errors) or poor results in specific subject areas. *This reexamination and analysis is of tremendous importance for effective test preparation.*

Practice Test 1 Analysis Sheets

Content Knowledge (Multiple-Choice Questions)				
	Possible	Completed	Right	Wrong
I. Literature and Language Studies	27			
II. Mathematics	27			
III. History/Social Sciences	24			
IV. Science	24			
V. Visual and Performing Arts	14			
VI. Human Development	9			
VII. Physical Education	9			
Total	134			

To get a rough approximation of your multiple-choice score range, total the number of correct responses. Do not subtract any points for questions attempted but missed, as there is no penalty for guessing. Now, refer to the broad-range score approximator on page 12.

Analysis/Tally Sheet for Questions Missed

One of the most important parts of test preparation is analyzing **why** you missed a question so that you can reduce the number of mistakes. Now that you've taken Practice Test 1 and corrected your answers, carefully tally your multiple-choice mistakes by marking in the proper column

	Reason for Mistake		
	Total Missed	Simple Mistake	Misread Question	Lack of Knowledge
I. Literature and Language Studies				
II. Mathematics				
III. History/Social Sciences				
IV. Science				
V. Visual and Performing Arts				
VI. Human Development				
VII. Physical Education				
Total				

Essay Checklist

Compare your short constructed-response answers to the answers given. A good short constructed-response answer will do the following:

_____ address the assignment

_____ be well focused

_____ use key words ("buzzwords")

_____ show an understanding of the subject

For each of your responses, check to see if your answer fulfills the criteria above. Fill in the following charts with the number of criteria fulfilled for each essay to get a general idea of the effectiveness of your answer. **These numbers do not represent a score** but are simply meant to help you evaluate your response.

Content Area Exercises 1 (Short Essay Questions)

	Essays Possible	Number of Essay Checklist Criteria Fulfilled			
		Essay 1	Essay 2	Essay 3	Essay 4
I. Literature and Language Studies	4				
II. Mathematics	4				
III. Visual and Performing Arts	2				
IV. Human Development	2				
V. Physical Education	2				
Total	*14*				

Content Area Exercises 2 (Short Essay Questions)

	Essays Possible	Number of Essay Checklist Criteria Fulfilled			
		Essay 1	Essay 2	Essay 3	Essay 4
I. History/Social Sciences	4				
II. Science	4				
Total	*8*				

ANSWERS AND EXPLANATIONS FOR PRACTICE TEST 1

CONTENT KNOWLEDGE

I. Literature and Language Studies

1. (A) The first line compares the sea to something that has been wrinkled and to someone or something that crawls without using *like* or *as*. These figures are metaphors. A simile would use *like* or *as;* antithesis is a contrast or opposition of ideas; a paradox is an apparent self-contradiction.

2. (B) Both a metaphor and a simile could compare two unlike objects, could compare an eagle and a thunderbolt ("the eagle is a thunderbolt" is a metaphor), and both are examples of figurative language. Only the simile would use *like*.

3. (D) There are three rhymes on the same sound, a triplet. A couplet has two rhymes, a ballad stanza is abcb, and blank verse is unrhymed.

4. (A) This line from *Hamlet* combines the metaphor of a battle with the metaphor of the sea. It has been suggested that *sea* should be *siege* or that the line alludes to a mad warrior of myth who attempted to fight against the waves that he imagined were enemy soldiers. Not all mixed metaphors are to be deplored.

5. (A) An aphorism is a pithy statement, a precept, an adage, a short general comment in a memorable form. It need not be taken from a poem as all four of these quotations are.

6. (B) Although *turning point* might be used in the discussion of a comedy, and possibly *flashback, point of view* (the angle from which a story is told, the narrator, the focus of narration) is much more likely to be used to discuss prose fiction, such as the novel or short story.

7. (C) A psychological reading is most useful when the focus of the work is characterization. Although a satiric comedy may have characters, they are often undeveloped. Given the choice between novel and satiric comedy here, novel is the better option.

8. (B) The Latin *stella* means *star*. The prefix *con* (*com*) means *with* or *together with*. The word *constellation* means *set with stars*.

9. (D) The lines use a simile, or an analogy, comparing judgments and watches. The figure is not a metaphor because it uses *like*. A personification is a comparison to a person, or living human.

10. (C) The lines compare poets with critics and genius with taste. Both genius in a poet and taste in a critic are unusual (*rare–seldom*).

11. (C) The lines say that poets of genius and critics with true taste are both rare, so most criticism would be inadequate. (A) is a tempting answer, since the first two lines say that we all believe our own judgments, but the poem does not explicitly say we should not do so, while (C) is a logical deduction from lines 3–4.

12. (B) The passage compares individuals and nations. They are alike, not opposed. The oppositions of the passage are *perceive–abstract, poetical–philosophical, particularity–generalization, knowledge–imagination,* and *theories–poems.*

13. (A) Since the passage argues that the more people know, the worse their poems, poetry ought to be best when people are *half-civilized* and go downhill as they acquire more knowledge. Contemporary poetry should be the worst, and the Old English poems the best.

14. (C) If, as the passage argues, in the modern period theory is better than ever before, and poetry is worse, a greater emphasis on theory than on poetry would be a reasonable consequence. None of the other results is really relevant to the ideas of the paragraph.

15. (B) A conditional phrase describes what might be as opposed to what is. *Yet* does not suggest uncertainty, as the other three terms do.

16. (B) The ā symbol would be used to represent the a in bait or bate. The rhyme, therefore, is rate.

17. (C) The phrase *this time* in (1) must refer to a time already mentioned, so (1) must follow (3), which refers to *hours.* The *Or* in (2) must follow some other possible action, so (2) must follow (4).

18. (B) This is the rhyme scheme of the sestet (last six lines) of a sonnet in the English rhyme scheme. Lines 1–8 would rhyme ababcdcd.

19. (B) A paradox, or apparent self-contradiction, is the misfit here. the three others are closely related and might be used as definitions of one another.

20. (D) The major premise, or first of the three terms of a syllogism, presents a general truth, such as *All reptiles are cold-blooded.* The second step, or minor premise, presents a particular instance, such as *Alligators are reptiles.* The conclusion is deduced from a combination of the major and the minor premise. This question supplies only the minor premise and the conclusion, but you can deduce that the major premise must be *All reptiles are cold-blooded.*

21. (D) Physical growth is not a factor in the acquisition of language.

22. (D) The passage is written in short, simple sentences, using commonplace diction. The author (whose identity need not be known to answer the question) is Ernest Hemingway.

23. (A) *Learning to recognize printed symbols associated with sounds or words* best fits a good definition of reading.

24. (C) The girl replaces every *f* in alfalfa with *ph,* thus suggesting her idea that all *f* sounds should be spelled with *ph.* Choices (A) and (B) contradict the girl's words, and because she does give spelling advice, she does not assume that she knows nothing about spelling.

25. (A) Choices (B) and (C) are explicitly contradicted by the boy's response to the girl's spelling, and there is no evidence that he believes correct spelling to be a mystery. His final remark, *too many letters,* suggests that he associates the spelling of a word with its pronunciation.

26. (B) The proper pronunciation is in tiṁ i date.

27. (C) Analogous means bearing some resemblance in the midst of differences. This is making a comparison.

II. Mathematics

28. (C) One way to solve this problem is to set up a ratio: 10 kilometers is to 6.2 miles as 45 kilometers is to how many miles? This is expressed in mathematical terms as

$$\frac{10 \text{ km}}{6.2 \text{ m}} = \frac{45 \text{ km}}{x}$$

Cross multiplying gives

$$10x = 6.2 \times 45$$
$$10x = 279$$

Dividing both sides by 10 gives

$$\frac{10x}{10} = \frac{279}{10}$$
$$x = 27.9$$

Another method is to realize that 45 kilometers is exactly 4½ times 10 kilometers. Therefore, the number of miles in 45 kilometers must be 4½ times the number of miles in 10 kilometers, or 4½ times 6.2. Thus $4.5 \times 6.2 = 27.9$.

29. **(D)** By simply sketching the times on a clock, it is evident that 12:15 gives an angle of approximately 90° between the two hands.

30. **(C)** Since the figure is a rectangle, its opposite sides are equal. To find its perimeter, first add the two sides, then double the sum (or double each of the sides and add the results).

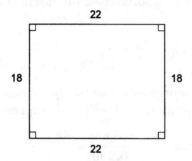

Now, to determine the side of a square with the same perimeter, simply divide by 4, since the side of a square is one-fourth its perimeter. Finally, to find the area of the square, multiply its side times itself (square it).

31. **(B)** If the price of the tie is x, the price of the shirt is $3x$, the price of the slacks is $3x$, and the price of the coat is twice the shirt, or $6x$. Totaling the x's gives $13x$. Since the total spent was $156, $13x = \$156$. Dividing both sides by 13 gives

$$\frac{13x}{13} = \frac{\$156}{13}$$

$$x = \$12$$

Therefore, the price of the pair of slacks, $3x$, is $3(\$12) = \$36$.

32. **(D)** The solution of two lines can be determined by the coordinates of the point at which the lines intersect. Lines l_1 and l_2 intersect at (2, 4). Therefore, $x = 2$ and $y = 4$.

33. (D) If Tom is four years older than Fran, if Fran's age is x, Tom's age must be four years more, or $x + 4$. Therefore, since the total of their ages is twenty-four,

$$\text{Fran's age} + \text{Tom's age} = 24$$

$$x + (x + 4) = 24$$

34. (C) Take some scissors and a piece of paper and try it.

35. (D) Solving the equation $2x + 4 = 3x + 3$, first subtract $2x$ from each side.

$$2x + 4 - 2x = 3x + 3 - 2x$$

$$4 = x + 3$$

Now subtract 3 from both sides.

$$4 - 3 = x + 3 - 3$$

$$1 = x$$

By plugging in the above value of x (that is, 1) for each of the answer choices, you will find that 1 satisfies all the equations *except* choice (D).

$$\text{Does } x = -1? \text{ No.}$$

$$x \neq -1$$

Therefore, (D) is the correct answer.

36. (B) Note that all choices except (B) are larger than $\frac{1}{2}$. Choice (B), $\frac{4}{9}$, is smaller than $\frac{1}{2}$.

37. (C) If an integer is divisible by both 5 and 3, it must be divisible by 15. The integers between 1 and 100 that are divisible by 15 are 15, 30, 45, 60, 75, and 90. This totals 6 integers.

38. (D) Since the chart does not distinguish how many houses are three years old or four years old, the answer cannot be determined.

39. (C) If the product of two numbers equals one of the numbers, then $(x)(y) = x$. If this product is more than zero, neither of the numbers may be zero. Therefore, y must be 1: $(x)(1) = x$.

40. (A) The sale of each bouquet yields a profit of $2.75 (since each costs $2.00 and is sold for $4.75). Therefore, the number of bouquets necessary to be sold to yield a total of $82.50 can be determined by dividing $82.50 by the profit from each sale, $2.75. Answer (D) is incorrect because in the order of operations division takes precedence over subtraction (is performed first).

41. (A) Since one angle of a square is 90° and the circle is 360°, the percent is $^{90}/_{360}$ or $^{1}/_{4}$ = 25%.

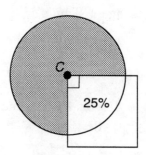

42. (D) Since the large square has side 4 cm, its area must be 16. By careful grouping of areas, you will see that there are four unshaded smaller squares and four shaded smaller squares (match the shaded parts to four squares). Therefore, half of the area is shaded, or 8 square cm.

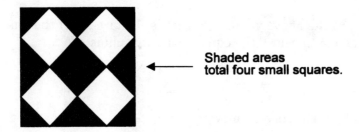

Shaded areas total four small squares.

43. (C) Note that only choice (C) raises one of the numbers by five while it lowers the other number by five. This gives the best approximation of the five choices.

44. (D) Using the probablilty formula,

$$\text{probability} = \frac{\text{number of ``lucky'' chances}}{\text{total number of chances}}$$

The chance of choosing a weekday = 5 weekdays/7 total days = 5/7.

45. (A) Note that since there is a mark between +7 and +9, that mark must equal +8. Thus, each mark equals 1. Counting back, point Q is at +5. Therefore, fifteen units to the left of +5 would be + 5 − 15 = −10.

46. (C) The *product of two numbers* indicates that the numbers must be multiplied together. Their *sum* means add. Therefore,

the product of two numbers equals five more than their sum.

$(A)(B)$ = $A + B + 5$

47. (C) Since each slot has ten possibilities and each are independent, simply multiply 10 × 10 × 10 = 1000.

48. (D) Since Brenda's sports car averages 35 miles for each gallon of gas, on 12 gallons she'll be able to drive 12 × 35, or 420 miles.

49. (A) To find the total number of paintings, use the equation

$$\frac{\text{is}}{\text{of}} = \%$$

and simply plug in the given values. The question is essentially this: 24 is 30% of how many? Therefore, 24 is the "is," 30 is the percent, and "how many" (the unknown) is the "of." Plugging into the equation,

$$\frac{24}{x} = \frac{30}{100}$$

(Note that the fractional percent is used to simplify the math.)

Cross multiplying,

$$30x = 2400$$

Dividing both sides by 30,

$$\frac{30x}{30} = \frac{2400}{30}$$

$$x = 80$$

50. (D) If each adult drinks a fifth of a gallon of lemonade, one gallon is consumed by each five adults. Since twenty-eight adults attend the picnic, 28/5 = slightly over five gallons.

51. (B) To make this problem less abstract, plug in numbers for a, b, c, and d such that they obey the relationship stated in the inequality. Starting from the right side, since $d < 0$, let d equal -1. Since $c < d$, let c equal -2. Since $b < c$, let b equal -3. Finally, since $a < b$, let a equal -4. Now determine which of the answer choices has the least value by plugging in these values. Choice (A), $1/a$, will therefore equal $1/-4$, or $-\frac{1}{4}$. Choice (B), $1/d$, will equal $1/-1$, or -1. Choice (B) is therefore less than choice (A) because (B) has a greater negative value. Choice (B) is negative and therefore will be less than choice (C), 0. In this way—plugging in your own values that obey the relationship given—you can determine which of the choices has the least value, choice (B).

52. (B) Note that on the graph a 35 degree drop in temperature (horizontal line) correlates with a 20% attendance drop (the fourth slash up the vertical line).

53. (A) The associative property of addition demonstrates that when adding numbers, they may be grouped differently and will still give the same outcome.

54. (A) Since the sum of the angles is 180°,

$$m + n + 72 + 25 = 180$$
$$m + n + 97 = 180$$
$$m + n = 180 - 97$$
$$m + n = 83$$

Hence, the sum of $m + n$ is 83°.

III. History/Social Sciences

55. (A) In November of 1993, Governor Wilson signed into law a bill that changed the date for presidential primaries in California from June to March. New Hampshire (a small electoral state), by holding its primary in March, has had a far greater impact on the direction of national politics than has California. In recent elections, both the Democratic and Republican candidates were basically determined prior to the California primary, in effect, disenfranchising California, the largest delegate state. Therefore, it was felt that by holding the primary in March, California would have a major voice in determining the course of national politics. None of the other choices would have a significant effect on national politics.

56. (C) The most serious objection to the Japanese relocation program centered on the fact that race was the sole factor in the decision to intern the Japanese. American citizens of Japanese ancestry were interned without a trial, thus calling into question basic constitutional guarantees. However, at the same time, American citizens of Italian and German ancestry were not interned or held without trials. Choice (A) was a reason *for* the relocation program. Choice (B) indicates the cultural bias that faced people of Japanese ancestry living in California, but it was not the most serious objection to the relocation.

57. (B) *Two Years before the Mast* by Richard Henry Dana gained national recognition as a vivid description of California under Mexican rule. The book not only chronicled the dangers associated with voyages around Cape Horn, but more important to this question, extolled the climate and potential wealth from California resources. Dana's book was instrumental in encouraging the pioneer migration to California and in this way served the same function as *Democracy in America.*

58. (C) The dress and head ornament are representative of ancient Egypt. The falcon is symbolic of Horus, the son of Isis and the avenger of Osiris. The relative size of the two figures also suggests the significance of religious deities in the daily life of ancient Egypt. Horus is often depicted holding an ankh (a symbol of enduring life). Choice (B) is incorrect because neither object is representative of Mesopotamia, and nothing in the representation suggests a cult figure.

59. (D) In free trade, all products (foreign and domestic) can be traded without government regulations that restrict the free flow of goods. A protective tariff, on the other hand, is designed as more than a revenue measure. Its purpose is to restrict foreign products from competing with domestic products and thus encourage the expansion of domestic industries. However, in the interdependence of world economies, protective tariffs often invite retaliation in the form of restrictive tariffs on American goods. Both the Reagan and Bush administrations resisted passing protective tariffs, even those directed against the Japanese auto industry. Instead, both presidents pursued free trade agreements and open markets with the Japanese.

60. (A) If the dollar were to rise sharply against other currencies, foreign imports to the United States would tend to be less expensive for Americans. The dollar would be "stronger" than competing currencies. U.S. exports, on the other hand, would tend to be more expensive, since it would take more yen, marks, pesos, etc., to buy American products. Answer (C), however, is incorrect because the question asks for the probable effect on the *U.S. economy,* not on the economies of other countries. A "weak" dollar (a drop in the dollar's value in relation to foreign currencies) would tend to make U.S. exports cheaper but would raise the price of imports to the United States. A weak dollar tends to reduce the U.S. trade deficit because it encourages foreign countries to buy U.S. products.

61. (B) Since the passage of the Twenty-sixth Amendment in 1971, the expected dramatic increase in the participation of younger voters (18–26) has not materialized. In fact, the young voter has consistently recorded the lowest voter turnout of any age group. Sociological and demographic studies indicate that the young voter is less familiar with candidates for public office than are other groups. Factors which contribute to a lack of participation by young voters in the election process include mobility, career interests, and candidates that are much older than the young voter.

62. (B) The Hellenistic Age (323 B.C. to c. 30 B.C.) was a time of great economic growth and expansion. Rhodes, Alexandria, and Antioch replaced Athens in commercial importance. Dynasties were established in Macedonia, Egypt, and Persia following Alexander's death. The new "Hellenistic" world saw the expansion of Greek culture, the rise of cities, and the virtual disappearance of the Greek city-state, or polis, as an administrative center.

63. (A) A careful reading of the chart shows overwhelming opposition to U.S. involvement in any venture that might entangle the United States in a foreign conflict. Therefore, the results of public-opinion polls taken in the middle 1930s strongly supported the continuation of isolationist sentiments. Congress, during this period, responded to the potential threat of a European war by attempting to remain neutral at almost any cost.

64. (C) The map represents Europe in A.D. 500, shortly after the fall of the Roman Empire. 100 B.C. represents Rome shortly before Julius Caesar, A.D. 200 Rome at the end of the two-hundred-year *Pax Romana* (Roman Peace), and A.D. 800 the Frankish Empire at the end of the reign of Charlemagne. A key to identifying the time period of this map is recognizing the change in territory once controlled by Rome. Choices (A) and (B) indicate the expansion of Rome, not its decline. Note that the Byzantine Empire was not established until the fourth century and recalling this information would limit your response to just two choices, (C) and (D).

65. (D) During the twentieth century, the traditional American family underwent profound social changes. Industrialization and urbanization had a fundamental impact upon the family structure. Rural America was rapidly replaced by an urban, industrial society. Some of the effects of this modernization on the family were greater emphasis on child-centered values; increased acceptance of alternative lifestyles; steady increase in the divorce rate; redefinition of the status of women; and greater social, political, and economic equality for minorities.

66. (B) The "war-guilt" clause included in the Treaty of Versailles (1919) was considered by the Germans as unfairly blaming them for a war that had multiple causes. In fact, the Germans felt that their honor as a people had been compromised, since Germany had to accept "sole responsibility" for causing World War I. Other points of the treaty forced Germany to pay large reparations, lose territory, demilitarize the Rhineland, and eliminate the merchant marine. Part of Hitler's rise to power was based on the harsh terms of the Treaty of Versailles.

67. (D) During World War I, over 50,000 black Americans moved from the rural South to the urban North to meet the unprecedented demand for wartime labor. Because immigration was temporarily interrupted by the war, the increased demand for black labor resulted not only in new jobs but also in substantial economic and social gains for blacks. This situation led to a racist backlash, exemplified by a revival of the Ku Klux Klan. Race riots erupted in many major cities in 1919.

68. (D) In 1964, two American destroyers were allegedly attacked in international waters by the North Vietnamese. Congress, based on the reports of the incident in the Gulf of Tonkin, authorized the president to "take all necessary measures" to repel any armed attack against the forces of the United States. President Johnson responded by ordering the bombing of selected military targets in North Vietnam. This action escalated the war. Later evidence brought into question whether the United States was actually attacked in international waters. Choice (B) was expressly prohibited by Congress.

69. (C) The question asks for the most logical extension of the philosophy implied in the political cartoon. Choice (A) is not the best answer because the effectiveness of the slogan is not addressed. The best answer, choice (C), is based on the assumption that the cartoonist, in drawing a parallel between clubs and guns, is implying that obvious truths often go unnoticed. Choice (D) is not supported by the information presented in the cartoon.

70. (A) This is the only choice that addresses the main focus of the statement (population growth will outstrip any increase in food production). Choice (B) is a misstatement of the information presented in the paragraph. Choice (C) goes beyond the scope of the original statement; there is insufficient information to justify either choice (C) or (D).

71. (B) Deferred gratification, a behavior pattern that encourages postponing immediate wants so that long-range goals can be achieved, is primarily associated with the middle class. For example, individuals in the middle class continue their education in order to achieve future economic success. Choice (A) is incorrect because the unstable economic environment of the lower class often makes long-term economic planning impractical. Choice (D) is incorrect because the term *minority* is too general to specifically answer the question.

72. (C) Pennsylvania had 26 electoral votes and Ohio had 21 for a total of 47. The electoral vote of a state is equal to the number of votes the state has in Congress (House and Senate). Thus, the most populous states have greater representation not only in the House (which is based on population) but also in the electoral college. It should also be apparent that in 1868 the most populous states would be in the northeastern and midwestern sections of the United States.

73. (B) The map is identified as the subcontinent of India, which should suggest to you that India is the largest country shown. India has a Hindu population of approximately 84 percent and consequently does *not* have a Moslem or Buddhist majority. (Nepal, not marked with a letter, also is predominantly Hindu.) The religious breakdown of the other countries shown is as follows: Pakistan (A) and Bangladesh (D) are predominantly Moslem. Bhutan (C) is predominantly Buddhist (as is Burma, which also is not marked with a letter).

74. (C) John Foster Dulles, secretary of state, based his foreign policy on the assumption that Soviet domination of Eastern Europe could be altered. Dulles also based his policy on the concept of "massive retaliation" in response to Soviet aggression.

75. (A) The sale of indulgences was an immediate cause of the Protestant Reformation. Martin Luther objected to this policy on both theological and moral grounds, and these objections became the basis of the Ninety-five Theses. After the Theses were circulated, Luther was excommunicated.

76. (C) The correct chronological order is Federalist Party (1789), Democratic Party (1824), Whig Party (1832), and Republican Party (1854). Simply by knowing which of the parties listed developed first (the Federalists) or which last (the Republicans) would allow you to eliminate two choices.

77. (C) Stratified sampling techniques are used in polling to ensure that the sample reflects the characteristics of the general population. All elements of the population are represented proportionately in the sample. Choice (A) is an example of random sampling.

78. (D) The law of diminishing returns states that as extra units of a varying input are successfully added to a fixed amount of another input, eventually the extra output per unit of additional variable will decline. In this case, adding one more unit of input of labor and capital (after 5) results in a decrease in the output of wheat (see input of labor and capital at point 6).

IV. Science

79. (B) A *dramatic* increase in atmospheric carbon dioxide would generate increased global warming. All life forms are carbon based. Therefore, the burning of coal, oil, natural gas, and wood and the decomposition of organic materials could increase the greenhouse effect, with possibly far-reaching environmental changes. For example, if the mean temperature of the earth increased only five percent, the polar icecaps would begin to shrink, resulting in extensive flooding in lowland coastal areas. Choice (A) is the opposite of the polar change that would be expected in this situation. Chlorofluorocarbons (CFCs) (C) are the primary contributor to ozone depletion, and while they add to global warming, they are not its main cause.

80. (C) The liquefaction of air can be accomplished by changing temperature or pressure or both. Lowering the temperature can change a gas into a liquid. Raising the pressure has the same result, since increased pressure forces molecules closer together. The most efficient procedure is to lower the air temperature while the pressure is increased.

81. (B) The formation of rust is the result of a chemical reaction. Rust, by definition, is iron oxide. When atoms of oxygen in the air come into contact with atoms in iron, a new compound results. Anything made of iron will eventually begin to rust if left outside long enough. Salt water would accelerate the process. Choice (D) is a true statement, but the paint inhibits, rather than causes, rusting.

82. (B) A deciduous forest, made up of broad-leafed trees such as oaks, maples, elms, and walnuts, is climatically associated with cold winters, warm summers, and abundant rainfall. The leaves of deciduous trees turn bright red, orange, or yellow each autumn and then fall from the tree by winter. In a coniferous forest (A), the trees are "evergreen," needle-bearing, such as pines and firs.

83. (C) Aerosol cans are under high pressure. When the top button is pressed, gas escapes to the lower pressure in the surrounding air, "pushing" the product out of the pressurized can. If an aerosol can is heated (B), the gases inside it expand, and in time, the expansion causes the can to explode.

84. (D) Sedimentation is the only *natural* process listed that would tend to destroy an existing lake. Sedimentation is generally a process (initiated by runoff) in which sediments such as clay, silt, and sand gradually accumulate. Chemical fertilizers (A) could rapidly destroy a lake, but this is not a natural process. Pollution of the *outlet* stream would not affect the lake from which it comes.

85. (B) The diagram of Charles's law shows a direct relationship between the volume and temperature of a gas. The law states that higher temperatures cause gas molecules to move rapidly. As the temperature of a gas increases, and the pressure remains constant, the volume of the gas also increases. An everyday demonstration of this relationship would be to place a tied-off balloon, half filled with air, in the sun. The sun's heat warms the air inside the balloon, causing the gas and balloon to expand.

86. (C) Earth movements (such as faulting, folding, and tectonic movements) have slowly lifted the land up for millions of years, a phenomenon evident along the west coast of North America. Old shorelines have been uplifted hundreds of feet above the present sea level. On the other hand, erosion and weathering are natural processes that, over millions of years, wear down hills and mountains.

87. (B) Sulfur from coal combines with oxygen in the air to form sulfur dioxide. Coal is the most common fuel in electric power plants; heat from burning coal produces steam, which is used to generate electric power. (Scrubbers, filters, are inserted in some smokestacks to reduce the sulfur dioxide problem.) Some electric power plants burn oil or natural gas, which also yield sulfur dioxide. Automobile engines (A) yield carbon dioxide, carbon monoxide, nitrous oxides, and some sulfur dioxides.

88. (A) The weight of an object does not affect the rate at which the object falls. Two objects of different weights, if they have the same shape, will fall at the same rate. This was the basis for Galileo's classic experiment involving the dropping of weights (perhaps from the Leaning Tower of Pisa). However, with objects of different shapes and weights, air resistance (wind and friction) does have an effect on falling rate, as you could see by dropping a flat piece of paper from a height. (In a vacuum, there is no air resistance, and any two objects would fall equal distances in equal times. In a vacuum, a feather and a piano would both hit the ground at the same time; they would accelerate at a uniform thirty-two feet per second squared.)

89. (C) Adaptations enable organisms to better survice in an environment. It is to the advantage of each insect species to avoid being eaten, and many have adapted by having bright colors for protection. From the information presented, one could logically assume that monkeys have learned that insects with bright colors taste bad. Even insects that don't taste bad would then find that bright colors are helpful protection. In nature, many species mimic a potentially dangerous species in order to protect themselves. For example, the "eye" markings on a butterfly's wings may scare off potential predators.

90. (D) The diagram shows the production of the color spectrum by shining sunlight through a glass prism. When light enters a prism, it is bent, or refracted, because the speed of light changes as it passes from one transparent medium to another (from water to air, from air to glass). White light enters the prism, but several colors of light leave the prism. The prism has *separated* white light into its basic colors, showing that white light is a mixture. The colors of the spectrum are visible in a rainbow because after a rainstorm, the air is full of tiny drops of water; each drop acts as a prism, *splitting* the light into the colors of the spectrum.

91. (B) The experiment describes how a solar still can act as a water purifier. The dirt that made the water muddy would *not* evaporate at the same temperature as would the water. Therefore, when water vaporizes by heat (changes from a liquid to a gas), it leaves the tiny particles of mud behind. Distillation is often used to separate substances in a mixture.

92. (C) Respiration is the central life process during metabolism. Oxygen is taken in, allowing stored chemical energy to be released. Respiration takes place within a cell. Photosynthesis (A) is the process opposite to respiration. In respiration, an individual inhales air rich in oxygen and exhales air rich in carbon dioxide. In photosynthesis, green plants take carbon dioxide and water from the atmosphere and release oxygen, water, and glucose as by-products.

93. (C) Some of the key characteristics suggesting classification as a life form are metabolism, growth, respiration, excretion, motion, and, most important, *reproduction*. Viruses can be classified both as living organisms and as chemical compounds. The fact that a virus can produce nucleic acids would argue for including it as a life form. Many nonliving substances can increase in size (D); for example, metals and gases can expand, and rocks can accumulate as conglomerates.

94. (A) The stamen is a pollen-bearing organ made up of a slender stalk and a pollen sac. The several stamens on a flower are the source of the male pollen cells. The bee gets coated with pollen as it enters and leaves the flower in search of nectar. The pistil (B) is the female seed-bearing organ.

95. (B) Ionic bonding exists in compounds containing both a metal (sodium) and a nonmetal (chlorine). In ionic bonding, the metallic atom gives up electrons, and the nonmetallic atom receives them. The transfer of electrons creates ions (charged atoms) of opposite charges. The attraction between opposite charges keeps the compound bonded together.

96. (B) The temperature of the soup remains the same. While the soup is boiling, both liquid and vapor are present in the covered kettle. The temperature of the liquid cannot be higher than its boiling point (212 degrees Fahrenheit), and the temperature of the water vapor cannot be less than the boiling point. Therefore, the soup stays at the boiling point.

97. (C) Water pressure increases with depth. The deeper the water, the greater the pressure. In the experiment, the water near the bottom of the bottle has the force of all water above it.

98. (D) The diagram shows the decomposition of water by an electric current (electrolysis). The purpose of an electrolytic experiment is to break down water into its elements, hydrogen and oxygen. Each molecule of water contains two hydrogen atoms and one oxygen atom. So the decomposition of water gives off twice as much hydrogen as oxygen.

99. (B) The age of moon rocks has been estimated at approximately five billion years based on the amount of radioactive material left in the rocks. Choice (C) is incorrect because carbon-14 dating can date only items that were once living organisms. Carbon dating is accurate to about fifty thousand years.

100. (D) Inertia is the tendency of an object to remain stationary or to be in motion. Objects resist any change in their motion. An object at rest will continue at rest, while an object in motion will continue moving in the same direction and at the same speed unless acted upon by some outside force, such as gravity or friction. Choice (D) results from the rotation of the earth.

101. (D) All planets and moons are visible *only* by the sunlight reflected from them. Only stars (suns) have an independent source of constant light, from the nuclear reactions taking place in their thermonuclear cores. All other planetary objects depend on reflected starlight to be seen. The exterior composition of a planetary object does, in part, determine how light is reflected. Mars is conspicuous for its red light, a result of the fact that the other colors in sunlight tend to be absorbed by the Martian surface. Choice (C) is incorrect because the statement deals with the *core,* which would not affect the reflected color.

102. (C) Choices (A), (B), and (D) are all examples of symbiosis, a relationship in which dissimilar organisms live in close association. Such relationships may be beneficial to both organisms or just to one. For example, in the symbiotic relationship between whales and barnacles, the barnacle attaches itself to the whale, getting both transportation and protection. The relationship between a fox and a chicken is an example of a predator/prey relationship, not symbiosis, because the two animals do not live in close association.

V. Visual and Performing Arts

103. (B) Isadora Duncan believed that the regimented and codified steps associated with classical dance are sterile and restrictive. Duncan also believed that all movement is appropriate to dance. She emphasized expressing the body in motion rather than adhering to the "correctness" of classical technique and is generally credited with initiating the modern dance movement (early twentieth century), calling for both free expression and the dancer's inner interpretation of the music to guide all dance movements. She considered the music of the great composers (such as Beethoven, Bach, Chopin, and Wagner) as particularly suited to her dance style (D). Prior to Duncan, the nonballet works of the great composers were considered inappropriate for general dance.

104. (C) Agnes de Mille's ballet *Rodeo* (1942) romanticized a traditional American character, the cowboy. Prior to de Mille, the American setting and contemporary American themes were not generally accepted as appropriate topics for ballet. Traditional ballet at this time relied on classic themes from fairy tales and legends. De Mille made use of American folk tradition in her ballets. Her most famous choreography was for the musical *Oklahoma!* (1943) for which she created dance sequences that were an integral part of the plot.

105. (A) An arabesque is a pose in which one arm is extended in front and the other arm and one leg are extended behind, with the leg straight and the toe pointed. Choice (B) refers to an attitude pose, (C) to an entrechat jump, and (D) to a pirouette.

106. (A) The tango originated in Spain, coming to the New World with Spanish colonization. By the early nineteenth century, the Spanish tango had developed into a solo dance for women. The ballroom adaptation of the dance originated in the area of Buenos Aires, Argentina, and although it was at first considered risque, it became enormously popular in the early twentieth century. The tango is characterized by a slow-slow-quick-quick-slow rhythm and the close position and unified movements of the dance partners.

107. (D) Kabuki is vibrant, energetic, and interactive theater. A characteristic of Kabuki is its use of elaborate costumes. Actors often wear layers of clothing which can be removed at critical points in the play to reveal changing or "new" characters. Other characteristics of Kabuki include: (1) The actors do not use masks but rely on heavy make-up to develop characterization. (2) The plots are generally complex. (3) Virtue is rewarded. (4) The actors strike a *mie* stance (a stationary pose) to direct the audience's attention to a key point in the play. (4) The plays last all day. (5) All roles are played by men (women being banned from the stage as undesirable elements). (6) Violent action is displayed in picturesque settings.

108. (A) All playwrights had to conform to the formal structure of an Elizabethan stage. Although theaters varied in size and were of differing shapes (round, square, five sided, eight sided), all recognized theaters shared the following features: a large platform that "thrust" out into the middle of the theater, a door at each side of the stage (stage left and stage right) and a door at the rear of the stage, a "discovery space" with an upper acting area above this space, windows on both sides of the upper stage (balcony area), and a third level that could be used by both actors and musicians. The use of balconies should be evident if you recall the famous scene from *Romeo and Juliet*.

109. (B) Shakespeare's *Hamlet* combines an unfolding mystery and a search for revenge. (Hamlet is determined to avenge his father's death after Hamlet's uncle is discovered to be the killer.) However, it is Hamlet's psychological turmoil that gives the tragedy its unparalleled strength and substance. Hamlet is in conflict with his own feelings, and he questions, to the point of indecisiveness, the consequences of each possible action. However, while waiting to act, he inextricably sets in motion a chain of events that will take the lives of both friend and foe. In the end, Hamlet has his revenge, but at the cost of his own life.

110. (C) In the early stages of blocking, a director would be *least* concerned with the speed of a specific scene. This refinement would be one of the final rehearsal adjustments. In blocking during rehearsals, a director choreographs the position of actors on the stage and is initially concerned with the actors' gross stage movements. As the rehearsals go on, more specific blocking refinements are made. When blocking on one scene is complete, the director continues the process until all scenes have been taken care of.

111. (A) A quartet is a musical ensemble consisting of four pieces or singers. The string quartet typically consists of a first violin, a second violin, a viola, and a cello. Music written specifically for the string quartet is quite common, such as that by Bach Mozart, Haydn, and Mendelssohn.

112. (A) The meter signature 3/4 characterizes a waltz, which is set in the time of one-two-three, one-two-three. The signature is a way to count time. In 3/4 time, 3 means three beats to the measure, and 4 means that a quarter note gets one beat.

113. (C) The primary feature of all rondo structures is a recurring main, or central, theme which alternates with one or more subordinate themes and which begins and ends with the main theme. A simple rondo has only two thematic subjects (AB). The most common rondo form follows the plan ABACA, containing two subordinate themes (B and C), which alternate with the main theme. Binary structure (A) is a two-part structure (AB) which involves two *main* themes. Theme and variation (B) refers to a melody in which the central theme is restated, but in each restatement, there are slight changes, or variations. A canon (C) is a single melody, which enters at different times (for example, as in "Row, Row, Row Your Boat").

114. (B) Complementary colors are directly opposite each other on the color wheel, as are blue and orange, red and green, or yellow and purple (with the first color of each pair here being primary and the second secondary). When mixed together in equal amounts, complementary colors produce brown.

115. (B) The Byzantine period marked a time of religious fervor. Paintings were austere and dehumanized in depicting religious icons to the common person. The art focused on helping the faithful understand their religion; it was not intended to be realistic. The people depicted were symbolic, flat, simplified, and not true to life.

116. (C) The term *asymmetrical* means *not symmetrical,* or *not equally balanced,* but the term does not imply imbalance of the whole. Although the elements on each side of the central line of an asymmetrical painting are not precisely balanced, this lack of pure symmetry makes the work vital and dynamic. Choice (B) defines the characteristics of dominance.

VI. Human Development

117. (A) The teacher is attempting to alter the child's behavior by reinforcing a positive tendency. This strategy is based on the principles of operant conditioning. Operants are defined as all responses that are not triggered by unlearned stimuli. In this example, the teacher waited for the desired operant (raising one's hand) in order to condition the behavior.

118. (B) According to child-oriented play theorists, play should emphasize the *means* (how a game is played) rather than the *ends* (the results of the game). Child-oriented play theorists believe that play activities should create intrinsic motivation and interest; play based solely on satisfying social demands should be avoided. Current research supports the premise that older children engage in more cooperative play activities, while younger children are more likely to play by themselves (D).

119. (A) An independent variable is one that causes or influences another variable. In this case, level of achievement in English is seen to influence self-image.

120. (B) Intelligence tests that favor children whose backgrounds are similar to the norm on which the test was based (that is, that give advantage to one group over another due to the experience of the group's culture) are considered culturally biased. For example, standardized intelligence tests in North America tend to favor white, middle-class children because the tests were standardized using that sample group. For this reason, most intelligence tests are considered unfair to a variety of minority students, a problem that could be addressed by including minority groups in a representative way in determining the sample to be normed.

121. (C) Piaget's stages of cognitive development are so imbedded in current curricular design that a fundamental knowledge of each stage is significant, not only for testing purposes, but also for understanding the conceptual basis for cognitive development. Mental combinations and problem solving and goal-directed behavior are associated with the later stages of the sensorimotor period. According to Piaget, the understanding of object permanence divides the sensorimotor (0–2 years) and preoperational (2–7 years) stages. Emergence of symbolic functions (organizing and forming concepts) cannot proceed until object permanence has been internalized.

122. (C) Most researchers believe that aggression is primarily a learned behavior. Violent cartoon characters often become models of aggression that children attempt to emulate. Bandura's research concluded that children who observe aggression are more likely to imitate aggression. Choice (D) does not specifically address the question asked.

123. (B) In criterion-referenced testing, a child's score is compared against a criterion, or goal, that the child must reach, not against the standard score of others (standardized test scores or nationally normed scores). It should be apparent that a criterion-referenced test cannot provide numbers comparable to an IQ score. Therefore, criterion-referenced testing can meet the guidelines of Public Law 94-142. Minimum-competency tests that set predetermined target scores are criterion based.

124. (B) Kohlberg's cognitive theory of moral development characterizes various attitudes and beliefs that individuals hold. These attitudes are then correlated to cognitive development stages. Kohlberg reasoned that moral thought evolves through a series of developmental stages. According to Kohlberg, the three levels of moral thought are preconventional, conventional, and postconventional. Kohlberg believed that moral development begins with preconventional thought. At this stage, fear of punishment, not moral reasoning, encourages children to obey rules.

125. (C) After conditioning has taken place, it can be assumed that the *conditioned stimulus* (ringing the bell) would elicit a *conditioned response* (salivation). The example represents the classical-conditioning experiment used by Pavlov to condition a dog to salivate at the sound of a bell. This question calls for an understanding of the terms: conditioned stimulus, unconditioned response, unconditioned stimulus (salivating at the sight of food before any conditioning takes place), and conditioned response. In education, behaviorists use conditioning techniques in the form of counterconditioning, extinction, and affective conditioning. Conditioning can alter preexisting attitudes and beliefs.

VII. Physical Education

126. (C) A rigid catching motion often makes catching any thrown object, such as a ball, difficult. When a person attempts to catch a ball, proper catching technique includes the following: the fingers are spread apart in a relaxed manner; the ball should be caught with the pads of the fingers; and the ball is visually tracked until the catch is made. By bringing the ball "into" the body after initial contact is made, the force of the object can be absorbed over a longer period of time. This is easily demonstated during an egg-toss game. A rigid catching technique results in a broken egg.

127. (C) A structured movement incorportes specific, quantifiable skills. Therefore, structured skills impose limitations on the activity being performed. Since the activity can be quantified, it can be judged as to its "correctness." Unstructured activities—(A), (B), and (D)— allow the individual to make fundamental decisions that determine the outcome of the activity.

128. (D) Anabolic steroids are derivatives of the male hormone testosterone. Steroids are used by athletes as "program enhancers" in that steroid use can increase body mass and muscular strength. The side effects of steroids are largely detrimental, including reproductive abnormalities, liver problems, increased body hair, and increased incidence of adult acne. Also, the potential for prolonged steroid use to induce adverse psychological side effects is well documented. High-density lipoproteins (C) are actually *decreased*. Anabolic steroids and related compounds have been banned by the United States Olympic Committee and are considered controlled substances in many countries.

129. (D) Breaking down an activity into its component parts facilitates learning. Individualized instruction provides the maximum opportunity to improve on the locomotor skill of skipping. Choice (B) could actually reinforce negative self-image.

130. (A) Rhythmics should be introduced in kindergarten and should represent approximately forty percent of all physical education activities. Rhythmic activities develop gross-motor movements and locomotor patterns and also aid in the development of social interaction. Movement expression through rhythmics and dance affords the primary-level child greater expression in interpreting his or her environment. A drum is a typical primary-grade object used to reinforce movement-in-time and rhythmics.

131. (C) Only brisk walking (of the choices given) would be considered an aerobic activity. The purpose of aerobic conditioning (continuous activities for at least thirty minutes at a time) is to improve the cardiorespiratory system. Aerobic activities should allow an individual to reach and maintain his or her target heart rate. Flexibility exercises (D) would not necessarily provide the basis for aerobic conditioning.

132. (D) All choices are beneficial aspects of proper warm-up exercises. Warm-up activities elevate the body's temperature and increase the breakdown of oxyhemoglobin. (Oxyhemoglobin provides oxygen to working muscles.) Decreasing muscle viscosity improves mechanical efficiency and power; injuries often result from connective tissues which are cold and have low blood saturation.

133. (C) A lateral deviation in posture indicates that the spinal column is asymmetrical. The spinal column often appears to resemble an S-curve, with one shoulder higher than the other. Choice (B) is an indicator of poor posture but does not signify a lateral deviation. The degree of the forward/backward plane of the body can also indicate improper posture.

134. (B) Mimetics, mimicking an action, is often used to develop basic concepts associated with learning new motor skills. The purpose of mimetics is to imitate an action generally carried out with an implement without actually using that implement (such as a ball or bat). The child using this approach can concentrate on the mechanics of the skill without the potential interference of an introduced object.

CONTENT AREA EXERCISES 1

I. Literature and Language Studies

1.   THE MAN HE KILLED

       "Had he and I but met
       By some old ancient inn,
   We should have sat us down to wet
       Right many a nipperkin!

(5)   "But ranged as infantry,
       And staring face to face,
   I shot at him as he at me,
       And killed him in his place.

       "I shot him dead because—
(10)   Because he was my foe,
Just so: my foe of course he was;
       That's clear enough; although

       "He thought he'd 'list, perhaps,
       Off-hand like—just as I;
(15) Was out of work, had sold his traps—
       No other reason why.

       "Yes; quaint and curious war is!
       You shoot a fellow down
   You'd treat if met where any bar is,
(20)   Or help to half-a-crown."

THOMAS HARDY

Discuss the meaning of the third stanza of the poem above and how it functions in the structure of the poem.

    The third stanza begins confidently but breaks off after the "because." The repetition of "Because" at the beginning of the second line suggests that the soldier is groping for an answer, and all he can come up with is the vague cliché "he was my foe." Even with this answer, he fails to convince himself, so he must insist to himself that this is a sufficient explanation: "Just so . . . of course he was." His hesitations convince us that he is not convinced. He insists that it is "clear," but the stanza ends suspended, hanging on the "although." This stanza is the turning point of the poem, revealing the doubts of the speaker, who seemed confident in the first two stanzas.

2. Name and discuss three major elements of the novel.

Three major elements of the novel include plot, setting, and characterization.

The plot is the story line, including all the events and their connection to one another. The events may be presented chronologically or by other methods such as the flashback. Plot is often said to move from exposition to rising action to climax to falling action to resolution.

The setting includes the physical location in which the action takes place (for example, New York City) , the time it takes place (for example, in December), and the historical era in which it takes place (for example, during World War II).

Characterization involves the depiction of the people of the novel including both their physical and mental attributes. Characterization can be achieved directly by the author, who tells us about the person, through the eyes of another character, through the eyes of the character himself or herself, and through dialogue.

3. Discuss the differences between analytical and descriptive writing.

Analytical writing is dissective writing. Its focus is on explanation of how something works—such as an argument, a problem, a philosophy, a machine, or a recipe. For example, in considering a poem, one might write an analytical essay dealing with what the poem means and how that meaning is created through diction, imagery, structure, and tone. In considering a problem in algebra, one might write an analytical discussion dealing with the background knowledge needed to solve the problem, the variables involved, and the steps required to solve for each variable. The tone of the analytical writing itself is often cool and reasoned.

Descriptive writing is evocative writing. Its intention is to evoke through its language both intellectual and emotional response from the reader. It frequently appeals to the senses, inviting the reader, through its images, to see, hear, smell, feel, and taste, Descriptive writing often uses the type of language that analytical writing might dissect.

4. The Inuit language has many different words for snow, while the English language has only a few. Explain why the Inuits would have so many ways to refer to snow.

Languages change as the cultures of those who speak them change. For example, consider the explosion of terms in late twentieth century English having to do with computers. We create words to reflect the world we find ourselves in.

Snow is a very important part of the Inuits' lives. Because of its significance, Inuits must have precise language to reflect the distinctions between different types of snow—for example, new-fallen snow, powdery snow, snow that's good for tracking, old snow, and icy snow. Since snow is not as significant in the lives of most English-speaking people, fewer distinctions need to be made; therefore, only a few words describing types of snow are necessary.

II. Mathematics

5.   **Total: 40 Hours of Office Work**

10 hours typing
4 hours clerical
20 hours computer data entry
6 hours telephone answering

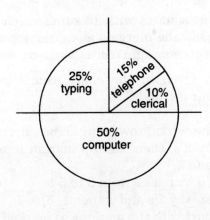

· Use the circle above to construct a pie chart showing percentages to reflect the office work. Explain the reason for the size of each of the sections.

10 hours of typing out of 40 total hours is 10/40 = 1/4 = 25%.

4 hours of clerical out of 40 total hours is 4/40 = 1/10 = 10%.

20 hours computer data entry out of 40 total hours is 20/40 = 1/2 = 50%.

6 hours telephone answering out of 40 total hours is 6/40 = 3/20 = 15%.

6. If x is an even integer, then $x(x + 1)(x + 2)$ is also an even integer. How do you know that this is true? Show and explain two methods.

To show that if x is an even integer, then x(x + 1)(x + 2) is also an even integer, simply select an even integer, plug in, and show the outcome.

Let x = 2.

Then 2(2 + 1)(2 + 2) = 2(3)(4) = 24, which is an even integer.

Another method is to realize that if x is an even integer, (x + 1) is an odd integer and (x + 2) is an even integer. Now, multiplying an even integer times an odd integer times an even integer gives an even integer.

7.

+	2	4	6	8
1	3	5	7	9
3	5	7	9	11
5	7	9	11	13
7	9	11	13	15

The chart above contains squares with 16 sums which result from the addition of positive integers located in the margins along the top row and the left side of the chart. These integers in each margin increase in a consistent pattern.

Using the information given in the chart, complete the chart, including the margins, and explain your methods.

Since the numbers in the second row going across increase by 2's and the numbers in the third row increase by 2's, then the top margin must increase by 2's. The top margin is therefore 2, 4, 6, and 8.

Since the second column increases from 3 to 5 to ____ to 9, it increases by 2's. The left margin must then increase by 2's and is then 1, 3, 5, 7.

So this is an addition chart with the margins as marked in the chart.

8.

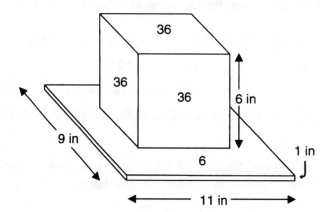

The cube above is glued onto a rectangular piece of wood one inch thick, which is sitting on a table. If you wanted to paint the complete surface that is exposed, except the one-inch edge of the rectangular piece of wood, what is the measure of the surface area that needs to be painted? Show your work and explain your steps.

To find the exposed area of the structure, find the surface area by section. First, find the surface area of the cube. Since the edge is 6″, then each face is 6 × 6, or 36 sq in. Multiply 36 sq in by 5, the number of exposed sides. So the exposed surface area of the cube is 180 sq in.

Next, find the exposed surface area of the rectangular piece of wood, excluding the edge. To do this, multiply the length times the width, which is 11″ × 9″, or 99 sq in.

Now, subtract 36 sq in, the area covered by the glued cube, and you are left with 63 sq in. Add this 63 sq in to the 180 sq in, and you have 243 sq in of surface area.

III. Visual and Performing Arts

9. How can stage lighting create mood and atmosphere in a modern theater production? Include specific examples to support your answer.

Stage lighting dramatically increases the artistic potential of any dramatic presentation. Theaters in the twentieth century are generally designed to be "light-tight." The lighting director can fully illuminate, partially illuminate, or withhold light to focus attention on a specific actor and control the visual focus of the audience.

Sidelights, overhead lights, and stage lights are interconnected in order to provide a coordinated visual and sensory effect for a scene. Theater lighting has the capacity to transform white light into a mood-altering array of colors. The proper use of the "mixing of light" can manipulate emotions and allow the audience to more fully experience the depth of a character.

10. Modern dance developed in the early 1900s. Briefly discuss specific reasons that leaders of this new movement broke with earlier dance tradition. How did Isadora Duncan influence the modern dance movement?

Isadora Duncan, who danced in the early twentieth century, was the classic exponent of this new, free, and expressive dance form. Her loose-fitting garments and stark stage backgrounds focused visual attention on the dancer's interpretation of the music. Duncan revolutionized dance interpretation by freeing the dancer from the restraints inherent in structured dancing. Duncan attempted to imitate nature in dance through experimentation and innovation, not rules and steps.

Modern dance, as Duncan envisioned it, had few restraints. She rejected traditional dance costumes (tutu, tights, and toe slippers) as obstructive to natural movement. The only limitation on expression was a dancer's ability to reach inward in "discovering" personalized movement. Tumbling and gymnastics could be incorporated into a dance routine. Dancers were also encouraged to experiment in creating patterns, angles, and shapes with their bodies.

IV. Human Development

11. Piaget discovered that there are developmental learning processes by which children arrive at answers to problems. How would Piagetian levels explain the following observation?

A child thinks the following two rows have a total of eight objects

OOOO
OOOO

but thinks that the following rows have a different total number of objects.

OO
OOO
OO
O

The example given represents Piaget's conservation of number stage. The child understands one-to-one correspondence and counting. This, however, does not mean that the child understands number. Children who reach the concrete operations stage (usually starting at the age of seven) are able to understand reversibility (the concept that the operation can be reversed) and conservation of number (the properties of objects). During this stage, operational thought appears; the child can order experiences into a whole.

This child did not establish "lasting equivalence." Perceptual factors (the way the symbols were arranged) caused the child to "see" different total number of objects. Through trial and error, children eventually begin to realize that objects that are spread out or bunched together do not change in number.

12. List the dominant abilities of the left and right hemispheres of the brain. What implications does this research hold for teachers?

Left-hemisphere functions: language, writing, logic, math, science, sequential ordering, and organization.

Right-hemisphere functions: spatial relationships, perception, aesthetics, art, music, dance, and fantasy.

Most researchers indicate that current educational practices emphasize left-hemisphere functions. This is evidenced by the importance in the core curriculum of the language arts, math, science, and logic. Left-brain people are able to see individual parts but have difficulty seeing the whole.

Right-brain functions are generally not emphasized in most curricular areas. Right-brain individuals have a strong connection to emotions and are better able to see patterns in things.

The goal of education should be to educate the whole child, or "both halves" of the brain. This would foster synchronous thinking and lead to self-actualization. Therefore, increased emphasis on the performing arts, aesthetic appreciation, and creativity should be incorporated into all curricular areas.

V. Physical Education

13. List six health-related risk factors for cardiovascular disease. How can a comprehensive health-related physical fitness program reduce health-risk factors? What does current research indicate about this subject?

1. Lack of exercise
2. Obesity
3. Heredity (a genetic component)
4. Smoking
5. Elevated cholesterol (above 200)
6. High blood pressure (diastolic above 115, systolic above 160)

A physical fitness program that emphasizes aerobic activities will reduce most health-related risk factors. By increasing the capacity of the lungs to transport oxygen to the body, cardiovascular fitness is greatly improved. This, in turn, improves coronary circulation, lowers the heart rate and blood pressure, reduces blood fat, and increases protective HDL lipids. Health-related fitness also leads to decreased body fat. A comprehensive fitness program also reduces stress and provides ongoing behavior modification for at-risk individuals.

Recent intervention studies conducted by UCLA and by the American Heart Association clearly indicate a direct beneficial relationship between proper exercise and preventing degenerative disease. This is especially evident in cardiovascular studies.

14. Briefly discuss two motor-development patterns that are prerequisites for a fourteen-year-old to efficiently throw a forward pass during a football game.

One necessary motor-development pattern is having adequate depth perception. Without depth perception, the passer cannot visualize proper pass routes or determine the appropriate distance to lead a receiver who is attempting to catch a pass.

Another motor-development pattern is reaction time. To effectively throw a forward pass during a game, there must be a split-second reaction between the time the passer receives the ball and correctly determines what to do with the ball. For example, the passer moves away from the line, adjusts the ball in his or her hand, and picks out a receiver in the context of moving bodies and defensive players attempting to stop the execution of the play.

CONTENT AREA EXERCISES 2

I. History/Social Sciences

1. In the 1988 presidential election, only fifty-three percent of eligible U.S. citizens voted. Briefly discuss four key factors to explain limited voter participation in national elections.

   1. Voter apathy is a primary factor in explaining the low percentage of registered voters who participated in national elections. Many individuals felt that a single vote made little difference in determining the outcome of an election.

   2. There is a distance on the part of voters from the decision-making process. For many, it is difficult to be involved directly in the election process due to financial limitations and time commitments.

   3. The similarity of the two parties promotes apathy. There are few substantive differences between the parties. This factor has led to increased voter disenchantment with the political process.

   4. Pre-election polls and the influence of the media foster the belief that the election outcome is predetermined.

2. Describe how the geography of Egypt influenced the area's historical growth.

   Egypt was called the "Gift of the Nile" and became an early "cradle of civilization" because of its favorable geographic features. The development of agriculture was linked to geography because the annual flooding of the Nile was predictable and nondestructive. Almost all Egyptians lived or worked on the banks of the Nile.

   Egypt was not generally subject to invasion because of its naturally defensible borders, the desert and the Mediterranean Sea. Egypt's distance from other civilizations in Mesopotamia and the fertile crescent also hindered invasion.

   Inventions and technology were tied to geography. The Nile was associated with the development of paper (papyrus), canals for irrigation, building materials, and the development of the sail and surveying. Geography also influenced religion because many gods were associated with the Nile.

3. The progressive reform movement swept America in the early twentieth century. Why was the presidential election of 1912 a bench mark for progressivism? Discuss three important progressive reforms at the national level implemented by the Democratic and Republican parties.

The progressive movement (1908–24) attempted to reduce the power of big business and make government more democratic. All major political parties in the election of 1912 favored some form of progressive reform. Even Taft, the Republican candidate, supported a minor progressive agenda. The election results overwhelmingly showed support for the progressive movement. Wilson, a progressive Democrat, easily won the election over Taft. Wilson was helped enormously by the third-party candidacy of Teddy Roosevelt, running on the Progressive party ticket.

Progressive reforms at the national level included the Seventeenth Amendment (the direct election of senators), which was intended to reduce "boss" rule, and the Nineteenth Amendment (women's suffrage). The Clayton Anti-Trust Act was passed by Congress to reduce the monopolistic practices of big business.

4. Discuss how the triangular trade connected New England, Africa, and the West Indies in the seventeenth century. Include in your answer the products exchanged and the significance of the "middle passage" as an example of inhumane practices.

The triangular trade was synonymous with the infamies associated with the slave trade.

There were three phases in the triangular trade. The first phase involved ships coming from Europe to Africa in order to exchange goods for black slaves. This segment was centered on the west coast of Africa. The next phase was the most horrific. During this "middle passage" to the Atlantic coast, human beings were kept in deplorable conditions. The slaves were chained below deck and packed together so tightly that disease and death were commonplace. Upon arriving, the slaves were sold for huge profits.

During the last phase, the traders purchased sugar, coffee, and tobacco in the West Indies for transport to Europe.

II. Science

5. Discuss three key characteristics of asexual reproduction. Give examples from the plant and animal kingdoms and include regeneration in your answer.

In asexual reproduction, both male and female reproductive organs are on the same individual. The production of an offspring is by one parent only, and ony one set of sex cells is involved. The sex cell splits into two cells. Asexual reproduction explains how, by regeneration, skin and bone cells reproduce and how damaged tissues regrow, as in the worm, sponge, or hydra.

Many fruits, vegetables, bulbs, and flowers reproduce asexually. Plant tissue is capable (usually on the tips and roots) of dividing into new cells, which explains why cuttings will propagate into new individuals. The genetic component is identical.

6. List and discuss four reasons that can be cited as evidence for the continental drift theory.

    1. Paleontology: Evidence indicates the similarity of fossils in the Americas, Europe, and Asia.

    2. Continental "jigsaw puzzle": The outlines of the continents seem to fit together—for example, the eastern coast of South America and the western coast of Africa.

    3. Ocean bottom: The ocean floor is not stationary. Continents, in response to ocean-floor movement, are spreading apart. The ocean floor expands in opposite directions, spreading continents apart and away from the mid-Atlantic ridge.

    4. Paleoclimatology (study of ancient climates): Glacial deposits suggest that a single glaciation covered the continents at the same general time. Also, ancient coral reefs (associated with warm water) are found in areas that could not currently support such growth.

7. Which of the following diagrams shows a situation in which more force would be needed, and which shows one in which less force would be needed? Discuss the lifting principles involved in the diagrams.

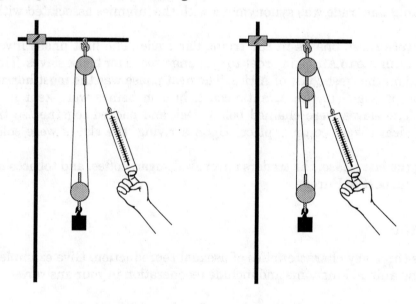

Diagram 1   *Diagram 2*

Diagram one would require more force.
Diagram two would require less force.

    The pulley device will change the direction of the force, or give the person using the device a mechanical advantage. The change of direction allows an individual to pull downward. The load (item lifted) can be raised only as high as the support holding the pulley.

Diagram one represents a double pulley. As effort is applied (pulling power), and the load (weight) is raised. In this system, the load moves only half the distance that the rope is pulled. However, the force raising the load is double the effort pulling the rope.

Diagram two represents a multiple-pulley system. In this system, less strength is used to accomplish the same lifting height as in diagram one. The work load does not change; however, less force, and consequently less effort, is needed.

8. The two structures below show changes in the earth's crust. Briefly discuss the forces present in each structure.

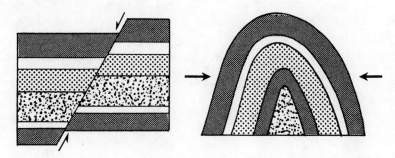

Structure one represents a vertical fault (one side of the fault is higher than the other side). A vertical fault forms when pressure within the earth's crust becomes so great that it causes associated rock layers to break. The fault slippage can be either upward or downward as indicated by the arrows.

Structure two represents forces within the earth's crust which cause associated rock layers to fold, or bend. Rocks that are deeply buried are subject to intense pressures and temperatures and can become plastic (fluid) and begin to fold. The folds are produced by tremendous horizontal compression. Some folds can be classified as being anticline (folded upward like an arch) or syncline (folded downward like a trough).

PRACTICE TEST 2

Answer Sheet for Practice Test 2

1. Ⓐ Ⓑ Ⓒ Ⓓ	35. Ⓐ Ⓑ Ⓒ Ⓓ	69. Ⓐ Ⓑ Ⓒ Ⓓ	103. Ⓐ Ⓑ Ⓒ Ⓓ
2. Ⓐ Ⓑ Ⓒ Ⓓ	36. Ⓐ Ⓑ Ⓒ Ⓓ	70. Ⓐ Ⓑ Ⓒ Ⓓ	104. Ⓐ Ⓑ Ⓒ Ⓓ
3. Ⓐ Ⓑ Ⓒ Ⓓ	37. Ⓐ Ⓑ Ⓒ Ⓓ	71. Ⓐ Ⓑ Ⓒ Ⓓ	105. Ⓐ Ⓑ Ⓒ Ⓓ
4. Ⓐ Ⓑ Ⓒ Ⓓ	38. Ⓐ Ⓑ Ⓒ Ⓓ	72. Ⓐ Ⓑ Ⓒ Ⓓ	106. Ⓐ Ⓑ Ⓒ Ⓓ
5. Ⓐ Ⓑ Ⓒ Ⓓ	39. Ⓐ Ⓑ Ⓒ Ⓓ	73. Ⓐ Ⓑ Ⓒ Ⓓ	107. Ⓐ Ⓑ Ⓒ Ⓓ
6. Ⓐ Ⓑ Ⓒ Ⓓ	40. Ⓐ Ⓑ Ⓒ Ⓓ	74. Ⓐ Ⓑ Ⓒ Ⓓ	108. Ⓐ Ⓑ Ⓒ Ⓓ
7. Ⓐ Ⓑ Ⓒ Ⓓ	41. Ⓐ Ⓑ Ⓒ Ⓓ	75. Ⓐ Ⓑ Ⓒ Ⓓ	109. Ⓐ Ⓑ Ⓒ Ⓓ
8. Ⓐ Ⓑ Ⓒ Ⓓ	42. Ⓐ Ⓑ Ⓒ Ⓓ	76. Ⓐ Ⓑ Ⓒ Ⓓ	110. Ⓐ Ⓑ Ⓒ Ⓓ
9. Ⓐ Ⓑ Ⓒ Ⓓ	43. Ⓐ Ⓑ Ⓒ Ⓓ	77. Ⓐ Ⓑ Ⓒ Ⓓ	111. Ⓐ Ⓑ Ⓒ Ⓓ
10. Ⓐ Ⓑ Ⓒ Ⓓ	44. Ⓐ Ⓑ Ⓒ Ⓓ	78. Ⓐ Ⓑ Ⓒ Ⓓ	112. Ⓐ Ⓑ Ⓒ Ⓓ
11. Ⓐ Ⓑ Ⓒ Ⓓ	45. Ⓐ Ⓑ Ⓒ Ⓓ	79. Ⓐ Ⓑ Ⓒ Ⓓ	113. Ⓐ Ⓑ Ⓒ Ⓓ
12. Ⓐ Ⓑ Ⓒ Ⓓ	46. Ⓐ Ⓑ Ⓒ Ⓓ	80. Ⓐ Ⓑ Ⓒ Ⓓ	114. Ⓐ Ⓑ Ⓒ Ⓓ
13. Ⓐ Ⓑ Ⓒ Ⓓ	47. Ⓐ Ⓑ Ⓒ Ⓓ	81. Ⓐ Ⓑ Ⓒ Ⓓ	115. Ⓐ Ⓑ Ⓒ Ⓓ
14. Ⓐ Ⓑ Ⓒ Ⓓ	48. Ⓐ Ⓑ Ⓒ Ⓓ	82. Ⓐ Ⓑ Ⓒ Ⓓ	116. Ⓐ Ⓑ Ⓒ Ⓓ
15. Ⓐ Ⓑ Ⓒ Ⓓ	49. Ⓐ Ⓑ Ⓒ Ⓓ	83. Ⓐ Ⓑ Ⓒ Ⓓ	117. Ⓐ Ⓑ Ⓒ Ⓓ
16. Ⓐ Ⓑ Ⓒ Ⓓ	50. Ⓐ Ⓑ Ⓒ Ⓓ	84. Ⓐ Ⓑ Ⓒ Ⓓ	118. Ⓐ Ⓑ Ⓒ Ⓓ
17. Ⓐ Ⓑ Ⓒ Ⓓ	51. Ⓐ Ⓑ Ⓒ Ⓓ	85. Ⓐ Ⓑ Ⓒ Ⓓ	119. Ⓐ Ⓑ Ⓒ Ⓓ
18. Ⓐ Ⓑ Ⓒ Ⓓ	52. Ⓐ Ⓑ Ⓒ Ⓓ	86. Ⓐ Ⓑ Ⓒ Ⓓ	120. Ⓐ Ⓑ Ⓒ Ⓓ
19. Ⓐ Ⓑ Ⓒ Ⓓ	53. Ⓐ Ⓑ Ⓒ Ⓓ	87. Ⓐ Ⓑ Ⓒ Ⓓ	121. Ⓐ Ⓑ Ⓒ Ⓓ
20. Ⓐ Ⓑ Ⓒ Ⓓ	54. Ⓐ Ⓑ Ⓒ Ⓓ	88. Ⓐ Ⓑ Ⓒ Ⓓ	122. Ⓐ Ⓑ Ⓒ Ⓓ
21. Ⓐ Ⓑ Ⓒ Ⓓ	55. Ⓐ Ⓑ Ⓒ Ⓓ	89. Ⓐ Ⓑ Ⓒ Ⓓ	123. Ⓐ Ⓑ Ⓒ Ⓓ
22. Ⓐ Ⓑ Ⓒ Ⓓ	56. Ⓐ Ⓑ Ⓒ Ⓓ	90. Ⓐ Ⓑ Ⓒ Ⓓ	124. Ⓐ Ⓑ Ⓒ Ⓓ
23. Ⓐ Ⓑ Ⓒ Ⓓ	57. Ⓐ Ⓑ Ⓒ Ⓓ	91. Ⓐ Ⓑ Ⓒ Ⓓ	125. Ⓐ Ⓑ Ⓒ Ⓓ
24. Ⓐ Ⓑ Ⓒ Ⓓ	58. Ⓐ Ⓑ Ⓒ Ⓓ	92. Ⓐ Ⓑ Ⓒ Ⓓ	126. Ⓐ Ⓑ Ⓒ Ⓓ
25. Ⓐ Ⓑ Ⓒ Ⓓ	59. Ⓐ Ⓑ Ⓒ Ⓓ	93. Ⓐ Ⓑ Ⓒ Ⓓ	127. Ⓐ Ⓑ Ⓒ Ⓓ
26. Ⓐ Ⓑ Ⓒ Ⓓ	60. Ⓐ Ⓑ Ⓒ Ⓓ	94. Ⓐ Ⓑ Ⓒ Ⓓ	128. Ⓐ Ⓑ Ⓒ Ⓓ
27. Ⓐ Ⓑ Ⓒ Ⓓ	61. Ⓐ Ⓑ Ⓒ Ⓓ	95. Ⓐ Ⓑ Ⓒ Ⓓ	129. Ⓐ Ⓑ Ⓒ Ⓓ
28. Ⓐ Ⓑ Ⓒ Ⓓ	62. Ⓐ Ⓑ Ⓒ Ⓓ	96. Ⓐ Ⓑ Ⓒ Ⓓ	130. Ⓐ Ⓑ Ⓒ Ⓓ
29. Ⓐ Ⓑ Ⓒ Ⓓ	63. Ⓐ Ⓑ Ⓒ Ⓓ	97. Ⓐ Ⓑ Ⓒ Ⓓ	131. Ⓐ Ⓑ Ⓒ Ⓓ
30. Ⓐ Ⓑ Ⓒ Ⓓ	64. Ⓐ Ⓑ Ⓒ Ⓓ	98. Ⓐ Ⓑ Ⓒ Ⓓ	132. Ⓐ Ⓑ Ⓒ Ⓓ
31. Ⓐ Ⓑ Ⓒ Ⓓ	65. Ⓐ Ⓑ Ⓒ Ⓓ	99. Ⓐ Ⓑ Ⓒ Ⓓ	133. Ⓐ Ⓑ Ⓒ Ⓓ
32. Ⓐ Ⓑ Ⓒ Ⓓ	66. Ⓐ Ⓑ Ⓒ Ⓓ	100. Ⓐ Ⓑ Ⓒ Ⓓ	134. Ⓐ Ⓑ Ⓒ Ⓓ
33. Ⓐ Ⓑ Ⓒ Ⓓ	67. Ⓐ Ⓑ Ⓒ Ⓓ	101. Ⓐ Ⓑ Ⓒ Ⓓ	
34. Ⓐ Ⓑ Ⓒ Ⓓ	68. Ⓐ Ⓑ Ⓒ Ⓓ	102. Ⓐ Ⓑ Ⓒ Ⓓ	

CONTENT KNOWLEDGE

Time: 2 Hours
134 Questions

Directions: Each of the following questions or incomplete statements is followed by four possible answers or completions. Choose the answer or completion that is best in each case.

I. Literature and Language Studies

Questions 1–3 refer to the following poem by John Milton.

> How soon hath Time, the subtle thief of youth,
> Stolen on his wing my three-and-twentieth year!
> My hasting days fly on with full career,
> But my late spring no bud or blossom show'th.

1. The subject and direct object in lines 1–2 are
   (A) "Time" and "wing"
   (B) "thief" and "wing"
   (C) "Time" and "year"
   (D) "thief" and "year"

2. The phrase "late spring" is a metaphor for
   (A) infertility
   (B) the speaker's hopes
   (C) a season of promise
   (D) the speaker's age

3. In line 4, both "bud" and "blossom" are examples of
   (A) personification
   (B) metaphor
   (C) paradox
   (D) literary allusion

4. (1) On the other hand, scores in the high schools have improved. (2) After four years of improvement, scores on reading tests for junior high school students have declined slightly. (3) They have vowed to do something about the decline right away. (4) Educators were dismayed by this change of direction.

Which of the following is the most logical order of the four sentences in the paragraph above?
(A) 1–4–3–2
(B) 2–3–4–1
(C) 2–1–4–3
(D) 4–2–3–1

5. Of the following elements, which is the LEAST likely to appear in a conventional gothic romance?
(A) A dark, mysterious hero
(B) A large mansion in a remote setting
(C) A young and innocent heroine
(D) A wicked stepmother

6. Which of the following historical events probably most influenced the English poets of the Romantic era?
(A) The defeat of the Spanish Armada
(B) The potato famine in Ireland
(C) The French Revolution
(D) The invention of steam-powered looms

7. All of the following terms refer to a kind of novel EXCEPT
(A) mystery
(B) picaresque
(C) epistolary
(D) epic

Questions 8–10 refer to the following poem by Ralph Waldo Emerson.

> The cup of life is not so shallow
> That we have drained the best,
> That all the wine at once we swallow
> And lees make all the rest.
>
> (5) Maids of as soft a bloom shall marry
> As Hymen yet hath blessed,
> And fairer forms are in the quarry
> Than Phidias released.

8. Which of the following best states the theme of this poem?
(A) Art is more lasting than the artist who created it.
(B) Human life is not in decline.
(C) So long as we remain hopeful, life will get better.
(D) The arts of the past surpass those of the present.

9. The Phidias referred to in the final line of the poem is
   (A) a writer
   (B) a sculptor
   (C) a military hero
   (D) a political figure

10. The poem uses a slant rhyme, or off rhyme, in all of the following EXCEPT
    (A) lines 1 and 3
    (B) lines 2 and 4
    (C) lines 5 and 7
    (D) lines 6 and 8

11. The root word "meter" (as in "perimeter") means
    (A) around
    (B) distance
    (C) weight
    (D) measure

12. All of the following words could be used to introduce the conclusion of an argument EXCEPT
    (A) unless
    (B) hence
    (C) thus
    (D) therefore

13. (1) According to recent studies, it certainly can. (2) Consequently, environmentalists are filing suit against six plumbing manufacturers. (3) Tests in Oregon have shown that lead contamination from faucets is a hundred times higher than the state's standard. (4) Can an old or new faucet be dangerous?

    Which of the following is the most logical order of the four sentences in the paragraph above?
    (A) 4–3–2–1
    (B) 4–1–3–2
    (C) 3–4–1–2
    (D) 2–3–1–4

14. In most dictionaries, the explanation of the meaning of pronunciation symbols is usually found
    (A) at the beginning of the dictionary
    (B) in an appendix of the dictionary
    (C) at the bottom of each page
    (D) with each word, before the definition of the word

15. Which of the following is not properly treated as a classic of children's literature?
    (A) *The Wind in the Willows*
    (B) *Gulliver's Travels*
    (C) *The Wizard of Oz*
    (D) *Grimm's Fairy-Tales*

16. In Italy, all operas, even operas written in English are sung in Italian. But in English-speaking countries, Italian operas are rarely sung in English.

    The passage above introduces a discussion of opera in English by means of a
    (A) metaphor
    (B) comparison
    (C) hypothesis
    (D) syllogism

17. A topic outline is unlike a sentence outline for all of the following reasons EXCEPT:
    (A) An entry may be only a single word.
    (B) All its entries are brief.
    (C) It begins with the main idea, or thesis.
    (D) Its entries are rarely written as complete sentences.

Questions 18–20 refer to the following excerpt from Shakespeare's *Hamlet*.

> *Hamlet:* Now I am alone!
> O what a rogue and peasant slave am I!
> Is it not monstrous that this player here,
> But in a fiction, in a dream of passion,
> (5) Could force his soul so to his own conceit
> That from her working all his visage wanned,
> Tears in his eyes, distraction in his aspect,
> A broken voice, and his whole function suiting
> With forms to his conceit?

18. This passage is an example of a
    (A) dramatic monologue
    (B) dialogue in verse
    (C) soliloquy
    (D) oration

19. The passage is written in
    (A) unrhymed couplets
    (B) blank verse
    (C) iambic hexameter
    (D) ballad stanza

20. All of the following are used synonymously in this passage EXCEPT
    (A) "fiction," line 4
    (B) "dream," line 4
    (C) "visage," line 6
    (D) "conceit," line 9

21. Which part of the word "infinitesimal" means "limited"?
    (A) in
    (B) finite
    (C) tes
    (D) mal

22.   How weary, stale, flat, and unprofitable
                        Seem to me all the uses of the world.

    The attitude expressed in the lines above is which of the following?
    (A) Resigned loyalty
    (B) Curious precision
    (C) Unqualified surrender
    (D) Absolute disdain

23.   No coward soul is mine,
                    No trembler in the world's storm-troubled sphere:
                        I see Heaven's glories shine,
                    And faith shines equal, arming me from fear.

    In the preceding lines of poetry by Emily Brontë, the word "arming" means
    (A) guarding
    (B) pushing
    (C) reaching
    (D) shaking

24. All of the following words connect contrasting ideas EXCEPT
    (A) in spite of
    (B) however
    (C) in addition to
    (D) although

25. The proper syllabication of the word "phenomenon" is
    (A) phen om en on
    (B) phe no men on
    (C) phe nom en on
    (D) phe nom e non

26. The word "anarchy" means lawlessness or lack of government and is derived from
    which of the following languages?
    (A) Anglo-Saxon
    (B) Greek
    (C) French
    (D) Hebrew

27. Which of the following is <u>not</u> a goal of written composition?
    (A) It will develop self-expression.
    (B) It will develop an appreciation for group dynamics.
    (C) It will develop punctuation skills.
    (D) It will develop basic grammar skills.

II. Mathematics

28. Four students received their scores on a math test. Alexis scored higher than Frank, and Caroline scored lower than Frank. Dominique scored higher than Frank but lower than Alexis. Which of the following, from highest to lowest, correctly represents the order of their scores on the test?
    (A) Alexis > Frank > Caroline > Dominique
    (B) Alexis > Frank > Dominique > Caroline
    (C) Alexis > Caroline > Frank > Dominique
    (D) Alexis > Dominique > Frank > Caroline

29.

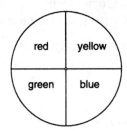

From the diagram of the spinner above, in spinning the spinner only once, what is the probability of spinning red, yellow, or blue?
    (A) 1/4
    (B) 1/3
    (C) 1/2
    (D) 3/4

30.

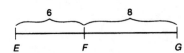

If H is the midpoint of segment EF and J is the midpoint of segment FG, which of the following segments has the greatest value?
    (A) EF
    (B) HJ
    (C) FG
    (D) JG

31.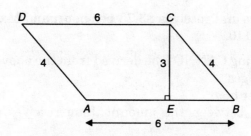

To compute the area of the figure above, one would use
(A) 6 + 3
(B) 6 × 3
(C) 6 × 4
(D) 12 × 3

32. All of the following ratios are equal EXCEPT
(A) 1 to 4
(B) 3 to 8
(C) 2 to 8
(D) 3 to 12

33. $$825.50 + 435.00 = 1260.50$$

Which of the following could be expressed by the number sentence above?
(A) The difference in the cost of housing in two cities, Chicago and Indianapolis
(B) The total amount of money earned in each of two months during the summer vacation
(C) The average of two months' earnings
(D) 435.00 is the result of taking the weight of 825.50 pounds minus some unknown.

34.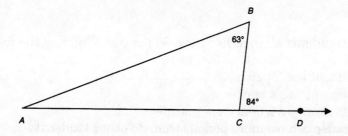

Given $\triangle ABC$ above with $\angle BCD = 84°$ and $\angle B = 63°$, what is the measure of $\angle A$ in degrees?
(A) 21
(B) 27
(C) 84
(D) 96

35. Juan works 8 hours and receives $3.75 per hour, and Mary works 24 hours and receives a total of $110.

    Which of the following CANNOT be derived from the above statement?
    (A) Juan's total wages
    (B) Mary's wage per hour
    (C) The difference between the amount Juan receives and the amount Mary receives
    (D) The hours Mary worked each day

36. The fraction 1/8 is between the numbers listed in which of the following pairs?
    (A) 1/10 and 2/17
    (B) .1 and .12
    (C) 1/9 and 2/15
    (D) 1 and 8

37.

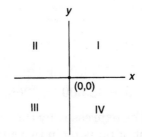

    In the coordinate graph above, the point represented by $(-3, 4)$ would be found in which quadrant?
    (A) I
    (B) II
    (C) III
    (D) IV

38. A class of 30 students all together have 60 pencils. Which of the following must be true?
    (A) Each student has 2 pencils.
    (B) Every student has a pencil.
    (C) The class averages 2 pencils per student.
    (D) Some students have more pencils than do other students.

39.

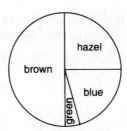

Sam constructs a pie graph as shown above representing eye color of his class-mates. In his class of 24 students, 6 students have blue eyes, 12 students have brown eyes, 5 students have hazel eyes, and 1 student has green eyes. His teacher tells him that his graph is not correct. In order to fix the graph, Sam should
(A) increase the amount of green and decrease the amount of blue
(B) increase the amount of blue and decrease the amount of hazel
(C) decrease the amount of blue and increase the amount of brown
(D) decrease the amount of hazel and increase the amount of brown

40. If D is between A and B on $\overleftrightarrow{AB}$, which of the following must be true?
(A) $AD = DB$
(B) $DB = AB - AD$
(C) $AD = AB + DB$
(D) $DB = AD + AB$

41.
AVERAGE FAMILY'S EXPENSES

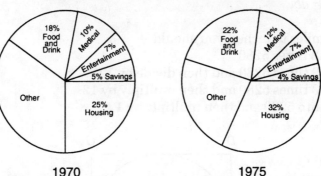

1970
Average Income $12,000

1975
Average Income $16,000

How much more moeny did the average family spend on medical expenses in 1975 than in 1970?
(A) $500–$600
(B) $600–$700
(C) $700–$800
(D) $800–$900

42. In a senior class of 800, only 240 decide to attend the senior prom. What percentage of the senior class attended the senior prom?
    (A) 8%
    (B) 24%
    (C) 30%
    (D) 33%

43. What is the probability of tossing a penny twice so that both times it lands heads up?
    (A) 1/8
    (B) 1/4
    (C) 1/3
    (D) 1/2

44. .0074 is how many times smaller than 740,000?
    (A)   1,000,000
    (B)   10,000,000
    (C)   100,000,000
    (D)   1,000,000,000

45. Which of the following demonstrates the distributive property?
    (A) $a(b + c) = (b + c)a$
    (B) $a(b + c) = a(c + b)$
    (C) $a(b + c) = ab + ac$
    (D) $a(b + c) = abc$

46. To change 3 miles to inches, you should
    (A) multiply 3 times 5280
    (B) multiply 3 times 5280 and then divide by 12
    (C) multiply 3 times 5280 and then multiply by 12
    (D) divide 3 into 5280 and then multiply by 12

47.

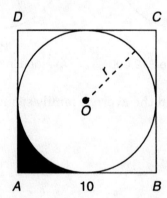

Circle O is inscribed in square $ABCD$ as shown above. The area of the shaded region is approximately
    (A) 10
    (B) 25
    (C) 30
    (D) 50

48. Angela has nickels and dimes in her pocket. She has twice as many dimes as nickels. What is the best expression of the amount of money she has in cents if x equals the number of nickels she has?
    (A) $25x$
    (B) $10x + 5(2x)$
    (C) $x + 2x$
    (D) $5(3x)$

49.

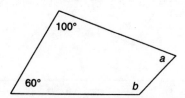

In the quadrilateral above, if the angles are as marked and angle a is less than 70°, the value of angle b must be
    (A) $170° > b > 140°$
    (B) $180° > b > 121°$
    (C) $169° > b > 110°$
    (D) $200° > b > 130°$

50. How many integers between 1 and 75 are divisible by both 4 and 6?
    (A) 4
    (B) 6
    (C) 8
    (D) 12

51. A color television set is marked down 20% to $320. Which of the following equations could be used to determine its original price, P?
    (A) $\$320 - .20 = P$
    (B) $.20P = \$320$
    (C) $P = \$320 + .20$
    (D) $.80P = \$320$

52. Which of the following is the most appropriate unit for describing the weight of a bowling ball?
    (A) Milligrams
    (B) Centigrams
    (C) Grams
    (D) Kilograms

53.

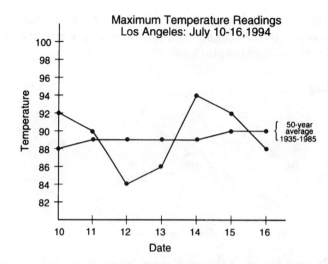

Maximum Temperature Readings
Los Angeles: July 10-16,1994

Of the seven days shown in the graph above, on approximately what percent of the days did the maximum temperature exceed the average temperature?
(A) 3%
(B) 4%
(C) 43%
(D) 57%

54. The sum of two numbers equals one of the numbers.

If the above statement is true, which of the following best represents the relationship?
(A) $x + y = y + x$
(B) $(x)(y) = 1$
(C) $x + y = 1$
(D) $x + y = y$

III. History/Social Sciences

55. The mission system in California was originally intended to be temporary. However, it lasted almost three-fourths of a century. How did the mission system fail to accomplish that for which it was designed?

I. It failed to teach Indians to speak Spanish and to adopt the values of the church.
II. It failed to train useful citizens who could practice a trade.
III. It failed to maintain a self-sufficient agricultural economy that produced a food surplus.

(A) I only
(B) I and II only
(C) II and III only
(D) I, II, and III

56. If a plane left San Francisco and traveled on a direct course to Lake Tahoe, the plane would cross which of the following geographical features?
(A) Mt. Shasta, Central Valley, Cascade Range
(B) Coast Range, Central Valley, Sierra Nevada
(C) Rockies, Mojave Desert, Sierra Nevada
(D) Coast Range, Mt. Whitney, Sequoia National Park

57. *The Octopus,* by Frank Norris, vividly describes the negative impact of which of the following industries on the lives of many California citizens?
(A) The meatpacking industry
(B) The fishing and canning industry
(C) The railroad industry
(D) The oil industry

58. "The proletariat will use its political supremacy to wrest by degrees all capital from the bourgeoisie, to centralize all instruments of production in the hands of the state. . . . The workers have nothing to lose but their chains. They have a world to win. Workers of the world, unite!

The statement above is most closely associated with
(A) Joseph Stalin
(B) Vladimir Lenin
(C) Karl Marx
(D) Leon Trotsky

59.

The wooden statue above is associated with a particular religion. A person who follows this religion would accept which of the following statements as true?
(A) All religions are equally acceptable to all people.
(B) Reincarnation is part of an extended life process.
(C) Meditation cannot replace confession in gaining enlightenment.
(D) The Koran is the direct word of God.

60. Which of the following economic systems would best facilitate the theories of social Darwinism?
    (A) Capitalism
    (B) Socialism
    (C) Communism
    (D) Facism

61.

A COMPARISON OF THREE STATE CONSTITUTIONS

	South Carolina	Pennsylvania	Massachusetts
	President	*Council*	*Governor*
Executive	2-year term, legislature elects, has full veto.	3-year term, voters elect.	1-year term, voters elect, 2/3 vote can override veto.
Upper House	Life term, lower house elects.	None.	1-year term, voters elect.
Judges	Life term, legislature elects.	7-year term, appointed by council.	Life term, appointed by governor.
Voting	100 acres or £60 or pay 10 shillings in taxes.	Pay taxes.	£60 or £3 income from real estate yearly.
Eligibility to Hold Office	500 acres in parish or 500 acres and 10 slaves in county, or £1000.	Pay taxes.	Governor—£1000 real estate; Senator—£300 real estate or £600; Representative—£100 real estate or £200.

Which of the following inferences can be drawn from information presented in the chart above?
(A) Land ownership and wealth were prerequisites to direct involvement in government.
(B) The framers of the state constitutions limited the term of the executive branch to three years.
(C) The legislative branch would dominate the political process.
(D) The state constitutions were modeled on the federal Constitution.

62. In reference to the British colonial empire in the late nineteenth and early twentieth centuries, which of the following bodies of water was called the "British Lake"?
    (A) Lake Victoria
    (B) The Mediterranean Sea
    (C) The Caspian Sea
    (D) The Indian Ocean

63.

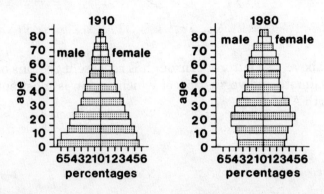

Based on the information presented in the population pyramid charts above,
    (A) in population pyramids, the chart is always in the form of a pyramid with the widest part at the bottom and the narrowest at the top
    (B) for the early twentieth century, the base of the pyramid reflects a smaller percentage of males and females at younger ages than at older ages
    (C) The amount of money spent on social-welfare programs in the last quarter of the twentieth century is directly related to the increased age of the population
    (D) from 1910 to 1980, the proportion of young people decreased as the proportion of people over 65 increased

64. Since 1965, which of the following U.S. geographical areas has shown the greatest increase in voter registration?
    (A) The Gulf states
    (B) The Southwest states
    (C) The Midwest states
    (D) The Northeast states

65. The Balfour Declaration (1917) is most closely associated with
    (A) the placing of Jerusalem under international control
    (B) the concept of a permanent Jewish homeland
    (C) British opposition to the creation of a Jewish state in the Jordan Valley
    (D) restricted immigration of Jews into Palestine

66. In the United States, if a bill is sent to the president during the last ten days of a legislative session and the president refuses to act on the bill, the bill
    (A) automatically becomes law
    (B) may be overridden by a two-thirds vote in both the House and Senate
    (C) cannot become law during that session of Congress
    (D) becomes law without the president's signature

67.

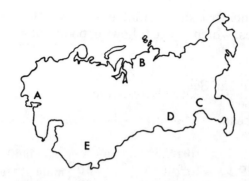

On the map above, the letters A through E represent regions of the former Soviet Union. The climate and vegetation of which region is most similar to the tundra region of North America?
(A) A
(B) B
(C) C
(D) D or E

68. During the "new nation" period of American History, Alexander Hamilton and Thomas Jefferson were the leaders of opposing political parties, the Federalists and the Republicans. Which of the following was not a primary objective of the Federalists?
(A) Protective tariffs
(B) Formation of a national bank
(C) Agrarian land reform
(D) Centralized national government

69. Assuming that the exchange rate between the United States and Canada favors the United States by twenty percent, the probable effect would be to
(A) encourage Canadian tourism in the United States
(B) encourage Canadian investment in the United States
(C) make U.S. products in Canada more expensive
(D) make Canadian products in the United States more expensive

70. The tomb of Tutankhamen is historically significant to archeologists primarily because
(A) the discovery provided the key to unlocking hieroglyphics
(B) the golden funerary mask represented the height of Egyptian material culture
(C) the mummified body of the pharaoh was remarkably preserved
(D) the religious and functional items had been left undisturbed and could be studied as a time capsule of privileged life in ancient Egypt

71. Assume the following.

   I. A majority of U.S. grain farmers produce an unusually large crop in a one-year period.
   II. There are no government price supports.
   III. Demand remains relatively constant.

Which of the following statements best represents the probable effect on farm income?
(A) Income would tend to gradually increase.
(B) Income would tend to fall.
(C) Income would remain relatively stable.
(D) There is insufficient evidence to predict the probable effect.

72.

`AFTER YOU!`...`NO, AFTER YOU!`...`NO, AFTER YOU!`...`NO, AFTER YOU!`...`NO, AFTER YOU!`..`NO...`

The main point of the above political cartoon is that
(A) the business community is a contributor to the inflationary cycle because it encourages the consumption of unnecessary items
(B) weight control clinics are inadequate in determining the basic causes of overweight
(C) the employer as well as the employee must compromise if inflation is going to be reduced
(D) people on a fixed income are most affected by inflation

73.

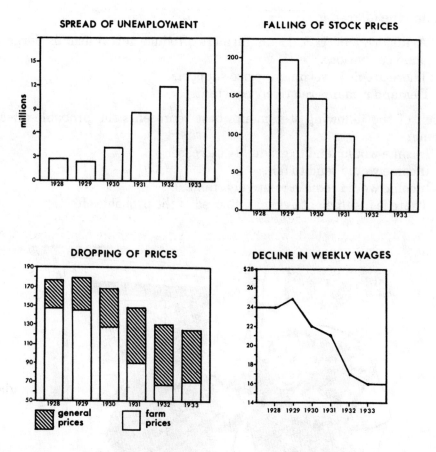

Based upon the data presented in the charts, which of the following is a true statement?

(A) The unemployment rate had only a moderate effect on weekly wages.

(B) The stock-market crash was not a basic cause of the Great Depression.

(C) Farm prices indicated that the agricultural section of the economy was substantially more affected than was the economy as a whole.

(D) The increase in inflation was directly related to the rapid increase in the rate of unemployment.

74.

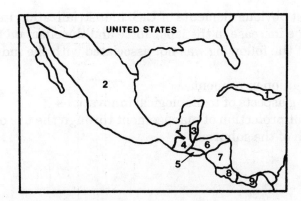

Historically, U.S. involvement in Central America was predicated on global considerations. In the year 2000, which Central American country will gain full control and sovereignty over an area under U.S. control once viewed as strategically important to the United States?
(A) 1
(B) 4
(C) 5
(D) 9

75. The people's right to know is a cornerstone of the American legal system However, media accounts of sensational criminal trials often result in prejudicial trial publicity.

This statement most clearly represents a basic constitutional conflict between which of the following?
(A) Freedom of speech and the right to privacy
(B) Freedom of speech and the right to a fair trial
(C) The right to an impartial jury and the equal protection of the law
(D) The due process of the law and the legal requirement of being charged with a crime

76. Which of the following religions is most closely associated with the development of a theocracy in America?
(A) The Catholics
(B) The Quakers
(C) The Anglicans
(D) The Puritans

77. Diffusion is the transmission of features of one culture to another and is a significant factor in cultural change. Which of the following is not an example of cultural change resulting from diffusion?
(A) The development of agriculture as it passes from one region to another
(B) The spread of Christianity from Spain to the New World
(C) The independent cultivation of root crops in Southeast Asia and Central America
(D) The production of modern furniture based on Renaissance design

78. Two of the most obvious elements of U.S. industrialization in the late nineteenth century were the increase in the labor force and the effect on the growth of urban areas. Which of the following was <u>not</u> associated with the industrialization of the United States?
    (A) The trade-union movement
    (B) Humanizing aspects of technological innovations
    (C) Government protection of management through the use of court injunctions
    (D) The growth of the suburbs

IV. Science

79. What is the chronological order of the evolutionary appearance of the following plants?
    (A) Fern, moss, rose, pine
    (B) Fern, rose, moss, pine
    (C) Moss, fern, pine, rose
    (D) Pine, fern, moss, rose

80. Which characteristic of a wave must change in order to affect the pitch of a sound?
    (A) Amplitude
    (B) Wavelength
    (C) Frequency
    (D) Crest

81. During exploration for petroleum, varying amounts of oil, water, and natural gas are found in a porous rock reservoir. The substances occur as separate, horizontal layers. In what order would a continuous drill find these three substances?
    (A) Gas, water, oil
    (B) Water, gas, oil
    (C) Gas, oil, water
    (D) Water, oil, gas

82. A commercial glass thermometer is partially filled with mercury. What physical principle best explains the use of mercury in thermometers?
    (A) The change in air pressure when air is heated moves the mercury.
    (B) Liquid mercury expands at regular intervals upon heating.
    (C) The liquid mercury expands more than the glass.
    (D) Gases expand more than liquids.

83. In what part of the cell is genetic material stored?
    (A) Vacuoles
    (B) Chromosomes
    (C) Cytoplasm
    (D) Membranes

84. Within a natural community of many different plant and animal species, which of the following is most likely to be true?
    (A) Competition between two species will upset the delicate natural balance.
    (B) Each species occupies its own niche in the environment.
    (C) The largest carnivore will command the greatest territory.
    (D) Owls hunt at night and therefore do not compete with nocturnal animals.

85. Most deposits of ore that are rich in copper, lead, and zinc are believed to have been formed from hot water solutions.

    Based on the information above, which of the following would not be considered a significant factor in exploration for these ores?
    (A) Exploration based on identifying the magnetic properties of the ores
    (B) Exploration based on recognizing the location of fissures and faults
    (C) Exploration based on the fact that nearby rocks display intense changes due to the presence of water
    (D) Exploration based on the fact that ore crystals contain microscopic bubbles filled with water

86. In experiments involving genetic engineering, which of the following relationships would make it more difficult to establish a connection between genotype and phenotype?

    I. One genetic characteristic is controlled by several genes.
    II. One gene controls one characteristic.
    III. One gene controls several characteristics.

    (A) I only
    (B) II only
    (C) I and III only
    (D) II and III only

87.

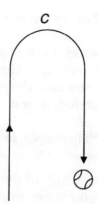

The diagram above shows the conservation of energy when a ball is thrown vertically into the air. Which of the following statements accurately describes the condition of the ball when it thrown perfectly straight up but before it reaches the peak of its upward flight at point C?
(A) The ball has no potential energy but increasing kinetic energy.
(B) The ball has maximum potential energy.
(C) The ball has decreasing kinetic energy and increasing potential energy.
(D) The ball has increasing kinetic energy and decreasing potential energy.

88. Which of the following factors most clearly separates a bread mold from a cactus plant?
(A) The ability to reproduce
(B) Body functions such as respiration and transpiration
(C) The ability to manufacture food
(D) A microscopic cell structure

89. What would be the most likely effect if the sun, moon, and earth, in that order, were directly aligned?
(A) Earthquake clusters
(B) Increased gravitational pull on the tides
(C) A lunar eclipse
(D) Slight tectonic plate movement

90. Which type of cloud indicates an upcoming thunderstorm?
(A) Cirrus
(B) Stratus
(C) Cumulonimbus
(D) Altostratus

91. Deoxyribonucleic acid is most closely associated with
(A) acid rain
(B) greenhouse gases
(C) genetic engineering
(D) cross-pollination experiments

92. Stars come in many colors. By identifying the color of a star, its surface tempera-ture can be determined. Which of the following places star colors in order of decreasing surface temperature?
    (A) Blue, white, yellow, orange, red
    (B) Red, orange, yellow, white, blue
    (C) Blue, yellow, orange, white, red
    (D) Red, orange, yellow, blue, white

93. Which of the following is the best example of a chemical reaction?
    (A) Hydrogen and oxygen combining to form water
    (B) A change in the atomic structure of carbon
    (C) Sugar dissolving in coffee
    (D) An electric light that flashes intermittently

94. During a moderate wind storm, a bridge collapsed. After studying the structural failure, the Army Corps of Engineers issued an order mandating that soldiers cannot march in step while crossing a bridge.

    What is the principle on which the order discussed above is based?
    (A) The cumulative effect of synchronized marching might cause small amplitude variations.
    (B) The sustained in-step marching might result in a change in the air pressure.
    (C) The sound produced by in-step marching might result in a series of different harmonics.
    (D) The marching might make the bridge vibrate at its own natural frequency.

95. A serious environmental problem facing the United States today is how to dispose of garbage.

    Which of the following items would take the longest to decompose?
    (A) A plastic bag
    (B) A cigarette butt
    (C) A glass bottle
    (D) A tin can

96.

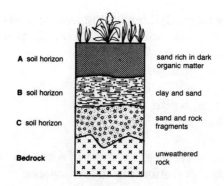

The diagram above shows a soil profile that might be exposed on the side of a recently dug trench. Notice the different soil zones. At the top of the profile, a long period of weathering has produced fine soil. Deeper into the profile, weathering is just beginning to produce fragments which will eventually become sand.

What does the profile suggest about the origin of soil?
(A) An accumulation of organic material leads to soil.
(B) The soil forms by the breakdown of bedrock.
(C) Soil results where much clay has been deposited.
(D) Soil requires an underground source of water.

97. A houseplant set near a window will in time turn toward it. Therefore, the plant must be consistently rotated to maintain its shape. The term that best describes the bending of the houseplant in response to an external stimuli is
(A) photosynthesis
(B) tropism
(C) parallelism
(D) gravity

98. All of the following must necessarily exist for all known forms of life EXCEPT
(A) air
(B) carbon atoms
(C) nucleic acids
(D) water

99. A piece of ice of unusual shape is dropped into a large glass of water and instantly floats. What is the best explanation for this occurrence?
(A) Ice contains microscopic bubbles of air.
(B) The atomic structure of ice and water produce different densities.
(C) Water contracts when frozen.
(D) The ice has a density of less than 1.0.

100. In which of the following locations would soft tissue most likely avoid decomposition and survive as a fossil?
(A) In desert soil
(B) In beach sand
(C) In river silt
(D) In lake-bottom mud

Questions 101–102 refer to the following diagram of a sealed jar and varied organisms.

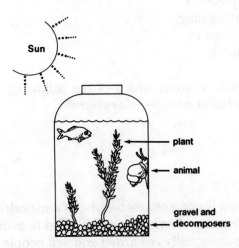

101. What is the major contribution of the plants to the welfare of the animals in this system?
    (A) They produce carbon dioxide needed by the animals.
    (B) They produce oxygen needed by the animals.
    (C) They produce carbon dioxide needed by the other plants.
    (D) They filter the water to maintain cleanliness.

102. Which of the following best shows the flow of energy through the system?
    (A) Animal to plant to sun to decomposers
    (B) Sun to plant to animal to decomposers
    (C) Decomposers to sun to animal to plant
    (D) Sun to animal to plant to decomposers

V. Visual and Performing Arts

103. Vaslav Nijinsky shocked Western dance audiences in his interpretation of *The Rite of Spring* (1913) because the choreography
    (A) restored the technical concepts of romantic ballet but in a menacing and forbidding format
    (B) employed primitive gestures and nonballetic movements in defining the theme
    (C) rejected the dissonance of the composition in favor of harmony and unity
    (D) incorporated ancient themes in a modern setting

104. Labanotation is used throughout the world to record ballet choreography and is considered an essential tool in preserving ethnic dance elements. Which of the following is most closely associated with labanotation?
    (A) Analyzing and notating patterns of physical movement
    (B) Analyzing tribal musical rhythmic patterns
    (C) Analyzing the oral history embodied in an ethnic dance
    (D) Analyzing ethnographic dance posters

105. Maypole dances were originally associated with
     (A) recreation and pleasure
     (B) winter and hunting magic
     (C) courtship and romance
     (D) fertility and rebirth

106. In the late nineteenth century, which of the following countries reached a high point in ballet while ballet declined elsewhere?
     (A) France
     (B) Russia
     (C) England
     (D) Spain

107. Which of the following is not a characteristic of a melodrama?
     (A) A good person from an elevated position is led to complete ruination.
     (B) Good people are eventually rewarded and evil people receive retribution.
     (C) The characters are clearly defined and do not lend themselves to intense psychological scrutiny.
     (D) The protagonist is an innocent victim of entangled circumstances surrounding him or her.

108. Stage directions are always given from the point of view an actor standing on stage facing the audience.

     Based on the above, which of the following would be considered an atypical stage direction?
     (A) Exit stage right and to the audience's left.
     (B) Move upstage and away from the audience.
     (C) Move upstage center to a position in the center area of the stage farthest from the audience.
     (D) Move downstage right to the area of the stage closest to the audience and to the audience's right.

109. Which of the following is not a Shakespearean tragedy?
     (A) *Romeo and Juliet*
     (B) *Macbeth*
     (C) *Richard III*
     (D) *King Lear*

110. Although there were many dramatic presentations during the Middle Ages, secular plays were limited. Which of the following types of productions performed during the later Middle Ages is considered secular?
     (A) Liturgical plays
     (B) Farces
     (C) Miracle plays
     (D) Mystery plays

111. Which of the following most closely characterizes a smooth, flowing musical presentation?
    (A) Legato
    (B) Staccato
    (C) Fortissimo
    (D) Pianissimo

112. A melody played or sung by several instruments or voices entering at different times best defines a
    (A) rondo
    (B) ballet
    (C) canon
    (D) carol

113.

    The melody shown above best represents the opening of which of the following songs?
    (A) "My Country, 'Tis of Thee"
    (B) "Row, Row, Row Your Boat"
    (C) "Three Blind Mice"
    (D) "The Star-Spangled Banner"

114. In art, contour lines move across the form of an object to indicate
    (A) distance and space
    (B) mass and volume
    (C) solid and void
    (D) strength and stability

115. Which of the following is true about a fresco?
    (A) A fresco is associated with meticulous brush techniques and is usually applied on wooden surfaces.
    (B) The binding material in fresco paint is egg yolk or some other viscous material.
    (C) The colors of a fresco are generally limited to earth tones because these pigments are usually not affected by the calcium in plaster.
    (D) A fresco allows the painter maximum flexibility in applying color.

116. If a composition uses overlapping shapes, receding color intensity, and lack of detail in the distance, the artist is probably attempting to
    (A) create an abstract landscape or seascape
    (B) control space by using the rules of perspective
    (C) create a flat, one-dimensional background
    (D) incorporate elements of solid and void

VI. Human Development

117. In what way did Piaget's cognitive-development theory influence American education?
    (A) It recognized that bright children should be accelerated by "skipping" a grade rather than by being enriched at the current grade level.
    (B) It emphasized a structured teaching approach when attempting to teach mastery of a basic skill.
    (C) It encouraged spontaneous discovery in learning a skill.
    (D) It was the basis for a comprehensive phonics program to decode words.

118. Tracking has been a common practice in primary education throughout most of the twentieth century. Which of the following is the most successful tracking configuration?
    (A) Ability grouping by subject area
    (B) Ability grouping based on intelligence testing
    (C) Ability grouping for core subjects only
    (D) Ability grouping for the visual and performing arts only

119. In disciplining a child, permissiveness can be an acceptable behavior-modification program.

    In which of the following examples would an educational psychologist most likely disagree with the above statement?
    (A) When nonphysical attempts to discipline the child have been met with inconsistent behavior change
    (B) When the child is engaging in excessive aggression
    (C) When the purpose of the discipline modification is to teach independence and assertiveness
    (D) When both parents come from single-parent homes

120. Erik Erickson's psychosocial stages of development make certain assumptions about human development. Which of the following statements would not be associated with Erickson?
    (A) A child's personality is determined mainly by parental input.
    (B) The entire life span of an individual is emphasized in understanding human behavior.
    (C) A young child must learn to feel competent because failure often brings feelings of inferiority.
    (D) Developmental stages influence the socialization process.

121. The desire to interact with peers is a normal part of the socialization process. In which of the following areas would an adolescent peer group most likely have greater influence on behavior than do adults?
    (A) Academic choices
    (B) Political philosophy
    (C) Sexual attitudes
    (D) Career orientation

122. A young child has used the following phrase correctly for several months: "Mommy come here." Shortly thereafter, the child alters her speech pattern by saying, "Mommy comed here."

What is the best explanation for this language shift?
(A) Regression is a normal stage in language development.
(B) The child is advancing in language development.
(C) Auditory discrimination is difficult for young children.
(D) Early language patterns were not sufficiently reinforced.

123. Which of the following is usually considered the most important factor in a child's observable classroom behavior?
(A) Heredity
(B) Sex
(C) Cultural background
(D) Self-concept

124. According to Bloom's taxonomy of educational objectives, which of the following categories represents the highest level of cognition?
(A) Knowledge
(B) Interpretation
(C) Synthesis
(D) Evaluation

125. Which of the following motivational theories views the consequences of behavior as a regulator and controller of an individual's actions?

  I. Behaviorism
 II. Humanism
III. Cognitivism

(A) I only
(B) II only
(C) III only
(D) I and III only

VII. Physical Education

126. Which of the following most accurately describes the proper follow-through body motion in the mature stage of throwing a ball?
(A) The feet remain stationary in preparation for the throw.
(B) As the trunk rotates, weight is completely shifted to the foot opposite the throwing side of the body.
(C) In the initial throwing motion, the person throwing steps forward with the foot that is on the same side as the throwing arm.
(D) The weight is shifted from the front to the back foot.

127. Which of the following physical principles are applicable to biomechanical analyses?

    I. Aerodynamics
   II. Hydrodynamics
  III. Force
  IV. Motion

   (A) I and II only
   (B) II and III only
   (C) II, III, and IV only
   (D) I, II, III, and IV

128. An early-primary-level child who exhibits poor perceptual-motor development would most likely have difficulty in all of the following EXCEPT
   (A) running for a sustained period of time
   (B) understanding the verbal directions for a game
   (C) skipping backward after learning how to skip
   (D) handling a bean-bag in a group activity

129. A female is considered mildly obese when the percentage of body fat (body-fat index) in the individual exceeds
   (A) 15 percent
   (B) 25 percent
   (C) 35 percent
   (D) 45 percent

130. In tracking an object, the visual concentration of a primary-level child will dramatically improve if
   (A) the object is circular
   (B) the object is thrown to the child with an arc, or loft
   (C) the child is familiar with the rules of the game being played
   (D) the child has modeled the expected outcome

131. In terms of cardiorespiratory fitness, which of the following is an incorrect pairing?
   (A) Abduction: raising the arms
   (B) Adduction: lowering the arms
   (C) Circumduction: circular motion of the trunk
   (D) Flexion: stretching the arms

132. The best reason for a "start-and-expand" activity in a physical education program is
   (A) to provide positive reinforcement in presenting a particular skill-based lesson
   (B) to introduce an activity at a low skill level and appropriately adjust the complexity of the skill
   (C) to individualize a lesson based on the goals of the student
   (D) to demonstrate a specific skill as part of an integrated unit

133. A kindergarten introductory physical education lesson includes the following activity. In succession, children touch their hands, feet, head, nose, back, and chest to the floor.

The primary purpose for this activity is to reinforce
(A) body imaging
(B) balance
(C) rhythmic movement
(D) hand-eye coordination

134. What is the physical-fitness rationale for testing youth fitness with timed, one-minute, bent-knee sit-ups?
(A) To evaluate upper-body muscle strength and endurance
(B) To evaluate static strength through repetitive flexion exercises
(C) To evaluate abdominal-muscle strength and endurance
(D) To evaluate arm and shoulder-girdle muscle strength and endurance

CONTENT AREA EXERCISES 1

Time: 2 Hours
14 Questions

Directions: On the actual MSAT, you will have a page and a half to two pages of 8½ × 11 paper on which to write each answer. For the following questions, use no more than two pages to write each response.

I. Literature and Language Studies

1. Discuss four different sound devices used in poetry.

2. Compare the one-act play to the short story.

3. Discuss two ways in which figurative language adds to the vividness of a description.

4. The following sentences are in "broken" English. Explain their meaning and give a situation in which this might occur in someone's writing.

   Yesterday him sing you some song.
   You sing some song to she.
   Yesterday you no sing song she want.

II. Mathematics

5. **Math Class Enrollment Comparison 1980–1990**

1980—20 students
1982—25 students
1984—20 students
1986—30 students
1988—40 students
1990—45 students

Use the grid below to graph the information given above. Explain your procedure in graphing.

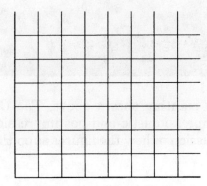

6. If a number is divisible by 2 and 3, it is also divisible by 6. Explain why this same number is not necessarily divisible by 9.

7.

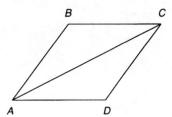

In the parallelogram above, line AC bisects angle C. With this information, give four deductions that can be made about the diagram.

8. Cars A and B each travel the same road to city X. Car A travels at 50 mph and leaves at 10 A.M., while car B travels at 60 mph and leaves at 11 A.M. Will car B overtake car A before it reaches city X, which is 310 miles away? Explain why or why not.

III. Visual and Performing Arts

9.

Briefly discuss how the painting shown above, *The Card Players,* incorporates elements of both the impressionistic and postimpressionistic periods. Include in your answer a brief discussion of how the figures support the intended effect of this composition.

10. Briefly discuss the advantages of the proscenium stage. Include relevant information on the historical background of this stage in your answer.

IV. Human Development

11. A teacher observes that a small number of students in a fifth-grade classroom do not do well on paper-and-pencil activities. Discuss two possible explanations for this behavior. Include in your answer educational interventions to address this problem.

12. Define behavior modification in terms of operant conditioning (responses on which stimulus-response learning theory is based). Briefly discuss implications for educators in determining how children will respond to operant conditioning.

V. Physical Education

13. A child is learning to catch a baseball. Briefly discuss how to overcome the avoidance reaction generally associated with catching a baseball. Include in your answer a discussion of the proper body mechanics involved in catching a baseball.

14. Briefly define aerobic and anaerobic fitness. Include appropriate examples in your answer.

CONTENT AREA EXERCISES 2

Time: 1 Hour
8 Questions

Directions: On the actual MSAT, you will have a page and a half to two pages of $8\frac{1}{2} \times 11$ paper on which to write each answer. For the following questions, use no more than two pages to write each response.

I. History/Social Sciences

1. "Reaganomics" was the dominant economic philosophy of the 1980s in the United States. Briefly discuss the rationale for Reaganomics.

2. Spartan women said the following when their men went off to war: "Come back with your shield or upon it."

   How does this statement reflect Spartan society? Include in your answer a brief discussion of how the state controlled the lives of its citizens.

3. One of the central features of American government is the principle of separation of power. Briefly discuss the reason the principle is important. Include in your answer the basic function of each branch of government.

4. Briefly discuss three major economic factors that would result in a strong U.S. dollar. Define appropriate terms and include one negative effect on trade resulting from a strong dollar.

II. Science

5.

THE HYDROLOGIC CYCLE

(A)_____
(B)_____
(C)_____
(D)_____
(E)_____
(F)_____

Fill in the blanks to the left of the diagram of the hydrologic (water) cycle in the correct configuration, using these terms: precipitation, evaporation, wind, condensation, percolation, runoff. Briefly describe the processes that make up the water cycle.

6. If a blue-eyed individual married a brown-eyed individual who carries only the dominant brown eye-color gene and no recessives, diagram the possible eye colors that can occur in the offspring of these individuals.

7. How do drops of water acting as prisms explain the appearance of a rainbow? Include refraction, dispersion, and color sequence in your answer.

8. Briefly discuss how chlorofluorocarbons are directly associated with ozone depletion. Include in your answer ozone-depleting products and three consequences attributed to ozone depletion.

ANSWER KEY FOR PRACTICE TEST 2

Content Knowledge

1. C	28. D	55. D	82. B	109. C
2. D	29. D	56. B	83. B	110. B
3. B	30. C	57. C	84. B	111. A
4. C	31. B	58. C	85. A	112. C
5. D	32. B	59. B	86. C	113. D
6. C	33. B	60. A	87. C	114. B
7. D	34. A	61. A	88. C	115. C
8. B	35. D	62. D	89. B	116. B
9. B	36. C	63. D	90. C	117. C
10. B	37. B	64. A	91. C	118. A
11. D	38. C	65. B	92. A	119. B
12. A	39. B	66. C	93. A	120. A
13. B	40. B	67. B	94. D	121. C
14. C	41. C	68. C	95. C	122. B
15. B	42. C	69. C	96. B	123. D
16. B	43. B	70. D	97. B	124. D
17. C	44. C	71. B	98. A	125. A
18. C	45. C	72. C	99. D	126. B
19. B	46. C	73. C	100. D	127. D
20. C	47. A	74. D	101. B	128. B
21. B	48. A	75. B	102. B	129. B
22. D	49. D	76. D	103. B	130. B
23. A	50. B	77. C	104. A	131. D
24. C	51. D	78. B	105. D	132. B
25. D	52. D	79. C	106. B	133. A
26. B	53. D	80. C	107. A	134. C
27. B	54. D	81. C	108. D	

Content Area Exercises

See the Essay Checklist on page 522 and the discussion of essay scoring beginning on page 16 to evaluate your short essays.

ANALYZING YOUR TEST RESULTS

Use the following charts to carefully analyze your results and spot your strengths and weaknesses. Complete the process of analyzing each subject area and each individual question for Practice Test 2. Examine your results for trends in types of error (repeated errors) or poor results in specific subject areas. *This reexamination and analysis is of tremendous importance for effective test preparation.*

Practice Test 2 Analysis Sheets

Content Knowledge (Multiple-Choice Questions)				
	Possible	Completed	Right	Wrong
I. Literature and Language Studies	27			
II. Mathematics	27			
III. History/Social Sciences	24			
IV. Science	24			
V. Visual and Performing Arts	14			
VI. Human Development	9			
VII. Physical Education	9			
Total	*134*			

To get a rough approximation of your multiple-choice score range, total the number of correct responses. Do not subtract any points for questions attempted but missed, as there is no penalty for guessing. Now, refer to the broad-range score approximator on page 12.

Analysis/Tally Sheet for Questions Missed

One of the most important parts of test preparation is analyzing **why** you missed a question so that you can reduce the number of mistakes. Now that you've taken Practice Test 2 and corrected your answers, carefully tally your multiple-choice mistakes by marking in the proper column

	Reason for Mistake			
	Total Missed	Simple Mistake	Misread Question	Lack of Knowledge
I. Literature and Language Studies				
II. Mathematics				
III. History/Social Sciences				
IV. Science				
V. Visual and Performing Arts				
VI. Human Development				
VII. Physical Education				
Total				

Essay Checklist

Compare your short constructed-response answers to the answers given. A good short constructed-response answer will do the following:

_____ address the assignment

_____ be well focused

_____ use key words ("buzzwords")

_____ show an understanding of the subject

For each of your responses, check to see if your answer fulfills the criteria above. Fill in the following charts with the number of criteria fulfilled for each essay to get a general idea of the effectiveness of your answer. **These numbers do not represent a score** but are simply meant to help you evaluate your response.

Content Area Exercises 1 (Short Essay Questions)

	Essays Possible	Number of Essay Checklist Criteria Fulfilled			
		Essay 1	Essay 2	Essay 3	Essay 4
I. Literature and Language Studies	4				
II. Mathematics	4				
III. Visual and Performing Arts	2				
IV. Human Development	2				
V. Physical Education	2				
Total	*14*				

Content Area Exercises 2 (Short Essay Questions)

	Essays Possible	Number of Essay Checklist Criteria Fulfilled			
		Essay 1	Essay 2	Essay 3	Essay 4
I. History/Social Sciences	4				
II. Science	4				
Total	*8*				

ANSWERS AND EXPLANATIONS FOR PRACTICE TEST 2

CONTENT KNOWLEDGE

I. Literature and Language Studies

1. (C) The subject of the sentence is *Time*, with *thief* in apposition to *Time*. The verb is *hath stolen*, and *year* is the object of the verb.

2. (D) The phrase is a metaphor for the speaker's age. He is now in his twenties but has not yet produced anything of note. Though it is not clear from the lines, the poet is concerned that he has not yet written notable poetry.

3. (B) The two words are metaphors comparing the bud and blossom of a plant to human productions. A personification is a figure comparing an inanimate object to a human; a paradox is an apparent self-contradiction; and an allusion is a reference or citation.

4. (C) The phrase *On the other hand* places (1) after (2). The *they* in (3) must refer to the educators of (4), so (4) must precede (3). The logical order is 2–1–4–3.

5. (D) The wicked stepmother is a stock figure of fairy tales. Although a wicked stepmother *might* appear in a gothic romance, the dark hero, innocent heroine, and remote mansion are more likely.

6. (C) The English Romantic poets flourished in the closing decade of the eighteenth century and the early part of the nineteenth century. Of the events listed here, the French Revolution affected them most strongly. The Spanish Armada was dispersed in the sixteenth century and the Irish famine came after the Romantic period.

7. (D) The mystery, picaresque (the story of a rogue), and epistolary (told in letters) are types of a novel, a prose narrative. *Epic* is a term for a genre of poetry.

8. (B) The poem argues that we have not drained the good wine of life, that maids are as beautiful as any, and that sculptures even better than those of ancient Greece are still to come.

9. (B) Phidias is the most renowned sculptor of ancient Greece. The correct answer can be inferred from the reference in line 7 to *fairer forms . . . in the quarry,* that is, sculptures that have not yet been carved.

10. (B) A slant rhyme is an approximate rhyme as opposed to one in which the vowel sounds are identical. The rhyme of *best* and *rest* is exact, but slant rhymes are used in *shallow–swallow, marry–quarry,* and *blessed–released.*

11. (D) The English word *meter* comes from the Greek for *measure*. The *perimeter* is the measure around, while the word *barometer* combines the prefix for atmospheric pressure with *meter*.

12. (A) *Hence, thus,* and *therefore* are all words that would logically introduce a conclusion. *Unless,* on the other hand, expresses doubt or a condition.

13. (B) The paragraph must begin with the question (4), which the rest of the paragraph answers. Sentence (1) needs an antecedent for the *it,* and the *can* answers the question of (1). *Consequently* in (2) is more logical after (3) than in the second position, so the order is 4–1–3–2.

14. (C) Most American dictionaries repeat the explanation of the pronunciation symbols at the bottom of every page so the reader can look from the word to the bottom of the page without having to look elsewhere in the book.

15. (B) Although the first book of *Gulliver's Travels* is sometimes expurgated for children, the corrosive satire of Swift's work was not intended for children.

16. (B) The statements here are literal, not metaphorical. They are not hypothetical or syllogistic, but they do compare operatic practice in Italy with that of English-speaking countries.

17. (C) A topic outline uses sentence fragments or even single words, but like a sentence outline, it begins with the main idea, or thesis.

18. (C) The passage is part of a soliloquy, as the phrase *Now I am alone* makes clear. A soliloquy is spoken by a character alone; a dramatic monologue has only one speaker, but the speaker addresses a specific audience.

19. (B) Like most of Shakespeare's plays, this passage is in blank verse, that is, unrhymed iambic pentameter.

20. (C) The *fiction, dream,* and *conceit* are the situation the performing player has imagined. A *visage* is a face.

21. (B) The word *finite* means limited. *Infinitesimal* means an infinitely small quantity.

22. (D) The speaker's attitude is obviously negative; therefore, all positive or neutral choices should be eliminated—(A) and (B). In the lines, the speaker does not explicitly or implicitly surrender but does express absolute disdain (dislike) for the world.

23. (A) The poem asserts that she is brave because faith guards her from fear. It is essential that you use the given passage to answer this type of interpretive question rather than rely on your prior knowledge.

24. (C) The words *in addition to* usually connect similar ideas and supporting material.

25. (D) The correct syllabication is phe nom e non.

26. (B) *Anarchy* is derived from the Greek word *anarchios—an,* meaning *not,* and *arche,* meaning *rule.*

27. (B) Written composition is generally an individual effort and would not contribute to an appreciation for group dynamics.

II. Mathematics

28. (D) Only this arrangement correctly reflects the statement about Dominique. She scored higher than Frank but lower than Alexis.

29. (D) There are three chances out of four of spinning either red, yellow, or blue. Thus, the correct answer is 3/4.

30. (C) Marking the midpoints H and J gives

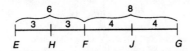

Thus, $EF = 6$; $HJ = 7$; $FG = 8$; and $JG = 4$. So FG has the greatest value.

31. (B) Figure $ABCD$ is a parallelogram. The formula for the area of a parallelogram is *area* equals *base* times *height.* Since the base is 6 and the height (a perpendicular drawn to the base) is 3, the area would be computed by 6×3, or answer (B).

32. (B) Ratios may be expressed as fractions. Thus "1 to 4" (A) may be expressed as 1/4. Notice that (C) and (D) are fractions that reduce to 1/4.

$$2/8 = 1/4$$

$$3/12 = 1/4$$

Only 3/8 (B) does *not* equal 1/4.

33. (B) The number sentence is an addition problem.

$$825.50 + 435.00$$

The only choice which expresses a problem in addition is (B).

34. (A) $\angle BCD = \angle A + \angle B$ (exterior angle of a triangle equals the sum of the opposite two angles). Then $84° = \angle A + 63°$, and $\angle A = 21°$.

35. **(D)** Mary worked a total of 24 hours, but we do not know in how many days. Therefore, we cannot derive the number of hours she worked each day. Each of the other choices can be derived from the statement.

36. **(C)** The fraction 1/8 equals .125.

$$8\overline{)1.000} \quad .125$$

Thus, it would lie between 1/9 (.111) and 2/15 (.133).

37. **(B)** Points plotted on a coordinate graph are expressed (x, y) where x indicates the distance forward or backward and y indicates the distance up or down. Thus, $(-3, 4)$ means 3 "steps" back and then 4 "steps" up. This will place the point within quadrant II as shown below.

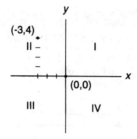

38. **(C)** The only statement which *must* be true is (C). The class averages 2 pencils per student. Notice that 30 students could each have 2 pencils, so (D) may be false. Likewise, just one of the students could have all 60 pencils. Therefore, (A) and (B) may be false.

39. **(B)** In order to have the pie graph represent blue-eyed students as 6 out of 24, the piece of the "pie" representing blue-eyed students should be 6/24, or 1/4. So the blue piece needs to be increased. Likewise, for hazel to represent 5/24, its piece of the pie should be slightly less than 6/24, so its size should be decreased.

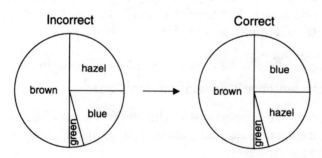

40. (B) Since D is between A and B on $\overleftrightarrow{AB}$, we know that the sum of the lengths of the smaller segments AD and DB is equal to the length of the larger segment AB.

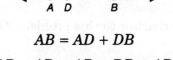

Hence,

$$AB = AD + DB$$

$$AB - AD = AD + DB - AD$$

$$AB - AD = DB$$

41. (C) In 1970, 10% of $12,000, or $1200, was spent on medical. In 1975, 12% of $16,000, or $1920, was spent on medical. Thus, there was an increase of $720.

42. (C) 240 out of 800 can be expressed as 240/800, which reduces to 3/10, or 30%.

43. (B) The probability of throwing a head in one throw is

$$\frac{\text{chance of a head}}{\text{total chances (1 head + 1 tail)}} = \frac{1}{2}$$

Since you are trying to throw a head *twice,* multiply the probability for the first toss (1/2) times the probability for the second toss (again, 1/2). Thus,

$$\frac{1}{2} \times \frac{1}{2} = \frac{1}{4}$$

and 1/4 is the probability of throwing heads twice in two tosses. Another way of approaching this problem is to look at the total number of possible outcomes.

	First Toss	*Second Toss*
1.	H	H
2.	H	T
3.	T	H
4.	T	T

Thus, there are four different possible outcomes. There is only one way to throw two heads in two tosses. So the probability of tossing two heads in two tosses is one out of four total outcomes, or 1/4.

44. (C) Changing 740,000 to .0074 requires moving the decimal eight places to the left. This is the same as multiplying by 1/100,000,000.

45. (C) The distributive property of multiplication over addition is demonstrated by multiplying each term on the inside of the parentheses by the variable on the outside of the parentheses.

$$a(b + c) = ab + ac$$

46. (C) To change 3 miles to feet, simply multiply 3 times 5280 (since 5280 is the number of feet in a mile). This will give the number of feet in 3 miles. Then multiply this product by 12, since there are 12 inches in each foot. The resulting product will be the number of inches in 3 miles.

47. (A) There are several approaches to this problem. One solution is to first find the area of the square.

$$10 \times 10 = 100$$

Then subtract the approximate area of the circle.

$$A = \pi(r^2) \cong 3(5^2) = 3(25) = 75$$

Therefore, the total area inside the square but outside the circle is approximately 25. One quarter of that area is shaded. Therefore, 25/4 is approximately the shaded area. The closest answer is 10 (A).

A more efficient method is to first find the area of the square.

$$10 \times 10 = 100$$

Then divide the square into four equal sections as follows.

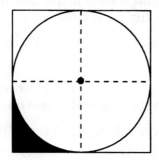

Since a quarter of the square is 25, the only possible answer choice for the shaded area is 10 (A).

48. (A) The number of nickels that Angela has is x. Thus, the total value of those nickels (in cents) is $5x$. Angela also has twice as many dimes as nickels, or $2x$. The total value in cents of those dimes is $2x(10)$, or $20x$. Adding the value of the nickels and dimes gives $5x + 20x$, or $25x$.

49. (D) Since a quadrilateral has 360° and two of the angles are 100° and 60°, which equals 160°, there are 200° remaining for angles a and b. If angle $a < 70°$, angle a could be 69°, so angle b could be 131°. Or angle a could be 1°, so angle b could be 199°. So angle b must be between 200° and 130°.

50. (B) To answer this question, you could list multiples of 6 and then check to see if they are divisible by 4.

Multiples of 6:

$$6, 12, 18, 24, 30, 36, 42, 48, 54, 60, 66, 72$$

Multiples of 6 also divisible by 4:

$$12, 24, 36, 48, 60, 72$$

There are 6 integers divisible by both 4 and 6. You might also have noticed that any number divisible by both 4 and 6 must also be divisible by 12.

51. (D) If the color television is marked down 20%, its current price is 80% of its original price. Thus,

$$.80P = \$320$$

52. (D) Kilograms could be used to approximate the weight of a bowling ball. The other units all weigh far less than a pound.

53. (D) There were four days (July 10, 11, 14, and 15) on which the maximum temperature exceeded the average. Thus, 4/7 is approximately 57%.

54. (D) The word *sum* indicates addition. The sum of two numbers is therefore $x + y$. If this sum equals one of the numbers, the equation will be either $x + y = x$ or $x + y = y$.

III. History/Social Sciences

55. (D) The mission system did not accomplish its primary goals: to make California Indians useful, productive, Christian citizens and to enable the mission to become a self-sufficient community capable of producing an agricultural surplus. The first missions were founded in 1769 by the Spanish. However, Mexico secularized all California missions between 1834 and 1836. The virtual land monopoly given to the missions as well as the forced relocation of the Indians ended with secularization. The Indians often found mission life intolerable due to a combination of culture shock, disease, cramped and forced living conditions, and the dictatorial and punitive policies of the church.

56. (B) A trip from San Francisco to Lake Tahoe (adjacent to Nevada) would cross the following: Coast Range, Central Valley, and Sierra Nevada. The Coast Range extends in a north-south direction from northern to southern California. The Central Valley is the most productive agricultural area in the state and separates the Coast and Sierra Nevada ranges. With the exception of the Rockies, the other choices are part of the physical geography/topography of California.

57. (C) Frank Norris described in *The Octopus* the far-reaching and destructive practices of the California railroad monopolies. The story chronicles the domination of the railroad industries by the "robber barons," who systematically destroyed, with unfair practices, small agricultural businesses. *The Octopus* had a direct effect on the California reform movement, which led to legislation to prohibit rebates and other unfair business practices.

58. (C) Karl Marx described the conditions of the working class in *The Communist Manifesto* (1848). Marx theorized that the existence of private property invariably leads to class conflicts. According to Marx, the proletariat, or working class, is always subservient to the oppressor class, or bourgeoisie, who control the industrial interests of the state. In western Europe in the mid-nineteenth century, Marx saw industrialization, especially in England, as the vehicle which could keep the working class in perpetual economic subservience. Marx further theorized that the proletariat would overthrow the industrialized governments of Europe. Marx viewed class revolution based on the ideals of socialism as inevitable. Lenin is associated with the phrase "Peace, Land, and Bread," which symbolized the internal turmoil in Russia during World War I.

59. (B) The statue is representative of a Buddhist priest at peace with himself. Among the beliefs of Buddhism are a belief in reincarnation, a belief that through meditation one can find freedom from suffering and enter Nirvana, respect for all living creatures, a belief in sacred animals (cow), and a belief in many gods. Choice (D) represents the Islamic religion.

60. (A) Proponents of social Darwinism expanded Darwin's theory of evolution to include society as a whole. Darwin in the *Origin of Species* (1859) theorized that evolution is a continuous process in which successful species (in order to survive) adapt to their environment. The social Darwinists viewed society as a "struggle for existence." Only the "fittest" members of society would survive. The accumulation of wealth was considered a visible sign of a successful adaptation, and virtue and wealth became synonymous. However, for social Darwinism to succeed, it was thought that a free and open economic system was needed. Capitalism (with the private ownership of land, freedom of choice, a competitive free-market system, and limited government restraints) was regarded as the "natural environment" in which "survival of the fittest" could be tested. The social Darwinists also believed that some races were superior to others, that poverty indicated unfitness, and that a class-structured society was desirable.

61. (A) The chart indicates that not all people were allowed to participate in government. Although the new state governments were the beginning of the democratic process, it is clear that only landholders were eligible to vote. There is insufficient evidence to support choices (C) and (D). Note that the information in choice (B) (that the executive branch was limited to three years or less) is *stated* in the table and that a stated fact is *not* an inference. The executive branch was restricted to a limited time to keep it from becoming powerful enough to restrict the rights of the people.

62. (D) The British colonial empire by the start of World War I controlled approximately a quarter of the world's land and population. The Indian Ocean at this time was economically, politically, and militarily dominated by England. Virtually all shores of the Indian Ocean were controlled by the British, which made it, in effect, a "British Lake." Choice (B) is incorrect because the Mediterranean, given the independent European countries using it, was not considered a British "possession."

63. (D) A population pyramid displays a frequency distribution of a population based on age and sex. Note that the 1980 pyramid indicates a relatively even distribution of the population at all ages, which is in sharp contrast to the 1910 profile. It should be apparent that the proportion of the population 15 and under is smaller in 1980 than it is in 1910. Factors that account for the change from 1910 to 1980 are a decreasing birth rate, increased longevity, and better health care. Choices (A) and (B) are not supported by the information presented in the chart, and while (C) might be true, the chart does not address money spent on social-welfare programs.

64. (A) The 1965 landmark Voting Rights Act virtually banned literacy tests as a prerequisite to voting and also authorized the use of federal registrars to guarantee African-American voting rights, in effect, enfranchising a voting majority in many southern states, including the Gulf states of Texas, Louisiana, Mississippi, Alabama, and Florida. Growing urbanization also changed voting patterns in the South. Choice (B) is incorrect because in this area a large number of Hispanic residents are not citizens and are therefore ineligible to vote.

65. (B) In 1917, British Foreign Secretary Arthur Balfour issued a declaration of sympathy with Jewish-Zionist aspirations to establish a homeland in Palestine. The Balfour Declaration came at a time when Germany was making overtures to Zionist leaders, promising a Jewish state as a reward for possible Zionist help during World War I. Britain was given a League of Nations mandate (control) over Palestine in 1923, a mandate which ultimately became the political framework for the successful creation of Israel as a nation (1948).

66. (C) The president has ten days (not including Sundays) to sign or veto a bill. If the president receives a bill from Congress during the *last* ten days of a legislative session and does not act on the bill (sign it or veto it), the bill automatically dies—a situation referred to as a pocket veto. If the president receives a bill from Congress and it is *not* during the last ten days of a legislative session, excluding Sundays, and no action is taken on the bill, the bill automatically becomes law *without* the president's signature.

67. (B) The tundra is an area of permanently frozen ground and is characterized by treeless topography. The tundra zone, which lies at high latitudes, is a region of low winter temperatures and limited precipitation.

68. (C) The Federalists did not pursue a policy of agrarian land reform. They *did* favor a national bank and protective tariffs. Fundamental disagreements over Hamilton's financial plan led to the creation of the American two-party system. Hamilton and the Federalists believed that a government based on the interests of the moneyed class would best serve the needs of the new nation. He was a proponent of expanding federalism and, as such, favored a national government based on a broad interpretation of the Constitution. Jefferson and the Republicans (Anti-Federalists) favored the farmers and a strict interpretation of the Constitution—one which would favor states' rights at the expense of federal power.

69. (C) The statement discusses a "strong dollar" in relation to Canadian currency. In this case, U.S. exports to Canada would tend to be more expensive because it would take more Canadian dollars to purchase American products. Choices (A), (B), and (D) are the opposite of what one might expect if the Canadian dollar were weak in relation to the U.S. dollar.

70. (D) Tutankhamen's (King Tut's) tomb, discovered by Howard Carter in 1922, is generally considered the richest royal tomb of antiquity ever found. Because the tomb had never been robbed, archeologists were provided with an undisturbed time capsule containing evidence of the culture of the "boy king" who ruled from *c.* 1371 to *c* 1352 B.C. The artifacts discovered were both functional and religious. Choice (A) is associated with the Rosetta Stone. Choice (B) is characteristic of Egyptian craftsmanship, but the mask alone would have only limited significance in interpreting ancient Egyptian society.

71. (B) If a majority of farmers produce unusually large crop surpluses in a particular year, that overproduction increases supply, and assuming that demand remains constant, the price of a crop, and incomes, would tend to fall.

72. (C) The cartoonist indicates that both prices and wages are too high (overweight condition of each person). The presence of the weight control clinic suggests that measures to reduce the rate of inflation are available. It is clear that in a program of effective weight loss, an individual must be committed to hard work and sacrifice. The cartoonist indicates that economic self-interest is keeping labor (wages) and management (prices) from initiating policies that would control the inflationary spiral.

73. (C) Farm prices during the Depression collapsed. In 1928, the farm price index stood at approximately 148. By 1932 it had dropped to a low of approximately 64, representing close to a sixty percent decrease in less than four years. During the early 1930s, total farm production declined by only six percent, but the purchasing power of farmers declined by over fifty percent. Choices (B) and (D) are beyond the scope of the data presented. Also, a careful reading of the charts makes it clear that 1929 marked the statistical high of the U.S. economy during the period 1928–1933. Among the causes of the Depression were unequal distribution of income, overinvestment in industry, overspeculation in the stock market, and short-sighted government policies that failed to address the disparity between farm and business income.

74. (D) Here, you must recognize that the question deals with the Panama Canal (an area once viewed as strategically important to the United States) and then be able to locate Panama on the map of Central America. In 1978, after thirteen years of discussion, the U.S. Senate ratified two treaties which provide for the transfer of the canal to Panama by the year 2000. The second treaty, establishing neutrality in the Canal Zone, was not popular in the United States and passed the Senate with only one vote above the needed two-thirds majority. The Canal Zone does not have the same strategic importance that it did when the U.S. acquired control of the territory in 1903. At that time, the canal alleviated the problem of having to maintain a two-coast naval fleet. Today, however, the changing technology of war, the hostility of many who view the Canal Zone as an unjustified extension of U.S. power, and the fact that supertankers cannot use the canal have combined to make it expendable.

75. (B) The right to an impartial jury is an essential ingredient of a fair trial and is protected by the Sixth Amendment. In recent history, the public's right to know, protected by the First Amendment (freedom of the press), has come into conflict with the Sixth Amendment. Lawyers have argued successfully that in certain cases pretrial or trial publicity can jeopardize a defendant's right to an impartial jury. The courts are the final arbiters in maintaining a balance between First- and Sixth-Amendment rights.

76. (D) The objective of the Puritan migration to America (1620s) was to set up a Bible commonwealth. In practice, Puritan New England was a theocracy (government by ecclesiastical authorities), with civil authority residing in members of the clergy. The social order and civil laws were predicated on religious concepts, with the Bible the overall regulator of society. Dissent was severely restricted.

77. (C) A careful reading of the statement provides sufficient information to answer this question. *Independent* (instituted without outside information) cultivation of root crops is the only example given of cultural change that does not result from diffusion.

78. (B) The industrialization of the United States was essentially dehumanizing and impersonal. Technological innovations resulted in more efficient, labor-saving machinery, but as machines replaced workers and factories grew larger, the labor-management relationship became increasingly impersonal. The quality of urban life as evidenced by slums, economic dislocation, alcoholism, and insecurity was a conspicuous reminder of the dehumanizing aspects of the industrialization of the United States.

IV. Science

79. (C) The moss and the fern are the two most primitive plants given. Neither reproduces by seeds, so you can assume that the chronological order had to begin with one of the two. Of the two plants with seeds (the pine and the rose), the plant with flowers is the most advanced. By knowing only the simplest and most advanced of the plants listed, you could eliminate all choices but (C).

80. (C) A wave's crest is the top of its "hill." A wave's amplitude is its height, the distance between its resting position and its crest. Wavelength is defined as the distance between two consecutive points on a wave (crest to crest). The pitch of a sound depends on how fast the particles of a medium vibrate. The number of waves produced in a given time is the wave's frequency.

81. (C) The three substances occur in their order of density, with the lightest substance on top and the heaviest on the bottom. Gas is lighter than the two liquids, so it is at the top. Oil floats on water, so it is second. On the bottom is the most dense substance, water. Always try to use information you already know to eliminate wrong answers. Here, you might recall seeing oil slicks floating on top of a body of water.

82. (B) The scale marks on the thermometer are evenly spaced. Such a simple scale is possible only because liquid mercury expands regularly when heated, expanding upward. Choice (C), although an accurate statement, does not identify the principle behind the use of mercury in a thermometer.

83. (B) Chromosomes contain all genetic material. Inside each chromosome is stored the long DNA molecule that carries the coded messages that control all inherited traits. The chromosomes are in the nucleus of a cell. The cytoplasm (C) makes up the majority of a cell and ranges in consistency from a fluid to a semisolid.

84. (B) In a natural community, a balance usually develops, allowing organisms to exist and reproduce. Each plant and animal occupies its own niche. Choice (A) is incorrect because competition is an ongoing natural process. Choice (D) is incorrect because owls *are* nocturnal animals.

85. (A) The question calls for determining the correct answer based on the information presented in the statement. Therefore, only choice (A), which deals with the magnetic properties of ores, can be eliminated. The other choices are consistent with the idea that deposits of ore were formed from hot water solutions seeping along underground cracks.

86. (C) Genetic scientists use the term *characteristic* for one feature of an organism, for example, eye color. Of the examples given, the simplest relationship is II, one gene controlling one characteristic. Both I and III involve multiple factors and are more common and more complicating in genetic research. Genotype is the genetic makeup of an organism, while phenotype refers to the physical characteristics exhibited by an organism.

87. (C) The maximum potential energy will be at point *C*. At the peak of the ball's flight, the ball will have zero kinetic energy (the energy of motion) and maximum potential energy. The ball slows as it reaches its peak and then comes to a stop before it starts downward. At this point, the ball is at rest.

88. (C) Molds are not green plants (producers) but are fungi and lack true leaves, roots, and stems. Molds do not contain chlorophyll and therefore cannot manufacture food. However, because molds are a life form, basic life elements such as reproduction, respiration, and cellular structure can be eliminated as correct choices, leaving the ability to manufacture food as the correct answer.

89. (B) The gravitational attraction of the moon (and to a much lesser extent, the sun) causes the tides. Since the moon is nearer to the earth than is the sun, the moon's mass attracts and distorts the oceans, causing the highest tides when the moon and sun are on the same side and aligned with the earth. Alignment also causes a lunar eclipse, but in this case the alignment is in the order sun, earth, moon.

90. (C) Cirrus clouds are featherlike clouds that indicate fair weather. Stratus clouds are smooth layers of low clouds that indicate a chance of drizzle or snow. Altostratus clouds are piled in waves and indicate rain or snow. Cumulonimbus clouds are large, dark clouds that indicate thunderstorms.

91. (C) Genetic science can isolate many genes that control crucial chemical activity in cells. A gene can be spliced into bacterial cells that then can be cultured and reproduced. Examples of genetic engineering are the synthesizing of such products as human insulin and interferons and the production of genetically engineered, frost-resistant strawberry plants. DNA, found only in the chromosomes of the cell nuclei and duplicated during reproduction, records genetic messages as a coded sequence of bases. The genetic information provides detailed signals that control the development and activity of cells.

92. (A) Stars with the highest surface temperature appear blue, while stars with the lowest surface temperature appear red. Choice (B) is incorrect because it lists stars in order of *increasing* surface temperature. Knowing that red indicates a cooler surface temperature and that white indicates a warmer surface temperature would help here in eliminating incorrect choices.

93. (A) Water is a chemical compound, produced when different elements join to form a new substance as the result of a chemical reaction. A burning candle and a rusting car are also examples of chemical reactions. Chemical compounds cannot be broken down into simpler substances by processes such as distillation, evaporation, or separation. Choice (B) describes a nuclear reaction, and (C) represents a solution.

94. (D) Sound travels in sound waves, which consist of different layers of air pressure. When something vibrates, the air surrounding the object also vibrates. A wind storm could cause a bridge to vibrate at its natural frequency, which all objects have. Once the bridge begins to vibrate in this way, it could begin to sway, a motion that over time could lead to structural failure and eventual collapse. Soldiers marching in step or a large group of people dancing in step could potentially cause such collapses. The same principle discussed here also explains why some singers can shatter glass. By singing at the natural frequency of the glass, they create strong enough vibrations to break it.

95. (C) The disposal of garbage is an important issue because of the limited number of landfills. A glass bottle would decompose after about one thousand years; a tin can, fifty years; a plastic bag, ten years; and a cigarette butt, less than five years.

96. (B) The information presented in the diagram and the statement is enough to answer this question correctly. The statement suggests that each soil zone is the result of a weathering, or breaking down, process in which bedrock is slowly transformed into fine soil material. Weathering may occur through chemical or physical processes and is a primary factor in soil formation.

97. (B) A tropism is a movement of a plant in reaction to a stimulus, usually a light source such as the sun, toward which, because of chemicals in the plant cells, a plant bends.

98. (A) Some organisms (including many yeasts and bacteria) are anaerobic, that is, existing without free oxygen. For these organisms, in the process of fermentation, glucose is changed into ethanol and carbon dioxide anaerobically. *All* forms of life require water for biochemical reactions, reproduce by means of nucleic acid (DNA), and contain carbon atoms.

99. (D) Any material with a density less than that of the liquid it is in will float. Since water has a density of 1.0, the ice must have a density of less than 1.0 in order to float. The unusual shape of the ice is not relevant. Choice (B) is incorrect because the atomic structure of water and ice is the same (two hydrogen atoms and one oxygen atom).

100. (D) Soft plant and animal tissues decompose quickly in the presence of decay bacteria, which exist wherever oxygen exists. Therefore, the correct answer will be the most oxygen-free environment listed. Lake-bottom mud prevents oxygen-rich air from reaching the tissues. Choice (A) is not the best answer because even in the driest desert environment some decay takes place—even in natural mummification, there is dessication.

101. (B) The diagram clearly involves the photosynthetic process, in which green plants (producers) manufacture food. In the example, the major contribution of the plants is to produce the oxygen needed by the other organisms. Sunlight provides continuing energy necessary for plants to produce oxygen, a process that produces most of the free oxygen in our atmosphere.

102. (B) The flow of energy starts with the sun, the source of energy needed for this system to survive (as it is for the closed system of the earth to survive). This energy is converted to food and oxygen through photosynthesis. Animals take this food energy and use it to live and reproduce, in turn giving off carbon dioxide and minerals (through decomposition), which are used by the plants.

V. Visual and Performing Arts

103. (B) Nijinsky shocked European audiences with his revolutionary choreography of Stravinsky's *The Rite of Spring*. The Nijinsky interpretation called for grotesque positions and awkward, quivering movements. Classical ballet techniques were thought not to be compatible with the composition, as Nijinsky sought to choreograph the intensity and striking rhythm of the music with an equally dissonant but compatible dance form. Nijinsky created movement patterns designed to evoke images of a pagan period in Russian history. The ballet was performed only six times, as European audiences were outraged by Nijinsky's irreverent approach.

104. (A) Labanotation is a technique used to record the movement of a dancer, including hand and foot movements, by using symbols to refer to the body as it moves in space. This method of notation has made it possible to acurately reconstruct the choreography of any dance performance. The location of the symbol on a center vertical line indicates the moving body part. Placement to the right and left of that line indicates position. The speed and direction of the dancer can also be noted by symbols. Labanotation has frequently been used by anthropologists to record primitive dance movements.

105. (D) Maypole dances were originally associated with fertility rituals. In primitive cultures, a pole was placed in the ground and consecrated during a religious ceremony. The maypole symbolized spring and the rebirth associated with the changing seasons. Maypole dancing is a recurring theme in most Western cultures. Individuals danced around the maypole, often holding long ribbons that were tied to the pole. The dances are also a link between folk dances and Stone Age dance rituals.

106. (B) Ballet had reached its high point in Europe during the Romantic period, with Paris considered the center of the ballet world. At this time in Russia, the economy was predominantly agricultural, and industrialization was in its emergent stages. A national folk dance tradition was still maintained there (unlike in western Europe), and the emphasis on dance extended to the ballet. By the end of the nineteenth century, Russia was unique in supporting a state-financed ballet program (the Imperial School) and had become the center of the ballet world. Many classic ballet dancers, including the French dancer Marius Petipa, emigrated to Russia. During this time of Russian ballet ascendancy, Petipa choreographed three of the world's classic ballets: *The Sleeping Beauty, The Nutcracker,* and *Swan Lake.*

107. (A) In a melodrama, a happy resolution is an essential ingredient. Complete ruination of the protagonist is generally associated with a tragic drama. By the end of a melodrama, on the other hand, it is the *antagonist* whose power is neutralized and who gets his or her "just reward." Virtue always wins out over evil.

108. (D) Stage geography can be defined with five basic terms: upstage, downstage, center stage, stage right, and stage left. The description of each area can be further refined, for example, downstage center or upstage center. The information given in the question tells you that all stage directions are from the point of view of an actor standing on stage facing the audience. So the only atypical (not normal) direction is (D). Downstage right *is* the area closest to the audience, but it is to the audience's *left* (the actor's right).

109. (C) *Richard III* is a Shakespearean *history,* not a tragedy, set in fifteenth-century England as the War of the Roses was drawing to a conclusion. The central theme involves the usurpation of power. Shakespeare portrayed Richard as a depraved and amoral individual.

110. (B) Secular, or worldly, plays, while not as significant as religious plays during the Middle Ages, did develop important theatrical forms such as the farce, which generally treated humankind with ridicule. Farces often used comic twists and satire (exposing human shortcomings) in the development of the plot. Liturgical plays (A) and miracle plays (C), the majority of church drama, were generally performed in Latin by the clergy. All church drama focused on the miraculous power of God in determining the direction of human events, with miracle plays dramatizing events taken from the lives of the saints. Mystery plays (D), also called medieval cycle plays, dramatized biblical stories. The word *mystery,* in this context, is of French origin and indicates a stage production performed by trade or craft guilds, *not* a suspenseful drama.

111. (A) *Legato* (A) refers to a smooth, flowing musical presentation, *staccato* (B) to one that is choppy, composed of separate sounds or elements. The term *fortissimo* (C) refers to loud sounds, *pianissimo* (D) to soft sounds.

112. (C) A canon, or round, is a melody played by several instruments entering at different times. Examples include "Row, Row, Row Your Boat" and "Three Blind Mice." One of the most familiar canons is by Pachelbel. A rondo (A) is a form in which a tune or theme is repeated three or more times. The form can be written as ABACADA.

113. (D) "The Star-Spangled Banner" is the only song that has a melody line that begins by descending and then immediately ascends. The rhythm patterns of this melody are also uneven, as shown by the dots and flags on the melody line.

The melodic contour of "My country, 'Tis of Thee" looks like this.

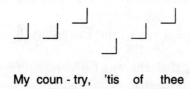

My coun - try, 'tis of thee

The first three notes in "Row, Row, Row Your Boat" are at the same level.

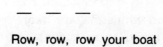

Row, row, row your boat

The first three notes in "Three Blind Mice" descend, followed by a repetition of this pattern.

114. (B) Mass is shown in art by the use of a line to indicate contour. A contour line separates an area from its surrounding background. Since contour lines follow both the interior and exterior structure, they can indicate shadows and textures.

115. (C) The key to this question is recognizing that a fresco is applied to wet plaster. Once it dries, it becomes a permanent part of the plaster, In fresco painting, the artist has limited flexibility in applying color. Choice (B) is associated with tempera painting.

116. (B) The techniques of using overlapping shapes, receding color intensity, and lack of detail in the background are most closely associated with showing depth, or perspective. Choice (A) is not the best answer because it limits the painting involved both to a landscape or seascape and to an abstract style.

VI. Human Development

117. (C) Piaget has had a profound influence on American education, and his stages of development have been incorporated into many curricular designs. Piagetian theory emphasizes creativity and flexibility, not reliance on structured teaching modes, and does *not* favor skipping a child, but rather extending the child's cognitive development through individualization of the curriculum. Only choice (C) is an accurate statement regarding Piagetian theory.

118. (A) Research has shown that the most successful tracking configuration is based on ability grouping by subject area, allowing for both flexible organization and accurate assessment of individual differences in children. The disadvantages of tracking include the negative emotional and academic effects of ability grouping on lower-tracked students. Alternatives to tracking include flexible grouping and cooperative learning opportunities.

119. (B) Permissive parents and educators are likely to treat children with tolerance and acceptance and to avoid punishment and strict controls as behavior-modification models. Permissiveness can encourage independence and autonomy and promote a democratic environment, but too great an emphasis on permissiveness can result in immature behavior and a lack of impulse control. When a child engages in excessive aggression (B), the behavior must be viewed in the context of the situation.

120. (A) Erickson's eight psychosocial stages of development emphasize social and cultural forces in shaping personality. He also postulated that failure at one stage of development did not have irreversible consequences. His psychosocial stages incorporate both sexual and social aspects of personality growth. In contrast to Erickson, Freud believed that a child's personality is largely determined by his or her parents (A).

121. (C) Research has shown that peers usually have a greater influence on adolescent behavior in the areas of sexual attitudes, group identity, interpersonal relationships, colloquial language, and clothing fads. Members of a peer group attempt to conform to the standards and values of that group.

122. (B) The child is advancing in language development. The past tense (ed) of a verb is a more complex grammatical morpheme than is the present tense. This usage also indicates that the child is attempting to imitate the syntactic skills of "conversational" role models. It is important to note that when the parent corrects the child's speech pattern (*come*, not *comed*), the parent generally corrects semantic comprehension, not grammar.

123. (D) An individual's self-image (whether positive or negative) is most directly related to observable classroom behaviors. When an individual has a poor self-image, acting-out behaviors often mask underlying self-concept issues. Maslow's theory of self-actualization identifies a hierarchy of human needs, with self-esteem given as a basic need that must be met before true intrinsic learning can take place.

124. (D) Bloom's taxonomy contains six major classes: knowledge, comprehension, application, analysis, synthesis, and evaluation. Evaluation (the highest level) is defined as quantitative and qualitative judgments about the extent to which material and methods satisfy criteria. Evaluation is placed at the end of the taxonomy because it involves some combination of all other behaviors, along with the addition of criteria and values.

125. (A) Behaviorism is primarily associated with the consequences of behavior as a determiner of one's actions. Extrinsic (external) rewards are emphasized. Humanism (II) is primarily associated with the dignity and worth of the individual. Intrinsic (internal) rewards are emphasized. Congitivism (III) is primarily associated with how individuals acquire information, make decisions, and think logically.

VII. Physical Education

126. (B) The concept of opposition is fundamental in developing efficient body mechanics used in performing throwing skills. In the mature stage of throwing a ball (usually developed by the age of seven), weight is shifted from the back foot to the front foot as the ball is being released. Weight transfer is essential in throwing, batting, and striking skills. A child who throws primarily with the arm (A) will not be able to generate power or distance. Shifting the weight from the front to the back foot (D) is associated with a pitcher's rocking motion as he or she prepares to throw a ball.

127. (D) All four factors are physical principles directly applied to biomechanical analyses, which focus on the mechanical factors that influence movement. Researchers in biomechanics apply physics to sports. The following are examples of this application: In aerodynamics, projection angle and flight velocity; in hydrodynamics, buoyancy and water resistance; in force, Newton's laws of motion (inertia, acceleration, reaction); in motion, linear displacement, velocity, and acceleration.

128. (B) Understanding verbal directions is not associated with perceptual-motor activities, but rather with auditory-discrimination ability. Characteristics of a student exhibiting perceptual-motor difficulties include problems with balance, lateral dysfunction (difficulty with one side of the body), and difficulty in hopping or skipping, in spatial orientation (accurately judging distances in reference to the individual's body), and in combining basic movements such as hopping and skipping.

129. (B) When a male's or female's body-fat index exceeds 20 percent, the individual is considered mildly obese. At 40 percent, the individual is considered moderately obese and at 100 percent, severely obese. Risk factors associated with obesity include elevated blood pressure, elevated levels of cholesterol, and increased risk of diabetes and cardiovascular disease.

130. (B) A young child's visual tracking is greatly improved if the child can easily see the flight of the thrown object. A ball thrown with an arc, or loft, allows additional time to adjust to any directional changes in the path of the ball. Other factors associated with visual tracking include the size and velocity of the object being thrown.

131. (D) *Flexion* refers to the bending of the body (*extension* refers to stretching activities). Circumduction (C) involves a circular motion of the hips, trunk, or shoulders. Adduction, abduction, circumduction, and flexion are used in warm-up activities.

132. (B) Start-and-expand techniques are based on the principle that the initial activity (start) should be so simple that all children can experience a measure of success in performing the skill. Expansion activities can be added to challenge capable students and to increase the complexity of the activity. Start-and-expand activities are most evident in beginning gymnastic programs. For example, an initial activity might simply involve jumping up and touching one's hands together while in the air. An expansion activity might involve jumping up, turning one's body, and clapping one's hands while in the air.

133. (A) An important goal of a primary physical education program is to assist children in perceptual-motor development. Body-imaging activities teach children to identify various body parts. A child walking on a balance beam is an example of a balance activity (B). A child keeping time to a drum beat is involved in a rhythmic activity (C). A child hitting a balloon with his or her hand while the balloon is still in the air is an example of a hand-eye coordination activity (D).

134. (C) The purpose of timed tests is to measure endurance and strength. Bent-knee sit-ups allow the evaluation of abdominal strength (and also strengthen the lower back). Choice (A) is associated with a traditional push-up. Choice (B) might involve a "donkey kick," a hyperextension exercise (repetitive flexion), which often causes lower-back problems.

CONTENT AREA EXERCISES 1

I. Literature and Language Studies

1. Discuss four different sound devices used in poetry.

Four different sound devices commonly used in poetry are meter, rhyme, alliteration, and onomatopoeia.

The meter of a poem is the rhythm and length of its lines. In Shakespeare's plays, for example, the meter often used is iambic pentameter, iambic meaning a foot of two syllables with the second syllable stressed and pentameter meaning a line of five feet.

Rhyme is the similar sound of two words, often the last words in a line. Words such as "run" and "fun" or "moon" and "spoon" are rhymes.

Alliteration is the use of the same letter sound, often at the beginning of a word. Examples are "big," "baby," and "back" or "field," "folly," and "phone."

Onomatopoeia is the use of words that, when spoken, sound like the thing to which they refer. For example, the words "buzz" and "hiss" sound like the noise itself.

2. Compare the one-act play to the short story.

The one-act play is like the short story because the one-act play is shorter than a full-length play and the short story is much shorter than a novel. Because they are short, both the one-act play and the short story usually have only one major plot and no subplots. Both have fewer scenes than a full-length play or a novel, often only one.

However, the words spoken in a one-act play are dialogue only, while in a short story, there may be a mix of narrative and dialogue or just narrative. One could probably read a one-act play in the same amount of time it takes to read the average short story.

3. Discuss two ways in which figurative language adds to the vividness of a description.

Figurative language is a comparison, such as in a simile or a metaphor. In a simile, two things are compared, and the comparison uses the word "like." "He runs like a deer" is a simile. A metaphor leaves out the "like" but still makes the comparison. "The runner is a deer" is a metaphor. This figure of speech is not to be read literally; that is, we are not to think that the runner is actually an animal, a deer. Rather, both the simile and the metaphor add vividness to a description because, based on the comparison made, the reader sees that the runner and the deer share something—in this case, perhaps, speed and grace. In addition, the use of figurative language directly involves the reader, who must be able to see the possible connections being suggested.

4. The following sentences are in "broken" English. Explain their meaning and give a situation in which this might occur in someone's writing.

Yesterday him sing you some song.
You sing some song to she.
Yesterday you no sing song she want.

The first sentence means "Yesterday he sang you a song." The second sentence means "You sing her a song." The third sentence means "Yesterday you didn't sing the song she wanted."

The sentences show confusion in word choice, case, and tense (for example, "no" instead of "didn't," "him" instead of "he," and "sing" instead of "sang." This type of writing might occur if the writer is a foreigner who is not familiar with the sentence structure of the English language.

II. Mathematics

5.

Math Class Enrollment Comparison 1980–1990

1980—20 students
1982—25 students
1984—20 students
1986—30 students
1988—40 students
1990—45 students

Use the grid below to graph the information given above. Explain your procedure in graphing.

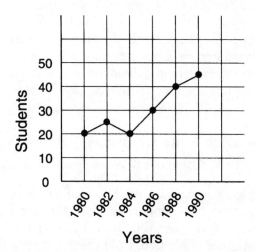

The vertical numbers on the left side represent the number of students, starting with 0 and increasing by steps of 10. The horizontal numbers along the bottom of the graph indicate the years of classes starting with 1980 and increasing by two-year intervals.

Since there were 20 students in math class in 1980, the graph would be marked at the 20 line in 1980. The year 1982 would be marked about halfway between the 20 and 30 line because the enrollment was 25. 1984 would be marked at the 20 line. l986 would be marked at the 30 line. l988 would be marked at the 40 line. And 1990 would be marked approximately halfway between the 40 and 50 line because the enrollment was 45.

6. If a number is divisible by 2 and 3, it is also divisible by 6. Explain why this same number is not necessarily divisible by 9.

   A number that is divisible by 9 is not necessarily divisible by 6 because to be divisible by 6, the number must be even. And although some even numbers are divisible by 9 and 6, some aren't. For example 18 is divisible by 9 and 6, but 30 is divisible by 6 but is not divisible by 9.

7.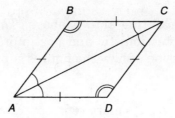

   In the parallelogram above, line AC bisects angle C. With this information, give four deductions that can be made abaout the diagram.

   (1) Line AC bisects angle A.
   (2) Angles A and C are congruent.
   (3) Angles B and D are congruent.
   (4) All sides are equal.

8. Cars A and B each travel the same road to city X. Car A travels at 50 mph and leaves at 10 A.M., while car B travels at 60 mph and leaves at 11 A.M. Will car B overtake car A before it reaches city X, which is 310 miles away? Explain why or why not.

   Since car A is going 50 mph and car B is going 60 mph,

$$50\overline{)300} 60\overline{)300}$$
$$6 5$$

So it takes car A 6 hours to go 300 miles, and it takes car B 5 hours to go 300 miles. Since car A leaves at 10 A.M. and car B leaves at 11 A.M., car A will overtake car B at 4 P.M. at the 300-mile mark, which is before it reaches city X, which is 310 miles away.

III. Visual and Performing Arts

9.

Briefly discuss how the painting shown above, *The Card Players,* incorporates elements of both the impressionistic and postimpressionistic periods. Include in your answer a brief discussion of how the figures support the intended effect of this composition.

The Card Players, by Cézanne, is more representative of the impressionistic period than of the postimpressionistic period. Characteristics of the impressionists are evidenced in that Cézanne was not concerned with depicting reality by reproducing exact shapes, lines, and textures found in nature. Also, the painting's style encourages the viewer to become more than a simple observer in what appears to be an ordinary event. However, since the painting emphasizes form, solidity, and structure, it also incorporates elements of the postimpressionistic period. In addition, detail is lacking, as the artist discarded anything he felt was unnecessary to record.

The figures of the two men are solid masses. The brush strokes look like large patches of light and dark. They are juxtaposed to indicate form. The men's arms are bent angularly, as if to frame the center area where the cards are being contemplated.

10. Briefly discuss the advantages of the proscenium stage. Include relevant information on the historical background of this stage in your answer.

The proscenium stage and arch (developed during the Renaissance) were created in response to an increasing demand to use scenery in stage productions. The "arch" is the most recognizable feature of a proscenium stage; it allows audiences to view stage events as if seen through an "opening" that leads to other scenes. It encourages a "forced perspective" through which the audience views the action. The proscenium arch is erected downstage and separates the audience from the central action. The key to the proscenium stage is the visual perspective gained by the audience, since most seats in this configuration face the proscenium arch. This allows the audience a visual intimacy with the actors.

IV. Human Development

11. A teacher observes that a small number of students in a fifth-grade classroom do not do well on paper-and-pencil activities. Discuss two possible explanations for this behavior. Include in your answer educational interventions to address this problem.

Assuming that the students have the intellectual ability to perform on these tasks, but consistently do not, the teacher should consider the possibility of specific learning disabilities. The inability to perform on paper-and-pencil activities can be related to fine motor coordination problems. This should be evident in how the individual "manages" his or her paper. Coordination problems can signal serious learning problems.

Attention-deficit disorders would be another avenue to investigate. Once the cause of the problem is discovered, the teacher could employ alternative learning modalities to meet the needs of the students—for example, using manipulatives, allowing students to explain how a problem could be solved and then using a calculator to solve it, designing paper-and-pencil tasks so that lining items up is not a distraction, etc.

12. Define behavior modification in terms of operant conditioning (responses on which stimulus-response learning theory is based). Briefly discuss implications for educators in determining how children will respond to operant conditioning.

Behavior modification (systematic measures to change a particular observable human behavior) is based on the principles of operant conditioning. Operant conditioning changes behavior by scientifically manipulating the environment. Behavior can be changed by either positive or negative reinforcement. Operants (all responses that are not reflexive) can be classified according to their effect on the learning environment.

Educators who incorporate operant conditioning are able to predict a desired learning environment and then attempt to control it. When a desired behavior is evidenced, the teacher should immediately provide a reward, either verbal or nonverbal.

Children respond to operant conditioning through observation and reinforcement. Although operant conditioning can employ both positive and negative (punishment) reinforcement to affect behavior, positive reinforcement provides more lasting behavior modification.

V. Physical Education

13. A child is learning to catch a baseball. Briefly discuss how to overcome the avoidance reaction generally associated with catching a baseball. Include in your answer a discussion of the proper body mechanics involved in catching a baseball.

A child will initially demonstrate a fear of thrown objects. For example, a child will generally turn away from a thrown ball as it approaches him or her. To overcome this typical avoidance reaction, the instructor should substitute a pineapple-size, soft foam ball or a small bean-bag as the thrown object. The "forgiving" nature of these objects encourages children to visually follow the ball.

After the avoidance reaction is reduced or eliminated, proper body mechanics can be taught. The arms are bent at the elbows; both hands are used to catch the ball; the fingers are shaped like a cup; the hands are relaxed, not rigid; the ball is caught with the pads of the fingers; both hands are brought together; and the ball is brought to the body to distribute the force over a longer distance.

14. Briefly define aerobic and anaerobic fitness. Include appropriate examples in your answer.

Aerobic activity is designed to elevate the heart rate and increase lung capacity. Typical exercises involve sustained locomotor activities such as running, swimming, cycling, jogging, and aerobics. The goal of aerobic activity is to increase the maximum amount of oxygen that the body can process in a specific time.

Anaerobic fitness essentially involves using muscle groups at high intensities (station-by-station weight lifting) or performing activities that require short bursts of speed at high power levels (running a hundred-yard dash). Anaerobic activities are usually high-intensity and low-duration events which do not require prolonged oxygen intake.

CONTENT AREA EXERCISES 2

I. History/Social Sciences

1. "Reaganomics" was the dominant economic philosophy of the 1980s in the United States. Briefly discuss the rationale for Reaganomics.

Reaganomics was based on the principles of supply-side economics. Proponents of supply-side economics argued that large tax cuts would stimulate the economy by encouraging both spending and investment. Increased spending would generate additional demand for products and therefore stimulate the supply side of the economy. An economic "ripple effect" would generate the need for additional workers to meet the increased demand for products.

The expanded work force, it was argued, by spending discretionary income, would generate additional product demand. By stimulating the supply side of the economy, substantially more individuals would be paying taxes. The largest tax cuts were reserved for the wealthiest Americans. This aspect of the plan was derisively labeled "trickle-down" economics.

2. Spartan women said the following when their men went off to war: "Come back with your shield or upon it."

How does this statement reflect Spartan society? Include in your answer a brief discussion of how the state controlled the lives of its citizens.

The statement reflects the belief that the survival of the state was the primary responsibility of every Spartan citizen. Death in battle was considered an honor; cowardice was considered a disgrace. Without a willingness to die to preserve the state, the fragile system of Spartan control might collapse.

Sparta was essentially a warrior state, dependent on a superior military machine and loyal soldiers to ensure order and maintain power. The rigid structure of Spartan society allowed the Spartans to rule, even though Spartan citizens were outnumbered by noncitizens by about ten to one. The state owned most of the land. Large families were discouraged. At birth, all Spartan males belonged to the state, and by the age of seven, they enrolled in military-style camps. It was not considered unusual for Spartan mothers to practice infanticide.

3. One of the central features of American government is the principle of separation of power. Briefly discuss the reason the principle is important. Include in your answer the basic function of each branch of government.

By having three distinct branches of government, the possibility of usurpation of power is reduced. This structure also encourages broad deliberation before legislation is passed.

The executive branch (president) is responsible for implementing laws. The judicial branch (courts) is responsible for interpreting laws. The legislative branch (congress) is responsible for making laws. The checks and balances inherent in this system are limitations on constitutional power.

4. Briefly discuss three major economic factors that would result in a strong U.S. dollar. Define appropriate terms and include one negative effect on trade resulting from a strong dollar.

(1) The dollar's value is essentially based on supply and demand. For example, if a foreign country invests large amounts in U.S. government bonds, that country must sell its currency to buy dollars. The result is an increased demand for dollars and, on a global scale, a rising dollar.

(2) Higher interest rates in the United States will attract foreign investors and push the dollar to higher levels.

(3) Political uncertainties in the world usually result in an increased value for the dollar. This is because the United States is seen as a stable political environment and therefore a safe haven for foreign investment.

A rising dollar can have a negative effect on the U.S. trade deficit. American exports become less competitive with foreign products and therefore less attractive to foreign investment.

II. Science

5.

THE HYDROLOGIC CYCLE

(A) wind
(B) precipitation
(C) runoff
(D) condensation
(E) percolation
(F) evaporation

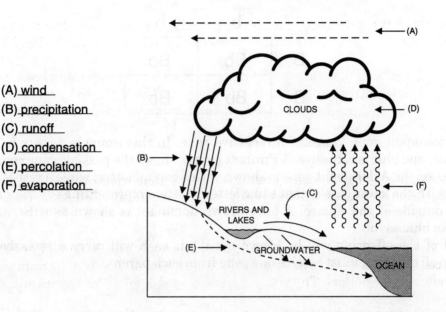

Fill in the blanks to the left of the diagram above of the hydrologic (water) cycle in the correct configuration, using these terms: precipitation, evaporation, wind, condensation, percolation, runoff. Briefly describe the processes that make up the water cycle.

The sun initiates the water cycle. The sun's rays warm the oceans, changing water into water vapor through the process of evaporation. Evaporation allows water from rivers, lakes, streams, etc., to escape into the atmosphere.

The moisture-carrying warm air rises to altitudes of lower pressure in the troposphere. The air expands and cools; the cooling results in the condensation of the water vapor, which forms into clouds. The clouds may be blown inland and cool further.

As the clouds become saturated, moisture is returned to the earth as precipitation (rain, snow, sleet, etc.). As the water is returned to the surface, the process begins again in a continuous cycle.

6. If a blue-eyed individual marries a brown-eyed individual who carries only the dominant brown eye-color gene and no recessives, diagram the possible eye colors that can occur in the offspring of these individuals.

	b	b
B	Bb	Bb
B	Bb	Bb

A dominant gene "masks" a recessive gene. In this example, brown is dominant over blue, and blue is recessive. A Punnett square shows the possible gene combinations in the example. A dominant gene is shown with a capital letter, while a recessive gene is shown with the lower case of that same letter . Letters representing eye color are placed on the outside of the square. A pure brown dominant is shown as (BB), and a pure recessive blue as (bb).

All of the offspring will be brown eyed, but each will carry a recessive for blue because all offspring must receive one gene from each parent.

7. How do drops of water acting as prisms explain the appearance of a rainbow? Include refraction, dispersion, and color sequence in your answer.

As light passes through a prism, it is refracted (bent) by very small amounts. White light going through a prism separates into red, orange, yellow, green, blue, indigo, and violet. The spreading process is called dispersion, and the spectrum is the resulting color sequence.

The atmosphere, following a storm or shower, is full of tiny drops of water. Each drop acts as a prism, splitting white light into the colors of the spectrum. Light is slowed down as it travels through transparent objects or substances. A rainbow is the total effect of refracted sunlight as it passes through the countless tiny drops of water suspended in air. The different colors are the result of light refracted at slightly different speeds.

8. Briefly discuss how chlorofluorocarbons are directly associated with ozone depletion. Include in your answer ozone-depleting products and three consequences attributed to ozone depletion.

   Chlorofluorocarbons (CFCs) escape into the atmosphere and destroy ozone molecules in the stratosphere by reacting with the protective ozone layer to form chlorine oxide. They are used in refrigeration, freon, aerosol spray cans, propellent gases, and many types of foam insulation.

Consequences of ozone depletion:

   (1) The ozone layer acts as a shield in preventing harmful ultraviolet (UV) radiation from reaching the lower atmosphere. The breakdown in this protective layer greatly increases the risk of skin cancer and eye cataracts.

   (2) Increased UV radiation can upset the delicate balance of all food chains because it can damage DNA, directly affecting our genetic makeup.

   (3) Many CFCs are linked to greenhouse gases. CFCs contribute to global warming.

Part V:
Supplemental Short
Constructed-Response
Practice and Analysis

SHORT *CONSTRUCTED-RESPONSE QUESTIONS*

Some of these sample short constructed-response questions are followed by information pertinent to answering the question, information similar to that which you might jot down before writing your essay. Use this information and any additional information you think appropriate to write your response. **Keep in mind that these lists of pertinent information are not given to you on the test.** Other sample questions are included for additional practice. Use no more than two sides of an 8½ × 11 sheet of paper and give yourself a maximum of eight minutes for each response.

Literature and Language Studies

1. Discuss three differences between free verse and blank verse.

Information

- Free verse:
  Has varying rhythms
  Has varying line lengths
  Can have from one to any number of syllables in a line
  Can have as many stresses as poet chooses as long as some sense of rhythm, or can follow regular rhythm

- Blank verse:
  Usually uses a ten-syllable line, with five accents, beginning with unstressed syllable
  Stress falls on even-numbered syllables: 2, 4, 6, 8, 10
  This meter called unrhymed iambic pentameter
  Lines are nearly the same length

2. Compare and contrast the Gothic and the Victorian novel. Address the setting, time period, and characterization.

Information

- Gothic novel:
  As term first used, meant the novel had a setting in Middle Ages
  Setting a place of mystery
  Characters not carefully developed
  Usually had beautiful, innocent heroine persecuted by sinister, noble man with designs on her physically or on her fortune

- Victorian novel:
  Usually focused on life in mid-nineteenth-century England, time of Queen Victoria
  Usually large cast of characters, well developed

Questions 3–5 refer to the following poem by A. E. Housman.

> Could man be drunk forever
> With liquor, love, or fights,
> Lief should I rouse at morning
> And lief lie down of nights.
>
> But men at whiles are sober
> And think by fits and starts,
> And if they think, they fasten
> Their hands upon their hearts.

3. Discuss the use of literal and figurative language in the first stanza of this poem. Explain what comparisons the figurative language makes.

4. Discuss the structure of this poem. What are its major parts and by what means are the parts related to each other.

5. Discuss the theme of this poem and explain why the poem is or is not effective.

6. List and discuss the major components of a persuasive essay.

7. What is the difference between denotation and connotation? Explain what this difference has to do with the effectiveness of words. Use specific examples.

8. Writers use a number of methods to "brainstorm" and organize their thoughts. Describe and demonstrate two of these methods.

9. In debating an issue, there are many ways to weaken someone's argument. Discuss three methods or techniques used to weaken an argument.

Mathematics

1. A motorist travels 120 miles to his destination at the average speed of 60 miles per hour and returns to the starting point at the average speed of 40 miles per hour. How would you find the average speed for the entire trip?

Information

- Destination 120 miles away and average speed = 60 mph
- Divide 120 by 60 to get average speed going = 2 hours
- Return 120 miles away and average speed = 40 mph
- Divide 120 by 40 to get average speed returning = 3 hours
- Total time going + total time returning = 2 + 3 = 5 hours total time
- Total distance going + total distance returning = 120 + 120 = 240
- Total distance 240 divided by total time 5 = 48 mph average

2. Not all numbers are prime numbers. What is a prime number and why are all odd numbers not prime? Give examples of five prime numbers.

Information

- Prime number is divisible by only 1 and itself
- Some odd numbers divisible by other numbers, so not prime
- Example: 15 not prime because divisible by 1, 15, 3, and 5
- Other prime numbers: 2, 3, 5, 7, 11

3. What is the value of $\frac{1}{3} + \frac{1}{8} + \frac{5}{6}$? Explain the method used to add these fractions.

Information

- To add fractions with different denominators must get common denominator
- Least common denominator of 3, 8, and 6 = 24
- Change all fractions to something over 24
- $\frac{1}{3} = \frac{8}{24}$; $\frac{1}{8} = \frac{3}{24}$; $\frac{5}{6} = \frac{20}{24}$
- So now add numerators: 8 + 3 + 20 = 31. And keep same denominator: $\frac{31}{24}$
- Change improper fraction to mixed number; divide denominator into numerator = $1\frac{7}{24}$

4. If Tom starts school on Friday, what day of the week was it 30 days earlier? Explain how you arrived at your answer.

Information

- One day earlier = Thursday; two days earlier = Wednesday, etc.
- One week earlier = Friday
- So divide 30 by 7 = 4 with 2 remainder
- Four weeks earlier = Friday
- Two days earlier than Friday = Wednesday, so was Wednesday 30 days earlier

5. A college student invests $2000, part of it at 7% in a savings account and part of it at 12% in a special money market account. The annual income from her investment is $200. Wilthout calculating the exact amounts, how can you tell if she invested more money in the savings account or in the money market account?

Information

- Can quickly see that $200 return on $2000 = 10%
- So more money would have to be at 12% to make up for less made at 7%
- So more money in money market

6.

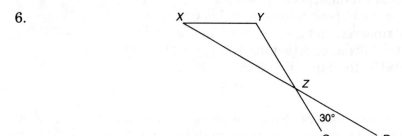

In the figure above, if $\angle YXZ = \angle QZR$, what is the measure of $\angle XYZ$? Show your work.

7. A teacher gave a test to a class, and all the boys averaged 82%, while all the girls averaged 85%. If there were twenty boys and ten girls in the class, explain a simple method for finding the class average.

8. One way to approximate the value for $.26 \times .67 \times .9$ is by using fractions. Without performing the calculations, explain how this method works and give an approximate answer.

9.

Family Income of $40,000

$20,000 salary
$ 4,000 interest
$10,000 rental property
$ 6,000 freelance consulting

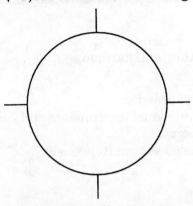

Use the circle above to construct a pie chart showing the percentages to reflect the family income.

10. What information is needed to solve the following problem?

A painting crew painted three rooms on Monday, five rooms on Tuesday, two rooms on Wednesday, and four rooms on Thursday. How many gallons of paint did the crew use?

11. Multiplying by ¼ is the same as dividing by what number? Explain how you arrived at your answer.

12. What is the value of x in the equation $5x + 7 = 17$? Give an answer and explain your method, step by step.

13. What is the approximate value of .27 × .5 × .73. Show your work and explain your steps.

Visual and Performing Arts

Music

1. Compare and contrast the Baroque and Classical musical styles.

Information

- Style includes melody, rhythm, and harmony
- Baroque style (1660–1750):
  Characterized by dramatic expression
  Emphasis on character of individual instruments and voices
  Strong rhythmic drive, energy
  Polyphonic, two or more melodies simultaneously
  Bach, Handel, Purcell
- Classical style (1750–1820):
  Homophonic, single melody with subordinate chords
  Elegance, clarity, symmetry over emotion
  More restrained, objective than Baroque
  Larger sectional groupings, balanced sections
  Emphasis on clear melodic line

2. What is a "spiritual"? Include in your answer the music style and historical development of the spiritual.

Information

- Folk song, African-American, oral tradition
- Emotional and religious
- Believed to be slave created, connected to "sorrow" songs of American slaves
- Inspired blues and jazz
- Mournful refrains, melancholy
- Often singing in unison, call and response pattern

3. Why is music referred to as an "international language"? Include in your answer a brief discussion of this statement in both aesthetic and performance terms.

4. Discuss how American jazz could be considered a unique American development in the field of music expression. Include appropriate time periods and individuals in your answer.

5. What is the importance of traditional folk songs in American culture? Include in your answer characteristics of folk songs.

Visual Arts

6.

Briefly discuss the imagery associated with the subject matter of the painting above. What specific techniques did the artist use to achieve unity, balance, and controlled space?

Information

- Formalistic rather than realistic
- Flat, linear, balanced
- Repetitive shapes—halos, wings, three vertical rows, slanted heads; stability, unity
- Placement and size of Madonna
- Overlapping but lack of depth
- Expressions stoic, gestures stilted
- Intent to depict religious symbols, not reality

7.

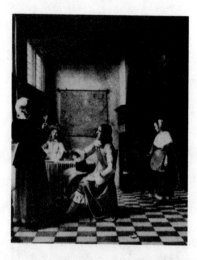

The artist who painted the picture above used light in a particular manner. Briefly discuss the artistic purpose achieved by the use of light and how the use of perspective helps create an overall balance in the composition. Discuss the various individual components that together create the picture's overall effect.

Dance

8. Briefly discuss the techniques used in classical ballet that separate this art form from other dance forms. Include appropriate terminology in your answer.

Information

- Movements result of extensive training
- Unnatural movements seem natural
- Harmonious form through body control, and development of balance
- Turnout position: heels together with toes outward, basic position which can be varied to such as arabesque and attitude poses
- Manner in which steps executed create wide range of moods

9. Discuss three characteristics of folk dancing that are shared by most cultures. Include in your answer how folk dancing developed over time and provide examples to support your answer.

10. Expert choreography is essential to any successful ballet production. List and describe three primary considerations that a choreographer uses to arrange the movements of a ballet.

11. Briefly discuss the origin, time period, and characteristics of the following dances: the Charleston and the twist. Include in your answer reasons for the development of each dance form.

Drama

12. Describe four key elements of a tragedy that characterized this dramatic form prior to the eighteenth century. Include one literary example to support your answer.

Information

- Serious mood throughout
- Protagonist suffers reversal of fortune because violates moral code
- Moral/ethical code reestablished by end of drama
- Tragic figure usually arouses sympathy and admiration at beginning
- Protagonist has character flaw, fated outcome
- Protagonist usually of ruling class
- Example: Oedipus, excessive pride, marries mother unknowingly
- Misfortunes in Thebes, Oedipus brings disaster to town, eventually learns truth of situation

13. Describe the role of the director in a modern theater.

14. Briefly compare and contrast a melodrama with a tragic drama. Include a brief discussion of characterization, moral issues, and dramatic conclusion in your answer.

15. Oedipus is considered a classic tragedy. Briefly discuss how a director might interpret the plot of this tragedy.

Human Development

1. How does positive reinforcement influence a child's ability to learn? Cite appropriate research to support your answer.

Information

- Reinforcement:
  Strengthens following response
  Classical conditioning experiments (stimulus-response) of Skinner, Watson, etc.
  Behavior reinforcement strong motivator in changing behavior

- Positive Reinforcement:
  Reinforcement for desired behavior
  Increases probability that desired behavior will be strengthened

- Research:
  For PR to be most effective, must immediately follow desired behavior
  Rewarded behavior repeated and strengthened
  Behavior developed by cues, is active process, therefore is reinforceable
  PR either intrinsic or extrinsic
  Teacher more control over extrinsic
  Classroom structure can foster intrinsic also

2. "A child who is motivated will learn."

Assuming new learning is to take place, list four techniques that would support the statement above. Include in your answer how teachers through proper motivation can reduce potential classroom management problems.

Information

- Be involved, enthusiastic, make students feel special
- Introduce material presented; visual aids; open-ended questions
- Relate new learning to previous learning
- Understand differences, vary learning modalities (kinesthetic, role-playing, etc.)
- Pace lessons so all successful
- Reinforce positive behavior, model behavior, no sarcasm
- Provide learning activities for divergent thinking
- Allow students to take responsibility for learning; stress problem solving

3. Briefly describe the basic hierarchical stages of cognitive development.

Information

- Bloom's taxonomy, educational objectives
  Stated in behavioral terms—define, convert, change, diagram, compose, etc.
  Progression of understanding—from simple recall and eventually progressing to evaluation
  Purpose to help teachers prepare questions to test critical thinking

- Steps of cognitive domain:
  Knowledge (simple recall)
  Comprehension (understanding meaning)
  Application (using material to solve problems)
  Analysis (breaking material down to individual parts)
  Synthesis (combining material to form new concept)
  Evaluation (making value judgments)

4. Studies show that many children lose their initial creativity by the age of nine or ten. Explain the reasons for this loss and provide appropriate examples to support your answer. What procedures would you follow to avoid this outcome?

5. "Discipline must be taught. Its ultimate goal must be self-discipline."

Design a program that will have as an outcome the development of self-discipline.

6. In reference to K–5 public school education, discuss current educational research on "tracking" by ability grouping. Include a definition of tracking in your answer.

Physical Education

1. Define the term "gross-motor coordination skill" and give specific examples to support your definition.

Information

- Gross-motor coordination:
  Involves entire body (uses big-muscle groups)
  Used in locomotor (moving body from one area to another) or nonlocomotor (stationary) activities

- Gross-motor activities:
  Locomotor activities include running, jumping, swimming, and other activities that use the major muscle groups
  Can involve controlling body in flight (jumping over obstacles), performing specific sports activities (kicking a football, hitting a baseball, platform diving), and all endurance activities
  Nonlocomotor (stationary) activities include flexibility exercises (bending, stretching, twisting, and turning) and weight-lifting exercises

2. What is the educational purpose of incorporating static balance activities in a comprehensive physical education program? Include appropriate examples to support your answer.

Information

- Static body activities:
  Are used to develop body coordination, body awareness, object handling
  Coordination involves ability to support body weight in evenly distributed position
  All movement activities involve balance
  Static body activities develop awareness of body in controlled space

- Static balance in kindergarten:
  Enhances perceptual-motor skills
  Examples: balancing on one foot, balancing manipulative on a body part (hand, foot, leg), completing a frog stand
  Is achieved when center of gravity is directly over base of support
  Extension of static balance activities involved in all sports
  Individual is aware of how body moves and adjusts to weight and space differences

3. Briefly discuss three reasons that would support the teaching of tumbling skills to first grade students. Define the mechanics of tumbling.

Information

- Definition:
  Involves controlling one's body in space
  Requires estimation of spatial relationships and coordination of speed and balance efficiently and safely
  Develops basic movements in response to space, time, force, and flow
  Involves movement as creative expression

- Reasons:
  Fear factor in older children but first graders more willing to experiment
  Excellent way to teach balance and coordination
  If exposed to skills early can progress to more challenging gymnastic activities
  Promotes activities that develop strength, flexibility, agility, and conceptual assimilation
  Skills, once taught, are lifetime skills and facilitate achievement in all sports activities

4. Analyze the following activity and discuss how a teacher would evaluate the appropriateness of the activity for third grade students.

   The teacher chooses two coed relay teams of four members each.

   The length of the relay is two hundred yards. Each student will run for fifty yards.

   A baton will be exchanged during the relay.

5. How can colorization of a primary playground four-square court enhance skill performance and improve socialization?

6. Give an example of one of the following and describe how the activity assists the physical education development of a child: perceptual-motor development, balance activities, rhythmic movement, hand-eye coordination.

7. Briefly describe three principles that are involved in enhancing skill performance.

History/Social Sciences

1. Hinduism is considered one of the world's major religions. Discuss the demographics of the Hindu religion. Also, include key beliefs that separate Hinduism from other major religions.

Information

- The religion:
  Approximately 650 million adherents
  Primarily in India, but also in Indian subcontinent and Southeast Asia
  Dates back to approximately 3000 B.C.
  Identified with no single religious figure
  Writings include vedas, epic poems, prayers, instructions, etc.
  Early writing in Sanskrit

- Basic beliefs:
  Polytheism (thousands of deities, including Brahma, Vishnu, and Siva)
  Belief in duality of many gods (good and bad side)
  The cow is considered sacred
  Respect for all living creatures
  Reincarnation

2. Briefly discuss three major military objectives of the North at the start of the American Civil War. Include basic strategy and geographic references in your answer.

Information

- Primary objective to capture Southern capital at Richmond, Virginia:
  Richmond was political symbol of the South
  Its capture would indicate to foreign countries that South was untenable political entity
  Thought that capture would force South to capitulate quickly
  Actually was four-year stand-off

- Blockade South's Atlantic seaports and cut off trade:
  In early 1860s, blockade ineffective
  By mid 1860s, North's superior industrial strength became evident
  South economically strangled

- Split the confederacy at the Mississippi River:
  Accomplished with the fall of Vicksburg
  Purpose to divide Southern forces east and west and prevent South from using Mississippi River
  Force South to fight a two-front war

- Capture the South's railroad lines:
  Chattanooga, Tennessee, was a major objective
  By splitting South's communications lines at Chattanooga and continuing to target railroads, South forced into more desperate defensive posture

3. Briefly discuss four demographic trends associated with current divorce statistics in the United States.

Information

- Divorce rate:
  Generally stable during past decade
  About five divorces per thousand population
  Ratio of divorced to married individuals has grown rapidly in recent decades
  About 8% of adult population currently divorced

- Divorce more prevalent in those under twenty-five years old, 50% from this age group

- Divorce most common in those married less than five years—the longer the marriage, the greater chance for success of the marriage

- More divorced women than divorced men; men tend to remarry more than divorced women

4. In comparison to European cultures of the seventeenth century, why is it difficult to reconstruct the history of sub-Saharan African cultures existing during the same period?

5. Evaluate the negative effects resulting from the building of the Great Wall on the long-term history of China. Support your answer with approximate dates and pertinent information associated with the building of the Great Wall.

6. Discuss three key differences between the Renaissance and the Middle Ages. Include economic implications and geographical references in your answer.

Science

1. Explain why a pin will sink in water but a steel ship can float.

Information

- Liquid exerts equal pressure on object immersed in that liquid
- Pressure increases with depth, upward pressure on bottom of object will be greater than downward force on top
- Object becomes lighter in water because of net lifting force of water
- Object will float in water if buoyant force equals entire weight of object
- Overall density of steel ship (total mass divided by total volume) is less than that of water

- Interior shape of ship and use of ballast affects overall density
- Object that is submerged displaces water and loses an amount of weight equal to weight of water displaced
- Pin has density greater than that of water displaced (greater than 1.0) and therefore will sink

2. The desert is a unique biome. Discuss four specific plant adaptations characteristic of this biome. Include a brief discussion of the term "adaptation" in your answer.

Information

- Term adaptation:
  Evolutionary change that benefits an organism
  Can also be classified as successful mutation

- To survive in region of limited water, desert plants have adapted uniquely:
  Some have waxy coats on leaves and stems to limit water loss by evaporation
  Some have seeds that won't germinate unless thoroughly soaked by water, sometimes dormant for years
  Trees temporarily drop leaves till water available
  Most desert shrubs have extensive roots to soak up available water; some have long, shallow roots parallel to ground to take advantage of water runoff
  Cacti can survive on limited water resources, have tiny needles to reduce water loss and limit animal grazing

3. Define the term "bacteria." Why are bacteria classified as living organisms? Include in your answer both useful and harmful aspects associated with bacteria.

Information

- Definition:
  One-celled plants able to live in water, air, and almost any environment

- Living organisms:
  Living cells and therefore exhibit all life processes
  Life processes include respiration, reproduction, metabolism, digestion, excretion, circulation, etc.
  Reproduce asexually by binary fission (splitting)
  For growth, need moist, oxygen-rich, moderately hot environment (in addition to food source and indirect sunlight)

- Useful/harmful aspects:
  Useful: soil formation, fermentation, ripening cheese
  Harmful: food poisoning, tooth cavities, diseases such as tuberculosis, typhoid, diphtheria

4. Using a pendulum as an example, explain the difference between potential and kinetic energy.

5. Discuss three key characteristics of sexual reproduction. Give examples from the plant kingdom to support your answer.

6. Discuss specific reasons that paleontology could be used as evidence to support the existence of evolutionary change.

7. How does a roller coaster demonstrate Newton's laws of motion and other principles of physics?

the final touches

1. Make sure that you are familiar with the testing center location and nearby parking facilities.

2. The last week of preparation should be spent on a general review of key concepts, test-taking strategies, and techniques.

3. Don't cram the night before the exam. It's a waste of time!

4. Arrive at the testing center with plenty of time before the exam.

5. Remember to bring the proper materials: identification, admission ticket, three or four sharpened Number 2 pencils, a nonprogrammable calculator, an eraser, several ballpoint pens, and a watch.

6. On each section, start off crisply, answering the questions you know first and then going back to try to answer the others.

7. On the multiple-choice questions, try to eliminate one or more choices before you guess, but make sure you fill in answers. There is no penalty for guessing.

8. Underline key words in questions. Write out important information and make notations on diagrams. Take advantage of being permitted to write in the test booklet.

9. Make sure you are answering "what is being asked" and that your answer is reasonable.

10. On the multiple-choice questions, cross out incorrect choices immediately. This strategy will keep you from reconsidering a choice that you have already eliminated.

11. On the short constructed-response questions, if you don't know the answer, at least try to give a partial response. You could get partial credit.

12. The key to getting a good score on the MSAT is reviewing properly, practicing, and getting the questions right that you should get right. A review of Part I and Part II of this book will help you focus during the final week before the exam.

sources

Sincere appreciation is given to the following authors and companies for allowing the use of excerpts from their outstanding works.

Theater, The Dynamics of the Art, by Brian Hansen. Reprinted by permission of Prentice Hall, Englewood Cliffs, New Jersey, © 1991.

Photographs of paintings and sculpture from *Great Museums of the World—National Gallery London,* Newsweek, Inc., and Arnoldo Mondadori Editore, photographs by Kodansha, Ltd., © 1969, and *Great Museums of the World—Louvre Paris,* Newsweek, Inc., and Arnoldo Mondadori Editori, photographs by Kodansha, Ltd., © 1967.

Cartoon by Frank Interlandi, © 1980 in the *Los Angeles News.*

The "Retail Prices" graph, from *Hammond Almanac.* Courtesy of Hammond Incorporated.

The "Distribution of Earned Degrees" graph by Bob Allen, © 1976, the *Los Angeles Times.* Reprinted by permission.

"Nonemployment Relationship," © 1977 by the *Los Angeles Times.* Reprinted by permission.

The "Anti-Inflation" cartoon by Auth, © 1978 by the *Philadelphia Inquirer.*

Chart of state constitutions, map of the elections of 1868, and the "Cattle Frontier" map from *America! America!* by L. Joanne Buggey, Gerald A. Danzer, Charles L. Mitsakos, C. Frederick Risinger, © 1977 by Scott, Foresman and Company. Reprinted by permission.

Literature terms from *Cliffs Advanced Placement Literature and Composition Preparation Guide,* © 1993 by Allan Casson.

Barefoot to Balanchine: How to Watch Dance by Mary Kerner, © 1990 by Mary Kerner. Used by permission of Doubleday, a division of Bantam Doubleday Dell Publishing Group, Inc.

Information contained in "Curriculum Objectives by Grade" derived from charts supplied by Beverly Hills Unified School District.